PRINTS AND THEIR CREATORS
A World History

Prints

AND THEIR CREATORS

A World History

*An Anthology of Printed Pictures and Introduction to the Study
of Graphic Art in the West and the East*

by Carl Zigrosser

CROWN PUBLISHERS, INC. • *NEW YORK*

To Laura

Originally published under the title *The Book of Fine Prints*.

© 1937 by Carl Zigrosser. Revised Edition © 1948, 1956, by Carl Zigrosser.
Second revised edition © 1974 by Carl Zigrosser.

Library of Congress Catalog Card Number: 74-80293

Published in the United States of America
Published simultaneously in Canada by General Publishing Company Limited

CONTENTS

A Note of Acknowledgment

Many people and institutions have helped me in the preparation of this book. I cannot enumerate them all, but I am grateful nonetheless. I have drawn upon my earlier writings, and wish to thank the University of Georgia Press, George Braziller, Alfred A. Knopf, Ben Wolf, and the Philadelphia Museum of Art for permission to use material published by them. I am also obligated to my editor, Herbert Michelman of Crown Publishers, for his encouragement and patience in the revision and enlargement of my old *Book of Fine Prints*.

This new work is really three books in one: a history of printmaking in Europe, in America, and in the Orient, from the beginnings to the present, thus covering the whole field within one volume. In addition, it is an anthology of printed pictures with 738 examples. The source of each picture is indicated (gratefully) in the index of illustrations. But I wish to thank specially the staff of my own museum from the Director downwards, and particularly the Curator of Prints, Kneeland McNulty, his secretary, Susan London, and the staff photographer, Alfred J. Wyatt, for their unstinting cooperation. Nor can I refrain from citing the many kindnesses of Lessing J. Rosenwald and the staff of the Alverthorpe and National Gallery, not to mention John McKendry of the Metropolitan Museum of Art, Louise Richards of the Cleveland Museum, and Harold Joachim of the Chicago Art Institute. The museums and specialized collections in America are indeed too numerous for me to mention them all.

Likewise my indebtedness to European museums is very great. I wish specially to thank Dr. Ekhart Knab of the *Albertina*, Dr. Dieter Koepplin of the Basel *Kupferstichkabinett*, and Dr. K.G. Boon of the *Rijksmuseum* for their valued cooperation, as well as the staffs of those institutions which were approached by correspondence, such as the Berlin *Kupferstichkabinett*, the Munich *Graphische Sammlung*, the Print Room of the British Museum, and many other places. Also I wish to thank Jan Tschichold, Arsène Bonafous-Murat, and Eberhard Kornfeld for valued help, and, last but not least, my wife Laura for her typing and advice. Indeed my dependence on books and people, both acknowledged and unacknowledged, is so extensive that I must cite Montaigne's words in my defense:

I name not my borrowings, but I weigh them.

1. Introduction

This is the story of certain scraps of paper, some old, some new, with curious marks of ink on them, but rare and precious in men's eyes, scraps of paper treasured in museums and cherished by collectors in many lands. These prints, for such they are, must indeed have something provocative and inspiring about them to have penetrated so deeply into our culture. What is the mysterious something that enhances so greatly the value of prints? It is not the intrinsic value of the paper and ink, for that is negligible. It is their power to move the beholder, not only to amuse or instruct him but also to stir the wellsprings of his being, to speak to him poignantly of his inmost thoughts and feelings, of religion, of sex, of war, of pride and pomp and power, of freedom and justice, of order and beauty. Prints share this power of evocation and inspiration with other great forms of visual art, but with the added virtue that they can be owned and enjoyed by many instead of few.

Prints have had many apologists and defenders, but none more charming than the anonymous author of *Sculptura-Historico-Technica*, or *The History and Art of Ingraving*, of 1747:

When I reflect on the Usefulness of this Art, I am surprised to find so few Gentlemen professed Admirers of it. It requires a large Fortune to make a fine Collection of Paintings, and great Judgment to avoid Imposition, and understand their Beauties; but Prints are adapted to all Ages, all Ranks of Men, and all Fortunes; they cost much less than Paintings, the Knowledge of them is more easily attained; and they comprehend all Sorts of Subjects, they are equally as useful as entertaining. . . .

Prints divert Youth, and instruct them at the same Time, by the lively Impression they make on their Minds; and this Instruction is not only more readily received but is more durable than that conveyed by Words. If you have a Child learn any Passage in Sacred or Profane History, by amusing him with a Representation of it, and explaining the Subject, he will rarely forget the Impression the different Characters that compose it will make on him. . . .

Prints are also as useful as entertaining; they represent absent things to us, as if they were present; they convey us instantly, without Hazard or Expense, into the most distant Countries, and make us as well acquainted with them as with our own; they communicate to us the Knowledge of many beautiful Objects in those Countries, which we must have been ignorant of, without their Assistance; and make us Contemporaries (in a manner) with the greatest Men of past Ages by giving us their lively Resemblance. . . .

Nothing is more proper to form a Taste than Prints: they give us a Tincture of the fine Arts; they assist us to arrive at the Knowledge of Paintings; for if we examine them attentively, they make us easily discover the different Manner affected by each School and Master. . . .

Lastly, there is hardly any Subject, with Regard to which we cannot either acquire some Knowledge, or enlarge that we already have, by the Help of this noble Art.

When our old author mentioned that prints can be both useful and entertaining, he hit upon a characteristic which prints share with books, namely their potential duality. Prints, like literature and the printed word, can serve both science and beauty—in Coleridge's famous distinction between science and poetry—as the communication of truth and the communication of immediate pleasure (in its widest sense as emotive power). Just as, among books, we can have both a manual of chemistry and a volume of poetry, so, among prints, we can have both a topographic map and a picture of timeless magic appeal. A print can be an original work of art even though not all prints are. Of the millions of prints which have been made since the beginning, only a small portion were ever intended to be intrinsic works of art. The vast majority were made by craftsmen and artisans for purposes of utility or instruction, to serve knowledge and science rather than art for its own sake. The emphasis was on use rather than beauty, although in the old days the distinction between the two was not as sharp as it is today. In science there is always progress: the old is superseded by improvement or by the invention of the new. But in the arts there is no such progress: we value the old equally with the new.

The graphic arts—comprising books and prints, in other words, those forms of visual art produced by printing methods—unquestionably have played an important role in the dissemination of knowledge and culture during the past six centuries. Indeed, one might venture to

assert that without the invention of printing and of printmaking in the fifteenth century, little if any of our present-day culture, our science, industry, and technology would exist. We would still be living in the Middle Ages. When Gutenberg, around the middle of the fifteenth century, perfected a method of printing from movable type, he transformed the unique handwritten manuscript, accessible to few, into the printed book, accessible to many. Of course, the Chinese had had the idea before him, but they could not profit by it because, with their use of a separate picture or ideograph for each word, they did not have a manageable alphabet. In the West, it became a process, quick, accurate, and cheap.

The same revolution took place in the making of pictures a little earlier, around the beginning of the fifteenth century. When some unknown craftsman devised a method of duplicating an image by printing, he transformed the unique drawing, accessible to few, into the printed picture, accessible to many. William M. Ivins has pointed out the importance and advantage of a precisely duplicable image. He cited the example of the botanist who wished to describe a plant to a fellow student in another country. He might write page after page of description, but unless he also sent along a drawing of it, he could not be sure that the other man would have a clear idea of how the plant or flower actually looked. Suppose, however, that instead of writing a letter, the botanist was writing a book, useful not only to his acquaintances but also to the many botanists whom he did not know, and to those of succeeding generations. He could not possibly draw all the pictures, nor could he write out all the books in longhand. Yet it was on the basis of this dissemination of ideas, this cumulative storing of knowledge—one scholar starting where others left off—that our science and technology and much of our civilization were built up. One could list examples from other fields, such as machine diagrams, building plans, mariners' maps, views and portraits, in addition to purely pictorial images. It is easy to see that the invention of a technique for making precisely duplicable images would benefit both science and art.

There have been collectors of prints for hundreds of years. Actually what are prints and why are they collected? The word *print* has only five letters, but it stands for a great many things. Literally, it means anything that is printed; and our life is surrounded by a multitude of printed things, for instance, postage stamps, paper money, stock certificates, illustrations in books, periodicals, and newspapers, photographs, posters and advertisements, printed textiles, colored reproductions of famous paintings, and the like. But we do not collect all these things, although stamps, money, and stock certificates have been collected with profit on occasion.

There are, however, certain kinds of prints, made by artists, that are collected because they are works of art. They are printed pictures, and the name is both descriptive and significant. The artist in general has many mediums in which to work: he may create oil paintings, watercolors, drawings, sculptures in wood or stone—or he may make printed pictures. The medium he chooses depends upon his inclination and training, but also upon the audience he intends to address. If he contemplates a single purchaser for his handiwork, he will draw, paint in oil or watercolor, or carve in wood or stone, because each work in these categories is unique, and can be possessed by only one purchaser. If he projects a wider circle of future owners—involving not one but numerous originals, each of which is truly an original—he will model and cast statues in metal or terra-cotta, or he will make prints, such as engravings, etchings, woodcuts, or lithographs. The essential characteristic of an artist print is that it is printed. The key to the method of making a print lies in the creation of a master design on a suitable base, such as a wood block or metal plate, which can be inked and printed to produce a quantity of identical prints. It is a device to produce multioriginals. The unique thing about prints is that they are not unique. In a sense printmaking is truly a democratic art, for it enables not one but many persons to own and enjoy a work of art.

Only an artist can make a work of art. It is not the medium but the esthetic intention that creates a work of art and gives it value. One can paint the side of a barn or one can paint a picture: the medium is the same, namely, oil colors. Similarly printmaking has both utilitarian and esthetic functions. In its early development, printmaking was quantitatively more utilitarian than artistic, furnishing (quite apart from religious imagery and other pictorial subject matter) all the illustrations in printed books of science, technology, natural history, architecture, models for furniture, textiles, and jewelry—that vast storehouse of visual knowledge about *things* upon which our civilization and culture are based. But throughout the history of graphic art, there have always been some artists who have made original prints more for pleasure and delectation than for utility. Such works are called fine or artist prints to distinguish them from the more prosaic variety. There is a special quality inherent in them—a heightened intensified communication cast in memorable form. Because the emotive potentialities are not exhausted in a single glance, we can look at great paintings or prints without surfeit or boredom. Prints and poems are alike in their power to kindle the imagination. Prints—without employing the same esthetic conventions as poetry—can have the same quality of concise and polished utterance, the same haunting

singing magic by which we can look at them again and again with unabated interest. It may be straining an analogy too far to liken a fine print to a broadsheet containing a poem. But one can say with assurance that original prints made by artists bear the same relation to general print production that high poetry and drama bear to general book production.

The pictures, which make up the main portion of this book, form an anthology, as it were, of more than ten centuries of artist prints. Out of the millions of prints that have been made in the course of time, 738 have been chosen for reproduction. It is hoped that they can be looked at with pleasure apart from the text as a portable exhibition of art, as it were, or "Museum without Walls." The groupings were made with a view to harmonious and significant arrangements on the page. In the selection I tried to maintain a balance between two different attitudes: that of the historian who searches for what is typical, average, and expressive of the time, and that of the artist who is interested in what is unusual, heightened, and timeless. In some rare instances, I believe, these seemingly divergent aims have been united in one and the same print that is at once timeless and nobly expressive of its time. Furthermore I have tried, as far as it is possible in the brief space allotted, to project prints against the background of history, to synchronize their production with that of the other arts and sciences, with the events of war and statecraft, economic and social life, in short to try to see them as their contemporaries saw them, as well as in the perspective of time. There is a give-and-take between the artist and his age: he leaves an impress on his contemporaries, and contemporary influences leave their impress on him. All this is mirrored dramatically in his works, more especially in such a medium as the print, which, being widespread and popular, reflects more accurately contemporary conditions. Two great factors have molded the actions of all men, economic conditions and ideology, stomach and mind. These inevitable strands of warp and woof are as evident in the tapestry of art as they are in the other activities of life. Art is one of the noblest of man's endeavors, but it is not supernatural; it is still essentially human, the product of the hand and brain.

Just as the connoisseur of food is interested in cookbooks, in how the delectable dishes are prepared, so the print lover should be interested in the techniques of the graphic arts, the "cookery" of fine prints. There are a number of principles or methods for duplicating designs. The relief method or woodcut is the oldest in point of time. The technique is relatively simple. The artist takes a block of wood, cut along the length of the tree and planed smooth, and proceeds to cut away all those portions of his design that he does not intend to print black.

When he has finished cutting on the wood, his drawing stands complete in relief, with the rest of the block cut down to a depth of about three millimeters. The artist then inks the surface of the block, lays a sheet of paper over it, runs it through a press, and the composition appears complete on the paper. The earliest woodcuts were printed not in a press but by rubbing with a burnisher or a spoon on the back of the paper in the way that all Japanese prints are made. In early times, too, there generally was a division of labor, the design being drawn on the wood by the artist and the cutting away being done by a professional woodcutter.

There is a variation and development of woodcut technique called wood engraving. In this instance the artist works on a block cut from the cross-section of a tree (thus avoiding the difficulties of cutting against the grain) and uses, among others, a burin or engraving tool which makes a white line against a background of black. There is some confusion and difference of opinion as to the exact meanings of woodcut and wood engraving. Some hold that the difference lies in the artist's fundamental conception of his picture: in a woodcut he conceives of the picture in terms of black lines against a background of white; in a wood engraving in terms of white lines against a background of black. It sometimes happens that the artist uses both methods in the same picture, and then it becomes difficult to say which predominates. The other school holds that the difference between the two lies in the technique. Woodcuts are printed from blocks sawed along the grain and cut with knives and gouges; whereas wood engravings are printed from end-grain blocks cut with a burin. This classification at least has the virtue of not being ambiguous; the artist cannot combine end-grain and along-the-grain on the same block. But it is not always easy to tell what kind of wood was used just by looking at a print. Dürer's woodblocks and Japanese prints are typical woodcuts. Bewick's blocks and Urs Graf's *Standard-Bearer* are examples of wood engraving. An early development of wood engraving is seen in the prints in the "dotted manner" or *manière criblée*. In these white line engravings, the solid blacks are often broken up by means of little white dots executed with a punch. Most of them were printed from metal blocks, such as copper, tin, bronze, or lead. Indeed the distinction between the two great processes of relief and intaglio lies not so much in the material as in the way of printing. Eric Gill has printed engravings from wood blocks, and William Blake etched copper plates for his "Songs of Innocence and Experience" in such a way that they could be printed as wood blocks.

The class of intaglio print includes metal engraving, etching, drypoint, mezzotint, stipple engraving, aquatint, and soft-ground etching. In engravings the lines are

incised into copper or other soft metal by means of a burin or graving tool. The technique of etching was perfected early in the sixteenth century in order to lighten the labor of cutting into the metal with a burin. It was discovered that it was possible to dig out the lines by chemical means instead of by manual effort. Therefore over the polished surface of the metal, a thin coating of an acid-resisting ground (consisting largely of wax) is laid; the artist makes a drawing upon the plate with a needle and thus lays bare the surface of the copper. The plate is then laid in a bath of acid (commonly nitric) which attacks the metal wherever it is exposed. It is this method of "etching" lines in metal that gives the process its name. One great advantage of etching over engraving is the greater freedom it gives in the drawing of the lines, since all manner of wayward and curved lines can be laid, which are exceedingly difficult to execute with the burin. Furthermore by "stopping out" some of the lines with an acid-resisting varnish and again inserting in the acid bath, it is possible to vary the biting and consequently the depth and quality of the line.

The printing principle of an engraving or etching is exactly the reverse of a woodcut. In a woodcut the lines stand out in relief and become the surface which is inked and printed. In an etching or engraving the lines are incised in the metal; the ink is forced into these lines and the surface of the metal is wiped clean. When a dampened sheet of paper is laid on the plate and the whole run through a press under considerable pressure, the paper is forced into the lines and picks up the ink therein; and the whole design is printed on the paper and becomes an impression, or proof as it is sometimes called, of an original etching. In an impression of an etching or engraving, the lines are ever so slightly raised above the surface of the paper, as can be proved by running the finger very lightly over the proof (though this action will grieve the true print lover!). This fact and the noticeable impression which the edge of the copper plate makes upon the paper, called the plate mark, are among the features which help to distinguish an etching or engraving from the woodcut processes. Etching is primarily a line technique, that is to say the etcher builds up his design by means of lines bitten to various depths. To amplify the technical means at the etcher's command, the process known as aquatint was perfected in the late eighteenth century. The technique is complicated but the principle is simple. Powdered rosin is dusted on a grounded plate, and the plate heated to melt the rosin. When the rosin cools it contracts, producing minute areas of exposed copper of characteristic pattern or grain. The plate is then bitten or rebitten in the usual way to produce areas of varying degrees of dark or light tones. By its use the etcher is enabled to draw not only with lines but also with washes or areas of tone, thus adding richness and variety of tonal color to his linear composition. Since both are etched with acid, it is easy to combine pure etching and aquatint. Aquatint was used to hold and define areas of colored ink in French eighteenth-century color prints, but even before its invention, roulettes, moulettes, and similar instruments were used to produce grained surfaces for the same purpose.

There is still another intaglio method designed to reproduce tones and not lines, namely mezzotint. A copper plate is covered with a multitude of tiny indentations made with a special instrument called a rocker. The plate, if it were inked at this stage, would print uniformly black. The engraver, by means of special instruments, scrapes away and burnishes out at will the minute indentations to establish his highlights, and working from dark to light, gradually creates a complete pattern of light and dark tones. It is a process particularly adapted to reproducing oil paintings, and was used almost exclusively for that purpose. It is printed like an engraving but does not yield as many impressions. Another technique, used largely to reproduce drawings and paintings, is stipple engraving or, similarly, engraving in the crayon manner. It is a variation of etching in which the design is built up by minute dots produced by means of a roulette and similar instruments. It can reproduce the texture and grain of a crayon drawing with great fidelity, but owing to its softness and lack of definition (even the lines are made up of tiny dots like a modern halftone) it found its widest use in sentimental and "fancy" subjects. Still another variation is soft-ground etching. A special and rather sticky ground is laid on the copper plate and upon this is laid a sheet of paper or silk or other textile. The lines are drawn over this, and when this is lifted off, the ground sticks to it wherever it was drawn upon. The plate is then bitten in the regular way. By this means a considerable variation in the textures of line work can be produced. It is sometimes used in conjunction with aquatint since its rather crumbly line is in keeping with the grained surface of aquatint. Lift-up soft ground can be used to produce areas as well as lines in varying textures. The possibilities of this method have been explored in recent times.

There is another modification of engraving called drypoint. Where the lines of an engraving are cut into the metal with a burin, in drypoint they are scratched into the surface with a steel needle or diamond point. In the process a furrow or shaving of metal, called the burr, is raised beside the line. The action of a burin also produces a burr but it is always shaved off in an engraving. When the burr is retained, it catches and holds more ink than the ordinary engraved line and imparts the rich and velvety black characteristic of the drypoint line. This burr

soon wears down and few good impressions can be pulled unless the plate is steel-faced. The technique was known in early times, Dürer and the Master of the Housebook having both made drypoints, but Rembrandt was the first to use the medium with a full realization of its possibilities. Drypoint is often used in conjunction with etching to give added richness and color to a composition.

The third great graphic method is lithography. It makes use of still another principle of printing. Its lines are neither incised in metal nor raised in relief on wood. It is called surface or chemical printing, and was invented around the beginning of the nineteenth century by a German, Aloys Senefelder. The process is based upon the well-known antipathy of grease and water. The artist draws with a greasy crayon on a slab of special limestone (found only in Bavaria) which has been grained to a requisite degree of fineness. When the artist has finished his drawing, the stone is turned over to a lithographer for printing. By a series of chemical steps which it will not be necessary to elaborate here, the greasy content becomes fixed in the stone. The stone is then moistened with a sponge. Wherever there is a greasy spot or mark the water will be repelled, but everywhere else the stone will absorb water and become damp. The stone is now ready for printing. A greasy ink is rolled over the surface. Wherever there is a greasy mark the ink will take, wherever the stone is damp and clear the greasy ink will not take. A sheet of paper is placed on the stone and the whole run through the press, with the result that an exact replica of the drawing appears on the paper. A certain kind of zinc plate can be used in place of the lithographic stone with equal success. Lithography is an exceedingly flexible medium with an enormous range of effects; lines with crayon or pen, washes, stump work, tonal values of all kinds can be rendered with fidelity and subtlety. It is well adapted for color printing, because linear and tonal effects can be produced on the same stone.

Another duplicating method employs the stencil principle, that is to say a hole in a masking surface. If any shape is cut in the masking material (such as a sheet of thin copper or plastic or even paper) and if that sheet is laid over a piece of paper, and if some pigment is brushed over the whole, an exact replica of the shape of the hole will appear on the paper beneath. This method, called *pochoir* in French and *Schablone* in German, has been used for coloring prints in quantity for many centuries in Europe and China (the red and yellow colors on the original of illustration No. 672 were probably applied through stencils). The crucial improvement in the process came about by fastening the master stencil to a piece of silk (later synthetic fabrics were used) stretched on a wooden frame. The open mesh of the silk allowed the pigment to flow through under slight pressure, and the silk, wherever attached to the stencil, gave it firm support on the delicate strips and promontories which otherwise were easily torn. The basic characteristic of the cut stencil—and its great limitation—was sharpness of outline. Subtle blending of tone and freehand irregularity of outline were impossible to achieve. The next great step in improvement was to dispense with the cut stencil entirely by creating its equivalent directly on the screen itself in the form of an opaque coating of glue or lacquer. This could be accomplished by the tusche-washout method: the artist draws his design (or the first of his color separations) on the stretched silk with lithographic tusche or crayon. Then he coats the screen with glue, and when the glue is set, he washes out the tusche drawing with kerosene or benzine which dissolves the tusche but not the glue. Thus an open-mesh stencil of the drawing is created, bounded by opaque areas of glue. For the printing, tempera or oil colors are used. A sheet of paper is laid on the wooden base to which the screen is hinged, and the screen swung over it. Then a generous portion of pigment is laid along the edge of the screen, and a squeegee (a rubber blade with a wooden handle similar to a window cleaner) is moved across the screen, forcing the pigment through the mesh and onto the paper. The characteristic mesh of the screen is visible when a print is examined with a magnifying glass: it is a distinguishing mark of the process. When the edition has been printed, the stencil can be washed out and the screen used over again. The process is well adapted for color printing since the registration of the successive printings is easy. It is also possible to photograph a design onto the screen. Stencil techniques do not involve the use of a press, but the meaning of the phrase *to print* has long since been enlarged to include numerous operations not dependent upon the pressure of a press, such as the printing of photographs or the printing of a wood block by hand with a burnisher or spoon. The prints made by artists with the silkscreen process are sometimes called serigraphs to differentiate them from commercial productions.

Photography is also a form of printmaking. In the early nineteenth century the researches of Daguerre, Niepce, Talbot, and others brought about the perfection of the photographic process—a device for fixing an image on paper, glass, or film by purely optical and chemical means, and then printing from that negative. The *daguerreotype*, being a unique positive, cannot be classed as a print. The camera can objectively and impersonally translate whatever appears before it in terms of light and dark upon the plate or film. If nature, or any object, is to be copied, photography can do it more quickly and

cheaply than any artist can, and seemingly more accurately, because the copyist's personality is not obvious. It must be remembered, however, that photography is really only another pictorial convention, and that the camera's eye also has a kind of "personality" or idiosyncracy, since its diverse-angled lenses and monocular vision (as opposed to human binocular or stereoscopic vision) produce not only variations but also distortion from "reality." But photography is so universally used and accepted that we have adopted its conventions as the last word in accuracy or "realism." Today, photography is the great documentary medium. Although most of its applications have been utilitarian, it has also been employed to create purposive works of art, in other words, artist prints. It has been said that photography could not be an art medium because all its operations are mechanical. All print mediums have mechanical elements, which the artist has learned to manipulate and control. There are enough variations in the steps of the photographic process to give the artist a wide repertory of expressive devices: lighting and arrangement of materials, choice of lenses, changes of focus, variations in development and printing, including solarization. There is no logical reason, then, why a photograph cannot be a work of art if it is made by a conscious artist.

In the last fifty years, printmakers have been much concerned with technique and technical innovations. In all mediums technical manipulation has been developed and raised to new levels. Experiments have been made in artificially creating blocks for relief printing by building up, from a plane surface, layer upon layer of synthetic plastics such as epoxy or acrylic, or by glueing cardboard, textiles, or string to the surface and covering with lacquer to be printed from (collographs, cellocuts, and the like). Similarly in intaglio printing, metal scrap, wire, netting, and other found objects are fastened to a metal plate and run through a press, either inked or uninked, to produce three-dimensional effects. The possibilities of embossing prints without ink have been explored. Textures derived from impresses of soft grounds have been created in wide variety. Aquatint has been given greater freedom of manipulation through the sugar-lift process. Printings by intaglio and by relief from the same plate have been combined to produce new effects. Photographic processes have been widely used, not only in transferring images, but also in preliminary stages of manipulation. In a *cliché verre*, for example, a drawing is made on a glass plate coated with a dark emulsion. Wherever the stylus makes a line through the coating, it appears as transparent glass. A facsimile of the drawing can be produced on photographic paper by exposure to light and development in the usual way. Caroline Durieux has experimented with a new method of color printing. It employs the principle of the *cliché verre* (using matrix film instead of glass) plus hand manipulation of the film (pushing the emulsion, freed from its support, into various pleats and creases to produce textural effects) and an extension of the dye-transfer process for color. With the technical aid of Professor H. E. Wheeler at Louisiana State University, she also developed a new medium, electron printing, making use of radioactive isotopes as the image-making agent. Only a few of the many variations and improvements in technique have been mentioned here. Those who want a fuller coverage of graphic processes are advised to consult the advanced technical manuals mentioned in the bibliography.

One final word on the use of the word *original*. Since it is used in two different senses, confusion sometimes occurs. It is used as an adjective in contradistinction to *reproductive*. An original etching is one which the artist designed and executed himself. A reproductive engraving is one in which the engraver has copied another artist's design or painting. This distinction has lost much of its force in recent years because photography and photo-mechanical methods have taken over the reproductive function of printmaking. In any case the distinction is invidious because some so-called reproductive engravings, Marcantonio Raimondi's after Raphael for example, are infinitely superior to a multitude of original etchings by mediocre artists. When used as a noun, original refers specifically to a print. Some people have the mistaken notion that all prints are copies of some hidden and mysterious original. Every impression of a woodcut, etching, or lithograph is an "original," the final and complete embodiment of the artist's intention, of which the plate, the paper, and the ink are the preliminary steps. The miracle of the graphic process is that there can be not one but many originals.

2. The End of Gothic

I. THE BEGINNING OF WOODCUT

During the fifteenth century—as far as it is mirrored in the history of prints—one great epoch ended and another began. In the northern countries, France, Germany, and Flanders, the Gothic era ended and the Renaissance began; in Italy the Rennaisance was in full bloom. In one sense, however, the classifications of late Gothic and early Renaissance are relatively minor distinctions: the very idea of making prints, a cheap multiplication of originals, like the idea of printing from movable type, was a development of the greatest cultural importance, and one that marked the transition between the medieval and the modern point of view. "The Gothic sun," as Victor Hugo said, "set behind the colossal press at Mainz." It was during the fifteenth century that both woodcuts and copper engravings in any quantity began to be made and printed and sold.

It is interesting to speculate why the idea of making prints should have been carried to a practical conclusion at that particular period in the annals of European history. It was not that the idea or the technique of engraving was a new one. There exist incised drawings by primitive man on mammoth tusks capable, when inked, of producing prints in our sense of the word. Likewise the Greeks and Etruscans sometimes engraved designs on the back of their bronze or silver mirrors which could easily serve as printing plates (illustration 1). And there are examples of Romanesque art such as the famous Chandelier of the Emperor Barbarossa at Aix-la-Chapelle of the twelfth century, parts of which contain metal plates with incised designs, as if made to order for the production of engravings. In the mid-nineteenth century, when this chandelier was taken down to be cleaned, someone conceived the idea of inking the plates and striking off a small number of impressions from them. One of these prints, the *Nativity*, in circular form, is reproduced in this book (illustration 2). The result might easily be taken for a true engraving in Romanesque style some three centuries before the earliest known engraving. Likewise, the technique of designing and cutting a wood block had already been perfected for the printing of textiles. There exist Coptic textiles of the sixth century which are stamped with wood blocks (illustration 3).

Printed textiles were common in the Middle Ages. Cennino Cennini described the technique in his *Book of Art* at the end of the fourteenth century.

One of the chief reasons why prints were not produced in the twelfth century was the fact that there was no cheap and efficient material on which to print, such as paper. Paper, to be sure, was known in Europe at the time. The earliest extant document on paper in Europe is a deed by King Roger of Sicily written in Arabic and Latin and dated 1109. Paper is officially recorded as having been invented in China in the year 105. It remained a Chinese secret until its manufacture in Samarkand in 757 and in Baghdad in 793 through knowledge gained from Chinese prisoners. This knowledge was later transmitted to the Saracens in Spain in 1150. The first paper mill in France was established at Hérault in 1189, in Italy at Fabriano in 1276, in Germany at Nuremberg in 1391. Much of the paper used in Europe, however, was still imported from the Saracen mills in Spain and Damascus, and it was not until the middle of the fifteenth century that paper was in general use in Europe. "There were few in Europe who could read," as Carter points out, "and the demand for a cheaper writing material, until the advent of printing, was small. It was the coming of paper that made the invention of printing possible, yet it was the invention of printing that made the use of paper general."

Indeed it is likely that the use of wood blocks to produce ornamental designs on textiles prompted a similar use of wood blocks to multiply pictorial images on paper. The transitional stage could be illustrated by a printed textile in the National Gallery of Art, Rosenwald Collection, *Lectern Cloth with the Marriage at Cana*, Austrian School ca. 1400 (illustration 4). Richard S. Field has well described its significance: "It is not only one of the very few surviving late medieval printed textiles, but it also is one of the earliest [European] woodcuts known. In both roles it strengthens the contention that printing on paper was a natural extension of the process of printing carved wooden blocks onto cloth. The technique of cutting developed from solid patterns printed from small blocks (or small motifs carved several times on one larger block, the

size of the cloth) to single scenes cut in outline on larger blocks. That development was paralleled by the increasing availability of paper, and the two seemed to have merged in the twenty years either side of 1400." This fragment (for it must originally have been longer) was probably used to drape over a lectern. It is another example of the advantage made possible by the duplicable image. Just as the printed book with printed illustrations became the poor man's version of an illuminated manuscript, so this lectern cloth was a less costly version of a woven or embroidered cloth for ecclesiastical use, or for use as a pattern for embroidery. The advantages were to grow greater with the increased use of paper.

Thus it is to be seen that a plentiful supply of cheap material such as paper was a conditioning factor in any widespread production of woodcuts and engravings. There was, however, still another factor to be considered, namely the demand on the part of the people. In the early Middle Ages the standard of living was very low. In that age of scarcity there was little demand for such marginal luxuries as pictures or the written word. Insofar as a demand for pictures existed, it was satisfied by the church, which was the meeting place and treasure-house of the whole community. Most of the people were scattered on the land; very little of the population was concentrated in towns. Furthermore, there was little trade. Each community was a self-contained economic unit. It produced, with considerable effort, all that it required for subsistence, but there was no surplus. It is difficult for us in this day and age to visualize such a state of society. There were no books or newspapers, no ready-made clothes, and few utensils, no shops or stores, few artisans who practiced their trade exclusively. There was practically no money: almost all trade was effected by barter. There was very little travel. The roads were bad, and there were many knights and nobles who made common practice of out-and-out brigandage, or, with some show of legality, of the exaction of tolls. A great many of the people could not travel at all since they were bound to the land as serfs or tenants. The standard of living in the manors and castles was more sumptuous but not much higher.

It is small wonder then that in such a milieu there was small demand for art for its own sake and no place for "art in the home." There were, however, several major historical developments which eventually succeeded in breaking up the stagnation of the feudal or manorial system. One of these was the Crusades; by increasing travel they introduced new ideas and cultivated a taste for the comforts and luxuries of the Orient. Another was the rise of free cities, which either retained or acquired exemption from feudal obligations incumbent on the peasantry. Concomitant with the growth of free cities

was a vast extension of trade both with the Orient and with various parts of Europe. The Italian cities, Genoa, Pisa, Amalfi, and chiefly Venice, grew rich through the Crusades and the oriental trade. The cities of Flanders, chiefly Bruges, were the meeting place of the northern and southern maritime trade, and at the same time the center of the woolen-weaving industry of Europe. Augsburg, Nuremberg, Ulm, Basel, Mainz, Frankfurt, and Cologne were cities that waxed prosperous along the river and overland trade routes from Venice to the north. All of these engaged in manufacture and trade—activities of the middleman as opposed to the agrarian and producer-consumer economy of feudalism. Their merchant and artisan guilds became wealthy and powerful, and their citizens acquired a taste for art and other luxuries. Albrecht Dürer, in his diary of his journey to the Netherlands in 1520, recounts how he was received in Bruges in the height of its prosperity:

Then they prepared a banquet for me, and I went thence with them to their guild hall; there were many honorable men gathered together, goldsmiths, painters, and merchants, and they made me sup with them and they gave me presents and sought my acquaintance and did me great honor.

And thus he describes a festival in Antwerp:

The Sunday after the Feast of the Assumption I saw the great procession of Our Lady's Church at Antwerp, where the whole town was gathered together, with all the trades and professions, and each was dressed in his best according to his rank; every guild and profession had its sign by which it might be recognized. Between the companies were carried great costly gold pole-candlesticks and their long old Frankish silver trumpets; and there were many pipers and drummers in the German fashion; all were loudly and noisily blown and beaten. I saw the procession pass along the street, spread far apart so that they took up much space crossways, but close behind one another: goldsmiths, painters, stonecutters, broiderers, sculptors, joiners, carpenters, sailors, fishermen, butchers, leather-workers, cloth-makers, bakers, tailors, shoemakers, and all kinds of craftsmen and workmen who work for their livelihood. There were likewise shopkeepers and merchants with their assistants of all sorts. After them came the marksmen with their guns, bows, and cross-bows; then the horsemen and foot soldiers; then came a fine troop of very gallant men, nobly and splendidly costumed.

It was in such free and vigorous city life that the practice of printmaking in the North took hold and spread rapidly. Prints, being produced in relatively large quantities, require, if not trading, at least an organized distribution over a wide area. Furthermore a prosperous middle class, which made up the urban population, was then and for many centuries to come the best customer for

prints. The peasant and laborer never had any margin above subsistence to buy more than an occasional religious image. And the nobles and the court circles, notably the Burgundian court of the fifteenth century and the rulers of the Italian cities, bestowed their greatest patronage on painting, sculpture, miniature painting, and architecture.

Of the two great genres of printmaking the woodblock was the first to be developed. Its actual beginnings are lost in the obscurity and anonymity that surround most popular art. Popular art, the obvious and omnipresent thing, the cheap common object, is generally quite literally worn out in use; little value is attached to it at the time, and it is preserved only by some happy chance. Those prints which have come down through the ages have sometimes been found in out-of-the-way places, pasted inside the bindings of old books, or pasted on doors and walls like wallpaper. Occasionally they are found pasted on the insides of little trunks or traveling cases (illustration 8). These boxes, as Hind suggests, were probably used by lawyers or merchants for their documents or accounts, or by priests to carry their breviaries and other requisites on their journeys, and even as portable altars. It is obvious that with such great lacunae in the record, the history of the woodcut in its origins is hard to determine. It is probable, however, that the idea of printing impressions on paper to supply a demand for a cheap multiplication of designs first gained currency around the end of the fourteenth century or the beginning of the fifteenth century. And demand there was, on two separate counts. One was for playing cards. Although there are no examples of woodcut playing cards extant before about 1450, cards by their nature being apt to wear out, there is every reason to suppose that there was a flourishing production of playing cards from the beginning of the century in Germany and Italy. An example dating from the second half of the fifteenth century and signed by J. de Dale of Lyons is reproduced as illustration 13. The more primitive cuts were in outline only and were designed to be colored either by hand or through stencils. An early representation of card playing, with a glimpse of the cards themselves, is given in illustration 22, from a book printed in Augsburg in 1472 by Gunther Zainer.

The second great demand for prints was for religious images, pictures of the saints, illustrations of the life of the Virgin or of Christ. Many of the early woodcuts were undoubtedly produced in monasteries by the monks themselves. The monasteries enjoyed immunity from guild restrictions, and at the beginning there undoubtedly was opposition by the guilds of artists and illuminators to a technique which threatened their livelihood. The great bulk of the work, however, was either made by regular artists by direct commission from monasteries or produced with an eye to the religious market at the great centers of print production, such as the cities of Ulm, Augsburg, Bamberg, Nuremberg, Cologne, Dijon, Avignon, Bruges, Salzburg. The religious orders and the churches, in any case, were among the chief customers for such prints. Hind quotes Luther's complaint against the Pope, in his pamphlet, *An den christlichen Adel deutscher Nation:* that he granted the revenues of a convent to some cardinal, who would leave a single monk in charge, one of whose chief duties was to sell pictures to pilgrims. The artists and printers also sold directly to the people at their shops or at the fairs. Dürer, when in Venice, wrote back to his friend Pirkheimer: "Now I commend myself to you, and tell my mother to be ready to sell at the Crown Fair."

The Buxheim *St. Christopher* (illustration 7) was for a long time famous as the first example of a woodcut actually bearing a date, namely 1423, though further research has discovered an earlier print, the Brussels *Madonna,* bearing the date 1418. It was found in the binding of a book in the Carthusian monastery of Buxheim and is probably of Bavarian origin. It is a dramatic rendering of the Christopher legend. In addition to the date below, there is a Latin inscription which may be translated as follows: "On whatsoever day thou hast seen Christopher's face, on that day, to be sure, thou shalt not die an evil death." This inscription furnishes a clue to the extraordinary popularity of images of St. Christopher: the sight of him was talismanic, and ensured, if not against death, at least against an unshrived or unsanctified death. It is interesting to discover in a painting of the Annunciation by a follower of Robert Campin, the Master of Flémalle, in the Brussels Museum, a print of St. Christopher hanging (with charming disregard for historical sequence) over the chimney. It illustrates the way in which these prints, unmatted and unframed, were used in the home, and also demonstrates why so few of them have survived. The anachronism of displaying a print of St. Christopher in a room where the Archangel Gabriel is foretelling to the Virgin the miraculous birth of Christ is characteristic of the age. This disregard of the unities of time or place is mirrored in the print of St. Christopher itself: various incidents in the life and miracle of St. Christopher are telescoped into one picture. The intention of the artist was not realistic but symbolic. The realistic touches that do appear in the picture are in the nature of corroborative or decorative detail. This approach to the solution of an artistic problem has been widely used by artists of all ages, including the twentieth century.

Art historians distinguish between two stylistic phases in fifteenth-century woodcuts. Characteristic of the ear-

lier style are the strong heavy outlines (almost like the lead in stained glass windows bounding the color areas to be painted in later by hand), the rounded facial types, the flowing decorative forms of drapery and the like, and the absence of shading or hatching. Typical are such prints as the *Rest on the Flight into Egypt* (Bohemian School, ca. 1410–25, illustration 5) or the *St. Dorothea* (Bavarian School, ca. 1410–25, illustration 6). Toward the end of the century more shading was employed and the forms of drapery became more angular. Many of the German book illustrations of the last quarter of the fifteenth century display elements of the late Gothic angular style (illustrations 16, 23).

Another development of relief printing in the late fifteenth century was the dotted print (*manière criblée* or *Schrottblatt*). The technique probably originated in the goldsmiths' workshops: metal plates (the surviving ones are of copper) were employed and manipulated with a burin and various punches of the kind used by goldsmiths. The design was usually conceived in terms of white line-work on a black background, but in many cases both white-line and black-line drawing appeared on the same plate. The heaviness of the dark backgrounds was enlivened by patterns of ornament created with the punches. The treatment was so consciously decorative that the question has been raised whether the plates were intended to be used for printing or whether the indentations were filled with colored enamel and the plate used solely as a decoration. Lettering, if it appears on the plate, could give a clue as to the intention. If the lettering was reversed, the plate presumably was designed for printing. From extant examples it would appear that the technique was used for both purposes. The same problem, whether for printing or for decoration, occurs in connection with *nielli*, a variety of intaglio print. In the dotted print, *Crucifixion* (illustration 9), the background is built up by the use of punches of several patterns, the figures are created by dots of various sizes, and the greensward with a burin and three-dotted punch. The faces and bare bodies are delineated by black line, whereas the rest of the composition is in white line. The other print, *Christ and the Woman of Samaria* (illustration 10), was probably made in Cologne, as is shown by the coat of arms of Cologne on the wall of the well. The design has been constructed entirely with dots, and pattern punches have been used only on the woman's dress. The big, simple forms, the decorative details, and the romantic glimpses (in the background) of towers, trees, and travelers all contribute to the picturesque effect and endow the print with the naive charm of folk art.

While on the subject of dotted prints, a mixed technique of white on black and black on white, one might consider the use of a pure white-line technique, a much rarer form, at least in the early days. Two examples of the art are shown. One of them, *Pomerium de Sanctis* (illustration 11)—like the print previously mentioned—has charm, not a naive winsomeness but the unworldly charm of the saintly or monastic life set in an enclosed orchard. The print, with its four roundels depicting the attributes of the four evangelists, was the frontispiece to a book of sermons by Fra Pelbartus, a monk of the Franciscan order. The other print is very much of this world, one might say, a picture full of worldly pomp and martial swagger, *Standard Bearer of Bern* by Urs Graf, 1521 (illustration 12).

The so-called block-books form an interesting phase in the history of the woodcut. In a block-book text and pictures were combined in one impression, the letterpress being also cut on the same block of wood. (In a few early instances, known as "chiro-xylographic," the space for the text was left blank, to be filled in by hand.) At one time the importance of these books was exaggerated, when it was thought that they formed a connecting link between printmaking and book printing. The deduction seemed logical. Printmaking, without question, was the earlier invention; then came the block-books, a combination of image with letterpress, and finally printing from movable type. Subsequent research has demonstrated, however, that the perfection of the art of printing from movable type proceeded quite independently of block-books. The subject is full of controversy. The documentary claims, for instance, in favor of Laurens Coster of Haarlem as against Gutenberg for the priority of the invention of printing, might perhaps be explained on the basis that Coster was concerned with the printing of block-books but not with movable type. A page from an *Apocalypse* and from a *Canticum Canticorum* are reproduced (illustrations 14, 15). Other titles are *Biblia Pauperum* and *Speculum Humanae Salvationis*. Still another one, *Ars Moriendi*, has engaged the attention of scholars for its connection with the intaglio sequence of Master E.S. Which came first? The consensus today seems to be that the designs in the block-book were based on those of Master E.S. The chief distinction of the block-books is their rarity: their merit as creative works of art is sometimes doubtful. Nonetheless they were popular in their day and copies were literally worn out by use.

Not many years after the invention of printing, the printers saw the possibility of using woodcuts for illustrating their books and thus competing more advantageously with the illuminated manuscript. From about 1470 onwards, woodcut books began to appear with increasing frequency in all the leading centers of book production. The number of illustrated *incunabula* (after 1500, the number is even greater) is large and offers an attractive field for the collector not only of books but also

of prints. The early *Einblattdrucke* (single prints, not from books) are excessively rare, and are to be found chiefly in old public collections. A few of them are great masterpieces, but the majority are crude and mediocre as works of art, and often in poor condition. On the other hand, single sheets from incomplete books are still fairly plentiful and above average in artistic merit. They are also much more easily datable (most dates for *Einblattdrucke* are attributions by scholars). One can get a fair idea of the art of the fifteenth century from book illustrations; one can get an even better conception—and a more fascinating one—of the life and customs of the end of the Middle Ages and Early Renaissance in all their variety and diversity. William Morris has aptly summed up their qualities: "It may surprise some of our readers to hear that I claim the title of works of art, both for these picture-ornamented books as books, and also for the pictures themselves. Their two main merits are first their decorative and next their story-telling quality; and it seems to me that these two qualities include what is necessary and essential in book pictures."

In my survey of fifteenth-century book illustration I have chosen twelve German works, two Dutch, and eleven French. I shall discuss the sixteen Italian fifteenth-century woodcuts more properly later in their context with Italian Renaissance prints in general. Here I shall treat only of the Gothic contribution. The first illustrated book with a date appeared in Germany. It is a collection of fables by Ulrich Boner entitled *Der Edelstein*, printed by Albrecht Pfister at Bamberg in 1461. Among the centers of German book production were Augsburg, Cologne, Lübeck, Mainz, Nuremberg, Strassburg, and Ulm. One of the most delightful of the Augsburg imprints is the *Spiegel des menschlichen Lebens* (Mirror of Human Life) by Rodericus Zamorensis, printed by Günther Zainer ca. 1475 (illustration 23). The subject was popular in the Middle Ages, treating of the condition and occupations of men and contrasting the good and evil sides of them. The woodcut has an elegance of design that is impressive; not all of the woodcuts in the book are as well cut as this one. I have already spoken of Ingold's *Guldin Spiel*, likewise printed by Günther Zainer in 1472 (illustration 22) in connection with playing cards. Of the two imprints from Ulm, one is the *Buch der Weisheit* (Bidpai), printed by L. Lienhart Holle in 1483 (illustration 18), a collection of Oriental fables, also known as the *Panchatantra*, compiled by Anthonius von Pforr from a Latin version based upon a Hebrew version, in turn based upon an Arabic translation from the original Sanskrit. The other is Conrad Dinckmuth's edition of Terence's *Eunuchus* of 1486 (illustration 16). In the woodcut shown, the houses and windows have been stylized into a pleasing pattern of black and white. It is interesting to compare this early print with a recent lithograph by the American, Niles Spencer, where the modern artist has also made a lively abstract pattern by conventionalizing house forms (illustration 620).

The introduction of printing and the expansion of the forces that led to the Reformation focused attention on the Bible. Not only were various editions of the Latin Vulgate printed, but many translations into Dutch, English, French, Czech, Italian, German (notably Luther's of 1522) were made and printed during the fifteenth and sixteenth centuries. The authority of God's Word in the vulgar tongue (as interpreted by each individual conscience) was invoked to controvert the authority of the Catholic Church in matters of salvation. One of the articles of the Schmalkaldic League, a band of German Protestant principalities, specified that "the articles of faith shall be based upon God's word and that of no one else, not even an angel's." Many of these popular Bibles were illustrated with woodcuts, some of only archaeological interest, others famous for their beauty and design. Four characteristic examples are shown here, two German, one French, and one Italian. Of the German books, the first is the *Adam and Eve and the Expulsion from Paradise* in the Cologne Bible, printed about 1479 by Quentel (illustration 20). It was the most ambitious undertaking of its time, and the blocks had considerable influence upon other artists; Koberger borrowed them (a not uncommon procedure of the day) to use in his edition of the Bible at Nuremberg in 1483; and both Dürer and Holbein borrowed and transformed some of the designs in their own series of biblical illustrations. The other German illustration is from the Bible printed in Lübeck by Steffen Arndes in 1494 (illustration 21). There are certain realistic touches and a certain interest in the psychological interplay of the characters—the embarrassment of Joseph's brothers in the presence, as they suppose, of a high Egyptian dignitary—that strike a rather new note in German illustration. Most early German illustration is schematic, a signpost, as Kristeller called it, a symbol rather than an illustration in the true sense of the word. They presented the bare bones of a subject but seldom clothed it in flesh and blood. The pictures were subordinate to the text and served as a quick method of locating a particular chapter or subject. In the *Nuremberg Chronicle*, for example, one and the same portrait cut was used to represent Thales, Paris the Trojan, Anastasius, Odofredus, and Dante. The *Chronicle* was a folio encyclopedia of world history and geography, profusely illustrated with 1,809 cuts of mediocre quality, few of them being distinguished either in design, in cutting, or in the arrangement on a page. Sydney Cockerell has analyzed the distribution of the cuts and discovered that there are really only 645, the other 1,164 being repeats, doing service for portraits and city

views without much regard for historical or scientific accuracy. The whole was intended to impress rather by its quantity than its quality. It sold bound for two Rhenish florins, and is an early example of mass production made possible by the fact that Koberger had agents in Paris, Lyons, and Toulouse for the sale of his books. A transition was taking place between the printer or craftsman who sold books at his printing shop and possibly at some of the local fairs or more important distant places, and the publisher with a regular selling organization and international affiliations. The capitalist nature of Koberger's undertaking is further emphasized by the fact that two rich men of Nuremberg, Sebald Schreyer and Sebastian Cammermeister, advanced money to be used in publishing enterprises, including Hartmann Schedel's *Liber Cronicarum*, familiarly known as the *Nuremberg Chronicle*. A cut from the latter is shown as illustration 130 in connection with map making; it is cited here in connection with the book as a whole. Koberger at one time employed twenty-four presses and over a hundred workmen. Koberger's was far from being an isolated example of capitalistic enterprise, since similar ventures have been recorded in Italy, Basel, and elsewhere. One other example from Koberger's press is shown, an amusing picture of *Solomon and His Wives at a Banquet* from the *Schatzbehalter* of 1491 (illustration 19). The name of the designer of the woodcut is known: he is Michael Wolgemut, the teacher of Albrecht Dürer.

From Mainz, the cradle of printing, came another book famous for its innovations, Breydenbach's *Peregrinatio in Terram Sanctam* (Voyage to the Holy Land) (illustration 25). It is the first book in which the illustrator's name is mentioned—Erhart Reuwich. The author, a rich canon of Mainz, took the artist along on his journey, and he made many drawings, later translated into woodcuts, of city views (some on large folding plates) and sketches of foreign peoples, Turks, Syrians, Jews, and the like. There is also a page of animals including a camel, monkey, giraffe, crocodile, and, amazingly enough, a unicorn; underneath is an inscription saying "these animals are accurately drawn as we saw them in the Holy Land." In spite of such occasional lapses, the book is not only lively and entertaining but surprisingly accurate. It is the first work of travel and geography that is based not on Ptolemy or Aristotle but on independent observation, and it inaugurates a long series of views and maps in printed form that were to extend man's knowledge of the globe and its inhabitants. The other Mainz imprint, the *Gart der Gesuntheit* or *Herbarius zu Teutsch*, printed by Peter Schöffer, Gutenberg's partner, in 1485, contains a handsome frontispiece designed unquestionably by the same Reuwich who went to the Holy Land. The *Gathering of Thirteen Physicians* (illustration 28) shows doctors assembled from many lands. Two more works of medical interest: one from a *Regimen Sanitatis* printed by Bämler, Augsburg, 1482, *Two Physicians Diagnosing a Patient*, displays a touch of satire in the delineation of the smug and learned doctor who does everything by the book (illustration 27). The other is a cut from Bartholomaeus Anglicus's book, *El Libro de Proprietatibus Rerum en Romance*, printed in Spanish at Toulouse in 1494 (illustration 26). Although the work is not as important as the Mainz *Gart der Gesuntheit* and other herbals and compendiums of natural history, it nonetheless reflects accurately the unscientific state of science at the time. Its illustrations, with their naive and decorative stylizations, have a charm that transcends their scientific interest.

Two examples of Netherlands presses are shown. The woodcut *The Author Dining with the Hermit "Understanding"* is from the *Chevalier Deliberé*, Gouda 1485, an allegorical and somewhat pedantic panegyric on the exploits of Charles the Bold (illustration 47). The other is *Sir Hercules Fighting Three Lions* from the *Histoire van Trojen*, Bellaert, Haarlem, 1485 (illustration 32). This woodcut, with its highly decorative pattern of black and white, is conceived in a sort of heraldic style with artistic conventions familiar to all students of heraldry. It is interesting to note that the hero wears the plate of armor which replaced the old-fashioned knee-length coat of mail around the beginning of the century. It was this style of armor that brought about the use of a separate upper and nether garment—shirt and hose or trousers—which has remained characteristic of male attire ever since.

Not only Bibles but other religious books such as Missals, Psalters, and Books of Hours, were adorned with woodcuts. The *Bible en Françoys* printed for Vérard about 1505, in its *Adam and Eve* (illustration 34), affords an interesting contrast to the similar subject from the Cologne Bible. The emphasis of the German work is on the moral question, whereas that of the French work is on a naive delight in the wonders of a terrestrial paradise. Among the most beautiful and touching productions in the whole history of prints were the *Horae* or Books of Hours, printed in Paris in the two decades just preceding and succeeding the turn of the sixteenth century. These *Horae* were prayer books chiefly for the laity, designed as cheap substitutes for the manuscript *Horae* which had been current for hundreds of years. They usually contained the Kalendar, extracts from the Gospels, the Canonical Hours or daily offices of the church, various other offices including the Office of the Dead, the Litanies, and the Penitential Psalms, and the whole furnished with a host of charming designs and pictures, following Pope Gregory's adage, *"Pictura est laicorum scriptura."* There might be large cuts of the Visitation, Nativity, Adoration of the Shepherds, and of the Magi,

Flight into Egypt, Dives and Lazarus, David and Bathsheba, and similar subjects traditionally associated with certain portions of the text. And there would be borders made up of small cuts of Gothic designs, scenes from the life of the Virgin and of Christ, the story of Susanna, or Joseph and His Brethren, images of saints, the procession of the *Danse Macabre*, the occupations of the months, glimpses of huntsmen and stags and dogs, of lovers and fools, of griffins and mermaids—a veritable kaleidoscope of imagery, austerely religious or enchantingly secular, to strike the fancy and delight the eye. The essence of the Middle Ages is distilled in these pages, the faint perfume of incense, the quiet and the coolness of churches, the perennial magic of an ancient legend sweetly told, a gallimaufry of sublime and grotesque. Three pages from books of hours are reproduced (illustrations 37, 38, 39). In one the dramatic story of *Dives and Lazarus* is set within a frame of beautiful Gothic ornament and this in turn is surrounded by a border of small cuts depicting the Cumaean Sibyl, the Marriage of Joachim and Anna, and three scenes of the Dance of Death, the Pope, the Emperor, and the Cardinal. In the second, the *Adoration of the Shepherds* is shown. This is genuine folk art, created by a nameless artist who gave expression to the simple joys and artless piety of humble folk. In spite of his anonymity the artisan is revealed as an artist in his masterly projection of character and his skillful use of Gothic ornament. Note how adroitly the engraver has varied the textures and avoided flat black areas so difficult to print from a metal surface. The third example depicts *Bathsheba in Her Bath* and King David in the role of *voyeur*. These books of hours were very popular at the time, about six hundred editions by various French publishers having been preserved and recorded, in addition to countless others that have been lost. They were one of the last fine flowerings of the Gothic spirit, and their popularity was short-lived. The impact of the Renaissance created an entirely new style of ornament and design, which is reflected in the *Horae* designed by Geoffrey Tory and printed by Simon de Colines in 1525 (illustration 40). Tory, famous humanist, typographer, and designer of type and woodcuts, author of *Champfleury*, was thoroughly imbued with the ideals of the Italian Renaissance. But these ideals were not in the long run sympathetic to a mode of expression so essentially medieval as the books of hours, and they eventually ceased to have any influence in the lives of the people. Though this later *Horae* does not suggest the religious feeling of the fifteenth-century book, from a typographical standpoint it is a beautiful work, the Renaissance ornament and open line-work harmonizing perfectly with the light roman type face.

The Dance of Death was a theme that haunted the medieval mind. And well it might, for the vision of sudden and inevitable death was a vivid and terrible reality in the later Middle Ages. There had been plagues in Europe before, but in 1348 the Black Death or bubonic plague swept through the whole of Europe in successive epidemics with an overwhelming loss of life. It is estimated that in England over half the population lost their lives; in Venice two-fifths of the people died; in certain districts of France only one-tenth of the population survived. There were two reactions possible toward this catastrophe: one licentious, "eat, drink and be merry, for tomorrow we die," and the other ascetic, "*memento mori.*" Both attitudes had their reflection in the art of the time, though the austere attitude predominated. An example of the first attitude is Boccaccio's *Decameron*, which as everyone knows were the tales told to pass the time away by a group of people who had retired to escape the plague. (This work is here represented by illustration 53, from the Venice edition of 1492.) The *Danse Macabre*, a typical expression of the more austere attitude, was immensely popular for several centuries to come. Not only was it literally performed as a Dance of Death, a sort of Mystery Play, but the sequence was painted on the walls of churches, cemeteries, and covered bridges, and appeared in innumerable prints and books. Perhaps the idea of death as the great leveler, before whom all ranks and privileges were abolished, unconsciously nourished certain democratic notions that were growing at the time. Typical of the earlier *Danses Macabres*, and indeed based upon the lost frescoes in the cemetery of Les Innocents at Paris, is the *Danse Macabre des Hommes* which Pierre le Rouge printed for Guyot Marchant in 1485 (illustration 29). Here the Doctor and the Lover are confronted with their dead selves in the shape of grinning corpses and skeletons. The series is completed by representatives of all walks and ranks of men, and was followed later by the equivalent panorama for women. Two other versions are shown (illustrations 30, 31), one from Lyons, giving a glimpse of a printing shop of the time, and the second from the *Loups Ravissans*, Paris ca. 1503, introducing a most amazing set of grinning death's-heads.

II. THE BEGINNING OF ENGRAVING

We must now return to an earlier period and trace the origin and development of the second great class of reproductive techniques, line-engraving on metal. The most important of those artists who, possibly inspired by the successful example of reduplication through woodcuts, first thought of engraving on copper for the purpose of multiplying his designs on paper, was an unknown whom scholarship has designated as the Master of the Playing Cards, so called from one of his outstanding works. That he was an artist of some power and sensibility is evident from such engravings as the *Sudarium* or *Handkerchief of Veronica* (illustration 59) and the set of playing cards, one of which, the *Queen of Flowers, B*, is reproduced as illustration 58. It is generally accepted that he was active from 1430 to 1455 somewhere in the Rhine Valley between Strassburg and Constance. He probably was more of a painter than a goldsmith, although he used the goldsmith's technique of simple hatching. Some authorities, Dorothy Miner and Hellmut Lehmann-Haupt, have advanced the theory that he may have executed a number of the miniatures in Gutenberg's Giant Bible of Mainz of 1452–53. It is possible that he lived temporarily in Mainz, but other details of imagery such as his use of the alpine cyclamen flower (which flourished around the Lake of Constance) suggest a sojourn farther up the river. His work stands out from a large group of somewhat mediocre work which has been associated by modern scholarship with such nebulous personalities as the Master of the Nuremberg Passion, the Master of the Banderolles, or the Master of the Power of Women. Two of them, however, deserve more than passing mention. The Master of the Balaam made an engraving of *St. Eligius*, the patron saint of goldsmiths, seated in a goldsmith's shop (illustration 60). The other is the Master of the Love Gardens, so named from his two engravings on the subject. He is amateurish in technique and awkward in drawing, but his work does reflect the sensibility and culture of the Burgundian court. Under the Valois dukes, particularly Philippe le Bon, the court of Burgundy attained a legendary magnificence. Poetry, music, and the arts flourished as never before. And so as one looks at the *Garden of Love* (illustration 63) one can almost hear the faint strains of a *rondeau* or *ballade* by Gilles Binchois or Guillaume Dufay.

The next important personality in engraving is Master E.S., who is assumed to have flourished from about 1440 to 1467 in the neighborhood of the Lake of Constance. Three hundred and seventeen different prints by this goldsmith engraver have come down to us. In spite of the fact that we have never been able to discover his name (the E.S. being a monogram found on some of his prints) a definite personality speaks through his work. His types of men and especially women have an easily discernible style, a mingling of sweetness and naïveté. One feels, somehow, the presence of a real human being, albeit vague and shadowy, behind these rare engravings, the figure of a man with likes and dislikes, a certain ideal of womanly beauty, some quiet touches of humor, a simple religious feeling combined with quite a sensuous appreciation of the lusts of the flesh (there are extant a half dozen rather free subjects engraved by him). He composed a whole alphabet of grotesque figures, a procession of saints, knights, ladies, gross-looking monks, grotesque animals, and the like. One of them, the letter Q, made up of mounted knights and villains, is reproduced as illustration 62. It is doubtful whether he realized the significance that might be read into the positions of the men of such different stations of life. An important and typical example of his religious work is the large *Madonna of Einsiedeln* of 1466 (illustration 61). At the Swiss monastery of Einsiedeln was a famous shrine of the Virgin much visited by the pilgrims. "Pilgrimages," as Douglas Percy Bliss has charmingly put it, "were a form of medieval holidaying, combining spiritual benefits with enjoyment. With the sweet showers of April, says the most famous of all pilgrims, Wives of Bath, Prioresses, and Millers all get restive—'Than longen folk to goon on pilgrimages.' And just as Chaucer's Pardoner, who had been at Rome, bore a pewter vernicle upon his hat and when he had got to Canterbury would pin an ampulla beside it, so if you went to a shrine or convent in Germany at a later date, you would buy a print or even, at some places, a block-book." On the print the Virgin and Child are seen enthroned between an angel and St. Meinrad, and in front are kneeling a male and female pilgrim with their staffs and hats and robes. Above, as if by a personal appearance from a balcony, are revealed the Trinity and the whole heavenly host. Altogether a most delightful picture. Other charming prints are the *Hortus Conclusus*, the *Virgin with Child Bathing*, and the *Nativity*, in which last the artist has suggested psychological reverberations in the characters of Joseph and Mary, similar in mood to the famous *Cherry Tree Carol*. Dürer later used a similar theme in his woodcut of the *Holy Family with Three Hares*.

The technique of Master E.S. is typical of the goldsmith's approach, based entirely on line, and showing cross-hatching and a loving preoccupation with ornament. His work is among the earliest bearing a signature

or monogram. It has been suggested that this monogram might be more in the nature of a hallmark (following the practice of goldsmiths), a guaranty of honest and masterly workmanship rather than a signature in the modern sense of the word. It may thus represent a transition stage between the complete anonymity of the Middle Ages or of Oriental countries like India, and the thorough capitalization of the individual artist's personality beginning with the Renaissance in Western art. In the medieval, and to a large extent in the Oriental conception of art, the artist's personality was completely submerged in his work; whereas in Western art, with the growth of capitalist society and the development of the artist as a trader, the artist's name became a valuable asset, and his work, issued under his trademark, became almost a special brand of merchandise. Under such a scheme questions of forgery and plagiarism become important; in the Middle Ages they were not. Artists copied and recopied each other's work without feeling that they were committing a crime; there were certain traditional ways of depicting things which were transmitted from artist to artist and generation to generation. Van Meckenem, as we shall see, acquired many of the coppers of Master E.S., retouched them, and put his own mark on some of them.

Only a few of the prints of Master E.S. were signed, and those late in his life; every one of the 115 engravings by Martin Schongauer, of the third generation of early German engravers, was signed with a monogram and distinctive mark. He was born around 1445 at Colmar. The son of a well-to-do goldsmith, he matriculated at the University of Leipzig in 1465. He must have given up scholarly pursuits to follow the career of artist. Although he was a painter, he still worked largely in the goldsmith tradition (illustration 64), and is better known for his engravings than his paintings. He was famous in his day: the young Dürer came to study in his workshop, only to find that he had come too late, for Schongauer died in 1491. Later, Vasari cites a number of his engravings and concludes as follows: "In another he did St. Anthony beaten by devils and carried into the air by a swarm of them, of the most curious forms imaginable, a sheet which so pleased Michelangelo when young that he began to color it." But he is still essentially the medieval artist, occasionally depicting devils and fantastic monsters as in the *Tribulation of St. Anthony* (illustration 73). In complicated compositions such as the *Death of the Virgin*, or *Christ Carrying the Cross*, he is not quite so successful, since he lacks the dramatic sense to subordinate detail for the sake of pictorial emphasis; he still has the goldsmith's conception of a flat linear pattern. He is at his best in the simpler compositions such as *Christ Appearing to the Magdalen* (illustration 65), the *Virgin and Child in the Courtyard, St. Michael*, and other saints and Madonnas, where his innate delicacy and refinement find full expression. In this class, too, falls his lovely *Nativity* (illustration 66), carried out in an exalted mood of adoration and beauty. It has all the grace, the enchanting unworldliness of a fairy story.

It was more or less customary to treat the birth of Christ in terms of fantasy and imagination. For a long time the Byzantine or Romanesque tradition held sway (see illustration 2). Toward the end of the fourteenth century a change in the iconography took place due to the *Revelations* of St. Bridget or Birgitta of Sweden. All her life she had had ecstatic visions, in one of which the Virgin Mary appeared and revealed to her the manner in which her Son came into the world. It was while she was in a trance of prayer and religious inspiration that Jesus was miraculously born. Schongauer has illustrated the theme literally. Furthermore he has added a few touches of symbolism, as Panofsky has pointed out: the lantern representing material light, has been dimmed by the radiance of the Divine Child, representing spiritual light.

On the other hand, it was more or less customary to treat the Birth of the Virgin realistically with a wealth of literal detail. A typical example by Israhel van Meckenem is reproduced as illustration 67. The theme was similarly treated by Dürer in his woodcut series of the *Life of the Virgin* (illustration 80). We see the newly born infant about to be bathed by a neighborly housewife who is testing the temperature of the water with her foot; we see roast chicken and drink being offered to the exhausted mother; we see the cradle and some utensils at hand—an interesting glimpse into the daily life of the fifteenth century. Van Meckenem is one of the most baffling artists in the history of engraving, as well as the most prolific of the fifteenth century, about 570 examples having been ascribed to his hand. He produced some of the most banal and mediocre engravings ever made, yet at times he was capable of work of considerable merit. We know what manner of man he was, since he has left a striking portrait of himself and his wife (illustration 75), not a particularly spiritual face, but a cheerful industrious type with a sense of humor and a keen eye for business. He must have been one of the earliest commercial professional engravers. He copied works by Master E.S., Schongauer, Master of the Amsterdam Cabinet, Wenzel von Olmütz, Hans Holbein the Elder, and Dürer. He acquired the original plates of Master E.S. on his death in 1467 (he had been his pupil in 1466 and 1467) and a number by the Netherlands Master F.V.B.; he retouched them and did a thriving business selling prints. He is one of the first engravers whose work shows any great variation in the number of states—a fact which has endeared

him to many modern collectors. He was born some time before 1450 and lived most of his life at Bocholt in Flanders. He died there in 1503. Among the best of his work, interesting chiefly as reflections of the life of the time, may be counted the large *Dance at the Court of Herod* (illustration 77), a most amusing series of genre subjects, such as *Lute Player and Harpist* (illustration 72), and *The Enraged Wife* (illustration 71). The latter might possibly be a satirical print, and is capable of several interpretations. In one, no doubt the most obvious, the wife is merely having a fit of temper and is belaboring her husband. In another interpretation she is fighting for her rights. This is not as absurd as it might appear. The woman has thrown her apron, her badge of servitude, upon the floor; she does not seem to be in a rage, in fact she may be smiling, she is merely making a gesture of defiance. Other similar instances could be cited from the fifteenth century. A variant of the theme, the feminine "Fight for the Trousers," can be traced from fifteenth-century prints down to the *imagerie populaire* of the early nineteenth century. Prints of satire against all sorts of follies, including man's opinion of women, were not uncommon in the fifteenth century, though not nearly as prevalent as religious imagery.

In the fifteenth century, engravings of ornament were —and continued to be for several centuries to come—an important class of nonreligious engravings (illustration 76). These ornament prints were designs to be followed, or models to be copied, by fellow artists and craftsmen, such as woodcarvers and carpenters, masons and stonecarvers, goldsmiths and metal workers, embroiderers, weavers, and other textile workers, decorative painters and the like. (It is known, for example, that El Greco as late as the seventeenth century copied compositional details from prints). There was a give-and-take between the painters and printmakers each giving ideas to the other or taking them from the other. For instance, the Netherlands Master I.A.M. reflects the aim and vocabulary of contemporary painting in his most moving engraving, *Lamentation over the Body of Christ* (illustration 70). Similarly Master L.Cz. was stimulated by the demons of Schongauer's *St. Anthony* to create an even more fantastic monster in his engraving the *Temptation of Christ* (illustration 74).

Two more examples complete the survey of Gothic engravings. Both are by an artist who was not apparently a professional engraver, but rather a painter who made a few plates. Thus he may be said to inaugurate a long and interesting line of graphic productions in which their authors brought to their task a freshness and breadth of view often lacking in the pure craftsman's approach. Little is known about the artist. He is variously designated as the Master of the Amsterdam Cabi-

net (where some eighty of his total eighty-nine engravings are conserved, many of them in unique impressions) or as the Master of the *Hausbuch*, a book containing some of his drawings at Wolfegg. He probably was active somewhere in the Middle Rhine from about 1475 to 1490. Little else is known about this personality who speaks so charmingly and attractively from his prints. He can hardly be classed as a professional engraver, since, owing to the extreme scarcity of his prints (many existing in only one impression), it is evident that he made comparatively little effort to multiply and sell his designs. Furthermore his technique was not that of the regular goldsmith engraver: it was more like a drypoint line (scratched into the metal) which would not hold up under many impressions. His approach is rather that of a painter having an eye for the figure as a whole and the interplay of light and color. But especially attractive are the freshness of his conception and the lovely lyric spirit that pervades his work. Seldom has the enchantment of love, the sweet and quiet delight of lovers in each other's company, been more charmingly depicted than in his print (illustration 68). Equally outstanding in their way are his *Young Man Confronted by Death* (illustration 69), the *Three Knights Confronted with Their Dead Selves*, the *Crucifixion, Two Men Talking*, and a delightfully realistic picture of a dog scratching himself, one of the first in that genre of prints. Altogether, the work of the Master of the Amsterdam Cabinet is one of the fresh and fragrant pages in the history of the graphic arts.

Henry Adams wrote:

The Gothic is singular in this: one seems easily at home in the Renaissance; one is not too strange in the Byzantine; as for the Roman, it is ourselves; and we could walk blindfolded through every chink and cranny of the Greek mind; all these styles seem modern, when we come close to them; but the Gothic gets away. No two men think alike about it, and no woman agrees with either man. The Church itself never agreed about it, and the architects agree even less than the priests. To most minds it casts too many shadows; it wraps itself in mystery; and when people talk of mystery, they commonly mean fear.

It is true that the Gothic era seems more alien to our modern temper than most of the other periods. To be sure, the Gothic, as reflected in the graphic arts, represented the latest period, its decadence so to speak. The great glory of the Gothic was the cathedral and the painting and sculpture that went into it. It was an age of faith and a Universal Church—which our age emphatically is not. It is difficult for us, brought up as we are from earliest childhood with the notion of a rational physical universe, to accept such impossible contradictions as simultaneous existence in two places, miraculous

changes without natural causes, anachronisms based upon ignorance of historical development, and the like. The Gothic was a credulous age of beautiful legend and little science, of touching faith and macabre humor, of unworldliness and chivalry and starving serfs, of uncertain life and violent death. The medieval artist sought to express an idea, not to imitate nature. As St. Thomas Aquinas said: "Art imitates nature [not in its form but] in its processes *(ars naturem imitat in sua operatione).*" It was symbolic in form and lacking in sensuous and realistic elements. When Worringer spoke of "the ceaseless melody of Northern line," he was referring particularly to architecture, but the phrase also has a certain aptness in regard to engraving. The Gothic line is calligraphic, that is to say it has a rhythm and melody of its own. The folds of drapery, for example, as depicted in a print or drawing, may not be at all naturalistic or revealing of the figure beneath; they may be arbitrary and abstract; but they have intrinsic beauty and vitality nevertheless. After all, graphic art, which expresses everything—color, form, atmosphere—largely by black and white lines, is in itself an abstract and arbitrary art.

In conclusion it might be useful to summarize the conditions that brought about the development of the graphic arts. In the first place there was the desire for religious images inculcated by organized religion. At the end of the Middle Ages the worship of a multitude of saints, and above all the Virgin Mary, reached its fullest development. Religion had been humanized. Every occupation and profession had its patron saint who was endowed with special virtues (as we have seen, for example, in St. Christopher). A canonized saint was a comforter in tribulation and a mediator between a sinner and a remote Godhead. Thus the saints and their attributes figured largely in the thoughts and feelings of the people. In a sense they personified them, as the feeling of tenderness and sweetness and mother love is personified in the Virgin and Child, as sorrow and affliction are personified in the drama of the Passion, as fear and terror are personified in the *Danse Macabre* and the Vision of the Last Judgment. Thus were the desire and the need for images provided, while economic conditions—a larger and larger number of people coming to enjoy a slight margin above a subsistence level—provided the means to satisfy the desire. Organized religion has at almost all times furnished a stimulus to the practice of the arts. It was likewise so, as we shall see in another chapter, when the spread of Mahayana Buddhism in China produced the demand for religious images and charms which had magical properties, and thus brought about the perfection of woodcutting and printing throughout the Chinese Empire as early as the eighth century. In addition to the religious stimulus, the graphic arts had other roots in the lives of the people. There were playing cards and prints of gallantry that ministered to the play instinct. There were prints of satire and caricature, those lightning rods that channeled the fury and resentment of the oppressed. Portraiture, a deep-seated desire in man, made a halting beginning in the fifteenth century, but was destined later to be one of the chief functions of prints. There were prints illustrating science and exploration. And finally there were prints of ornament, the trade secrets which the artists circulated among themselves. All these prints were purposive; there was no thought as yet of art for art's sake.

3. The Renaissance

I. IN THE NORTH

The dramatic transition from Gothic to Renaissance can be personified in the life and works of one man —Albrecht Dürer. He began in the Gothic tradition and died a painter and engraver of the Renaissance, acclaimed in Germany, Flanders, and even in Italy, the home of the Renaissance. Distinguished as he was as an artist, he was even greater as a dramatic figure, as a man in whom the tremendous forces of his age had their play and interplay, all the more so because he has left such a voluminous documentation of his thoughts and feelings. Many of the qualities which we particularly associate with the Renaissance—intellectual interests, passion for the antique, self-conscious interest in fame, pride in individual achievement, proficiency in diverse professions ("the man of virtu"), devotion to science as well as to art, a preoccupation with proportion and perspective— found their expression in his many-sided personality.

He was born in Nuremberg in 1471, the son of a goldsmith. Of himself Dürer wrote:

And my father took special pleasure in me, because he saw that I was diligent to learn. So he sent me to school, and when I had learned to read and write he took me away from it, and taught me the goldsmith's craft. But when I could work neatly, my liking drew me rather to painting than to goldsmith's work, so I laid it before my father; but he was not well pleased, regretting the time lost while I had been learning to be a goldsmith. Still he let it be as I wished, and in 1486 on St. Andrew's Day my father bound me apprentice to Michael Wolgemut, to serve him three years long. During that time God gave me diligence, so that I learned well, but I had much to suffer from his lads.

Having served his term with Wolgemut (who had supplied designs to Koberger for the *Schatzbehalter* and the *Nuremberg Chronicle*) and thus become steeped in the Gothic tradition not only from him but from his goldsmith father, he spent four years wandering about as a journeyman. It is not known what places he visited, but it is reasonably certain that he spent some time at Basel designing woodcuts for the publishers, notably two series of illustrations for the *Ritter vom Thurn* and for Sebastian Brant's *Ship of Fools*, both satiric commentaries on the foibles of mankind. One of these, about the fool who miscalculates his costs in building a house and finds his workmen walking out on the job, is reproduced herewith (illustration 79). There is little to distinguish these works from a number of Gothic illustrations except possibly a certain competence of drawing and gusto of observation. It is generally assumed that from the fall of 1494 to the spring of 1495 he made a trip to Venice. Before this, while still in Nuremberg, he had seen (interesting sidelight on the international trade in prints) and copied in pen and ink two engravings by Mantegna and one by a North Italian engraver of the *Death of Orpheus*. At any rate, from about this time a new note came into his work, a stronger painterlike feeling (thinking in terms of color, and painting in watercolors), a preoccupation with tactile form instead of the calligraphic line characteristic of the Gothic North. And in the woodcuts and the copper engravings (in which he seems to be largely self-taught) he gradually began to perfect the style associated with his name. In the series of fifteen large woodcut illustrations of the *Apocalypse*, issued in 1498, this style may already be seen in its completeness. When a print like the *Four Horsemen of the Apocalypse* (illustration 82) is compared with a similar subject from, say, the Cologne or Nuremberg Bible (illustration 81), the measure of his achievement is obvious. The print is conceived as a complete picture within the bounds of a rectangle, the figures and the details disposed within that space with the most telling dramatic effect. There is a sense of movement and of color; the figures are drawn in the round with some regard for realistic tactile values. Dürer managed to perfect a system of representation, a combination of the calligraphic and ideographic elements of Gothic art and the more painterlike pictorial qualities of the Renaissance, which became the prevailing idiom in Germany and the Netherlands for a century to come. Of course, in comparison with the work of Mantegna or Raphael, Dürer's style as a whole seems Gothic. Nevertheless it will always remain an exemplar of a striking and effective mode of graphic expression.

About 1500 he met in Nuremberg the Italian painter Jacopo de' Barbari (illustration 168) and wrote of him thus:

I can find no one who hath written aught about how to form a canon of human proportions, save one man, Jacopo by name, born at Venice, and a charming painter. He showed me the figures of a man and woman, which he had drawn according to a canon of proportions; and now I would rather be shown what he meant than behold a new kingdom. If I had this canon, I would put it into print in his honor, for the use of all men. Then, however, I was still young and had not heard of such things before. Howbeit I was very fond of art, so I set myself to discover how such a canon might be wrought out. For this aforesaid Jacopo, as I clearly saw, would not explain to me the principles upon which he went. Accordingly I set to work on my own idea and read Vitruvius, who writes somewhat about the human figure. Thus it was from, or out of, these two men aforesaid that I took my start, and thence, from day to day, have I followed up my search according to my own notions.

From that time on indeed he gathered, with more zeal perhaps than style, the notes, measurements, and researches, that eventually were published in his book *On Human Proportions*. Meanwhile, in 1504, making use of his studies in the ideal figure, he engraved his famous *Adam and Eve* (illustration 87), which he proudly signed "Albrecht Dürer of Nuremberg made this 1504." In it he expressed his dream of an ideal Adam and Eve, prototype of Man and Woman, and his nostalgia for the antique, Apollo and Venus transformed into the First Pair—the Adam indeed is based upon the Apollo Belvedere. This print typifies the emancipation of the North from a medieval contempt for the flesh, a sensuous interest and a freedom in the handling of the nude, characteristic of Renaissance artists. A half-century before, such a picture would have been unthinkable, except in Italy, which had the advantage of a more or less unbroken tradition from the antique. Not only were the medieval artists restricted in depicting the nude and seminude to such subjects as the Last Judgment, Adam and Eve, the Crucifixion, a few saints like St. Sebastian, and biblical stories like David and Bathsheba, but there was also little opportunity to draw from the nude. Professional models were unknown. For male models the artists often used themselves or their apprentices, for female models their wives and mistresses and occasionally prostitutes and the attendants in the public baths (which had none too respectable a reputation even as late as Casanova's time). Drawings exist by Pisanello, Dürer, Dirick Vellert, and others, of bath attendants, and Dürer made a woodcut of a men's bath. Professional models first came into use in Carracci's Academy. During the Renaissance there was a general feeling that the male body was superior in beauty and proportion to the female. Michelangelo used male

models for a number of his Sibyls. And Dürer in his engravings worked with more *esprit* on his Adam than on his Eve. He, however, retained an interest in the nude of both sexes till the end. In 1520 he was at Antwerp and witnessed the triumphal entry of Charles V.

He afterwards described to Melanchthon the splendid spectacles he had beheld, and how, in what were mythological groups, the most beautiful maidens figured almost naked, and covered only with a thin transparent veil. The young Emperor did not honor them with a single glance, but Dürer himself was very glad to get near, not less for the purpose of seeing the tableaux, than to have the opportunity of observing closely the perfect figures of the young girls. As he said, "Being a painter, I looked about me a little more boldly."

Meanwhile he led a busy and industrious existence in Nuremberg, doing portrait commissions, engraving sacred and profane subjects, Madonna pictures and the like. Two of the most beautiful and charming of these are the *Nativity* (illustration 84) and the *Virgin and Child with the Monkey* of about 1498 (illustration 83) with its lovely landscape background of the Weierhaus, which was copied by Giulio Campagnola in his engraving of *Ganymede*. Dürer's fame had spread far into Italy; many of his prints were sold and copied there, so much so that he was moved to make a second journey to Venice to protest against the wholesale forgery of his prints by Marcantonio Raimondi (no less than seventy-eight in all).

Marcantonio [wrote Vasari] began by imitating the things of Albert, studying all the prints which he had bought, which for their novelty and beauty, were sought by everyone. Having engraved on copper, all the Passion and Life of Christ in thirty-six sheets, with the A.D. with which Albert signed his works, Marcantonio succeeded in making them so like that no one could tell the difference, who did not know; and they were sold and bought as Albert's works. On being informed of this, one of the counterfeits being sent to Flanders [Vasari was vague about geography outside of Italy], Albert flew into such a rage that he left Flanders and came to Venice, and complained of Marcantonio to the Signoria. But all he obtained was that Marcantonio should no longer use his signature.

Dürer's letters to his friend Pirkheimer give a picture of his life in Italy. He exerted himself (perhaps in vain) to show that he was a great painter as well as a great draughtsman and engraver. He encountered the jealousy of the Italian painters; Bellini alone wished him well. He found everything expensive. Yet he wrote, "How I shall freeze after this sun! Here I am a gentleman, at home only a parasite." He made a pilgrimage to Mantua to visit Andrea Mantegna, whom he greatly admired. "But," as Camerarius wrote, "before he could reach Mantua, Andrea was dead, and Dürer used to say that this was the

saddest event in all his life." An interesting sidelight on Dürer's relations with Raphael is given on a Raphael drawing which has the following inscription in Dürer's handwriting: "Rafahel de' Urbin, who is held in such high esteem by the Pope, he made these naked figures and sent them to Albrecht Dürer at Nuremberg to show him his hand." Raphael had, we are told by Lodovico Dolce, drawings, engravings, and woodcuts of Dürer's hanging in his studio; and Vasari quoted Raphael as saying, "If Dürer had been acquainted with the antique he would have surpassed us all."

There is not space to recount all of Dürer's contacts with the writers and humanists, Erasmus, Melanchthon, Luther, Hans Sachs, Conrad Celtes, Stabius, Camerarius, with the great merchants, the Imhofs and Fuggers and Paumgartners; with the Court of the Emperor Maximilian. Dürer's portrait of Pirkheimer, patrician, humanist, and councilor of Nuremberg, and his lifelong friend, will have to typify his contacts with the learned world. Pirkheimer was a ponderous, pompous, irascible individual, and the engraving (illustration 93) does give a suggestion of this, though it lacks any sense of style. The textures are built up in a rather dull and literal way, and Dürer indulges in the somewhat flashy trick of showing the reflection of a window in the subject's eyes. But Dürer was no flatterer. The Gothic North has a fairly honorable reputation in this regard, being on the whole more interested in "character" than in elegance. Later, Titian, Van Dyck, and the French portrait engravers marked the beginning of the elegant style which eventually developed into the official or fashionable portrait, an art of flattery pure and simple. Dürer's engraved portrait of Erasmus was no likeness at all. Erasmus, when he saw it, politely excused its deficiency by saying that no doubt he had changed somewhat in the years since the drawing was made. The truth of the matter, however, probably was that the artist engraved the portrait some five or six years after he had made the preliminary drawings and he had simply "gone cold" on the subject. He had hoped to compensate for this by overelaborating all the accessories. Whether Pirkheimer liked his portrait or not is not known. He had the plate in his possession and no doubt had proofs printed as one would of a photograph today. It later passed into the hands of the Imhof family (Pirkheimer's daughter married an Imhof), and was sold by Hans Imhof in 1636 to the Earl of Arundel for forty Reichsthalers.

Dürer designed or engraved several great series besides the *Apocalypse*, such as the Large Woodcut Passion (12 blocks), the Little Woodcut Passion (37 blocks), the *Life of the Virgin* (20 blocks), all three published by Dürer himself in 1511 (though some of the individual blocks were completed before that), and the Copper Plate Passion (16 plates). These and a number of single blocks and plates proved a considerable source of income to him. When he made his journey to the Netherlands in 1520, he took a large quantity of prints with him which he sold, exchanged, or gave away, as we learn from his detailed diary. He even sold to a dealer at wholesale prices:

Sebald Fischer bought of me at Antwerp sixteen small Passions [woodcut] for four florins, thirty-two of the large books [sets of the Apocalypse and Large Passion] for eight florings, also six engraved Passions [on copper] for three florins.

He exchanged prints with other artists: "I gave eight florins' worth of my prints for a whole set of Lucas' [van Leyden's] engravings." Again: "I gave to Tommaso of Bologna a whole set of prints to send for me to Rome to another painter, who will send me Raphael's work [engraved by Marcantonio] in return." Occasionally he jotted down retail prices: "I sold a woodcut Passion for twelve stivers [about $5.00], besides an Adam and Eve [copper engraving] for four stivers [about $1.65].

Dürer, ever interested in new techniques, executed three drypoints. Because of the fragility of the burr, drypoints are very rare and must be seen in early impressions. The *St. Jerome by a Pollard Willow* (illustration 86), in the proof in the Albertina, has all the richness and color of a perfect impression. St. Jerome is surrounded by a velvety pollard willow, a grassy bank, and a most enchanting lion, so much more real than fifteenth-century beasts.

One of the most famous of the later engravings is the *Melancholia* (illustration 88), more or less uniform with two other famous engravings, the *St. Jerome in His Cell*, and the *Knight, Death, and the Devil* (illustration 85). It is possible that Dürer intended to illustrate in a series the various temperaments of man such as the phlegmatic, choleric, and melancholic. The idea of melancholy is capable of extended and diverse elaboration as readers of Burton's *Anatomy of Melancholy* well know. Much has been written about the significance of Dürer's strange plate, but nobody has succeeded in producing a complete and satisfying interpretation. Dr. Panofsky has come as close as anyone:

Dürer was, or thought he was, a melancholic. . . . He was also an artist-geometrician who suffered from the very limitations of the discipline he loved. In his younger days, when he prepared the *Adam and Eve*, he had hoped to capture absolute beauty by means of a ruler and compass. Shortly before he composed the *Melancolia* he was forced to admit: "But what absolute beauty is, I know not. Nobody knows it but God." . . . Thus Dürer's most perplexing engraving is the objective statement of a general philosophy and the subjective confession of an individual man. It fuses two great representational and literary traditions, that of Melancholy as one of the Four Hu-

mors and that of Geometry as one of the Seven Liberal Arts. It typifies the artist of the Renaissance . . . who feels "inspired" by celestial influences and eternal ideas, but suffers all the more from his human frailty and intellectual finiteness. But in doing all this it is in a sense a spiritual self-portrait of Albrecht Dürer.

In the early sixteenth century a new technique was developed for making prints. It was called etching, and the hint probably came from the armorer's craft. In those days fancy tournament armor was decorated with ornamental designs bitten into the iron with acid. The piece was first coated with red lead and the design drawn with a stylus; the exposed parts then bitten with acid. Some craftsman may have been struck with the possibilities of printing a flat iron plate on paper. And that craftsman might have been Daniel Hopfer (illustration 91). He came from a family of armorers and he made a number of etchings. The first etching with a date is by Urs Graf 1513, but it is quite likely that Hopfer made etchings before him even though he dated few of his prints and those were all later.

Dürer tried his hand at the new technique, and made in all six etchings, two of which are reproduced herewith: *Christ on the Mount of Olives* of 1515 and *The Great Cannon* of 1518 (illustrations 89 and 90). The former is one of the noblest of Dürer's works. The storm-tossed tree mirrors the psychological drama of Christ's Agony, and the whole is conceived and executed with a fury and spontaneity rare in his work. The *Cannon* represents a showpiece called the Nuremberg Serpent, popular at the moment, and was made in etching as a quick means of supplying an immediate demand. The Turks for whom, as pictured, the cannon was a warning and a threat, were the great bugaboo of the time. The first siege of Vienna by the Turks occurred in 1529. The landscape in the background is quite charming in spite of its lack of subtlety, and the print is prized not only because it is one of the earliest etchings but also because it is one of the earliest examples of the growing interest in landscape.

The idea of pure landscape did not emerge as a theme until the early sixteenth century. Albrecht Altdorfer, around 1525, etched a few transcriptions from nature without figure interest, and he thus was the earliest printmaker to make a picture of pure landscape (illustration 92). To be sure, there were delineations of landscape in prints and paintings during the fifteenth century, but only as background, never as the main theme. The full development of the landscape print, however, was to come with the Dutch etchers of the seventeenth century and with Bruegel and Rubens in engraving and Titian in woodcut. Besides Altdorfer, other precursors were Hirschvogel in the 1540s and Lautensack in the 1550s. In his prints the former used the device known as aerial perspective whereby the lines grow thinner as they recede in the distance. It is supposed that the artist used needle points of varying thickness to achieve this result.

Dürer died in Nuremberg in 1528 after a life of unremitting application to his craft. He was a great draughtsman and technician. If we sometimes miss in his work the fire of a great emotion, we nevertheless must be impressed by his insatiable preoccupation with the representation of all natural objects. It may be questioned whether his scientific interests, the canon of proportion, the mathematics and mensuration, the military engineering, all the things he wrote about in his books, did not affect his art adversely. Leonardo's scientific interests were even greater than Dürer's, and they may have affected the quantity but certainly not the quality of his art. The matter goes deeper: Dürer pinned his faith too much on externals. "To paint," he wrote, "is to be able to portray upon a flat surface any visible thing whatsoever that may be chosen." He was, par excellence, the extrovert artist. The world was too much with him. His power of description and analysis stood in the way of a vitalizing synthesis. He attempted to storm Heaven with a peddler's pack of literal details. That he searched all his life for some elusive secret of art is in itself revealing. Yet withal he is a most engaging figure, in Melanchthon's words, "a wise man, whose genius as a painter, were it ever so brilliant, would be the least of his gifts." His pride and his humility, his wisdom of life, his childlike delight in all natural objects, his systematizing capacity and technical skill, and his recording instinct make him one of the most fascinating men of art that the world has ever known.

One of the most famous of Dürer's friends was Lucas van Leyden, born at Leyden in 1494. Dürer exchanged prints with him and drew his portrait during his visit to the Netherlands. Lucas was a precocious artist, having engraved his first plate, *Mahomet and Sergius*, at the age of fourteen. He engraved many religious subjects, but like Schongauer and Dürer, also executed several genre scenes or illustrations of popular life. One of the most delightful of these is *The Milkmaid* of 1510 (illustration 101). He also designed a number of distinguished woodcuts (illustration 100). One of his masterpieces is the portrait of the Emperor Maximilian of 1520, based on Dürer's portrait (illustration 94). In addition to its masterly characterization and draughtsmanship, the plate has a technical interest. It is one of the earliest examples of a combination of etching and engraving. The earliest etchings had been made on iron, which could be engraved only with difficulty. By using copper instead of iron, it was possible to combine etching and engraving on the same plate. Lucas van Leyden's plate inaugurated that technical procedure of etching the preliminary work and

finishing up with the graver, that reached its culmination in the engravings of the eighteenth and early nineteenth centuries. In his later work Lucas assimilated the technique of Marcantonio, and with it gave up Dutch raciness for a rather empty Renaissance allegorical style. He died at the early age of thirty-nine. Another Flemish artist whom Dürer mentions in his diary is Dirick Vellert, painter, glassworker, engraver. He made about nineteen engravings and etchings, many of them small in size. One of the most charming of these, the *Faun on a Wine Barrel*, 1522, is reproduced as illustration 119.

The Emperor Maximilian, "the last of the Knights," was a great patron of the arts, and commissioned a number of elaborately illustrated works designed to glorify his person and his exploits, often imaginary: the *Genealogy*, the *Theuerdank*, the *Weisskunig*, the *Freydal*, the *Triumphal Arch*, and the *Triumphal Procession*. Dürer, Burgkmair, Altdorfer, Springinklee, Beck, Schäufelein, and others were employed on these works. Much of it is heraldic and ponderously contrived, of interest chiefly to the historian. Some of the works were left unpublished at the death of Maximilian. The contrast, for example, between the *Triumphal Procession* and Mantegna's *Triumphs of Caesar* (which perhaps inspired it) shows up the heavy-handedness of the Court and the crippling effect of committees of pedants issuing directives to the artists. Too many cooks are apt to spoil the broth. A page from the *Weisskunig*, left unpublished at Maximilian's death, is reproduced as illustration 102. It was designed by Hans Burgkmair, the most Italianate of the German printmakers, a typical court painter, witty, elegant, courtly, competent to undertake any subject upon request. He made a St. Sebastian (illustration 103) elegantly designed in a niche with Renaissance ornament, but with little feeling for the saint's martyrdom. The unusual thing about the print is that it was also signed by the woodcutter or *Formschneider*, Jost de Negker. Usually the woodcutter remained anonymous. Negker was a craftsman of exceptional ability, and he also collaborated with Burgkmair in the production of color prints. Burgkmair's portrait *Maximilian on Horseback* of 1508 is the first dated single-sheet color print (color prints were made in books by Ratdolt before that date) with printings of armor in black, gold, and silver for the Emperor. There will be a further discussion of color printing in connection with Ugo da Carpi and Italian chiaroscuro prints. After Maximilian's death in 1519, Burgkmair went back to work for the Augsburg book publishers.

Lucas Cranach was also a court painter (he entered the service of the Elector of Saxony around 1505). He designed on wood an outstanding set of the *Passion*, together with an impressive but very rare variant of the *Agony in the Garden*. His later work (and that of his son of the same name) suffers from the dilution so often attendant upon official renditions, but at its best it is charming, sensuous, elegant, and saturated with real feeling for nature (illustrations 104 and 105). The title of his engraving, the *Penance of St. John Chrysostom* requires some explanation. Bishop John, the Golden-mouthed (*Chrysostom*) was one of the "Four Greek Doctors of the Church" whose life was a paragon of piety and chastity. There is a legend, however—no doubt apocryphal since the saint could not have been a more unlikely protagonist —that he once seduced a woman. She retired to the forest to have a baby, who grew up as a child of nature. The saint is seen crawling on his hands and knees in the background. The story must have appealed to artists, for a number of them have illustrated the legend. Cranach also experimented with color printing, and made several charming chiaroscuro prints (illustration 179). Through his residence in Wittenberg he came in close contact with Martin Luther and other leaders of the Reformation. He designed woodcuts for the first edition of Luther's German Bible in 1522 and also engraved on copper the vivid portrait of 1520 (illustration 95) which fixes for eternity the warm, fanatic, yet human personality of the miner's son who defied Rome and established the written form of the German vernacular.

The sixteenth century was a warlike one. According to Sombart there were only twenty-five years which did not witness a war somewhere in Europe. Soldiers were everywhere, including a new kind of soldier, the mercenary. Erasmus wrote that the German disorders were "partly due to the natural fierceness of the race, partly to the division into so many separate States, and partly to the tendency of the people to serve as mercenaries." The insolent swaggering type and his female counterpart have been pictured by many German artists: Dürer, Virgil Solis, Burgkmair, Huber, Nicholas Manuel, Beham, Holbein, and Cranach. But most typical of all were the woodcuts of Urs Graf, who was himself a Landsknecht and fought in the murderous battle of Marignano. He led a violent and undisciplined life, was repeatedly brought before authorities "because of his licentious life that he openly and shamelessly leads with strumpets," and once was made to promise that "he would no longer push, beat, crush, or pinch his lawfully wedded wife, the daughter of an honorable tanner, who married against the will of her parents." Much of this wild and wayward energy, of this bluster and swagger, of this excess of animal spirits, is carried over into his prints, *The Soldiers and Death* (illustration 111) and the *Standard-Bearer of Bern* of 1521 (illustration 12). This last is a wood engraving, conceived as a white line engraving, and is an interesting anticipation of the method which Bewick later made famous.

Hans Holbein was born in Augsburg but spent most of his mature life in Basel. He was renowned as the painter at the court of Henry VIII and for his sanguine drawings of worthies of the realm, later copied by Bartolozzi in stipple. But he is equally famous for his work for the Basel publishers—Froben and others—for the drawings illustrating his friend Erasmus's *Praise of Folly*, and for his woodcut designs for the Bible and the *Dance of Death* (illustrations 106 through 110). In these last he carried the method of Dürer to its classic perfection, the completest expression of the German Renaissance. In his set of the *Dance of Death*, the obvious dance form has been discarded in favor of a more subtle and imaginative juxtaposition of death and the victim. The illustrations, dramatic in conception, masterly in drawing, and beautifully cut in wood by Hans Lützelberger, are justly famous in the annals of printmaking. It was perhaps the last great sequence of the *Danse Macabre*, and was copied many times. Other artists have since touched upon the theme, but usually in single examples rather than in a connected series.

In strong contrast to Holbein's classic feeling of balance and restraint is the demonic energy of Hans Baldung, surnamed Grien. Comparatively little is known of his life. He was born in 1476 near Strassburg; he was a friend and possibly a pupil of Dürer; he later fell under the spell of that strange genius Grünewald; and he probably died at Strassburg around 1540. His fame has suffered strange mutations. In his lifetime he achieved considerable acclaim and reputation; Baldung's prints were the only ones outside of his own that Dürer took with him for trade on his Netherlands journey. But in the seventeenth and eighteenth centuries his name and work were practically forgotten. In the early nineteenth century his name was again discovered, and at one time even Grünewald's masterpiece, the *Isenheimer Altar*, was ascribed to him. The twentieth century has resurrected his works and accorded them high praise. Indeed, in such works as *Adam and Eve*, the *Fall of Man*, the *Conversion of St. Paul*, the *Ascension of Christ*, the *Nativity*, the *Lamentation*, the *Witches*, the *Horses*, and the *Groom Bewitched*, there is an emotional intensity of conception, an originality and appropriateness of composition, a passionate and sensuous expression, and above all a wild and haunting power that are peculiarly appealing to the modern temper. Consider, for example, that most vivid drama of the flesh—the color and sensuousness of it—in the *Fall of Man* (illustration 118); the breathtaking asymmetry of the *Conversion of St. Paul* (illustration 115); the tenderness and sympathy of the *St. Sebastian* (illustration 116) in such contrast to Burgkmair's version (illustration 103). Or the demonic overtones, the bold recession of planes, in the *Groom Bewitched* (illustration 113); the swirling lines of force in the

Witches (illustration 180); or the wild and elemental energy of the *Horses in the Wood* (illustration 114). And finally the dynamic balance of forces, the thrusts and parallelisms of the lines in that dramatic illustration of the Fifth Commandment, *Thou Shalt Not Kill* (illustration 112). Baldung was a fiery partisan of the Reformation but he also seems to have been one of a circle, with Brunfels (illustration 117), Indagine, and Johannes Has, interested in chiromancy, astrology, and magic. He made several woodcuts and drawings of witches, notably the famous chiaroscuro already mentioned. The belief in witches which had been growing for centuries was crystallized and officially encouraged by the growth in power of the Inquisition and the publication of the *Malleus Malificarum*, or *Inquisitor's Manual* in 1489. The belief in and punishment for witchcraft continued through the seventeenth century.

There was another group of artists most of whom had had some contact with Dürer either as pupil or as indirect influence. From the small size of most of their prints, they are generally called the Little Masters. Three of them, Georg Pencz and the two brothers, Barthel and Hans Sebald Beham, got themselves in trouble for atheistic utterances and sympathies for the Peasant Revolt, and were banished from Nuremberg. An interesting reflection of this is seen in H.S. Beham's *Drummer and Standard-Bearer* with an inscription "In the Peasant War 1525" (illustration 123). Barthel Beham, who was less prolific but more pictorially creative than his brother, executed a charming little *Virgin and Child by the Window*, one of the jewels of German engraving (illustration 122). The Little Masters were very much interested in applied art of all kinds, and much of their work consists of prints of ornament and models for other arts, such as goldsmith's work or costume. Heinrich Aldegrever was one of the most talented, and produced some of the best Renaissance ornament in Germany, as well as some elegant costume studies of patricians, wedding dancers, and the like. The engraving, *Ornament with Lettering* (illustration 128), has been chosen to represent his work because it touches upon a field which had great interest during the sixteenth century. It was the period when the forms of letters were being established and experiments were being made with new variations. First there were the theoreticians on the shaping of Roman letters, Fra Luca Pacioli in 1509, Sigismondo de' Fanti in 1514, Dürer in his *Treatise on Mensuration*, 1525, Tory in his *Champfleury*, 1529. The growth of trade and culture in the middle class produced a demand for correct models for various types of script, legal, notarial, chancellery, and ornate, as used in various countries and languages. The first practical book of this kind was by Ludovico Vicentino, the official scribe at the Papal Court in Rome, in 1522. Similar books were produced in Italy, France, Spain, Holland, Ger-

many, and England during the sixteenth, seventeenth, and eighteenth centuries by Tagliente (illustrations 127 and 129), Palatino, Yciar, van de Velde, and many others. The class of prints known as bookplates has found practitioners from the fifteenth century to the present. One of the earliest, that of Hilprand Brandenburg, ca. 1480 (illustration 24) was pasted in the books given by him to the Carthusian monastery at Buxheim (where the famous *Einblattdruck* of St. Christopher was found). Another interesting phase of applied art was the costume books and the model books for lace and embroidery. The *Corona delle Nobili et Virtuose Donne*, published at Venice in 1592 (illustration 133), may serve as representative of the pattern books published by Gastel, Sibmacher, Quentel, Pellegrino, Vavassore, Pagan, Osthaus, Vinciolo, Parasole, Franco, and others. The *Corona* was issued by Cesare Vecellio, a cousin of Titian, and he also published in 1590 a famous work on costume, the first indeed with any pretense to historical or scientific accuracy, though similar works had been issued previously by Vico, de Bruyn, Boissard, Weigel, and Amman. Venice occupied during the sixteenth century, as Max von Boehn points out, a position as an emporium of luxury and fashionable amusement similar to that of Paris during the eighteenth and nineteenth centuries.

Another aspect of applied art is treated in the model for a highly ornamented bed, 1533 (illustration 132), by the Swiss-German woodcarver, architect, and maker of woodcuts, Peter Flöttner. He designed, and undoubtedly cut with his own hand (as evidenced by the woodcutting tools which he introduced in many of his pictures as his trademark) a considerable number of woodcuts of architectural ornament and models for intarsia or inlay work. Many books of herbals were issued to satisfy popular demand. One of the most noteworthy was the *Herbarum Vivae Eicones* by Otto von Brunfels (whose portrait Hans Baldung cut in wood, illustration 117). The woodcuts of the plants, the most accurate of their time, were designed by Hans Weiditz (illustration 126). The works of this master, whose name and personality were rediscovered only in recent times, are among the most appealing and charming in the history of prints. He illustrated several popular moralizing works compiled from Petrarch and Cicero, extolling the solid bourgeois virtues of thrift, prudence, moderation, piety, and the like. He was a born storyteller, and he illustrated these dull books with such zest and charm, above all with such a wealth of observation, that they have become a treasure-house of the manners and customs of the Augsburg of his day. He had what the historian loves above all else—a talent for the obvious. He rarely shows any great gift for design, but he more than makes up for this lack by his talent as a narrator and observer. Two characteristic woodcuts

are reproduced here, from Petrarch's *Consolation in Fortune and Misfortune*, Augsburg, 1532 (illustrations 124 and 125), one of them illustrating the story of the man who was so proud of his wife's unadorned beauty that he showed her off to a friend. Incidentally it reveals the norm of female beauty that was prevalent in Augsburg at the time.

One more of the Little Masters still remains to be considered, the most important of the group—Albrecht Altdorfer, who flourished at Regensburg on the Danube as a painter, engraver, architect, and city councilor, from about 1505 till his death in 1538. There is something very personal and appealing in his style, filled with homely feeling and endowed with a simple love of nature. There is also something a bit amateurish about his engravings, as if he did them for his own pleasure: his draughtsmanship at times leaves something to be desired. In 1515 he executed (for it is believed that he cut many of his own blocks) a series of forty small woodcuts of the Passion which have truly the distinction of being *multum in parvo*. They display an imagination, a dramatic power, and a depth of feeling that have been seldom surpassed. In the example here reproduced, the *Death of the Virgin* (illustration 138), note how the weight of the composition presses down upon the dying woman. The lovely and serene *Holy Family at the Fountain* of 1520 is also reproduced (illustration 135). Notable among his copper engravings are the *Crucifixion*, the *Virgin and Child in a Landscape* (illustration 134). As an example of his burin work in a sweet and tender vein the *Virgin and Child with St. Anne* is reproduced as illustration 137. Altdorfer also experimented with color printing. In some impressions of the woodcut *The Beautiful Virgin of Regensburg* he printed as many as seven blocks or colors, making it the first full color print on record (illustration 136).

With the consideration of Altdorfer the survey of German graphic art of the Renaissance comes to a close. At its best it was of brief duration: by the middle of the century there were no important German artists. Thereafter German art merits no serious consideration for several centuries to come. Some critics, among them William Morris, have ascribed this to the injurious influence of the Italian Renaissance upon so alien a culture as that of the Gothic North. Although it is true that the Renaissance, and likewise the Reformation, produced first a quickening and later a depressing effect on German art, there were nevertheless other factors that contributed strongly to its downfall. The political, social, and economic conditions in Germany at the middle and end of the century were not conducive to the cultivation of art. The country was in a state of anarchy, torn by the religious factionalism of Catholic against Protestant which culminated in the disastrous Thirty Years' War of

the seventeenth century, broken up into a multitude of avaricious, cruel, and warlike principalities, checked by practically no central authority. Travel was unsafe. The trade which had flourished so auspiciously in the previous century had been impaired by two events of far-reaching importance: the Portuguese development of a sea trade route around Africa to India, and the closing of the overland caravan routes by the conquests of the Suliman Turks which ruined the Venetian monopoly on Oriental trade. With the decline of the Venetian trade and the rise of Dutch naval commerce, the Hansa merchants and the Free Cities along the overland German trade route suffered a disastrous decline. In addition, the vast influx of silver and gold from the Spanish colonies caused a serious depreciation in the value of the precious metal mined in Germany. From these considerations it is easy to see that art suffered a blight that took centuries to overcome.

France contributed relatively little to the history of prints during the sixteenth century. The chief school of the first half of the century was the School of Fontainebleau, largely an importation from Italy, and in the second half-century France was rent with civil strife. The *Diana* (illustration 139) by Master L.D. after Primaticcio is characteristic of the work of the Fontainebleau School. One strange and mysterious figure stands out, however, among the early French engravers—Jean Duvet. This goldsmith-engraver was born about 1485 probably at Dijon, and died after 1561 at Langres. He executed some goldsmith's work as a present from the town of Langres to François I, and was honored with the title of Goldsmith to the King. He made some sixty engravings including a series of the *Apocalypse* and the *History of the Unicorn*, an allegory bearing some relation to the amours of Henri II and Diane de Poitiers. But this summary recital of his work gives no hint of the particular quality of his genius. He was a mystic, one of those extraordinary figures whose prints are moving not by what they say but by what they imply. As with many mystics, his expression is often turgid and confused, often his very language and forms are derivative—mystics are indifferent to such matters, since mundane expression bears the same relation to inner light as a candle does to the sun. But through these naive and clumsy engravings shine breathtaking illumination and fiery emotion. His conception is so much greater than his execution that he sometimes leaves his plates unfinished in despair. His plates of the *Apocalypse* (illustration 143), with their swirling forms and phantasmagoric appearances, seem more akin to the spirit of that great mystical document than Dürer's more prosaic versions, from which many of the details are borrowed. In a serener, more joyous vein is the *Marriage of Adam and Eve* (illustration 144). It is inter-esting to compare this with Dürer's *Adam and Eve* for a further contrast between the mystic and the man of the world.

Jean Cousin, painter, sculptor, engraver, architect, glassworker, mathematician, and writer, made a small number of engravings, notably *The Lamentation* (illustration 141), distinguished for its moving arrangement of figures against a background of classical landscape. His *Book of Perspective* of 1560, with its charming and precise woodcuts, bears witness to the great interest that existed in that branch of science. But the first French work, indeed the first printed work on perspective in any language, was issued at Toul in 1505 by Jean Pélerin. Pélerin, or Viator, was Canon of the Cathedral, had been in the service of the historian Philippe de Comines, and wrote books on Ptolemy as well as on devotional subjects. It is not known how he achieved the miracle of working out to perfection the complete system of perspective, but he did and illustrated it with a series of woodcut diagrams of a room (illustration 142), bridges, a courtyard, Notre-Dame Cathedral, et cetera. The book was popular and went through several editions, and was pirated in a Nuremberg edition of 1509. The work was dedicated to artists, and in the dedication he mentions some that he considered worthy in his day. They are, as far as they can be identified, as follows: Mantegna, Leonardo, Raphael, Michelangelo, Perugino, Bellini, Lucas van Leyden, Cranach, Dürer, Baldung Grien, Hugo van der Goes, Schäufelein, and Fouquet.

In Antwerp and later at Brussels there lived a man who was one of the world's greatest artists, Peter Bruegel. He was born about 1525 and studied with Pieter Koeck van Aelst, whose daughter he afterwards married. He undoubtedly derived inspiration in his macabre aspects from Hieronymus Bosch. In 1551 he was enrolled in the artists' Guild of St. Luke at Antwerp, and was furnishing designs to the print publisher, Jerome Cock. He made only one original etching, the *Rabbit Hunters* (illustration 149): the rest of his designs were engraved by others. Most of our knowledge of his life comes from the almost contemporary account of Karel van Mander.

With [his friend and patron] Franckert, Bruegel often went on trips among the peasants, to their weddings and fairs [illustration 148]. The two dressed like peasants, brought presents like the other guests, and acted as if they belonged to the families or acquaintances of the bride or groom. Here Bruegel delighted in observing the manners of the peasants in eating, drinking, dancing, jumping, making love, and engaging in various drolleries, all of which he knew how to copy very comically and skillfully.... He was astonishingly sure of his composition and drew most ably and beautifully with the pen ... Bruegel was a quiet man who did not talk much, but was jovial in

company, and he loved to frighten people, often his own pupils with all kinds of ghostly sounds and pranks that he played. . . . He painted a *Massacre of the Innocents*, in which there is much to see that is done true to life—a whole family, for instance, begging for the life of a peasant child whom a murderous soldier has siezed in order to kill it; the grief and the swooning of the mother and other events appear realistic. . . . Many of Bruegel's strange compositions and comical subjects one may see in his copper engravings. But he has made many skillful and beautiful drawings; he supplied them with inscriptions which, at the time, were too biting and too sharp, and which he had burned by his wife during his last illness, because of remorse, or fear that the most disagreeable consequences might grow out of them. In his will he left his wife a picture of a Magpie on a Gallows. By the magpie he meant the gossips whom he delivered to the gallows. In addition, he had painted a picture in which Truth triumphs. According to his own statement, this was the best thing painted by him.

Bruegel had a deep and abiding love for humanity, for the peasant and common man, for life in its essentials. But it was not a patronizing attitude, something he could exploit cynically or commercially for his own ends. It grew out of his innate sympathy for all the manifestations of life, high and low, the eternal verities of man and woman. He also had a great love for nature, its trees and rocks, its rivers and mountains, its fertile plains, as his many landscapes show (illustration 145). But he was also a great intellect, one of the world's greatest pictorial designers in line and color in space; like Bach, whom he resembled in many respects, a master of noble and intricate contrapuntal effects. Above all he was a philosopher who meditated on first and last things, who was capable of those profound syntheses of human experience which he clothed in archetypes of the most convincing realism. He gave his allegiance to no faction but to humanity as a whole. He pursued his way serenely in troubled times with an enduring faith in Truth and Man. And perilous times they were: the presence of sudden and cruel death, bitter religious strife, rapine and wanton destruction, the horrible oppression of the Spanish rulers and soldiery. That he felt all these things is evident from the inscriptions he destroyed and from the nostalgia that permeates his *Luilekkerland* (illustration 147), the "Land of *Cocaigne*," the "Rock-Candy Mountain," that land of milk and honey where sorrow and effort and care are banished. But he also faced the facts with unflinching realism in the *Massacre of the Innocents* and in that magnificent synthesis of *Justice* (illustration 146) where are assembled all the tortures of the Inquisition. He never took sides in the narrow sense. Is this the role of the artist? At any rate, it is one solution of the artist's problem. It must be remembered that the issues were not as clear at the time as they are to us in perspective; even the oppressed were disorganized and torn with opposing factions, and he died before the Spanish fury had reached its climax. He never took sides, but he always believed that his greatest painting was the *Triumph of Truth*.

II. IN ITALY

The Italians, set in the midst of natural loveliness and among the ruins of ancient art, had never wholly lost the sense of beauty; they may have paid but slight attention to what was about them, but they lived lifelong in the daily sight of fair scenes and beautiful forms, which impressed their senses and molded their nature, so that, when with the revival of letters they felt the native impulse of humanity toward the higher life stirring once more in their hearts, they found themselves embued with powers of perception and appreciation beyond any other people in the world. These powers were not the particular possession of a well-born class; the centuries had bred them unobserved into the nature of the race, into the physical constitution of the people. The artisan, no less than the prince, took delight in the dawn of art, and welcomed it with equal worship. Nor was this artistic instinct the only common acquisition; the enthusiasm for letters was likewise widely shared so that some of the best manuscripts of the classics have come down to modern times from the hands of humble Florentine workmen. Italy, indeed, was the first country where democratic civilization had place; here the contempt of the Northern lord for the peasant and the mechanic had never been widespread, partly because mercantile life was early held to be honorable, and partly because of peculiar social conditions. The long, uninterrupted intercourse with the remains of Roman civilization in the unbarbarized East, the contact with Saracenic civilization in the South, the culture of the court of the Two Sicilies, and the invariably leveling influence of commerce, had made Italy the most cosmopolitan of European countries; the sharp and warlike rivalry of small but intensely patriotic states, and the necessity they lay under of utilizing for their own preservation whatever individual energy might arise among them, perhaps most of all the powerful example of the omnipresent Church in which the son of a swineherd might take the Papal Throne, had contributed to make it comparatively easy to pass from lower to higher social ranks; the aristocratic structure remained but the distinction of classes was obscured, and the excellence of the individual's faculties, the energy and scope of his powers, were recognized as the real dignities which were worthy of respect. In this recognition of the individual, and this common taste for art and letters, lay the conditions of new and vigorous intellectual life; they resulted in the great age of Italy. It was this in the main that made possible the popular fervor

for the things of the mind in the Italian Renaissance, to which nothing else in the world's history is comparable but the popular enthusiasm of the modern Revolution for liberty. Dante gave his country a native language, the Humanists gave it the literature of Rome, the Hellenists the literature of Greece; poets sang and artists painted with a loftiness and dignity of imagination, a sweetness and delicacy of sentiment, and energy and reach of thought, a music of verse and harmony of line and color, still unsurpassed. The gifts which these men brought were not for a few, but for the many who shared in this mastering, absorbing interest in the things of the mind, in beauty and wisdom, which was the vital spirit of the Italian Renaissance.

Thus did the poet and scholar George Edward Woodberry summarize the background of the Italian Renaissance, from which sprang, about the middle of the fifteenth century, the art of engraving apparently quite independently of Germany. Just as in the northern countries, its development was bound up with the goldsmith. Modern scholarship has distinguished two schools or workshops of goldsmiths in Florence where the new art probably had its origin. The first workshop, traditionally associated with the names of Maso Finiguerra (to whom indeed Vasari mistakenly attributes the invention of engraving) and Baccio Baldini, produced prints in the "Fine Manner." The distinguishing characteristic of this technique was a system of cross-hatching by fine lines giving somewhat the effect of a wash drawing. One of the outstanding works of this school is a series of *The Planets* with their attributes and influences on daily life. The *Planet Mercury*, patron of commerce and art (illustration 153), presents a delightful picture of the flourishing state of the arts in Florence. In the foreground a sculptor is carving a portrait bust. To the left is a goldsmith's shop with an artist making an engraving, and a customer bargaining for a handsome goblet. Above on a scaffolding an artist is painting a fresco while his assistant is grinding colors. In the background is an astrologer with an astrolabe. To the right scholarly pursuits are illustrated. In the foreground a richly dressed youth is feasting in the company of the innkeeper. Truly a paradise for artists and scholars! Similar in technique is a class of goldsmiths' work known as nielli. These were small plates, usually of silver, in which a decorative design had been engraved and filled with a kind of enamel of contrasting color. The artist sometimes kept a record of his design by inking the plate and making a proof on paper or other material; from this—another transition step in the art of printmaking—he got the idea of making plates for the specific purpose of printing off designs. Two later tiny ornament prints, in the style of nielli, by Peregrino da Cesena are reproduced as illustrations 158 and 160. Another charming group in the Fine Manner are the so-called Otto Prints, from the name of an early owner

(illustration 159). They were round ornamental engravings and were perhaps designed for decorative purposes just as we might paste designs on a candy box.

The second large group of Florentine engravings is in the "Broad Manner," from the workshop of Francesco Rosselli. They are differentiated from the Fine Manner engravings by the use of parallel lines of shading, giving somewhat the effect of a pen-and-ink drawing. An example of the Broad Manner is shown in the *Assumption of the Virgin* (illustration 155). It is one of the finest and largest of the early Italian engravings and was undoubtedly based upon a design by Botticelli. The composition is noble and distinguished, and the engraving manages to translate some of the linear movement, rugged characterization, and lyric beauty that are associated with Botticelli in his last period.

One of the most important productions of the North Italian School is the set of so-called *Tarocchi Cards* of Mantegna which, as Hind points out, are neither cards nor Tarocchi nor by Mantegna. They are a series of fifty instructive prints divided into five series classified as *Ranks and Conditions of Men, Apollo and the Muses, Arts and Sciences, Genii and Virtues,* and *Planets and Spheres. The Primo Mobile,* or *Angel of the Ninth Sphere,* of the last-named series is reproduced as illustration 157. The engravings were probably made at Ferrara around 1465. Dürer made a copy of this print on his first journey to Italy; the drawing is preserved in the British Museum. The greatest artist of the North Italian School was Andrea Mantegna. He was born of humble parentage near Padua about 1430. He studied at the studio of Squarcione, a mediocre painter and dealer in antiquities, whose shop was the meeting place of the scholars and humanists of Padua. It was in this atmosphere that he developed the admiration for the works and culture of Roman civilization which became the ruling passion of his life. In Vasari's words, "Andrea always maintained that the good antique statues were more perfect and beautiful than anything in nature." He lived in an ideal world of his own imagination, the world of Rome, in which moved figures of incomparable nobility, dignity, and grandeur. And he set out to embody his dreams with all the tactile feeling, the sculpturesque power, the knowledge of nature and of representation, all the resources of a supremely creative temperament. His engravings, so seemingly dry and austere, are in truth loaded with emotion: every line is saturated with feeling. Never have tenderness and brooding protection been more superbly expressed than in the *Virgin and Child* (illustration 161). For breathtaking grandeur *The Risen Christ Between St. Andrew and Longinus* has never been surpassed (illustration 162); for the expression of sorrow and lofty sense of tragedy, his three *Entombments* (illustration 163). Consider also

those re-creations of the antique, the *Battle of the Sea Gods*, and the *Bacchanal with Silenus* and the *Bacchanal with Winepress* (illustration 164), with what solidity and tactile reality these types are rendered concrete. There they are—brought into being by Mantegna to live forever like the figures on Keats's urn—types of revelry, types of tenderness, types of grandeur, types of sorrow and tribulation. The concrete embodiment of types is creation of a high order, much higher, in fact, than realistic representation of natural objects, because it requires a much greater concentration of mental and emotional faculties. So, in spite of the smallness of his *œuvre*, seven engravings in all and the score that are associated as engravings of his school, Mantegna ranks as one of the supremely great artists in the history of prints. A word should be said about his burin technique. He engraved his outlines deeply, and the color areas in between, lightly. The latter soon wore out, leaving only the bare outlines. As William Ivins has said, it is a tribute to the power of his design that even his poor impressions are valued by collectors.

Mantegna established a reputation with some twenty prints, but Pollaiuolo became famous for only one, the *Battle of the Naked Men* (illustration 154). Antonio del Pollaiuolo was born in Florence about 1432 and was one of the most famous goldsmiths, sculptors, and painters of his time. "Antonio's treatment of the nude," says Vasari, "is more modern than that of any of the masters who preceded him, and he dissected many bodies to examine their anatomy, being the first to represent the proper action of the muscles." Berenson's famous appreciation of this engraving, one of the world's greatest masterpieces, is well known:

What is it that makes us return to this sheet with ever renewed, ever increased pleasure? Surely it is not the hideous faces of most of the figures and their scarcely less hideous bodies. Nor is it the pattern as decorative design, which is of great beauty indeed, but not at all in proportion to the spell exerted upon us. Least of all is it—for most of us—an interest in the technique or history of engraving. No, the pleasure we take in these savagely battling forms arises from their power to directly communicate life, to immensely heighten our sense of vitality. Look at the combatant prostrate on the ground and his assailant bending over, each intent on stabbing the other. See how the prostrate man plants his foot on the thigh of his enemy, and note the tremendous energy he exerts to keep off the foe, who, turning as upon a pivot, with his grip on the other's head, exerts no less force to keep the advantage gained. The significance of all these muscular strains and pressures is so rendered that we cannot help realizing them; we imagine ourselves imitating all the movements, and exerting the force required for them—and all without the least effort on our side. If all this without moving a muscle, what should we feel if we too had exerted ourselves! And thus while under the spell of this illusion—this hyperaesthesia not bought with drugs, and not paid for with cheques drawn on our vitality—we feel as if the elixir of life, not our own sluggish blood, were coursing through our veins.

Some of the charm and enchantment of the School of Giorgione are carried over in the engravings of Giulio Campagnola, born at Padua about 1482. The son of the writer, Girolamo Campagnola, Giulio was precocious and many-sided in his development: painter, engraver, poet, musician, scholar, and designer of type. About 1507 he settled in Venice and may have had some direct contact with Giorgione. He died after 1515. Of the sixteen plates that he engraved, some are quite banal, being copies after Dürer and others; but there are about a half dozen that are among the most exquisite prints of the period, the *Shepherds in a Landscape*, the *Stag at Rest*, the *Young Shepherd*, the *St. John the Baptist*, and *Christ and the Woman of Samaria*. It is hard to analyze wherein the magic of an engraving like the *Christ and the Woman of Samaria* (illustration 167) lies, but it is equally obvious that the enchantment exists. Perhaps it lies in the perfect identification of matter and form (in Walter Pater's words) or in the mood of serene and pure beauty that it so elusively suggests. The *St. John the Baptist* (illustration 165)—the landscape Giorgionesque, the figure deriving its nobility from Mantegna—likewise manages to convey a definite emotion in purely pictorial terms. Campagnola's work is distinguished not for intensity or strength but for sensibility and grace. Some of his works like the *Young Shepherd*, the *Stag at Rest* (illustration 166), or the *St. John*, are executed with an exquisite placement of every detail, including the lettering of the name. In this embodiment of sensibility and good taste as a creative principle, Campagnola is the exemplar of a long line of artists reaching to the present day. His technique is noteworthy also for its use of dots and flick-work combined with greater or lesser amounts of regular graver work to blend and soften his effects. It is an interesting anticipation of stipple engraving, not so much in its method as in its final result.

The allegories and mythological conceits dear to the Renaissance and Humanist temperament were depicted by a number of secondary yet charming engravers such as Master I.B. with the Bird, Nicoletto da Modena, Jacopo Francia, Christofano Robetta, Benedetto Montagna, Master of 1515, and others. Robetta is represented here by his *Adoration of the Magi* based upon Filippo Lippi (illustration 169), and Montagna by his *Apollo and Pan* and his *St. Benedict Teaching His Rule to His Monks* (illustrations 184 and 171). The famous *Rule of St. Benedict* has been published, and is a guide to the monastic life. The Master of 1515 is interesting for his extensive use of

drypoint (illustration 170). The man who was destined to make engraving into a professional system was Marcantonio Raimondi. He was born in Bologna about 1480 and studied with the goldsmith-painter, Francesco Francia. In due course he left his native city to seek his fortune in the big world. He was a facile engraver and had a great talent for assimilation. In Venice, most cosmopolitan of cities, he discovered the work of Dürer and, as we have already heard, copied much of it. "Arrived at Rome," in Vasari's words, "he made a beautiful copper engraving of a drawing of Raphael, representing Lucretia killing herself (illustration 173), executed with such beauty and diligence that, when it was shown to Raphael, the artist was disposed to issue some prints himself from his own designs." This was the beginning of a long and fruitful partnership between artist and engraver in the dissemination of designs, which had enormous influence on art for centuries to come. It established a practice of reproductive engraving which was to last until the perfection of photographic reproductions. It was in the form of reproductive engraving that a large portion of art was made accessible to other practicing artists. Not only did Marcantonio, in collaboration with Raphael, establish the practice, but he also, through his pupils, laid down a system of technique. As Ivins points out, "Marcantonio combined the German linear scheme for representation of textures and rotundity with the Italian feeling for volumes, and in so doing gave engraving its pictorial enfranchisement." Two of the greatest examples of these two artists' collaboration are the *Judgment of Paris* and the *Morbetto* or the *Plague* (illustrations 174 and 178). They are marvels of space composition, rhythmic movement and balance, linear design and felicitous handling of the figure. The *St. Cecilia* (illustration 175) is also after Raphael. The *Singer with a Lute* (illustration 172) is an early work. The engraving *Two Fauns* (illustration 176), based upon the antique, shows the extent to which Renaissance decoration deviated from medieval ornament. After the death of Raphael, Marcantonio's work suffered a marked deterioration, and this decline was completed by his financial ruin in the sack of Rome in 1527. He fled to Bologna and died a broken man.

Another engraver who collaborated with Raphael in still another form of reproductive engraving was Ugo da Carpi. Vasari credits da Carpi with the invention of chiaroscuro wood engraving or the use of several blocks in color for the reproduction of drawings. It is a matter of record, however, that the Germans—Burgkmair, 1508, Cranach, 1509 (illustration 179), Baldung Grien (illustration 180), Altdorfer (illustration 136), Wechtlin, and others —had perfected the process either previously or contemporaneously with the Italian. The methods of the two schools were nevertheless slightly different. The Ger-

mans in general worked up the black and white key block to its completion so that it could function as a woodcut independently (see illustration 104) and then added color blocks to heighten the effect, whereas the Italians conceived the whole in terms of color and made less use of detailed black and white accents. In the *Miraculous Draught of Fishes* by da Carpi after the drawing by Raphael (illustration 181) the details are treated so broadly and so completely in terms of color, that the key block would have no meaning independently of the other blocks. Another example, the *Saturn*, by da Carpi after Pordenone, is reproduced as illustration 182. Other practitioners of the art in Italy were Andreani, Vicentino, and Antonio da Trento (illustration 183), who also turned up in the School of Fontainebleau as Fantuzzi.

Mention of the woodcut leads us back half a century to trace the development of the art in Italy. Single woodcuts of the fifteenth century were not so frequent in Italy as in Germany, though woodcut playing cards are mentioned as a flourishing industry at Venice as early as 1441. The illustrated book, however, soon developed into one of the most important achievements of the Renaissance in Italy. One of the earliest illustrated books in Italy was Valturius, *De Re Militari*, printed at Verona in 1472. The designs of this early and important book on military engineering have been attributed to the medallist Matteo de Pastis or to Valturius himself (illustration 54). As an example of the pictorial treatment of another of the arts, the *Organist* from Gafurius, *Theorica Musicae*, printed in Milan in 1492, is reproduced as illustration 55. Bergomensis' *De Claris Mulieribus*, 1497 (illustration 57) with its charming series of woodcuts of famous women was issued in Ferrara.

The two great centers of book production in Italy, however, were Venice and Florence. The illustrators of Venice perfected a kind of engraving in outline not only intrinsically charming and graceful but also perfectly in keeping with the roman type face. The *Decameron* of 1492 has already been mentioned (illustration 53). One of the most distinguished examples of Venetian illustration is Ketham's *Fasciculus Medicinae* of 1493 (illustration 49). This noble and dignified work gives us a glimpse of the medical practice of the time: we see the doctor visiting the patient ill with the plague, being careful not to come too close for fear of infection. Perhaps the most famous Venetian book was the *Hypnerotomachia Poliphili*, or the *Strife of Love in a Dreame*, as an Elizabethan translated it. It was printed by Aldus in 1499 at the expense of Leonardus Crassus (illustration 51). The text by Colonna is a mélange of humanist and classical conceits, and the book is now remembered only for the beauty of its woodcuts and the harmony of its type and illustrations. The work has been a model to many subsequent illustrators, nota-

bly Ricketts and Maillol in modern times.

In Florence, among other things, were published a large group of illustrated books which bear the same relation to the Renaissance, in their perfection of a popular art, that the French Books of Hours bear to the Gothic spirit: the essence of the Renaissance is distilled in their pages. These woodcuts, like the cuts of the *Horae*, possess a distinctive and easily recognizable style. And curiously enough, the period of their greatest production coincided almost exactly with that of the French books, that is to say the ten years before and the thirty years after the beginning of the sixteenth century. Like them, too, the names of the artists or engravers are not known. Many of the Florentine cuts appeared in little booklets, manifestations of popular art, *Rappresentazione* or sacred mystery plays, sermons, poems, little novels—an enormous range of subject matter. The daily life of Florence is re-created before our eyes. Hundreds of scenes, the events, the gestures, the characters of everyday life are transformed into decorative pictures of lasting charm. We see a group singing before an image in church, we see the swain bringing his sweetheart a flower (illustration 45), we see the citizen at the shoemaker's shop or at the fishmonger's buying fish during Lent (illustration 41), we see young bucks carousing. We see dramatic incidents from the lives of the saints, we see Savonarola preaching in church (illustration 42), nay, we almost hear him as he holds his audience spellbound by his eloquence:

Women, you may rejoice in being beautiful. Be beautiful, it is woman's greatest delight. But tell me in what does beauty consist? In colors? No. In contours? No. It is in the harmony between them. And how is that harmony revealed? By light. Beauty is light. You see happy spirits; their beauty consists in light. You know, God is light: He is beauty also. The more truly that creatures participate in the beauty of God and approach it, the more beautiful they become. . . .

And the whole panorama is depicted with such charming decorative effect, such color and vivacity, such zest and *joie de vivre*, such unerring balance between particular and universal, that they have never been surpassed in the history of prints.

Single sheet woodcuts were not made in great quantities in the sixteenth century in Italy except for a few in Venice. Here Titian was the dominant influence. The five sheets of the *Triumph of Faith*, dated 1508, and the twelve sheets of *Pharaoh's Army Submerged in the Red Sea*, of 1549, are epoch-making works, grand both in size and significance. These works are too huge for reduction on a small scale, and two other works by Titian (illustrations 187 and 189) have been chosen for reproduction, cut by Nicolo Boldrini, the *Venus and Amor*, and the *Landscape with the Woman Milking a Cow*. They are faithful translations into wood of the characteristics of Titian's drawing, and one of them shows Titian's pastoral interest and method of treating pure landscape, which probably influenced Bruegel and Rubens when they came to take up the same theme. Titian was also indirectly involved in one of the landmarks of medical history, the book by Andreas Vesalius, *De Humani Corporis Fabrica*. The book was printed in Basel in 1543, but the many woodcut illustrations were designed and cut in Venice, and perhaps in Titian's workshop. The woodcuts indeed have been attributed to Titian, but modern critical opinion holds that they are by several hands close to Titian, including Vesalius himself, Jan Stephan van Calcar, and Domenico Campagnola for the landscape backgrounds to some of the woodcuts (illustration 188). In certain sections of the work, Vesalius had the artist as much in mind as the physician. He himself wrote: "These plates display a total view of the scheme of muscles such as only painters and sculptors are wont to consider." Titian's portraits were famous for their penetration of character, their decorative fullness, and nobility of style. Typical of these is Titian's portrait of his friend, the great poet, Ariosto, cut in wood by Francesco de Nanto and published in an edition of his *Orlando Furioso*, Ferrara, 1532 (illustration 190). Incidentally Ariosto mentions Titian in his poem. The great Venetian died in 1576 at the age of ninety-nine, rich in honors and achievement, one of the first professional artists in the modern sense of the word.

A distinguished portrait of Titian was engraved by Agostino Carracci (illustration 191), one of three brothers who founded the Eclectic School of Bologna, and who also were among the first to introduce the Academy system of teaching to replace the older master-apprentice method. The Carracci, dominant in the second half of the sixteenth century, represented the eclectic and somewhat decadent tendency that followed the great outburst of the Renaissance. Two other painters whose work anticipated and led up to some of the qualities associated with Baroque art were Parmigianino and Baroccio. Francesco Mazzuoli, called Parmigianino, was the first Italian to practice etching. His etchings, dating from about 1520 onwards, have the spontaneity and charm, the refinement and feminine grace of his drawings (illustration 194). He was one of the first of the Mannerists. Federigo Baroccio (1528–1612) made about four etchings, notably the large *Christ Appearing to St. Francis* (illustration 195). This plate is rather theatrical in style but executed with considerable subtlety of biting. Baroccio was to have considerable influence on the religious painting of Boucher and other artists of the eighteenth century. Mention should be made of two artists whose woodcuts have a fresh and original quality, Giuseppe Scolari and Luca Cambiaso.

Scolari may have cut his own blocks. At any rate he shows a feeling for the idiosyncracies of wood: not translations of pen line into wood but a painterly manipulation of dark masses, which he breaks up with white line. He executed a poignantly expressive *Ecce Homo* and a *Rape of Proserpina* full of Mannerist swagger (illustration 192). Cambiaso's woodcuts, however, are translations of his line drawings, but his drawings are executed with huge gusto, *allegro con brio* (illustration 193).

The early illustrated books had been decorated with woodcuts. But at the end of the sixteenth century woodcut illustrations were being replaced by intaglio or copperplate engravings. There were several reasons for this. Copper engraving became more fashionable than woodcuts. But there also was a growing differentiation in the purpose of the book: between the book as a cheap popular work and the book as an object of luxury. In the fifteenth century the differentiation had been between the cheap printed book and the sumptuous illuminated manuscript. Now the differentiation was made between the cheap woodcut book and the expensive copperplate book. There was no doubt that the copperplate book was more expensive to produce: it required more than one printing, the plates took longer to print and could not yield as many impressions as a woodblock. Thus the illustrated book became intaglio in character and luxurious and expensive in production. The woodcut went underground, as it were, and continued an unbroken tradition from the fifteenth century to the nineteenth century in the chapbooks, broadsheets, *images populaires*, and fugitive prints of the people. Of course in certain kinds of scientific work, such as maps or architectural illustrations, where the greater precision of copper engraving was desirable, there were reasons other than economic for the change. By the middle of the sixteenth century the technical difficulties in the way of using intaglio illustrations had been more or less overcome. Three books may be used to typify the new tendency. The first, catering to an aristocratic luxurious class, is Gualterotti's *Description of the Royal Fête at the Marriage of Christina of Lorraine with Don Ferdinando de' Medici, Grand Duke of Tuscany*, published at Florence in 1589. It was a sort of souvenir book of the ceremonies describing all the pageants, mimic battles, balls, triumphal arches, and allegories that were part of the festivities. There were sixty-seven paintings made of the various incidents by a number of court painters, and for the book they were etched with great zest and vigor by some unknown hand. The illustration chosen (200) represents the actual wedding ceremony, and was painted by Giovanni Balducci. The etching is carried out with a breadth and power, an incisive line and flair for style that is truly a delight to the eye. Incidentally, at this same wedding a number of

musical *intermezzi*, precursors of opera, were produced. One of them, *The Harmony of the Spheres*, was composed by Emilio del Cavaliere, who later produced the first oratorio.

The second example is midway between the scientific and the sumptuous book: *Della Trasportazione dell' Obelisco Vaticano*, published at Rome in 1589 (illustration 199). This work, written by Domenico Fontana, the architect of Pope Sixtus V, describes the engineering feat of transporting the obelisk to its present location in the Piazza S. Pietro, and is illustrated with a number of engravings by Natalis Bonifaccio after Fontana's designs. The plates were executed with gusto and a fine balance between scientific and pictorial interest. The artistic treatment of scaffolding, building construction, "the wonder of work," has been generally assumed to be of modern origin. Although the scientific aspect is stressed, it is probable that it was considered more as a sumptuous gift book given out by the Pope and his friends. The third example is more specifically of scientific interest, a page from the great Atlas of Ortelius, the *Map of the Pacific Ocean* of 1589 (illustration 131), printed by the famous Antwerp printer, Plantin, of whom we shall hear further in connection with Rubens. It is interesting to contrast this map with the Nuremberg map of the world in 1493 and trace the growth of man's geographical knowledge (illustration 130). In 1492 Columbus discovered America; in 1497 Cabot discovered Newfoundland; in 1498 Vasco de Gama sailed to India around Africa; in 1499 Amerigo Vespucci discovered Venezuela; in 1513 Balboa discovered the Pacific at Panama; in 1514 the Portuguese were in China and in 1542 in Japan; in 1520 Magellan sailed around the world; from 1539 to 1577 the explorations of de Soto, Coronado, Cartier, Frobisher, and Drake took place. Ortelius was one of the first cartographers to issue maps that were based on actual scientific observations. Yet withal the map is beautifully designed, with a fine sense of placement of the decorative cartouches and other accessories. The ship in the Pacific represents Magellan sailing around the world. Ortelius drew at a time when the truth about geography was still beautiful. Later on it was to become strictly utilitarian.

This concludes the survey of the Renaissance as expressed in prints. The astonishing thing about the Italian Renaissance was the extent to which all the people participated in it. There are always a few cultivated and creative people in every age, but when these qualities are spread among all the people, it becomes a great period. Artists and craftsmen of great talent sprang up on every hand; but there were also a great demand for and encouragement of their work. Time and time again one comes across passages in Vasari like this: "Agnolo Doni was then in Florence, and though sparing in other things,

spent willingly upon paintings and sculpture, of which he was very fond." Or the following: "All of which brought Marcantonio such fame that his things were more valued than those of the Flemings for their good design, and the merchants found them very profitable." It was in Italy that the printseller-publisher first developed. There were Il Baviera (Raphael's agent), Nicolo Nelli, Antonio Salamanca, Antoine Lafrery, C. Duchetti, Jerome Cock of Antwerp (illustration 197), and others. Even the commonest books and pamphlets were beautiful. But in the mutations of man's fate, this widespread cultivation of the beautiful did not last for long. We marvel at the calmness and casualness with which Vasari mentions the sack of Rome in 1527. Italy had been broken up into many rival cities and principalities, and the Hapsburgs vied with the rulers of France for their domination and control. Italy was undoubtedly the most civilized country of Europe, civilized not only in the sense of culture and refinement but also in the sense of commerce and manufacture. Italy gave much to Germany and Flanders and especially to France through the encouragement of its rulers from François I to Catherine de' Medici. With the development of these countries, Italy's prestige and its trade gradually declined. The dominant power in the second half of the sixteenth century was Spain with all the wealth of the Americas at its command, and its policy was reactionary and monarchial, definitely opposed to the relatively democratic cultures of Italy, England, and Flanders.

4. The Seventeenth Century

The seventeenth century has sometimes been called the century of the Baroque. And although an art period or style cannot be precisely delimited by centuries, many of the artists of the time display qualities that are associated with this style. The Baroque developed from the Renaissance and to a certain extent was a reaction against it. It was the age of the Counter-Reformation, a reaffirmation of faith and dogma, initiated largely by the Jesuits against the individualist interpretations of the Protestant Reformation. It has been claimed that the Baroque had a relation to the Gothic in its stress upon emotional elements. It is true that both Gothic and Baroque were ages of faith; but in the one case it was naive faith, a primary and creative impulse, in the second case it was a faith in established dogma, a secondary or derivative impulse. The Baroque would have been impossible without the Renaissance. A definite convention, a dogma, had been firmly established—a convention that embraced not only religious but also social and artistic forms, absolute monarchy, forms of building and painting, forms of social life—and the Baroque was the individual's reaction to this. The dogmas were not challenged: they were taken for granted; and with that foundation they were either expanded into a swelling system as with Rubens, or embroidered with grotesque themes as with Callot. The Baroque was a product of leisure and luxury, a slackening of the terrific outburst of energy of the Renaissance. The fires had died down; what remained were the flickerings of fantasy. The artists of the Renaissance expressed their ideas in attitudes and gestures energetically and beautifully appropriate to the occasion, the natural outgrowth of the action expressed. In the Baroque the gesture became important for its own sake; the artists played with it, they heightened it or exaggerated it, played variations on it, till it became largely devoid of logical meaning. The gesture became a mannerism, a form often employed purely for compositional effect. They were bored with austere or tragic effects; they craved novelty and ingenious invention. The positive, the affirming, the best side of the Baroque was expressed by Rubens.

Peter Paul Rubens, the Prince of Painters, lived and breathed in the grand manner. His work is one grand *largesse*, which was not with him a mannered attitude only: out of his fecundity, his incomparable zest, he endowed his forms with swelling pulsating life. He was a man of action: he painted pictures as a general would direct an army or a prince would rule a principality. He had vast organizing skill: he organized his pictures into masterly compositions, he organized his pupils and assistants to execute them; on both his instrument and his creation he put his own impress. He did not innovate, he summed up. He did not create new forms, he used the material at hand, he worked in the spirit of the age. He lived, as Fromentin said, *"en pleine lumière,"* in full light —never a shadow of skepticism or doubt. Born in 1577, he started his career as a court page; he died in 1640 the most renowned painter of his time. He studied with three masters and went to Italy to complete his education. At thirty-three he was a successful man with a beloved wife and children and an imposing house filled with art treasures. He became a diplomat, working consistently to maintain peace between Protestant Holland and Catholic Belgium. He was the courteous friend of Philip II of Spain, the companion of the art-loving Charles I, the painter of the *Triumphs of Marie de' Medici*, the confidant and trusted agent of the Infanta Isabella of Belgium. He engaged in vast correspondence in Latin, Spanish, Italian, and Flemish on many matters of diplomacy, business, antiquities, collecting, but never any speculation on art. We have a contemporary account of his daily life by the Dane, Otto Sperling:

We paid a visit to the very celebrated and eminent painter, Rubens, whom we found at work, and, while he went on with his painting, listening to a reading from Tacitus and dictating a letter. We kept silent for fear of disturbing him; but he spoke to us without stopping his work or the reading or the dictation, and answered our questions as if to give us proof of his powerful faculties. Then he ordered a servant to conduct us round his magnificent palace and show us his antiquities and the Greek and Roman statues of which he owns a great quantity.

It is natural that such an expansive and practical nature should, like Raphael, see the advantage of publishing engravings of his work under his own auspices. He set about to train and employ a school of engravers of whom Soutman, Vorsterman, Pontius, and the two Bolswerts were the most famous. In the Bibliothèque Nationale in Paris, there exist proofs of their engravings containing corrections and emendations in Rubens's hand. It is doubtful whether he ever handled the burin himself. One etching, however, is ascribed to him with considerable certainty—the superb *St. Catherine* with its monumental swelling forms (illustration 204). The more than eight hundred engravings that were made after his works did much to spread Rubens's fame throughout Europe. As an example of landscape with genre interest the *Village Dance* engraved by Bolswert is reproduced as illustration 203. As an example of a religious subject, *The Temptation of Christ* from the plafond of the Jesuit Church in Antwerp, cut in wood by Christophel Jegher, is reproduced as illustration 202. In the archives of Plantin-Moretus Museum in Antwerp is preserved Moretus's account referring to the printing of this very woodcut on September 2 and 8, 1633, "*item, doibt pour l'impression de 2000 images de bois avec le papier etc. Florins 72*" (item, cost of printing 2000 proofs of woodcut with paper 72 florins).

Anthony van Dyck was Rubens's most talented pupil. Before he settled permanently in England as a court painter to Charles I in 1632, he began an ambitious undertaking known as the *Iconography* or collection of one hundred portraits of the famous men of his day. He executed eighteen of these in etching, of which five remained unchanged (*Peter Bruegel the Younger, Erasmus, Snellinx, Suttermans,* and *Josse de Momper,* illustration 205), six others were later supplied with engraved backgrounds (*Jan Bruegel, Franken, van Noort, Pontius, Vorsterman,* and *de Wael*) and the balance completely reworked by professional engravers. He initiated a new style of portraiture, the freely etched portrait, concentrating on certain features of the face with open lines and dots, and leaving the body and background lightly sketched in. But the prevailing taste of his day was for the more formal portrait, and the balance of the *Iconography* was executed by the engravers of the Rubens School after his own drawings. It was not until several centuries later that the etchings themselves were appreciated. Van Dyck perfected a method for setting down the external features of a sitter without prying too deep into his essential character, which made him the eminently successful and fashionable portrait painter that he was. Even in his early days before the formula had mastered him completely, and when he was portraying his friends and fellow-painters, he could not resist endowing them all with a flattering dignity and nobility. It is known that van Dyck painted Charles I forty times and his Queen Henrietta thirty times. After the Countess Sophie of the Palatinate had been presented to the Queen and her attendants she recorded her naive astonishment at the discrepancy between fact and fiction: she had had such a different impression of the court from van Dyck's portraits.

Van Dyck died in 1641 just before the Great Rebellion in England. Another foreign etcher, Wenzel Hollar, allied himself with the Cavalier cause and fought in some of its battles. He was born in Prague in 1607 and studied with Mathias Merian. In 1637 he came to England under the patronage of the Earl of Arundel, who employed him to reproduce treasures in his collection. Born in a noble family which had lost everything in the Bohemian wars, Hollar took up etching as his life profession: he made about 2700 plates, characterized by sobriety, precision, and great technical skill. He married a lady-in-waiting at the Court and was very much interested in depicting costume, as for instance in the famous series of the *Theatrum Mulierum* of 1643. Characteristic is the *Winter* (illustration 206) of the set of the *Seasons*. The background shows a view of Cornhill and the Old Exchange in London. Underneath are four lines of verse in the spirit of the court of Charles:

> "The cold, not cruelty makes her weare
> In Winter, furrs and Wild beasts haire,
> For a smoother skinn at night
> Embraceth her with more delight."

After the Restoration he fell into poverty and worked for the book and print publishers at twelvepence per hour. According to his friend, Francis Place, "he had a method of working not common. He did all by the hour, in which he was very exact, for if anybody came in, and kept him from his business, he always laid the hourglass on one side, till they were gone." He died in extreme poverty in 1677.

As a foil to the almost feminine daintiness of Hollar one might put forward the masculine exuberance of Hendrick Goltzius. Born in 1558 of a long line of artists, he early developed an artistic temperament, and many stories are told of his pranks, of his posing as a cheese merchant before the engraver, Sadeler, of making engravings in the style of Dürer and Lucas van Leyden which fooled many would-be connoisseurs, of making his servant pose as the master while he in the role of servant listened to unguarded comments about the master. In his engraving he perfected the system of the swelling line, or minute variations in the thickness of each engraved line, which enabled him to render surface textures and color with more facility. This carried engraving further in the direction of a purely reproductive or

copying technique in contrast to the systems of Dürer and Marcantonio which were more in the nature of translations of one medium into the conventions of another. Nevertheless his technical proficiency brought him great fame. He was one of the few seventeenth-century artists who also made chiaroscuros and woodcuts, of which the *Landscape* (illustration 150) is a charming example. In his figure work he carried the Baroque tendency of mannered gesture, of swelling out and puffing up forms to the limit, as may be seen in the typical engraving of the *Statue of Hercules in the Farnese Palace in Rome* (illustration 152). With its glimpse of the visitors gazing in admiration at the statue, it affords a delightful suggestion of the *tourisme* of the time. John Evelyn in his diary thus records his visit in 1644:

In the first place, our sight-man (for so they name certain persons here who get their living by leading strangers about to see the city) went to the Palace Farnese, a magnificent square structure built by Michael Angelo.

...Descending into the court, we with astonishment contemplated those two incomparable statues of Hercules and Flora, so much celebrated by Pliny.

Italy and its many art treasures were still the goal of artists and cultured tourists. The names of two great French etchers of the early seventeenth century were intimately associated with Italy: Callot and Claude Gelée le Lorrain.

Callot [wrote Meaume] when a child of thirteen ran away from his home at Nancy, meaning to journey to Rome and study art. It was in the spring of 1606 the young fugitive departed on foot, almost without money, and quite without influence, relying entirely on his face and his good luck. He was soon obliged to join a troupe of gypsies who were going to Florence. There he was recognized by merchants from Nancy and was taken home to his parents. He ran away a second time and was again brought home, this time by his brother. In 1608 Callot's parents finally permitted him to go to Rome where he studied under Thomassin.

In 1611 he left Rome for Florence and entered the service of Cosmo II de' Medici. Eleven years later he returned to his native Lorraine where he remained with brief outside excursions till his death in 1635. Callot was a great etcher, and perfected the technique of repeated bitings to secure effects of great delicacy and subtlety. He made use of the tough varnishes employed by the lute and violin makers to devise a firmer and harder etching ground that would not flake off and cause foul biting. A *chef d'œuvre* such as *Impruneta* or the *Great Fair at Florence* (illustration 217) (said to contain well over a thousand figures) would not have been possible without a reliable ground. Callot was also a great Baroque artist in his predilection for the grotesque, as in the *Temptation of St. Anthony* (illustration 216), for masks and pageants (in *Florence and Nancy*), for mannered religious engravings (the series of *The Saints*, *The Passion*, and *La Bénédicité* (illustration 207), and in his research into the characters of the *Commedia dell'Arte*. Faithful reflections, too, of the movements of his time were his numerous war pictures, the *Military Exercises*, the three huge *Sieges of Breda*, the *Island of Ré*, and *La Rochelle*, and the larger and smaller *Disasters of War*. It is said that after the invasion of Lorraine in 1633, Louis XIII asked him to commemorate the siege of Nancy in another huge battle piece, but Callot refused to "do anything against the honor of my prince and my country." At any rate he had seen enough of the horrors of war during the French invasion in 1632 and 1633 to execute his two bitter series of *Les Misères de la Guerre* while his memory was still vivid. They are the first of a series of terrific indictments of war that have been drawn up by artists. No greater contrast could be imagined than between the brutality of the subject and the exquisite delicacy of the treatment (illustration 210). Not only were the savage lusts of murder and plunder depicted but also the equally devastating starvation and poverty. The social system of the age was rich in contrasts, and Callot has faithfully recorded its full range, from the *Garden at Nancy* (illustration 215) and the *Costumes of the Nobility* to the studies of *Beggars* (illustration 212), card sharpers, and wandering gypsy life (illustration 211). But in no respect was he so much a child of his age as in his picturing of the *Commedia dell'Arte* (illustration 213). The *Commedia* was the quintessence of the Baroque: it was improvised, often extravagant and satiric, antiintellectual and antirational, stressing emotional values, raising the caprice to an art form, playing variations on an accepted theme, a comedy of attitudes and gestures. In the *Commedia dell'-Arte* certain types (Harlequin, Columbine, Isabelle, Scaramouche, Pulcinella, Pantaloon, Brighella, Mezzetino, Scapin, Sganarelle, Cantarina, Inamorata, Soubrette, Pierrot, El Capitan, The Doctor) with attributes known to everyone played their parts in dramatic situations which again were familiar to all. The dialogue was not written down or fixed, but was improvised by the actors following patterns that were well established. Thus the emphasis and charm of the art form lay not in the significance or meaning or the drama, but in its expression, in the gestures and pantomime of the actors, and in the wit, the satire, the *double entendre* of their speech. The *Commedia* flourished chiefly in the Latin countries during the seventeenth and eighteenth centuries.

Before leaving Lorraine for Rome again, mention should be made of another artist from Lorraine, Jacques

Bellange (illustration 208) whose mannerist gestures and extravagant emotionalism are much admired nowadays.

According to legend, Callot's contemporary, Claude, was a pastrycook's apprentice who longed for Arcadia and found it. Claude Gelée, called Lorrain, was born in the Vosges in 1600. Left an orphan at twelve he wandered about Italy, Germany, Switzerland, and Lorraine, engaging in many adventures and misadventures, falling sick, being several times robbed, and picking up here and there a knowledge of the technique of art. In 1627 he settled down in Rome where he lived a quiet and uneventful life. He did not associate with the French academicians in Rome, or perhaps they would not associate with him, though he occasionally went on painting excursions with Poussin; he was no courtier, said Sandrart, and he had but few intimates like Swanevelt, Bombaccio, Andries Both, and Sandrart. He never married, all his passion went into his work, the task of rendering visible his dream of Arcadia, where all is peace and beauty and order. Sandrart wrote:

He applied himself with great earnestness and industry to perfect himself in his art and learn the secrets of nature. Day after day he would spend in the Campagna, from sunrise till long after nightfall, noting the tints of the dawn and the splendor of the setting sun. . . . As a master of aerial perspective, he well knew how to blend the sharp division of colors to make them appear like nature's. And at his studio he would sit long hours in reverie till there came to him those grand conceptions which grew in his mind so saturated with images of life and nature.

Claude made about twenty-seven etchings. He was no great technician, and some of his plates suffer from foul biting and poor printing. But the best of them are among the masterpieces of the art. Claude was the first great Impressionist in etching. He knew how to suggest the play of light on objects, and shimmering quivering atmosphere. His plates are sometimes heroically composed, like the *Sunrise*, the *Seaport with Tower*, the *Herd in a Storm*, or the *Rape of Europa*, or touched with soft arcadian charm like the *Le Bouvier* (illustration 249), the *Dance under the Trees*, or the *Dance by the Waterside*. One etching, *Campo Vaccino* (illustration 250), is a little more realistic and shows what the Roman Forum looked like in the seventeenth century. Fortunately success came to him later in life (he never could have carved it out for himself) and he died in peace at the age of eighty-two—a simple, naive, unlettered man who dreamed a sweet and beautiful dream.

There was another foreign artist living in Rome whose works display creative power and imagination but whose life ended tragically at thirty-two after years in a debtor's prison—the German painter, Adam Elsheimer. Both Rubens and Rembrandt admired his work. His small paintings of religious and mythological subjects have a strange and moving quality, which has been successfully carried over into black and white by his friend, the amateur engraver, Count Goudt, who also seems to have suffered a mysterious and tragic fate. Goudt engraved seven plates, all after Elsheimer, among them the large *Tobit and the Angel* with its lovely sky, the *Aurora* with an equally lovely sky, the mysterious *Mocking of Ceres*, the *Flight into Egypt* copied by Seghers, and finally the *Philemon and Baucis* (illustration 225). This last engraving, so beautiful in composition and magical in its chiaroscuro, illustrates the legend of Philemon and Baucis as told in the eighth book of Ovid's *Metamorphoses*. It is one of the most beautiful stories of hospitality ever told. Jupiter and Mercury disguised as travelers wandered into a Phrygian village. Asking for hospitality they were turned away at every door until at last they came to the humble dwelling of Philemon and Baucis. Here they were received with genuine hospitality by the aged couple. They bustled about to minister to their comfort and set before the weary travelers what provisions they could muster from their slender store. During the repast the old folks were astonished to see that the wine, as fast as it was poured out, renewed itself in the pitcher. Struck with terror, they recognized their heavenly guests and implored forgiveness for their poor entertainment. And they replied, "We are gods; this inhospitable village shall pay the penalty of its impiety; you alone shall go unpunished." They destroyed the village and transformed the humble dwelling into a beautiful temple, and Jove in a benign mood asked the mortals what boon they might wish of him. And, counseling with Baucis, Philemon replied, "Grant us to be priests and guardians of this your temple; and since here we have passed our lives in love and concord, we wish that one and the same hour may take us both from life, that I may not live to see her grave, nor be laid in my own by her." And their prayer was granted.

Another great personality in print history with an equally tragic maladjustment to his surroundings was the Dutchman, Hercules Seghers. He was born about 1590 and died about 1640 as the result, it is said, of an accident while trying to drown his sorrows in drink. "He approached his art," related his contemporary, van Hoogstraaten, "with incomparable zeal." The outstanding mark of his work is its emotional quality, its intense identification with nature. Like a Chinese mystic he became one with rocks and brooks in forbidding Alpine valleys (illustration 221), with straggling larch trees (illustration 223), with crumbling ruins, with sunny fertile plains, with tiny ships battling alone on a desperate sea. Nature became the *mise en scène* for the tortured drama of

his soul. There was something in him that was akin to his countryman van Gogh, something of his passionate absorption, something of his rhythmic vibrant manner of drawing. He was no doubt a bit unbalanced: he felt too keenly, he went too deeply into things. The baffled public would have none of his work; they did not know what it was all about. At that moment they preferred realism to imagination, with the result that his life was one continuous struggle against poverty and despair. Today we look at the little that has been preserved of his work with more favorable eyes. Take for example that masterpiece, *The Three Books* (illustration 222), existing in only two impressions, both printed with brownish black ink on yellow-colored linen with the background painted black; how simple it is, how beautiful in composition, with what emotional overtones of brooding and mystery. Seghers was a great experimenter; he apparently conceived many of his etchings in terms of color. He worked with various colored inks on various colored papers and even on linen, and often colored the prints still further by hand. He was one of the first Dutch artists to take up etching and especially to fall under the spell of wild mountain scenery. Some sixty etchings have come down to us, many of them existing only in one or two impressions. But we value him today not so much for his technical experiments as for his spirit, for the imagination and the emotional *timbre* with which his work is so richly endowed. And we couple his name—not in equality but in kinship—with that of Rembrandt, who admired his work and owned some of his pictures.

Rembrandt was the greatest etcher who ever lived. No one had a greater range and greater mastery within that range than he. Religious subjects, portraits, landscapes, nude studies, still life—in all of these he created masterpieces. In the field of genre alone he did not produce much, unless we consider his studies of beggars, the *Hog*, and his *Jews in the Synagogue*, as genre pictures. We learn little from him of the externals of life as lived in Amsterdam, but we learn much about humanity, the essentials of life which do not change from age to age. He was the visionary, the man apart, who moved above contemporary life. To the Holland of the seventeenth century he was an enigma; it took the world several centuries to catch up with him. Rembrandt Harmenz van Rijn, the miller's son, was born in Leyden in 1606. His parents were ambitious that he become a scholar, and he entered the University of Leyden in 1620. But he had no call for letters and he left within a year to enter a painter's studio. After studying with three different masters, he set up for himself, and in 1628 he received his first pupil, Gerard Dou. In 1631 he moved to Amsterdam. Three years later he married Saskia van Ulenburch, a woman of some wealth and position. He was successful; he sold

his pictures and obtained portrait commissions; his studio was crowded with pupils. He bought a house and filled it with treasures, jewels and rich robes for his Saskia, with sculpture and oriental carpets, Dutch and Italian paintings, engravings by Lucas van Leyden and others. This period of prosperity was checked by two events, the death of his wife and the debacle of the *Night Watch* in 1642. Thereupon his material affairs went into a decline which culminated in his bankruptcy in 1656. He always had been generous and impractical, he always had been a passionate and extravagant collector of art works. His last years were solaced by the affection and care of his serving maid, Hendrickje Stoffels (to the scandal of pious folk!). Forgotten or ignored by the burghers of Amsterdam, he was driven more and more into himself. Hendrickje died in 1664 and his son Titus in 1668. In 1669 Rembrandt himself died, possessing, as the formal inventory records: "alleenlijck sijne cleederen van linnen en wollen en't schildergereetschap"—only certain linen and woolen garments and his painting materials.

Rembrandt's first etchings are dated 1628. His early work, with a few notable exceptions, is not especially distinguished. He was learning his metier, his language. Rembrandt had great capacity for self-development; he could profit by his mistakes in art, however badly he managed in practical life. The process went slowly, for he was building up an independent art form: he raised etching into a major art. It was he who gave to etching the significance and direction it was subsequently to take. The following are but a few of the artists (cited by Lumsden) who show his influence: Bauer, Bone, Bracquemond, Cameron, Forain, Geddes, Goya, Haden, Jacque, John, Jongkind, Legros, McBey, Ostade, Potter, Tiepolo, and Whistler. He gave to etching the freedom and spontaneity and subtlety of drawing; and because his drawing was distinguished, dramatic, and noble he proved that an etching could be as lofty a work of art as a painting or statue. Most prints before Rembrandt had been translations, as it were, from another medium; he composed directly in the language of etching itself. In him we see the beginning of the modern attitude.

His early work consisted largely of studies of single figures: beggars (illustration 214), portraits of his father and his mother (illustration 226), studies of "picturesque" types, expression studies, mostly of himself, in every attitude, grimace, and costume. Many of these were obviously experimental, for the sake of his own training or for teaching purposes. There were also some compositions that were fumbling and petty, without the grandeur of his later work. The *Self-Portrait Leaning on a Stone Sill* (illustration 227) perhaps inspired by Raphael's portrait of Castiglione, and made in the height of his prosperity in 1639, shows that he could equal van Dyck at his

own game. But Rembrandt went on to make the supremely self-revealing *Self-Portrait by a Window* (illustration 228) in 1648, which van Dyck never could have done. With the skill and freedom of expression acquired in these early experiments, fortified by the development of his inner nature, he went on to execute the great portraits where the inner character, the breathing essence of the sitter, is revealed in the outward form, the *Jan Sylvius* of 1646, the *Clement de Jonghe* of 1651, the *Older* and the *Younger Haaring* of 1655, the *Tholinx* and *Lutma* of 1656.

The illness and death of Saskia apparently turned his interest temporarily in the direction of nature. He had already made a few landscapes, inspired possibly by the example of Seghers: the *View of Amsterdam*, the *Cottage with Hay Barn*, and the *Mill*. And in 1643 he etched the *Three Trees*. If, as Ivins penetratingly remarked, Bruegel is the Bach of landscape, then Rembrandt is its Beethoven. Rembrandt in these and his other etched landscapes, *Six's Bridge*, *Landscape with Square Tower*, *Gold Weighers' Field* (illustration 233), and *Landscape with Sportsman*, displays the emotional power and the transmutation of natural forms into perfect artistic expression that is characteristic only of genius. How marvelously the freshness of the passing shower has been suggested in the *Three Trees*; how enchantingly the pattern of light and dark and rhythmic line is arranged in the *Landscape with Farm Buildings and Tower* (illustration 232). Most landscape prints before Rembrandt were composed of heroic landscapes; he took the intimate themes familiar to all and turned them into songs of lasting beauty.

Like most emotionally creative types, Rembrandt had a strong dramatic sense, and this was the quality that vitalized his mythological and religious pictures. Take the *Dr. Faustus*, for example (illustration 229), in his study gazing at the magic disk, the intensity and suspense, the way the painter emphasizes, dramatizes by means of line, by means of light. His approach to the religious picture is unique and personal; he serves no religious dogma. He retells the sacred story in human terms. He makes the characters live with incomparable art and dramatic effect: with tenderness in the *Rest on the Flight*, lightly etched, or in the *Holy Family with Cat* (reminiscent of Mantegna in the *Virgin and Child*); with humor in *Abraham Entertaining the Angels*, and *Christ among the Doctors*; with pathos in the *Blindness of Tobit*, the *Christ Carried to the Tomb*, the *Entombment in the Vaulted Chamber*, and the *Descent from the Cross by Torchlight*; with splendor in the *Presentation in the Temple* (illustration 234); with epic monumentality in the *Three Crosses* (illustration 231), *Christ Healing the Sick*, and *Abraham's Sacrifice*. One of the most satisfying and completely realized of his religious works is the *Christ Preaching* (illustration 230). The composition is exceptionally beautiful, and the range of characters

delineated is almost as great as that of the *Hundred Guilder Print*, and expressed in more purely linear terms. The vista into the courtyard beyond shows what Rembrandt could do in rendering buildings. In all these representations there is no touch of theatre: all is pure drama, the perfect fusion of stirring theme and expressive form.

There has been much difference of opinion about Rembrandt's nudes. To many they are inexpressibly ugly and realistic. But in such early plates as the *Naked Woman on a Mound* (the Adam and Eve is, I am convinced, just a parody), Rembrandt was not interested in drawing a so-called pretty figure; he wanted to learn how to etch flesh, and he took what models he could find. It was not always easy to find handsome models, as Raphael records in 1515 in a letter to Baldessare Castiglione (who evidently had made some complimentary remarks about the model for the *Galatea*):

As far as the Galatea is concerned I would consider myself a great master if only half of the things you said about it were true. I recognize in your words the high regard you have for me. However I must tell you that whenever I have to paint a beautiful woman, it is necessary that I see a number of beauties (with the stipulation that you be present to choose the most beautiful!). Since, however, there is a dearth of such accomplished connoisseurs of women, as well as of beautiful women themselves, I depend upon a certain ideal and idea that I have in my mind. If this be an artistic advantage I know not, nevertheless I strive to attain it.

The question of the esthetic qualities of nudes, especially of the female sex, is a very complex one; when people say that a particular nude drawing is not artistic they often mean something else. It is questionable whether Rembrandt ever intended to emphasize the sexual attractiveness of a nude (as, for example, Zorn did) although the painting of *Danaë* in the Hermitage is quite as sensuous as Goya's *Maja*. In his later etchings of the nude, the *Woman Beside the Stove*, the *Woman Bathing with a Hat Beside Her*, the *Woman with the Arrow* (illustration 235), he aimed to present just Woman, the wholeness of a human being in an intimate pose. In these later etchings he came closer to that fusion of universal (Raphael's idea and ideal) and particular (convincing detail) which is the mark of great art.

Rembrandt's influence on succeeding generations has not been in every respect beneficial. His early etchings of picturesque types were the starting point of a flood of mediocre and sentimental and patronizing exploitations of the theme. His many experimental sketches, probably made with no thought of wide publication, became the excuse for countless trivialities by subsequent artists. In his endeavor to make etching an important and indepen-

dent mode of creative expression, he sometimes forced the medium far beyond the limits of appropriateness, as in the *Portrait of Jan Six*, the various night pieces, and even the *Hundred Guilder Print*. It is to be regretted that he was not familiar with the technique of mezzotint and lithograph. Nevertheless he was one of the titans of art, a visionary who lived most truly in the world of his imagination. Fortune smiled on him for a while and then turned her back to him. It would have been better perhaps if she had not noticed him at all. He posed as a man of the world, yet he never was, and the world soon found him out. Like Claude he was no courtier; he consorted with humble folk and beggars and doctors and preachers. His influence on his immediate contemporaries was negligible. Amsterdam in the seventeenth century was a tough place to live for one not of this world. Like his friends, Roghman and Seghers, and like his contemporary, Spinoza, whom he never met, Rembrandt died neglected and in want.

Now that we have sketched some of the outstanding personalities of the seventeenth century we shall take up the broader aspects of its schools and tendencies. The most flourishing and homogeneous movement of the first half of the seventeenth century was the Dutch School. The Dutch had emerged victorious from their desperate struggle against the domination of Spain. Their independence had intensified their national consciousness. They were vigorous, industrious, and enterprising. They became a great trading nation and entered upon a period of unparalleled prosperity. They were practically supreme on the sea. They had vast colonial possessions; they carried the world's goods in their vessels. Their cities were the commodity markets of Europe; they were the first to institute the practice of auction sales. They took the lead in the development of the banking system which originated in the seventeenth century: through the extension of bills of exchange and the practice of leaving money and gold on deposit with the goldsmiths for safekeeping and carrying on commercial transactions by means of checks and credit, they became the bankers of the world. All of which is by way of saying that they became rich and prosperous. And so they bought art. John Evelyn relates in his diary for 1641:

We arrived late at Rotterdam, where was their annual mart or fair, so furnished with pictures (especially landscapes and drolleries, as they call those clownish representations), that I was amazed. Some of these I bought and sent to England. The reason of this store of pictures, and their cheapness, proceeds from their want of land to employ their stock, so that it is an ordinary thing to find a common farmer to lay out two or three thousand pounds in this commodity. Their houses are full of them, and they vend them at their fairs to very great gains.

There was monetary inflation and so they invested their money in art. It was a special kind of art. As they acquired and rejoiced in tangible possessions, so they demanded of art that it be a representation of tangible objects, familiar scenes in daily life or landscape. No doubt other factors beside the economic entered into this predilection. It was a secular and not a religious art, because the tradition of religious art had been broken, not only by iconoclasm and the destruction of Catholic art during the wars, but also by the Protestant-Puritan attitude toward religious art in general. The general tone was bourgeois and middle class because there was no outstanding court to set the fashion. It was realistic, literal, and factual; it was technically accomplished, but not inspired by any tremendous depths of feeling. It is easy now to see why Seghers and Rembrandt did not fit into the scheme. Nevertheless within its limits it was an art of great distinction and charm, and the world is richer for the picture it gives of the Holland of the seventeenth century.

The work as a whole can be classified into several general groups. The first is the picture of daily life, the genre scene, which the Dutch may be said to have invented. One of the outstanding artists in this field was the painter and etcher, Adriaen van Ostade (1610–85). He etched fifty plates, not all equal in merit, but at their best displaying fine draughtsmanship and compositional effect and considerable feeling. Two characteristic examples are reproduced, *Painter's Studio* (illustration 236) and the *Fisherman* (illustration 237). His tradition was carried on by Dusart and Bega (illustration 240). Contrasting with Ostade's and Teniers's representations of peasants and artisans (illustration 242) is Willem Buytewech's etching of *Lucell and Ascagnes* (illustration 209) executed in an elegant, mannerist, almost caricatured manner. The next group are the landscape etchers, Pieter Molyn, Roelant Roghman (illustration 239), A. Waterloo (illustration 246), A. van Everdingen (illustration 247), the painters Jan van Goyen and Jacob van Ruysdael (illustration 238) important in the landscape tradition. Jan van de Velde's etchings (illustration 245), though executed in a dry formalized technique, have a charm of textural variation and inventive composition. The van de Veldes were precursors of Rembrandt in the molding of a pure landscape tradition. There were some etchers who specialized in pictures of the sea, and of these Renier Nooms, called Zeeman (so much admired by Meryon), and Rudolph Backhuysen were outstanding. Zeeman (illustration 243) could portray marine effects with great skill, and Backhuysen in his *Distant View of Amsterdam* (illustration 244) has admirably rendered a breezy day and a choppy sea. Then there were the etchers of animals and pastoral life, Claes Berchem, Karel du Jardin, and above all Paul Pot-

ter (illustration 248). Another and slightly overlapping group are the Italianizers, such as Breenbergh, Jan Both, and Swanevelt, who had been to Italy and sought to impose the arcadian tradition of Claude upon the realism of Holland.

The journeyings of these later Dutchmen bring us back to Italy again. Italian art of the *seicento* lacked the force of the preceeding centuries. There is undoubted sweetness and charm in the etchings of Guido Reni (illustration 254) and his pupil Cantarini, and Giovanni Barbieri, called Guercino (illustration 255). But they represent the gradual ebbing away of the religious tradition. Castiglione (illustration 251) in his etchings was influenced by both van Dyck and Rembrandt. The Venetian, Carpioni, did a few charming plates. José Ribera, Lo Spagnoletto, Spanish-born, but living in Naples, represented the naturalistic school of Caravaggio, in his few but very accomplished etchings (illustration 253). Caravaggio himself made only one etching, a rough but vigorous sketch (illustration 252). Salvator Rosa, also of Naples, had a wild and adventurous enough life. Poet, painter, musician, he took part in the insurrection of Masaniello against the Spanish rule, and lived for a while with bandits. His etchings have the mannerism and show of force of the Baroque style but in their delineation of wild and rugged scenery they anticipate to a certain extent a favorite theme of the Romantic School.

The etchings of Giovanbattista Bracelli are rare and curious, as is evidenced by the plates from his *Bizarie*, 1624 (illustration 259). The resemblance to cubism in his works, as in those of Dürer, Erhard Schön, and Cambiaso, is merely superficial. As Kenneth Clark has said: "Bracelli has combined three *seicento* discoveries—mannerism, mechanism, conceits. If he had never lived it would have been necessary to invent him."

In France during the first half of the seventeenth century, the foundation was laid for the reign of Louis XIV, which for its patronage of arts and letters Voltaire called "the most enlightened age the world has ever seen." The build-up was favored by the policies of the Queen Mother Marie de' Medici, Cardinal Richelieu, founder of the French Academy, and Cardinal Mazarin, patron of art, music, and the theatre. It was firmly established by Louis XIV and his minister Colbert upon his accession in 1661. Colbert believed "that it was by the standard of monuments that one measured kings." The Academy of Painters was founded: artists and craftsmen were encouraged with pensions and given lodging in the apartments of the Louvre and the Gobelins. The Gobelins, a state institution, was the center not only of the finest tapestry manufactured in Europe but also of the manufacture of furniture, metalwork, and jewelry. It was also a training school for artists, and in this way a high standard of craftsmanship was maintained. The seventeenth century witnessed a vast extension of luxury which found its reflection in ornament prints, models for jewelry (illustration 258), lace, leatherwork, metalwork (illustration 261), vases, furniture and wall decoration, formal gardens with grottoes, and the like (illustration 263) were laid out in greater and greater numbers. Ornament itself, in keeping with the Baroque style, tended to become exaggerated, grotesque, bursting with swelling bands and fantastic cartouches (illustration 260). All these exuberant elements were organized and somewhat restrained into a standardized and coherent system of great taste and decorative value by the artists and craftsmen under Louis XIV.

For a faithful picture of comfortable French life during the Regency and early part of the reign of Louis XIV, one must turn to the etchings of Abraham Bosse. He was typically the artist of the upper middle class, and he depicted their manners and customs with peculiar fidelity, sobriety, and vividness (illustrations 218, 219, and 220). The upper middle class is in general the backbone of the culture of a nation. It is they, through their opportunities for higher education, who supply the learned professions, law, medicine, and theology. They stand midway between the frivolousness of the court and the indigence of the proletariat. It is they who buy books and pictures, who patronize the theatre, who cultivate music. A charming picture of a musical gathering is given in Bosse's engraving, *Hearing*, from the series of the *Five Senses*. In the sixteenth and seventeenth centuries music was still a language familiar to many cultivated amateurs. Many of the charming compositions of the contrapuntal schools, part-songs, madrigals, motets, and the like, were performed in company with accomplished musicianship. The century also witnessed the development of stringed instruments (Stradivarius, Corelli, Vivaldi), and also a form of dramatic music which eventually became opera. Another picture of the time is given in the contrast between the two accouchement scenes portrayed by Bosse and by Callot in his *Gypsies* (illustration 211). Bosse made about 1400 engravings and is also famous for his textbook on the art of etching and engraving. Bosse and Hollar have much in common.

There was a great development of drama in the seventeenth century, not only in France with Corneille, Racine, and Molière, but also in England with Shakespeare and the other Elizabethan dramatists, and in Spain with Calderon and Lope de Vega.

The portrait received great impetus in the seventeenth century, and in France there grew up a school of portrait engraving that has never been surpassed. The earliest practitioner was Claude Mellan who developed Goltzius's linear system into an instrument of great power, as

may be seen in the portrait of Michael de Marolles, the great print collector (illustration 266). He also engraved a famous technical showpiece, the *La Sainte Face* (illustration 265), with a single spiral line starting at the nose. The drawing is developed by varying the width of the line. Jean Morin (illustration 267) engraved some colorful portraits such as that of the printer, Antoine Vitré. But Robert Nanteuil was the chief glory of the school. He was quartered in the Gobelins, and Louis XIV also granted in his favor the famous Edict of St. Jean-de-Luz which declared that engraving henceforth was to rank as a liberal and not as a mechanical art. He engraved over two hundred portraits, including eleven of "le Grand Monarque" (illustration 268), and a host of great men of the time, Richelieu, Mazarin, Cardinal de Retz, Jacques Amelot, Colbert, Fouquet, Loret (illustration 269), Gassendi, John Evelyn. Sometimes his portraits were used to decorate the thesis of a wealthy doctoral candidate (illustration 268). He usually received about two thousand livres per plate (about four hundred dollars). He set the style of portraiture which was followed by his pupils and associates, Masson, Edelinck, Poilly, Pitau, van Schuppen, and others. A consummate draughtsman, he concentrated, as Thomas points out, on the expression of character by the head. There is nothing spontaneous about these portrait engravings: every detail is studied and calculated. It is the opposite extreme of the candid camera shot: it is the "set portrait," where the sitter looks and appears as he would like to be, noble, dignified, in the grand manner. Mlle. de Scudéry wrote a quatrain which sums it up:

> Nanteuil en faisant son image
> A de son art divin signalé le pouvoir.
> Je haïs mes traits dans mon miroir,
> Je les aime dans son ouvrage.

(Nanteuil in his pictures has shown the power of his divine art. I hate my features in the mirror, I love them in his work.) Pepys in his *Diary* for January 1668 records: "My wife showed me many excellent prints of Nanteuil's and others, which W. Batelier hath, at my desire, brought me out of France, to my great content." As the prevailing taste changed from the sober delineation of character to a greater ostentation and display, so the portrait changed from the head to the full-length figure in gorgeous array of silks and satins. Drevet's *Bossuet* or Bervic's *Louis XVI* are characteristic of this tendency. However, Drevet's portrait of the architect, *Robert de Cotte*, is reproduced (illustration 270) because (as Kimball points out) he, though not the inventor, was a figurehead in the invention of the Rococo style. As a companion, there is Wille's portrait of the Marquis de Marigny, the

brother of La Pompadour, who played a similar role in the spread of the "Classical" style of the later eighteenth century (illustration 271). The French School of portrait engraving was the most distinguished in Europe; it drew many foreign artists, notably the Fleming, Edelinck, to Paris. Comparatively little portraiture of merit was made during the century outside of the engraved portraits of Paris or the etched portraits of Rembrandt and van Dyck. An exception must be recorded, however, in the charming portrait engravings of Ottavio Leoni of Rome in the first quarter of the seventeenth century. The portrait of the astronomer Galileo, who got in trouble with the Inquisition, is reproduced in illustration 256. Mention should be made of another pioneer work, Jan van de Velde's portrait *Oliver Cromwell* which anticipated the technique of aquatint by well over a hundred years (illustration 257).

The seventeenth century witnessed a further widening of the breach between rich and poor. The extensive wars of this and the preceding centuries contributed greatly to the spread of capitalism by nourishing that one great form of luxury, the army. Not only was a military career a direct avenue to riches through the opportunities for plunder and exaction of indemnities (Wallenstein when he was assassinated was worth nine million gulden), but the army encouraged lucrative capitalist enterprises through the contract system and large-scale production of food, clothing, guns, and ammunition. Wealth was becoming more and more concentrated in the hands of a few, while the great mass of the people were being ground down in abject poverty. Holland was the exception to this rule, but there it was the middle class which was acquiring wealth. Elsewhere the Court, the Church, and the rich were the chief supporters of art. Rubens's chief patrons were the Church, the extravagant Charles I and his favorites, and Philip of Spain whose income came from the gold of America. The seventeenth century saw the emergence of the collector of prints on a vast scale. To be sure, there had been collectors in the previous centuries, the Fuggers, Imhoffs, Welser (Dürer and van Leyden complete), Paul Praum, 1548–1616 (Dürer and Italian masters); and prints were included among the contents of the countless *Wunderkammern*, or Chambers of Curios, along with shells, insects, minerals, stuffed animals, cameos, and the like. (Evelyn, as late as 1651, notes: "I went to see the collection of one Monsieur Poignant which for variety of agates, crystals, onyxes, porcelain, medals, statues, relievos, paintings, tailles-douces [prints], and antiquities, might compare with the Italian virtuosos.") And artists such as Dürer and Rubens, as we have seen, and Rembrandt, who at one time owned over one hundred paintings and a huge collection of prints by Mantegna and many other artists, were passionate collec-

tors. But the first real print collector was Claude Maugis, Abbé de St. Ambroise, 1600–58, who spent forty years amassing a collection which eventually passed into the hands of Michel Marolles. Michel Marolles, Abbé de Villeloin, who had been given a fat living by Mazarin, was one of the world's great print collectors (illustration 266). No sooner had he disposed of his first huge collection, than he started all over again. As he wrote:

God has given me grace to devote myself to pictures without superstition, and I have been able to acquire a collection numbering more than 70,000 engravings of all subjects. I began it in 1644, and have continued it with so much zeal, and with such an expense for one not wealthy, than I can claim to possess some of the work of all the known masters . . . I have found that collecting such things was more suited to my purse than collecting paintings, and more serviceable to the building up of a library. Had we in France a dozen such collectors among the nobility, there would not be enough prints to satisfy them all, and the works of Dürer, Lucas, and Marcantonio for which we now pay four or five hundred écus when in perfect condition would be worth three times that amount.

In 1666 his collection had grown to 123,400 prints and drawings by over six thousand artists. The entire collection was bought by Colbert for the King and became the foundation of that huge public collection numbering over four million prints now housed in the Bibliothèque Nationale. In England there were collectors like Lord Pembroke and the Earl of Arundel (Hollar's patron), but it was in Paris that Marolles's suggestion was really followed. In 1673 there were eighty-five collections of prints, often in connection with libraries; toward the end of the century there were one hundred and thirty. It became so much the fashion that La Bruyère took note of it in his "Characters":

You wish to see my prints, says Democenes, and he forthwith brings them out and sets them before you. You see one that is neither dark nor clear nor completely drawn, and better fit to decorate on a holiday the walls of the Petit Pont or the Rue Neuve than be treasured in a famous collection. He admits that it is engraved badly and drawn worse, but hastens to inform you that it is the work of an Italian who produced very little, and that the plate had hardly any printing; that, moreover, it is the only one of its kind in France; that he paid much for it, and would not exchange it for something better. I am, he adds, in such serious trouble that it will prevent any further collecting. I have all of Callot but one print, which is not only not one of his best plates, but actually one of his worst; nevertheless it would complete my Callot. I have been looking for it for twenty years, and, despairing of success, I find life very hard indeed.

5. The Eighteenth Century

The history of eighteenth-century prints may be summed up as a year in Paris, a month in London, and a weekend in Italy. France was the artistic center of Europe, and France meant Paris. No city was ever so documented by its artists as Paris. It was an urban culture, highly civilized and highly artificial. Paris was the apex of the pyramid which rested on the broad base of the peasants of France. The flowers that grew in the hothouse at the apex had no strong roots in the free soil of the country. Nevertheless they were in many respects beautiful flowers, among the most extraordinary the world has ever seen. The documentation of Paris may be said to have proceeded on four separate levels. At the top, the most artificial and the most completely documented, was the life of the court. Below was the life of the middle class, sober, industrious, and urbane, untainted by the excesses of the court. The third was the life of the artists themselves, another aspect of the middle class. Below all these, the most meager in detail, yet represented by the *Cries of Paris*, the depiction of the lower artisan class, and by the *imagerie populaire*, was the level of the workers.

At the beginning of the century there lived and dreamed a rare artist, Antoine Watteau. His work may be said to symbolize, in its most ideal and beautiful aspects, the spirit of Louis XV. He was born in Valenciennes of Flemish ancestry in 1684. He died of consumption at the age of twenty-seven. He was supported by wealthy patrons like M. de Julienne; he had access, through his friend, the great collector Crozat, to drawings and paintings by Rubens, Titian, Giorgione, and Campagnola. Out of the leisure which good fortune brought him and out of the contacts with the great art of the world, and impelled by the heartbreaking nostalgia of the consumptive, he proceeded to make concrete one more dream of an ideal world. It was the world of the *fête galante*, the *Embarkation for the Isle of Cythère* (Love), exquisite glimpses of picnics in beautiful gardens, of couples in amorous conversation, of music and dancing and the theatre in the open. He made a few unimportant etchings: he poured himself out in his drawings and paintings. It was his lifelong friend, M. de Julienne, who undertook at his expense to have his work engraved by

the best engravers of the time and published in four huge volumes in 1734 at a price of five hundred livres. It is from this magnificent *recueil* that our three reproductions are drawn (illustrations 272, 273, and 274). Never has the spirit of play, of cultivated pastime, the *otium cum dignitate* of the ancients, been clothed in more enchanting dress. This escape from reality, this flight to a carefree island of love and beauty, strikes a responsive chord in every one of us at some time in our lives. It is Watteau's great achievement that he made the dream so tangible and so beautiful. All his contemporaries, Gersaint, De Caylus, testify to the unhappiness of his personal life. He was melancholy, irritable, and diffident. It was only when he was actually painting or drawing, said De Caylus, that he was the Watteau of his own pictures. It may be, as Wilenski suggests, that this unhappiness was due not only to the inroads of his malady, but also to his dilemma as a creative artist. He had every reason to be grateful to his rich patrons who had rescued him from a life of hackwork (he had started as a painter outside the pale of the all-powerful Academy) and to his dealers Sirois and Gersaint (illustration 273) for their affectionate and continued assistance, but they were all men of the world and did not look at a picture in the way he looked at it, nor see what he saw in it. He lived in the apartments which Crozat provided for him in his palace, but after a year he ran away. The world was not fashioned according to his heart's desire, and he was driven to his dreams. Yet, curiously enough, in this instance, the world, that is to say the court of Louis XV, tried to imitate his dream. Such a utopia as Watteau's Isle of Cythère can exist only in the world of art or imagination. When its happy irresponsible existence was translated into reality, it predicated the support of countless servants or slaves. Its grace and sensibility, its tender note of ideal love became tainted with wanton extravagance and display, sordid intrigue, and unbridled licentiousness. And so it was, as history tells us, at the court of Louis XV. Yet comparatively little of the sordid side is carried over into the pictorial record by the artists of the time. The obverse of the shield we discover from other sources and from the fact that suddenly the whole system collapsed. The art-

ists set out to glorify the reign of Louis XV as they had that of the Grand Monarch, and they did a magnificent job. They did it in two ways: by embellishing the setting and by recording it.

First of all there were the decorators, Boucher, for example. François Boucher (1703–70) was one of the most accomplished artists in France, director of the schools of the Academy and of the tapestry manufactory of Beauvais and the Gobelins, painter of murals for the king and for Mme de Pompadour. We know his features from the striking portrait by Roslin, an unassuming, somewhat cynical man of the world with able hands and piercing eyes. He is represented by the decorative composition engraved by Demarteau, *Venus Desarmée par les Amours* (illustration 276), and an original etching *Le Petit Savoyard* (illustration 278). We all remember Renoir's estimate of Boucher as recorded by Vollard:

As if being a decorator made any difference! Why Boucher is one of the painters who best understood the female body. What fresh youthful buttocks he painted, with the most enchanting dimples. It's odd that people are never willing to give a man credit for what he can do. They say they like Titian better. Good Lord so do I! But that has nothing to do with the fact that Boucher painted lovely women superbly. A painter who has the feel for breasts and buttocks is saved!

The second decorator, Jean Honoré Fragonard (1732–1806), was typical of the more frivolous spirit toward the end of the century. Pupil of Chardin, protégé of Boucher, influenced by Rembrandt and Tiepolo, he painted decorations for Du Barry and other fashionable women, and made countless drawings and paintings. He made among others a series of four etchings of *Bacchanals* (illustration 275) of great spirit and charm in a form probably suggested by the *Caprices* of Tiepolo. Some delightful engravings were made from his paintings, including the *Chiffre d'Amour*, *La Bonne Mère*, and the *Happy Accidents of the Swing* (illustration 277), frivolous yet charming, and filled with a certain gallant suggestiveness.

The setting was embellished in many ways. The enormous impetus given to architecture and the applied arts had its repercussion in ornament prints. There were two trends of ornament in the eighteenth century: one, the Rococo, was a development of the Baroque, carrying its mannerism and eccentricity to even greater limits, and the other a reaction against it in favor of the antique (stimulated perhaps by the excavations at Herculaneum and also by Adam and Piranesi) which culminated in the severely classic style of the Directoire and Empire. In flower arrangement and design there was a range from Casteels, 1730 (illustration 283) to Prévost (illustration 284). Characteristic Rococo ornament was supplied by Meis-

sonier, Oppenordt, Gillot, Watteau, Oudry, Huet, Huquier, Nilsen, Habermann, and notably in the delightful inventions of Pillemont (illustrations 279, 280). Chinoiserie and other exotic notes were fashionable. Among the notable furniture designers in France were Oppenordt, Toro, Pineau, and Cornille; in England Heppelwhite, Sheraton, Chippendale (illustration 281), Ince and Mayhew, and Robert Adam (illustration 282). The classic style in France was developed by Neufforge, Delafosse, Forty, Babel, and Lalonde. One field was specially cultivated, under the patronage of the Regent, Philippe d'Orléans, and of Madame de Pompadour (both of whom dabbled in design), namely the illustrated book. Sumptuous and expensive editions were published, illustrated with engravings and vignettes by the best artists of the time: *Molière's Works* illustrated by Boucher (illustration 287), the *Fermiers Généraux* edition of La Fontaine (an allusion to the source of its financing) illustrated by Eisen and others (illustration 285), Corneille's *Works* illustrated by Gravelot (illustration 286), Voltaire's *Works* illustrated by Gravelot (illustration 288), the *Metamorphoses* of Ovid illustrated by Boucher, Eisen, Gravelot, Moreau, and Choffard, 1767–71, *Les Baisers* illustrated by Eisen, 1770 (illustration 289), the *Choix de Chansons* de M. de la Borde illustrated by Moreau le Jeune, 1773 (illustration 290), one of the most beautiful books ever made, Rousseau's *Works*, 1774–83, also illustrated by Moreau le Jeune, and G. Bernard's *Works*, 1797, illustrated by Prud'hon (illustration 291). And so "Monsieur" and "Madame" were provided with books to look at (though perhaps not to read), furniture, wall decorations, jewelry, costumes, china, gardens, coaches, and rooms to live in, designed and executed by the greatest talent in France.

How they looked and acted amid these luxurious surroundings we discover from *Les Estampes Galantes, Estampes de la Mode*, and *Gravures des Mœurs*. There is a close resemblance between these engravings and Dutch seventeenth-century prints. There is the same factual literal representation of a contemporary scene. There is, to be sure, a greater perfection of execution, a more magnificent sense of style, a more effective feeling for the dramatic aspect in the French engravings, but the ultimate aim is the same—it is "giving the customers what they want." In spite of certain notable exceptions there is a spiritual poverty about both, a lack of creative conviction or passion on the part of the artists that prevents the work from being classed with the world's greatest art. It was a faithful, impersonal, and businesslike reflection of the age, and since the milieu was hardly a spiritual one, the art never rose above it, as the works of the greatest artists and thinkers always do. Incidentally Dutch genre pictures of the seventeenth century were collected by French amateurs of the eighteenth century. Both groups

catered definitely to a certain class: the Dutch seventeenth-century prints to a rising middle class, the French *estampes galantes* to the nobility and the underlying strata which imitated them. Who was it that bought these French prints? Certainly not the impoverished peasants and workers, for they had no money, nor even the lower middle class. Nor was it in general the principal personages of the court; there was no reason why they should buy pictures of the scenes they saw every day. It was rather that class which had a slight or indirect contact with the court and had grown rich through it, that sought these prints in order perhaps that their wives and daughters might see the latest fashions. Or it was the roué who bought the *sujets grivois*, the suggestive subjects, to add piquancy to his relations with his mistress in the sumptuous apartment where he maintained her. Or it was the rich amateur with a taste for art and nothing to do who succumbed to the collecting mania.

French eighteenth-century prints have been the subject of much argument pro and con. Even in their day, they, and the paintings from which they were often derived, were savagely attacked by Diderot as a symbol of a society of which he disapproved. Diderot incidentally was one of the first of the professional art critics. It was in the eighteenth century (1699 to be exact) that official exhibitions of paintings and drawings by many artists were inaugurated by the Academy. Gabriel de St. Aubin made a delightful etching of the "Salon" of the Academy held at the Louvre in the year 1753 (illustration 308). Of course pictures had been exhibited, as we have seen, at the fairs and markets in Germany, Italy, and Holland, and also at the Foire de St. Germain in Paris, but these had no official recognition. Therefore when society was confronted with several hundred pictures at a Salon which it was *de rigueur* to attend, the writers stepped in, as has been said, to tell it what to talk about, and thus art criticism, or rather art journalism, began. Unquestionably, the tone of society, pampered and protected as it was from reality, was highly artificial and frivolous. In Chamfort's words: " 'A genuine sentiment is so rare,' said M. de V——, 'that when I leave Versailles I sometimes stand still to see a dog gnaw a bone.' " French eighteenth-century prints, on the other hand, have had apologists who maintain that their licentious and irresponsible tone has been exaggerated, and point to the number of prints which extol the virtues of happy family life (illustration 297). Even those subjects, which are rather free, are never gross: they tell their story as a *double entendre*, with subtlety and a proper regard for the conventions. It is quite likely that the moral degradation of the age has been exaggerated, that it was confined to a few sensational and destructive examples at the court, and that the main body of the people went on in their accustomed ways. After all, even in our day financiers have kept mistresses and squandered fortunes without having overthrown the structure of society. In either case the prints themselves build up a complete picture of a mode of life that is elegant, refined, and luxurious. It is only when we go beyond the picture to examine its implications that we are compelled to exercise moral judgment. Incidentally it is interesting to discover that nearly all the engravers welcomed the Revolution and some took an active part in it.

After this rather philosophic preamble let us visit Paris and with the artist to give us entrée, let us visit the court and participate in its functions. First, having been introduced to Augustin de St. Aubin and his charming wife paying each other compliments in *Au Moins Soyez Discrets* and *Comptez sur mes Serments*, we accompany him to the *Concert* or to the court ball, *Le Bal Paré* (illustration 294), following an invitation engraved by Choffard. With the Swede Lavreince we might visit two other functions *chez le Duc de Luynes*, the *Assemblée au Salon* and *Assemblée au Concert*, or listen to Beaumarchais reading extracts from his *Figaro* in *Le Mercure de France*, or explore with him such crises of sentiment as *Consolation de l'Absence* (illustration 292), *L'Heureux Moment*, *L'Indiscrétion*, or *L'Aveu Difficile*, or, entering the more formal salon, hear *Qu'en dit l'Abbé* or see the furtive passing of the *Billet Doux* (illustration 295). Walking through the park with Baudouin, we might glimpse a charming *tête-à-tête* in *La Soirée des Tuileries* (illustration 296) and witness in the boudoir an intimacy close to the border line in *Le Danger du Tête-à-tête* and especially in *Le Carquois Épuisé (The Empty Quiver or Receptacle)* with its double meaning (illustration 293), or participate in the dramatic scenes, *La Couche de la Mariée* or *L'Enlèvement Nocturne*. We might see and purchase the latest portraits of the king and queen, or Pompadour, or Du Barry (illustration 323) or as a novelty that of Mr. Franklin, the new Philosopher from America who made such a hit at court and among the savants (illustration 302). We might with Carmontelle patronize the concert of a new infant prodigy of music, the seven-year-old Mozart (illustration 303). With the Swiss artist Freudeberg we might trace the round of daily life in luxury: *Le Lever*, *Le Bain*, the charmingly domestic *Le Petit Jour*, and *Le Coucher*. For a taste of gallantry there are Baudouin's *Marchez Tout Doux*, and *L'Épouse Indiscrète*, Fragonard's *Le Verrou*, Boilly's *L'Amant Favorisé*, Boucher's *La Courtisane Amoureuse*, Debucourt's *L'Escalade*, or Lavreince's *La Comparaison*.

Jean-Michel Moreau le Jeune was perhaps, all things considered, the finest and most accomplished designer and engraver of French manners. He was born in 1741 and studied engraving with jolly old Le Bas. In 1760 he married the daughter of Pineau, the furniture designer.

In 1770 he was appointed *Dessinateur des Menus-Plaisirs du Roi* and in 1781 he was made an associate of the Academy. His engravings, the *Coronation of Louis XVI* in 1776, the *Festin Royal*, the *Bal Masqué*, the *Feu d'Artifice* (the last three are in the Chalcographie du Louvre), and his engravings of *La Couche de la Mariée* and *Le Modèle Honnête* after Baudouin are well known, but his chief title to fame rests on his book illustrations and the great *Monument du Costume* of 1776 and 1783. Confronted with the problem of designing a series of costume plates, he composed them as scenes from daily life with such perfection of draughtsmanship and incomparable dramatic power that the twenty-four plates may almost be said to sum up a complete age and mode of society. Certainly the society of Louis XVI has never been displayed in a better light. The young king and queen were weak and mildly benevolent characters; they believed in a happy family life and asked nothing better than to play at being shepherds and shepherdesses in an irresponsible pastoral life. They merely reaped the whirlwind that was sown by the grandfather. Thus, true happiness, *Le Vrai Bonheur*, is visualized in the Monument as a happy farmer surrounded by his family and his pet animals. No more charming picture of domestic felicity has been made than the *Délices de la Maternité* (illustration 297). Has there ever been a more charming dinner party than *Le Souper Fin* (illustration 298)? The grace and glamour, the polished and distinguished manners of an aristocratic court will live forever in such plates as *Les Adieux*, or *La Sortie de l'Opéra* (illustrations 300 and 299). They seem like concrete embodiments of the maxims of one who was perhaps the most eloquent apologist of the courtly manner, Lord Chesterfield:

Courts are the best keys to character; there every passion is busy, every art exerted, every character analyzed; jealousy, ever watchful, not only discovers, but exposes, the mysteries of the trade, so that even bystanders, *y apprennent à déviner*. There, too, the great art of pleasing is practiced, taught, and learned, with all its graces and delicacies. It is the first thing needful there; it is the absolutely necessary harbinger of merit and talents, let them be ever so great. There is no advancing a step without it. Let misanthropes and would-be philosophers declaim as much as they please against the vices, the simulation, and dissimulation of Courts; those invectives are always the result of ignorance, ill-humor, or envy. Let them show me a cottage, where there are not the same vices of which they accuse the Courts; with this difference only, that in a cottage they appear in their native deformity, and that in Courts, manners and good breeding make them less shocking, and blunt their edge. No, be convinced that good breeding, the *tournure, la douceur dans les manières*, which alone are to be acquired at Courts, are not the showish trifles only, which some people call or think them; they are a solid good; they prevent a good deal of mischief; they

create, adorn, and strengthen friendships: they keep hatred within bounds; they promote good-humor and goodwill in families, where the want of good breeding and gentleness of manners is commonly the original cause of discord.

From the court to the middle class—from Moreau to Chardin. Jean-Baptiste Siméon Chardin was born in Paris in 1699 and died there in 1779. He was a simple kindly man who loved the city and its ways—especially the middle-class life that he lived and knew. He poured into his simple genre pieces and still lifes such a wealth of feeling, such love and tenderness, such consummate craftsmanship and perfection of design and placement that they seem to come to life before our eyes. He had much in common with Vermeer of Delft. About fifty engravings were made after his paintings, which had considerable vogue in his day. Among the best known are *Le Bénédicité*, *Le Dessinateur*, *L'Ecureuse*, *L'Etude de Dessin*, *La Mère Laborieuse*, *La Pourvoieuse*, *La Bonne Education*, and *L'Instant de la Méditation*. All of them have an intangible quality, a certain inwardness that haunts the imagination. We identify ourselves with the characters, and experience in a magic moment the simplicity and charm they so beautifully express. Two of the most charming are reproduced here, *La Gouvernante* and *Le Négligé* (illustrations 306 and 305). When the painting of *Le Négligé* was exhibited in the Salon of 1741, Charmarande reviewed it as follows: "No woman of the third estate of the Realm stands before one of Chardin's canvases without discerning a reflection of her own morals, manners, and daily avocations, of the ways of her children, of her household gods and wardrobe." Furthermore there is a story that "when Le Bas [the engraver of this picture] was asked what instructions the painter had given him for the interpretation of his colors, he, knowing very well that for the complete harmony of a picture there can be no fixed rule, replied: to use sentiment."

Chardin, sure of himself, pursued his own quiet way, and, though an academician through the influence of Largillière, seldom exhibited with them and had little sympathy with their historical grand manner. There was one other, a profoundly original artist and a rare personality, who did not fit into the academic mold—Gabriel de St. Aubin (1724-80). He had a brother, Augustin de St. Aubin, who was a man of the world and became *Graveur du Roi* and an artist of influence (illustration 294). But Gabriel, after competing unsuccessfully for the Prix de Rome, renounced academic ambitions and was content to remain an obscure professor of drawing at Blondel's School of Architecture.

He drew [recounts his brother] at all times and in all places. If he was taking a walk his crayon would be taking note of the

passersby. The lectures of the Academy were for him but a moving tableau for his sketches. One holiday, having placed himself in the nave of Notre Dame to hear a celebrated preacher, he drew out his sketchbook from habit and started to draw the orator. People nearby watched him as he worked; those in front of him turned around, those behind raised themselves in their chairs. Finally the attention of the listeners was so completely distracted that the preacher, interrupting his discourse, said, "When the eyes have been satisfied, I hope you will lend me your ears." This passion, joined to the desire to see everything and know everything, made him extremely negligent of his person and his health. He died completely worn out at the age of fifty-five. He was singular, bizarre: often before going out, he would rub white chalk from his crayons either on his hair to powder it or on his stockings to whiten them. He left a great number of curious drawings. We have several prints engraved after his designs and some etchings which display his genius.

He was in truth a singular and profoundly original artist. In an age and country where line engraving was supreme, he gave his preference to etching and made some fifty plates, probably largely for his own pleasure and amusement. At a time when all expression was keyed up to the grand manner, he came out with modest little etchings singularly free from pretense, each one a masterpiece of mood and atmosphere. His work strikes a very modern note: he is concerned only with entering into the spirit of a scene and reflecting with rare art his personal impression of it. Since he was an artist of great feeling and sensibility, his "impressions" have great charm for us. Take, for example, the *Spectacle des Tuileries* (illustration 307); with what subtlety and penetration he has invoked the spirit of the scene, the summer night under the swaying trees, the cool fragrance, the buzz of the conversation, the play of shadows and half-lights. On one proof of this etching St. Aubin wrote the following quatrain:

Le faste de repose en ces jardins charmants;
Les cercles sont formés autour de chaque belle.
Nonchalamment assis, mille couple d'amants
S'y jurent à leur age un flame éternelle.

How simply and effectively he has re-created an eighteenth-century coffeehouse in *Les Nouvellistes* (illustration 310). It could almost be an illustration for that marvelous literary projection of character and milieu, Diderot's *The Nephew of Rameau*. "There are," wrote the traveler Nemeitz in 1727, "an infinite number of coffeehouses in Paris, often ten or twelve on the same street. . . . There are still others where one finds *les nouvellistes* (newsmongers) who discuss the news and the latest affairs of the state. Since there are a number of idlers in Paris, some

of them do nothing else all day but frequent the cafés to hear the latest bit of news or gossip." Daumier later took up the same theme in his *Coffeehouse Politicians*. Two contemporary theatrical representations form an instructive contrast: Moreau le Jeune's *The Crowning of the Bust of Voltaire* (illustration 304) and St. Aubin's *Théâtre Italien* (illustration 311). The first is brilliant and polished, a showy panorama of stage and audience with Voltaire in a box bowing to the applause; the other is simple and unpretentious and enters into the very spirit of Harlequin and Columbine. St. Aubin's picture reminds one of Degas's studies of the essential gesture, the "magic moment" in his pictures of ballet dancers. In fact, in many of St. Aubin's works we find anticipations of the modern point of view.

Another charming little etching is the *Académie Particulière* (illustration 309), a glimpse of the artist drawing from a model. There were many delightful pictures made of artists' life in the eighteenth century, such as for example, the *Cabinet d'un Peintre* (illustration 317) by the Polish engraver Chodowiecki living in Berlin. The engravers generally lived uneventful lives concerned with apprenticeship, technique, commissions, and the like, and were more or less conscious of their middle-class station. The younger Cochin in his memoirs, when recounting a dispute with the Comte de Caylus, said, "I was met by that contempt which, I know only too well, is felt by men of birth, in spite of their fine seeming politeness, for all who are, like artists, but of the bourgeoisie." Cochin was one of the most attractive personalities in the history of the graphic arts. An excellent engraver and accomplished draughtsman—Diderot called him *le premier dessinateur français*—Cochin was also a scholarly writer, a *bon vivant*, and man of affairs who, by his amiable disposition and many talents, not to mention good fortune (the friendship and confidence of the Marquise de Pompadour), achieved great success at the court of Louis XV. In later years his duties as Keeper of the King's Drawings and Secretary of the Academy, as well as his extensive social life, prevented him from engraving much himself, but he made countless drawings, including a series of portraits of the notables of his time which comprised an artistic iconography of the eighteenth century, comparable in scope and importance to that made by Van Dyck a century earlier. He also was a writer on art and partisan of the "classical reaction" in favor of a simpler, supposedly antique style. In doing so, he repudiated, as it were, his earlier vital work in the rococo manner to become involved in academic allegories. His last years were saddened by failing eyesight and the ruin of the society he loved. He died in 1790, a relatively poor man, for he never used his enormous influence for personal aggrandizement.

The diary of J. G. Wille abounds in illuminating passages relating to contemporary life. He was an uninspired, rather mannered, and highly successful reproductive engraver (illustration 271) but he was a delightful social historian. He tells of his contacts with patrons and dealers, of the immense speculation in art at the time, how long it took to engrave a plate (two years and four months on the *Family Concert)* and the prices he received for his work (six livres or about $1.20 for the same print). Like many of the engravers, such as Cochin, Tardieu, Poilly, Chereau, and others, he was his own dealer, that is to say he also sold prints from his engraving studio. Pierre François Basan, a glimpse of whose shop is given in Choffard's engraving (illustration 316), was more a dealer than engraver. He was the first to establish the practice of printing a large number of "proofs before letters" to supply the vast demand on the part of amateurs for such "rarities." He acquired a number of the coppers by Rembrandt and other Dutch etchers which he published in collected form. He organized auction catalogs in the modern manner of such important collections as those of Bouchardon, van Loo, Marigny, and Wille. But the most important sale of all under Basan's management was that of the tremendous private collection of Pierre Jean Mariette in 1775 and 1776. The three generations of the Mariette family, the grandfather Pierre, the father Jean (illustration 319), and Pierre Jean (illustration 318) were among the great print dealers of the world. They had dealings with Marolles, Charles I, Crozat, and the genial Prince Eugène of Savoy whose own enormous collection of prints was eventually housed in the Imperial Library at Vienna under the curatorship of Adam von Bartsch (illustration 320) and formed the basis of Bartsch's monumental catalog of prints still in use today. Another important engraver, publisher, and dealer was Gabriel Huquier, whose shop was the center for the ornament prints of France. Still another dealer, C. F. Joullain, in his *Réflexions sur la Peinture et la Gravure accompagnées d'une courte dissertation sur le commerce de la curiosité et les ventes en général,* offers further sidelights on the traffic in prints, the psychology of collecting, the excitements of auction, and a complete description of how unscrupulous dealers formed a ring to control prices at an auction. In the eighteenth century picture-selling had become the business that it is today.

In the eighteenth century several discoveries in print-making technique were made which resulted in a widening of the range of its expression. Chief of these was the perfection of aquatint. This process allowed for a wider use of tonal effects in intaglio printing and also made possible one form of color printing which was developed and perfected by Janinet (illustration 322), Descourtis, Alix, Jazet, and Sergent-Marceau. The most original of these perhaps was P. L. Debucourt (1755–1842) who engraved much after his own designs. He seems to have had no strong political convictions since he issued plates that found favor with the *Ancien Régime,* the Revolution, Napoleon, and the Restoration. Perhaps he had a contempt for the whole human race, and political convictions did not matter, since much of his work has a strong satiric tendency. He spent his last years raising rabbits, pigeons, and chickens which he allowed to run wild and never would kill. Among his most famous plates are *Les Deux Baisers, Le Menuet de la Mariée,* and *La Noce au Château, La Matinée du Jour de l'An,* and *La Promenade de la Galerie du Palais Royal.* But his greatest print undoubtedly is the *Promenade Publique* of 1792 (illustration 324), a vivid panorama of society in the picturesque and stirring days of the National Convention. It is probable that Debucourt received the impulse to make his picture from Rowlandson's equally famous color print, *Vauxhall* (illustration 364). Still another technique developed in the eighteenth century was the stipple and crayon process. The crayon manner was developed by François and Demarteau (illustration 276) to reproduce the effect of crayon drawings, and by Marin-Bonnet (illustration 323) to reproduce the quality of a pastel drawing. The most famous practitioner of the stipple technique was Francesco Bartolozzi, an Italian who settled in London in 1764 (illustration 343). Indeed, stipple engraving was popular chiefly in England (illustration 344), where it was used to reproduce the sweet and sentimental works of Cipriani, Cosway, and Angelica Kauffmann, and the famous *Cries of London.* Soft-ground etching was used by the Swiss artist Liotard to approximate the texture of mezzotint (illustration 331).

Another technical discovery was the invention of the Physionotrace about 1768 by the court musician Gilles Louis Chrétien. The machine is really an adaptation of the pantograph idea to the making of outline silhouettes of the head. By this means the foundation of a good workmanlike likeness can be made in a sitting of less than five minutes. This tiny drawing could then be worked up on a copper plate with roulette work and etching into a complete portrait from which any number of prints could be taken. The speed of its production and its consequent cheapness ensured to the process an immediate success, especially with the rising middle class. Hitherto portraiture had been necessarily confined to distinguished people or to those few who could afford to commission an artist for a regular portrait. With the new process people of moderate means could afford to have portraits made of themselves. In addition to Chrétien there were other practitioners of the art, Quenedey and the émigré, Fevret de St. Memin, who came to America and made about eight hundred portraits (illustration 321).

St. Memin charged thirty-three dollars for the original drawing, the copper plate, and twelve impressions.

Meanwhile, side by side with all these activities of the *haute monde*, flowed the daily life of the people. Some reflection of this—patronizing to be sure—was given in several series of *Cries of Paris* or pictures of various crafts and professions by Boucher and Bouchardon, and in such genre pictures as *La Place des Halles* and *La Place Maubert* by Jeaurat. These were prints of the people but not for them. Such prints as they had were the rude woodcuts from chapbooks, in direct tradition from the fifteenth century through generations of obscure craftsmen, such as the *Notre Dame de Bonne Délivrance* (illustration 329) of which 500,000 proofs had been printed by 1766. Or they were the peepshow prints *(vues d'optique)* exhibited by wandering showmen, such as the *View of Fontainebleau* (illustration 328). See Le Prince's aquatint *La Vue* (illustration 327) for a general idea of the method of display.

In 1789 began the debacle of the *Ancien Régime*. Very many of the artists and engravers such as Moreau, Choffard, Debucourt, Ponce, welcomed the ideas of the Revolution; some of them, like Sergent, took an active part in it; but trained as they had been in the faithful delineation of an old order, they were unable to transfer their new convictions to their art. In spite of the eloquent appeal to artists by Minister Benezech (an artist turned political; who has heard of him since?) on the ninth Floreal of the Year IV ("Liberty invites you to retrace its triumphs. . . . You should acquire a national character in order that succeeding generations cannot reproach you with not having been French in the most remarkable epoch of our history"), most of the work was cold and uninspired. New forms were required for a new conception of society, and the academic Roman classicism of David or Regnault was not adequate. There was a great deal of documentation of the Revolution, much of it interesting to the historian rather than to the art-lover. *The Revolutionary Committee under the Terror*, engraved by Berthault after the younger Fragonard (illustration 326), does manage to dramatize some of the emotional currents of the Revolution—members of the nobility, often innocently suffering for the sins of their class, on the defensive before a group of "roughnecks" of the Terror. Such minor tragedies are enacted in every revolution. One of the most vivid pictures of those stirring times is Sergent-Marceau's color print, the *People Running Through the Streets* (illustration 325). The tenseness of passions unloosed, the uncertainties of alarms and excursions have been admirably suggested. Antoine François Sergent, called Sergent-Marceau (for he added his wife's name to his own), was a fiery and picturesque character. He married the sister of General Marceau, Maria Marceau, to

whom he paid the tribute of the ardent devotion of a lifetime. On her death at the age of eighty he published a pamphlet giving a detailed description of her mental and physical charms. When the Revolution broke, he threw himself into the thick of it, was one of the deputies who voted for the death of the king, celebrated at Chartres Cathedral the Festival of Reason, was instrumental in preventing the destruction or mutilation of many works of art during the Terror. After the reaction of the ninth Thermidor he fled to Switzerland; he returned later and was again exiled after the eighteenth Brumaire, and lived in Italy for the rest of his life. Eight days before his death in 1847, totally blind and ninety-six years of age, he declared to Carnot that "far from repenting his revolutionary activity, he considered it, on the contrary, as his chief title to fame."

We have had little to say about printmaking in England during the centuries. The country had been backward as far as the visual arts were concerned; its genius was expressed in other ways, in literature and science, in empire-building, in commerce and manufacture. Whatever production of art there had been was through foreign talent such as Holbein, Hollar, Sir Anthony van Dyck, Sir Peter Lely, and Sir Godfrey Kneller. But in the late seventeenth century and in the eighteenth century there was perfected a new printmaking medium eminently suited to the English taste—mezzotint—and native artists quickly sprang up to develop its possibilities. The process was invented by Ludwig von Siegen (1609–76) and the first dated (1642) mezzotint was a portrait of the Landgravin of Hesse (illustration 264). The secret of the process was communicated to Prince Rupert, to whom Evelyn in his "Sculptura" gives the credit for its invention by what appears to have been a willful juggling with the facts. A. Blooteling (illustration 241) perfected the technique by inventing the rocker for laying uniform and rich tone areas. The romantic Prince Rupert executed several plates, and though he did not invent the art, he encouraged its development in England with the result that in due course of time mezzotint was practiced chiefly in England, and labeled as "the English manner" everywhere on the Continent. The mezzotint process, based upon gradations of tone, was particularly suited to reproduce paintings. Since the English were interested chiefly in portrait painting, the great bulk of mezzotints are portraits.

In Holland [wrote Hogarth] selfishness is the ruling passion; in England vanity is united with it. Portrait painting therefore ever has, and ever will succeed better in this country than in any other; the demand will be as constant as new faces arise. . . . Upon the whole, it must be acknowledged that the artists and the age are fitted for each other. If hereafter the times alter,

the arts, like water, will find their level.

And Horace Walpole wrote to Sir Horace Mann:

Another rage is for prints of English portraits: I have been collecting them above thirty years, and originally never gave for a mezzotint above one or two shillings. The lowest are now a crown; most, from half a guinea to a guinea. . . . In short, we are at the height of extravagance and improvements, for we do improve rapidly in taste as well as in the former. I cannot say as much for our genius. Poetry has gone to bed, or into our prose; we are like the Romans in that too. If we have the arts of the Antonines—we have the fustian also.

England had become a prosperous nation, that is to say there were many noblemen, owning much of the land, who had grown rich through the enclosing of communal lands for sheep raising, and through the improvements in agriculture during the seventeenth and eighteenth centuries, and there were many merchants who had grown rich in commerce. Manufacture, chiefly of woolen cloth, had made great strides in the seventeenth century and had been aided materially by the influx of great numbers of skilled artisans possessing considerable capital, the Dutch and Flemish weavers who fled from the Spanish invasion, and the Huguenots, the pick of France's industrial population, who were expelled from France by Louis XIV. The beginning of the eighteenth century witnessed the naval and commercial supremacy of the English over the Dutch and Spanish; henceforth Britannia ruled the waves. In the conflict between the French and the English over India, England emerged victorious with the whole of India in her possession, an enormous source of wealth procured at very little cost. Furthermore, in 1769, James Watt took out his patent for a steam engine; and further inventions by Hargreaves, Arkwright, and Crompton benefited the spinning and weaving industries and brought about the Industrial Revolution, the full effects of which were not felt until the nineteenth century. All of these factors combined to make England the richest nation in Europe. And how did the English spend their money? The merchants invested theirs for further profits, but many of the noblemen, with the Grand Tour in Italy as a traditional part of their education, posed as collectors, dilettantes of the arts, connoisseurs or virtuosi, as they were called. Unfortunately they purchased chiefly Italian pictures, since there was little native art which had any prestige. The only native art which they patronized was portrait painting, and the fact that they patronized this one branch was largely due to the achievement and personality of one man, Sir Joshua Reynolds.

Sir Joshua, shrewd man of the world, suave member of Dr. Johnson's circle, dignified first President of the Royal Academy, continued the aristocratic tradition of van Dyck. As a portrait painter he substituted for elegance the glamour of the Grand Manner. He evolved an eclectic style based upon the achievements of the Venetian and Flemish schools, believing that genius was a power acquired by long labor and study.

Study consists in learning to see nature [he said] and may be called the art of using other men's minds. . . . We should to the last moment of our lives continue a settled intercourse with all true examples of grandeur. Their inventions are not only the food of our infancy, but the substance which supplies the fullest maturity of our vigor.

On which Blake commented later:

Reynolds endeavours to prove that there is No such thing as Inspiration and that any Man of plain Understanding may be Thieving from Others become a Mich. Angelo. . . . Reynolds Thinks that Man Learns all he Knows. I say on the Contrary that Man Brings All That he has or can have Into the World with him. Man is Born Like a Garden ready Planted and Sown. The World is too poor to produce one Seed.

Reynolds was not a great artist, but he was a successful one. He had enough tricks of the grand manner to impress his contemporaries, and envelop his fashionable portraits with a flattering dignity. Through his connection with the Academy and his *Discourses*, his careful cultivation of friends, and his countless commissions, he exerted enormous influence on the London art world, and hundreds of mezzotints were made after his paintings by such skilled engravers as McArdell, Houston, Fisher, J. Watson, T. Watson, Green, Dickinson, Jones, Walker, and others. A typical example is the portrait of *Lady Bamfylde* engraved by Thomas Watson (illustration 334). Regarding Reynolds's portrait of Dr. Johnson, the sitter expostulated to Boswell: "He may paint himself as deaf as he pleases, but I will not go down to Posterity as Blinking Sam" (illustration 336). Reynolds set the style of fashionable portrait which was continued with minor variations by Hoppner, Romney (illustration 335), Gainsborough, Raeburn, Wright, Lawrence, and their engravers. There is a certain sameness about all these mezzotint portraits, due partly perhaps to a limitation of the medium which emphasizes softness and smoothness at the expense of honest or subtle delineation of form, but also due to the fundamentally artificial approach of the painter to his problem. It is a highly aristocratic and superficial art, grandiloquent, flattering, and sentimentalizing, and without that exquisite taste and sense of style which gives distinction to the equally aristocratic art of France. Joseph Wright's mezzotints stand apart by

reason of his lighting effects in landscape and in illustrations of scientific instruments (illustration 337).

It is with some sense of relief—a touch of reality or a breath of fresh air—that one turns to the work of Gainsborough and Hogarth. With regard to Gainsborough, it is not so much the portraits (though most of these are executed with more originality and feeling than is visible in the other portraits of his time) as it is the landscapes which he executed for his own pleasure. "I'm sick of Portraits," he wrote to a friend, "and wish very much to take my viol-da-gamba and walk off to some sweet village where I can paint landskips and enjoy the fag-end of life in quietness and ease." He made a small number of soft ground etchings which were published in 1797 by Boydell after his death. They have caught the charm and freshness of the English countryside (illustration 342), and thus stand as precursors of the development of the English landscape school which took place in the nineteenth century.

The artist who placed himself most directly in opposition to Sir Joshua Reynolds and what he stood for was William Hogarth. He espoused a popular tradition as against the aristocratic and academic tradition of Reynolds. His genius found its completest expression in the creation of universal types under the stress of dramatic situations rather than in fashionable portraits or in historical compositions in the grand manner. Hogarth was born in 1697, and like Reynolds was the son of a schoolmaster. He was apprenticed to a silversmith and later studied at the academy of Sir James Thornhill. In 1729 he ran away with Thornhill's daughter. In 1733 he moved to a house in Leicester Fields, in which he lived until his death in 1764. Meanwhile he had painted in 1731, and a year later engraved, the series of six pictures entitled *Harlot's Progress.* They had such a widespread success that he became reconciled to his father-in-law Thornhill, who said, "the man who can furnish representations like these can also maintain a wife without a portion." It is recorded that there were over one thousand two hundred subscriptions entered for the engravings at a guinea per set. In describing the inception of this work Hogarth wrote that portrait painting, to a conscientious and self-respecting artist, was "not sufficiently profitable to pay the expenses my family required."

I therefore turned my thoughts to a still more novel mode, namely painting and engraving modern moral subjects, a field not broken up in any country or any age. . . . I have therefore endeavoured to treat my subject as a dramatic writer; my picture is my stage, and men and women my players, who by means of certain actions and gestures, are to exhibit a *dumb show.* . . . This I found was most likely to answer my purpose, provided I could strike the passions, and by small sums from many and by the sale of prints which I could engrave from my own pictures, thus secure my property to myself.

The pictures were much copied and pirated; so much so that Hogarth with other artists, Vertue and Vandergucht, petitioned Parliament to pass a law vesting in the artist the exclusive right to his own designs and restraining reproduction without consent. This Copyright Act was passed in 1735, and Hogarth's next series of engravings, *Rake's Progress,* appeared under that protection, the first prints to bear the inscription *Published according to Act of Parliament.* There had been previous attempts by artists, such as Rubens and others, to prevent plagiarism of their works, and some of them were successful in obtaining exclusive privileges from the king or ruler, but in every case they were "privileges" obtained by influence or favor, as the correspondence of Rubens clearly shows. For the first time the general principle of copyright was established: any artist could avail himself of its protection. The third famous picture sequence was *Marriage à la Mode* satirizing high society in the same manner that he had dramatized episodes in the life of a harlot and a rake. The six prints were published in 1745 but were not engraved by Hogarth himself. Plate II, the *Morning After,* engraved by Baron, is reproduced herein (illustration 338). The setting is supposed to have been copied from the drawing room at No. 5 Arlington St., once occupied by Horace Walpole. The theme of the series is the tragic unfolding of a marriage of convenience between an earl and his rich but plebeian wife.

Hogarth was in the habit of specially engraving some little subject and presenting it to the subscribers of his various large prints or series of prints, as a subscription receipt. One of these, the receipt for *Rake's Progress,* entitled *Laughing Audience,* is reproduced (illustration 341). It is a most delightful print, perfect in composition, and expressive of character by the simplest means. Hogarth engraved many famous single plates such as *The March to Finchley, Southwark Fair, Strolling Actresses Dressing in a Barn* (illustration 339), *Midnight Modern Conversation, Beer Street and Gin Lane,* and *Garrick as Richard III.* Hogarth also made political caricatures, being one of the first to cultivate that form of printmaking, specially favored in England and later developed by Rowlandson, Gillray, Dighton, and others. Allied to these, though not a caricature, was his *Portrait of Lord Lovat* (illustration 340), just before his execution for high treason. It was quickly etched to satisfy a popular demand so great that he sold prints, priced at one shilling, at the rate of two hundred and forty per day for many weeks. For vigor of characterization it ranks among the greatest portrait prints of the world.

Hogarth was not a realistic artist; he worked rather in

the style of the dramatist or comic writer like Fielding. He combined realistic elements for a theme that was either humorous or moral or descriptive. He was not the first artist to depict low life or the contemporary scene, nor the first to conceive of a picture sequence as connected episodes with a central theme, as we know from the many series of the Passion which preceded him. But he combined the two ideas with such vigor and dramatic power that he may be said to have perfected a new form. His painting has been called literary or didactic. This is true only of his less successful work; at his best it expresses its theme in purely pictorial terms rich in observation of life and character. His book *The Analysis of Beauty* shows him to have been a theoretician and technician of considerable ability and common sense. To say that his work has mankind for its central theme is merely to point out that it has social content. This is thoroughly within the legitimate province of art, although many critics disagree, just as in literature the purists are more likely to relish "Kubla Khan" than *Tom Jones*. For a print or picture to have a meaning should be an advantage, not a disqualification. Hogarth was in many respects typically English: he had the Englishman's contempt for foreigners as his caricatures of the French testify. His training was more or less indigenous; he never traveled abroad. He allied himself with the democratic tradition of Bruegel and the seventeenth-century Dutch. He aimed for expressive character, never for ideal beauty or elegant style, though, as Dobson says, when beauty came his way he drew it. It was a curious quirk of his character that although he despised the historical painters, he tried to beat them at their own game—with lamentable results. His genius was of a different order. One of the first great partisans of the bourgeois or middle class, he found his patrons among the many instead of the few.

Life in eighteenth-century Venice—if we believe the memoirs of Casanova, Carlo Gozzi, and Goldoni—was one long *fête galante* or carnival interrupted by short periods of Lent equally picturesque and beautiful. At any rate it was somewhat in this spirit that Giambattista Tiepolo (1696–1770) worked at his decorations for villas and palaces and occasionally for churches. He was a facile painter and draughtsman, and inventions came bubbling from his fertile brain. In the midst of a busy career he found time to etch about thirty-eight plates. They are truly what he called the two leading series of his etchings: *Capricci* and *Scherzi*, or whimsical inventions (illustration 345). The subject matter is most varied and fanciful, scenes of magicians, occultism, satyrs, Roman soldiers, Pulchinello, and the like, all executed with a light and airy grace, with much spirit and little meaning. The Tiepolos must have been a happy, jolly family: Giambattista married Cecilia Guardi, the sister of the

painter Francesco Guardi. It is said that she was such a gamester that once during the absence of her husband she gambled away all his sketches and even their country house with all his frescoes in it. They had nine children, two of whom, Domenico and Lorenzo, assisted their father with his decorations, and etched a number of plates after his paintings. Domenico was an able artist in his own right, and composed a series of twenty-five etchings entitled *Idee Pittoresche sopra La Fugga in Egitto*, 1753 (illustration 346), an elegant and fluent lenten meditation suffused with soft Italian atmosphere and charm.

If the Tiepolos may be said to have pictured the actors in the Venetian carnival, then Canaletto may be said to have provided the setting or backdrop. His thirty-odd etchings, also made in the intervals of a busy painting career, depict scenes in and around Venice, and are filled with brilliant sunshine and quivering atmosphere. Such plates as the *Torre di Malghera* (illustration 347) and the *Porch with the Lantern* are justly famous, but some of the smaller plates, the *Terrace* (illustration 348), the *Prison*, the *Market on the Giudecca*, are equally attractive. Canaletto had numerous contacts with English connoisseurs and collectors, and the collected edition of his *Vedute* or etchings was published with a dedication to Joseph Smith, the British Consul at Venice.

The third great name in eighteenth-century Italian etching was Giovanni Battista Piranesi. He too was a Venetian, born in 1720, the son of a stonemason. He was educated to be an architect but the great passion of his life was Roman antiquities. And passion was a mighty force in a man of his fiery temperament, if one can judge from the anecdotes told of him. How, for instance, when sketching in the old Roman Forum he saw a young girl who he was convinced was descended from the noble Romans, and how, after a cyclonic courtship lasting five days, was married to the daughter of the gardener of Prince Corsini. How he threatened to kill the doctor called in to minister to a member of his family if the patient did not recover within a few days. How when he was absorbed in the making of an etching, his wife and five children suffered agonies of hunger, not daring to disturb him or eat without him. It was in Rome, the city of his dreams, that he spent most of his life, pursuing his archaeological researches and bringing to completion his stupendous œuvre of over one thousand three hundred huge etchings. He became an authority on Roman archaeology throughout Europe, and exercised an influence on the development of the classic style in the France of Louis XVI and in England through his friendship with Robert Adam. His mastery of draughtsmanship and perspective, his knowledge of Roman antiquities, the sense of drama suggested by the picturesque figures with which he peopled his romantic ruins, and above all his

epic imagination all combine to make his etchings the most effective dramatization of Rome's past grandeur ever known. Piranesi also made many etchings of the Rome of his day; typical is the *Piazza Navona* (illustration 352) looking much the same as it does today. Early in his career he etched a series of fourteen (later sixteen) large etchings called *Carceri d'Invenzione* or *Prison Scenes* (illustrations 349 and 350). They seem at first to have been architectural caprices pure and simple. Fifteen years later, he reworked many of them, creating a new, fantastic, and visionary mood with dark and dramatic accents. De Quincey, in his *Confessions of an English Opium Eater*, mentions these prints in a celebrated passage, which probably reads into it meanings which were not in Piranesi's mind. In spite of its distortions it does manage to convey something of the spirit of these etched phantasmagoria:

Many years ago, when I was looking over Piranesi's *Antiquities of Rome*, Mr. Coleridge, who was standing by, described to me a set of plates by that artist, called his *Dreams*, and which record the scenery of his visions during the delirium of a fever. Some of them . . . represented vast Gothic halls, on the floor of which stood all sorts of engines and machinery, wheels, cables, pulleys, levers, catapults, and the like, expressive of enormous power put forth and resistance overcome. Creeping along the sides of the walls, you perceived a staircase; and upon it, grasping his way upwards, was Piranesi himself; follow the stairs a little further, and you perceive it comes to a sudden, abrupt termination, without any balustrade, and allowing no step onwards to him who had reached the extremity except into the depths below. . . . But raise your eyes, and behold a second flight of stairs still higher, on which again Piranesi is perceived, by this time standing on the very brink of the abyss. . . . With the same power of endless growth and self-production did my architecture proceed in my dreams.

6. The Nineteenth Century

The nineteenth century was a drama of personalities, and Goya, working in two centuries, wrote its prologue. The outstanding qualities of the nineteenth century were its diversity and its emphasis on personality. There were, to be sure, movements and schools of artists, plenty of them in bewildering succession, but they were usually grouped around a few outstanding personalities. Hitherto an art style or epoch lasted for a century or longer, now it lasted for a generation. Once the epoch molded the artist, now the artist created the style. Classicism, Romanticism, Realism, Barbizon, Impressionism, Postimpressionism all had their say within a hundred years. The nineteenth was the century of rugged individualism.

Francisco de Goya y Lucientes was a picturesque and outstanding personality who, in expressing himself, also expressed truths about mankind. He was a combination of court painter and satirist, of philosopher and *aficionado* of the bullring, that could occur only in Spain. Spain has always been a strange and mysterious land where all things are possible. As Joseph, who tried to rule the country for six years, ruefully said to his brother Napoleon: "*L'Espagne n'est pas un pays comme les autres.*" A backward and reactionary country, priest-ridden and king-ridden, its peoples displayed in many respects an astonishing wisdom of life, a real feeling for life as a fine art. Its beggars had the manners of grandees. Nowhere in Europe were bourgeois ideas and ideals so completely discounted and ignored as in Spain.

Goya was born in Fuente de Todos in Aragon in 1746. There are many legends of his early life, a record as violent and vivid as Cellini's, filled with love affairs, murderous quarrels, exploits in the bullring, travels in Italy. In 1776 he was settled in Madrid, married to Josepha Bayeu, who was to bear him twenty children, leading an active, hard-working life, designing cartoons for tapestries saturated with the gay spirit of Madrid life, painting murals and portraits of the nobility and the royal family. In 1780 he was elected to the Academy of San Fernando; in 1789 he was made *Pintor de Camara*; in 1799 he was *Primer Pintor de Camara*, chief painter to the king. He enjoyed the friendship and patronage of the Duke and Duchess of Ossuna; he had an intense love affair with the alluring but fickle Duchess of Alba. In all these years he drew and painted incessantly, tried his hand at etching copies of Velazquez. But his direct and passionate temperament also had opportunity to reflect on the pageant of human folly as he saw it: greed, fickleness, pride, lust, cruelty, stupidity. In 1791 the secret of aquatint etching had been published to the world in the *Encyclopédia Méthodique*. Goya must have come across it, and in the aquatint process he found a medium eminently fitted to reproduce his pen and wash drawings. In the last years of the century there began to crystalize in his mind the idea of a series of satiric compositions executed in etching and aquatint. The miracle of it was that he should want to publish to the world, in Spain of all places, such a series of prints. Perhaps he had to do it to keep his self-respect amid the corrupt and artificial surroundings of the court; perhaps he was a bit *afrancesado*, tinged with French revolutionary ideas. In any case, the series was announced to the public in 1797 in a prospectus containing the following explanation written, if not by Goya, by Cean Bermudez under the inspiration of his ideas:

Believing that the criticism of human errors and vices, although first and foremost the business of rhetoric and poetry, may also come within the province of painting, the author has chosen as subjects for his work some of those extravagances and stupidities, common to all classes of society, some of those prejudices and falsehoods, hallowed by custom, by ignorance or by interest, such themes indeed as seemed to him to offer matter for ridicule and scope for the free play of the artist's imagination. As the subjects are idealized it may not be too daring to assume that their faults will be leniently judged by people of intelligence. . . . I crave the public's indulgence in consideration of the fact that the author has made use of no strange models, nor even of studies from nature. The imitation of nature is as difficult as it is admirable if one can really attain it and carry it through. But he also may deserve praise, who has completely withdrawn himself from nature and has succeeded in placing before our eyes, forms and movements which have hitherto existed only in our imagination. . . . Painting, like Poetry, selects from the universe what she can best use for her own ends. She unites, she concentrates in one fantastic figure cir-

cumstances and characters which nature has distributed among various individuals. Thanks to this wise and ingenious combination the artist merits the title of an inventor and ceases to be a mere subordinate copyist.

Two years later the set of eighty plates of the *Caprichos* was put on sale at 320 reals (about $25.00)—one of the world's masterpieces of graphic art, a savage yet detached commentary on humankind. For once the facade was ripped off and the essential type laid bare (illustration 356). Yet not only types were attacked, but society, which allowed certain things to happen, as in *Will No One Unbind Us?* (illustration 355). In spite of Goya's disclaimer that the satire was general and not particular, there were rumors—as was natural in a society where gossip and the malicious story were raised to a fine art—that certain reigning court favorites and even the king and queen were attacked. Furthermore there were certain inquiries and investigations by the Inquisition, for some of the shots at superstition and fanaticism had hit a bull's-eye. Goya deemed it prudent to dedicate the series to the king, Charles IV, who graciously accepted it and duly rewarded the artist. Nowhere but in Spanish countries could such a thing have happened, in Spain where the technique of the deadly thrust in the bullring is appreciated with discriminating connoisseurship, where skepticism and faith, idealism and materialism, Don Quixote and Sancho Panza go hand in hand, and where flourishes the ironic laugh, the *vacilada* of the Mexicans, that is relished by its victims if only the sally be delivered with sufficient art. The frontispiece of the set was a portrait of Goya himself (illustration 354). We see him as he appeared at the height of his powers, the piercing, all-seeing eyes, the protuding underlip, the determined chin —the master of illusion and disillusion. Deafness was already upon him, that deafness which was eventually to cut him off from all society except a few intimates. Meanwhile things were happening in Spain. In 1808 Napoleon invaded Spain to establish his brother Joseph upon the throne. The Spaniards should have welcomed him, for any rule would have been preferable to the old regime of Spain, but most of them did not, and there ensued a guerrilla warfare of unparalleled savagery on both sides. For six long years it lasted, aided by Napoleon's implacable enemy, England, until finally reaction, bigotry, cruelty, and the Inquisition returned triumphantly in the person of Ferdinand VII in 1814. Goya watched it all and set it down in a series of etchings which were not published until long after his death as the *Disasters of War*. Not all the plates refer to the Napoleonic War; several are covert satires against the French and against Ferdinand; still another group refers to the great famine of 1812, indirect consequence of the war, when over twenty thousand people died in Madrid alone. A reflection of this is given in that magnificent composition *Thanks to Millet Seed* (illustration 360). "Men, women, and children," says Romanos in his *Reminiscences*, "lay dying in the streets, they begged for a scrap of green stuff, for a potato, for a drop of soup, however thin and bad. It was a scene of despair and pain." But most of the etchings relate to the invasion (illustrations 361 and 363), a terrific and awe-inspiring indictment, not of the enemy, but of war itself, its senselessness and incredible brutality. Only a Voltaire, in *Candide*, could do justice to the scope of Goya's savagely ironic portrayal:

He crept over a heap of dead and dying and at last reached a neighboring village which he found in ashes. It was a village of the Avares and the Bulgarians had burnt it down according to the rules of the international game. Here aged men, sinking beneath the blows that were showered upon them, saw their wives throttled to death, pressing their children to their bleeding breasts to the last. There girls lay dying, their bellies ripped open when they had served to satisfy the lust of conquering heroes; others, half burned, begged for death. On the ground one saw splashes of scattered brains and limbs lopped from bodies.

Goya worked on, more and more withdrawn into himself in the *Quinta del Sordo*, the deaf man's villa. On one of his *Caprichos* there was an inscription, "The Sleep of Reason Produces Monsters." Dreams and nightmares seemed to haunt him, visions far more fantastic and monstrous than those he pictured in the *Caprichos* (illustration 353). Out of pleasure or necessity he recorded them on the walls of the Quinta and in the series of twenty-two etchings and aquatints known as the *Disparates*, or *Extravagances*. Like Titian and Rembrandt, Goya suffered no diminution of imaginative power in his old age. The *Disasters* were realistic, the *Caprichos* were a mixture of realism and fantasy, but the *Disparates* were pure fantasy, a direct outpouring of his unconscious. What powerful and haunting visions they are, a group of people huddling on a rotten branch, a stallion biting a woman, flying men (illustration 358), a man haunted by demons! One of them, entitled *Disparate de Bestia* (illustration 359), shows priests and lawgivers anxiously holding a law code before an elephant who may or may not symbolize the People unconscious of their strength. It is a breathtaking composition.

In 1825 he was in Bordeaux for his health—old, in a strange land, deaf, with eyesight failing, "but very pleased with life and anxious to meet people." "He obstinately continued to work," wrote his friend Moratin, "painting everything that comes into his head and unwilling ever to correct what he paints." In his seventy-

ninth year he made a number of lithographs, then a comparatively new medium, including the four great bullfights (illustration 357). He had already etched forty good-sized plates (thirty-two of which were published in 1815) as a sort of illustrated history of the *corrida de toros* and its heroes. But his invention continued undiminished. These four great stones are a veritable orgy of bullfighting, the compositions built up with broad strokes and large masses, brimming with energy. They are amazingly spirited achievements from a man almost eighty and count among the great masterpieces of lithography. Goya had extraordinary energy and an indomitable will; in a letter he excused his bad penmanship, "I have neither sight, nor pulse, nor pen nor inkpot, I lack everything, only my will survives." But even the will to live was quenched by a stroke in 1828 brought on, it is said, by joy over the arrival of his son Xavier.

On one of the preliminary drawings for the *Caprichos*, the one which originally was to serve as the frontispiece, Goya wrote *"Idioma Universal."* Universal language, the ultimate aim of the print, that was what was in the back of his mind, and he came as close to it as any printmaker ever did. His only peers are Rembrandt and Daumier who approached humanity from the side of love and understanding. Goya perhaps probed deeper into the unconscious, into those devious but powerful forces that motivate our every action. He has brought into the light of day and made concrete in the shape of recognizable types certain essential drives that lie buried in most of us, impulses of vanity, pride, greed, gluttony, lust, cruelty, and the like. There is nothing like war or the vision of sudden death for uncovering the essence of man. This is strong medicine and bitter: many people will be repelled by Goya's work. But for those who can accept one aspect of reality without sugarcoating, it can become a most illuminating catharsis.

Another personality who was active in two centuries was Thomas Rowlandson. He was born in London in 1756, the son of a fairly prosperous merchant. He studied at the Academy School for a short time. In his sixteenth year, about 1771, he was sent to Paris to live with his aunt, née Mlle Chattelier, whose favorite he became. He learned to speak French like a native, plunged with eagerness into the life of the gay capital, and entered the Ecole de l'Académie Royale to continue his art studies. He became acquainted with Debucourt, and with Janinet, a fellow pupil at the Ecole. In 1775 when he was nineteen, he returned to London and continued his studies at the Royal Academy. Angelo in his *Reminiscences* recounts:

Bannister and Rowlandson were prankish youths. The latter once gave great offense by carrying a peashooter into the life academy, and, whilst old Moser was adjusting the female model and had just directed her contour, Rowlandson let fly a pea, which, making her start, threw her entirely out of position, and interrupted the gravity of the study for the whole evening.

In spite of such pranks Rowlandson was well liked; and a great future was predicted for him by the academicians, two presidents, Reynolds and West, having expressed the greatest admiration of his talents. In 1775 he exhibited for the first time at the Royal Academy, and continued to do so for about a dozen years. He gradually, however, lost interest in the so-called serious or historical art in favor of a more free and easy and rollicking social commentary, partly through the influence of such friends as Bunbury, Wigstead, and Gillray, and partly through the bent of his own temperament. He launched into a career of extravagance and dissipation aggravated by the receipt of a legacy of over seven thousand pounds from his French aunt. Yet his wild life did not interfere with his production: it rather spurred him on to tap the apparently inexhaustible sprints of his fancy. His work combined French elegance with English animal spirits. He had a ready gift for characterization combined with a rich knowledge of life gained from actual experience. His opulent and exuberant forms exactly mirrored his uncommon zest for life. His *Vauxhall Gardens* (illustration 364) has been mentioned as having influenced Debucourt. Vauxhall was a famous London amusement resort of the eighteenth century, and Rowlandson is supposed to have introduced caricatures of many well-known people in his picture. The two fashionably dressed women under the singer on the balcony are supposed to be the Duchess of Devonshire and her sister, Lady Duncannon. Farther to the right the man whispering into the ear of a lady linked to a deformed husband is the Prince of Wales, afterwards George IV. In a supper box Dr. Johnson is oblivious to everything but the pleasures of the table, with the ever-watchful Boswell diagonally on his left. On the right of Johnson, the blue-stocking Mrs. Thrale may be seen talking to Oliver Goldsmith. Rowlandson made many illustrations, chiefly for Ackermann's publications, the *Dance of Death*, the *Dance of Life*, the various *Tours of Dr. Syntax*, and the *Microcosm of London* (illustration 365) in collaboration with Pugin who supplied the architectural features. This last is a survey of the activities of a great city in 104 plates, furnishing a wealth of information regarding the manners of the time. For such publishers as Ackermann, Fores, and Tegg, he produced several political caricatures (illustration 366) and countless social caricatures, etched on copper and crudely colored by hand. *A Seriocomic Scene in Norwich* (illustration 367) is typical of these and of the robust humor of the time. The caricatures of Gillray,

Bunbury, Dighton, and Cruikshank are in the same vein.

Rowlandson also did a few sporting prints, a genre that was popular in the early nineteenth century in England. The hard-drinking, hard-riding English country squires and the young bucks of the city were collecting art, and the demand was ably supplied. The appreciation of these connoisseurs, however, was strictly limited: they demanded that a picture be factual, accurate, and pleasant, and, in subject matter, entirely within the range of their experience, either genre pictures of the English countryside (Morland and Ward), or sporting pictures, hunting, shooting, racing, or coaching prints. A large group of able, decorative but esthetically limited prints were produced by Alken, Pollard, Wolstenholme, Howitt, and others. Two prints, *Hare Hunting* by Hodges (illustration 368) and *False Alarm on the Road to Gretna Green* by Newhouse (illustration 369), may serve as representative of the class. There were other groups of prints appealing to a specialized public, such as flower prints (illustrations 370 and 371). Thousands and hundreds of thousands of specialized prints have been made, relating to science, natural history, travel, genre, illustration, which in their humble way have contributed to the amusement and instruction of mankind.

A new and cheap printmaking medium was perfected at the beginning of the century which was greatly to extend the range of popular prints—lithography. The inventor was Aloys Senefelder. He was not an artist, but was ambitious to write for the stage. Being poor, he saw no way of getting the world to look at his work unless he became his own publisher. In the course of his attempts to find a cheap method of printing plays with engraved plates, he happened upon the germ of lithography. In his own words:

I had just ground a stone plate smooth in order to treat it with etching fluid and to pursue on it my practice in reverse writing when my mother asked me to write a laundry list for her. The laundress was waiting but we could find no paper. My own supply had been used up by pulling proofs. Even the writing ink was dried up. Without bothering to look for writing materials, I wrote the list hastily on the clean stone with my prepared ink of wax, soap and lampblack, intending to copy it as soon as paper was supplied.

Curiosity as to the possibilities of this chance application of ink on stone led him to further experiments till he had evolved the complete process. Later unscrupulous promoters were to defraud the unworldly inventor of some of his just benefits and dues, but in the end he received a pension from the King of Bavaria, and painstaking biographers and autobiographers have set the whole record straight for the benefit of grateful posterity. In Germany and Austria the new medium did not stimulate any far-reaching response. At the beginning of the century these countries were in a state of depression artistically, economically, and politically. Schinkel made a few prints (illustration 419) and the Quaglios some romantic scenes including an interesting portrait of Senefelder printed with two stones like a chiaroscuro (illustration 373). The portrait, dated 1818, was undoubtedly done from life and thus punctures the legend that Hanfstängl's lithograph of 1834 was the only life portrait. The legend is that Senefelder had a deadly fear of having his picture taken: Hanfstängl persuaded him to sit for a portrait, and three days later he sickened and died. Strixner, Piloty, and Hanfstängl used lithography to reproduce paintings. Portrait lithographs were made by Reuter, Krüger, Schadow, and the Viennese Kriehuber, who drew the charmingly romantic *Une Matinée chez Liszt* (illustration 374) with portraits of Liszt, Berlioz, the pianist Carl Czerny (remembered for his Etudes), the violinist Ernst, and Kriehuber himself. It is one of the most famous of musical portraits.

It was in France, however, that lithography first came into its own. Not only was art in demand there, but there were also distinguished artists who were willing to try their hand with the new medium, Prud'hon, Guerin, Géricault (illustration 376), Baron Gros. Distinguished amateurs took it up (as they had the physionotrace). They included the Duc de Montpensier, brother of the future king Louis-Philippe, and Vivant Denon (illustration 375), one of Napoleon's savants who gathered together in the Louvre famous paintings from all over Europe as spoils of war, and of whom it was said that his chief occupations were *"la gravure et les femmes."* But lithography flourished in Paris chiefly because it satisfied a popular need. Amid all the ups and downs of the Revolution, the Directorate, the Empire, and the Restoration, the middle class had been slowly and steadily gaining in power and influence. A quick and inexpensive reproducing medium was needed in order to reach the bourgeoisie for purposes of propaganda. Woodcut and etching, as Edouard Fuchs has pointed out, were too complicated and costly; lithography was as if made for the purpose. Political caricature flourished as never before at the beginning of the reign of le *Roi Bourgeois.* Furthermore, the middle classes had still other uses for lithography beside political propaganda; they wanted pictures, decorations for their walls, and illustrations for their books. Thackeray in his *Paris Sketch Book* has drawn a pretty picture of this aspect of French bourgeois culture:

The same love of ornament which is shown in their public places of resort, appears in their houses likewise; and everyone of our readers who has lived in Paris, in any lodging, magnifi-

cent or humble with any family, however poor, may bear witness how profusely the walls of his smart *salon* in the English quarter, or of his little room *au sixième* in the Pays Latin, have been decorated with prints of all kinds. In the first, probably, with bad engravings on copper from the bad and tawdry pictures of the artists of the time of the Empire; in the latter, with gay caricatures of Grandville or Monnier: military pieces, such as are dashed off by Raffet, Charlet, Vernet; or clever pictures from the crayon of the Deverias, the admirable Roqueplan, or Decamps. . . . We get in these engravings the *loisirs* of men of genius, not the finikin performances of labored mediocrity, as with us: all these artists are good painters, as well as good designers; a design from them is worth a whole gross of *Books of Beauty*. . . . Can there be a more pleasing walk in the whole world than a stroll through the Gallery of the Louvre on a fête-day; not to look so much at the pictures as at the lookers-on? Thousands of the poorer classes are there: mechanics in their Sunday clothes, smiling grisettes, smart dapper soldiers of the line, with bronzed wondering faces, marching together in little companies of six or seven, and stopping every now and then at Napoleon or Leonidas as they appear in proper vulgar heroics in the pictures of David or Gros. The taste of these people will hardly be approved by the connoisseur, but they have *a* taste for art. Can the same be said of our lower classes, who, if they are inclined to be sociable and amused in their holidays, have no place of resort but the tap-room or tea-garden, and no food for conversation except such as can be built upon the politics or the police reports of the last Sunday paper? So much has Church and State puritanism done for us—so well has it succeeded in materializing and binding down to earth the imagination of men, for which God has made another world (which certain statesmen take but too little into account)—that fair and beautiful world of art, in which there *can* be nothing selfish or sordid, of which Dulness has forgotten the existence, and which Bigotry has endeavored to shut out from sight.

Thackeray, in speaking of onlookers, might also have been describing the group in front of *Delpech's Lithograph Shop* (illustration 372), so apt is his account. It is interesting to note the boy carrying a lithograph stone on his head. Carle Vernet, who drew the lithograph, was of a long line of artists reaching back to the *Ancien Régime*. He also was one of the artists, along with Raffet, Charlet, Marlet, and Bellangé, active in building up what was called the Napoleonic Legend. Almost a generation had passed since the great wars, and the old soldiers now indulged in fond and pleasant recollection. Nor was the comfortable bourgeois averse to tasting a little vicarious glory. Hundreds of lithographs were brought out, anecdotes of the war, details of uniforms, of battles, anecdotes of the emperor presenting him in a grand or kindly light, all executed with zest and a big dash of sentimentality. One of the most imaginative is Raffet's *Revue Nocturne* (illustration 362) where a phantom emperor nightly reviews his phantom troops. The reality of the Napoleonic legend we get in Goya's *Disasters* (illustration 363).

Another large-scale enterprise carried through with the aid of lithography was the *Voyages Pittoresques et Romantiques dans l'Ancienne France*, in twenty-four huge folio volumes brought out by Baron Taylor, Inspector General of the Fine Arts and of the Museums of France. Taylor was quite alive to the possibilities of lithography: "Bourgeois showed me his first lithographs. I saw in this new art a means of realizing an idea which was to occupy the greater part of my life: I believed I could forsee that lithography was to be for the arts of drawing almost what typography had been for literature." The 2700-odd lithographs included in this stupendous work cover every part and province of France, recording picturesque scenes and romantic ruins, and were made by the best artists of France and England: Ciceri, Isabey, Charlet, Vernet, C. Nanteuil, Ingres, Bonington, Prout, Boys, Harding, Haghe, and others. Two examples of this work, which did so much for landscape lithography, are reproduced (illustrations 377 and 378), Bonington's *Tour de la Grosse Horloge* at Evreux, and Eugène Isabey's *Eglise de St. Nectaire* in Auvergne, of which Pennell wrote: "The gems of the collection are the drawings of Eugène Isabey. The way he could seize upon the most pictorial point of view and use chalk, stump and scraper, or anything to work up his design until one hardly knows how his effect has been obtained, how he managed to fill it with color and light and air and beauty, is truly marvelous."

The technique of color lithography had been developing along with lithography in black and white, and reached perhaps its highest technical proficiency in the Paris portfolio of Thomas Shotter Boys (illustration 379). Color printing as a sensitive art was again revived at the end of the century by such artists as Toulouse-Lautrec, Bonnard, Vuillard, and Signac. Lithography found another great field in the genre pictures, the social commentary, the gay caricatures that Thackeray speaks about, by Monnier, Lami, Decamps, Deveria, Beaumont, Travies, and Gavarni.

Sulpice-Guillaume Chevalier, called Gavarni, was born in Paris in 1804 and died there in 1866. In him the wit and elegance and feminine grace of Parisian life found a worthy interpreter. One of his most famous prints is his portrait of the two de Goncourt brothers (illustration 380). His name is often coupled with that of Daumier. In a sense they complement each other: although Gavarni has none of the virility or depth or grandeur of Daumier, he has a delicacy and a flair for a pretty woman and a modish dress that is lacking in the work of the great caricaturist (illustration 381). He also anticipated the costume and bearing of our youth of today (illustrations 382 and 383).

It is said that when Balzac saw some of Daumier's work he exclaimed: "This fellow has a lot of Michelan-

gelo inside of him." It is quite true that there is much of Michelangelo's heroic and plastic monumentality in his work, as there is of Rembrandt's deep feeling for humanity. Daumier presented the complete drama of humanity in the dress of the middle class. Never has the life of the solid bourgeois and his equally solid wife been presented in greater detail or with greater understanding and humor. All its hopes and fears, its virtues and prejudices, its little crises of happiness or unhappiness found expression in Daumier's crayon. As Baudelaire pointed out, Daumier was the pictorial complement to Balzac's *Comédie Humaine*. There were limitations to his range: neither the extremes of proletarian poverty, starvation, and degradation nor the elegance of the demi-monde (so delightfully portrayed by Gavarni) nor the luxuries of the ruling class were pictured by Daumier. Daumier was the middle class writ large, the bourgeois in his noblest aspect, the tireless fighter for political freedom against censorship and monarchical reaction, against war and extreme exploitation, ecclesiastical obscurantism, against police brutality and the venality of the law. Insofar as the middle class represented the ideals of humanity —and it has come as close to it as any single class ever has —Daumier was a universal artist. *"Je suis de mon temps,"* he said—I am of my own time. No heroics, no ideal figures, no search for the beautiful or the sublime, merely scenes and incidents of daily life, topical, factual, often of ephemeral interest. But through his genius he has made these scenes live for all time. We turn to them again and again, long after the stimulus that gave them birth has been forgotten, as inspiring and illuminating pages in the history of mankind—fresh and pertinent today as they were the day they were published.

Honoré Daumier was born in Marseilles in 1808, the son of an impecunious glazier with poetic aspirations. In 1814 the family moved to Paris, and young Daumier grew up in the great city whose life he so heroically depicted. He wanted to draw; the family finally consented, but not until he had served his term as a bookseller's clerk and as a process-server in a lawyer's office (where perhaps he got his first insight into the legal mind). He entered the studio of Lenoir and drew ears and noses from casts. But this was not to his liking either, and he went out into the streets of Paris to watch and observe and store his memory with impressions of life. He had a visual memory astonishing even for an artist. An anecdote is told of him later that illustrates this forcibly. He was out one Sunday with the Daubignys at Valmondois. He asked if there were any ducks to be seen, since he had to draw some in one of his lithographs. They led him to the canal where there was a whole flock of the birds, and after he had observed them for a few minutes, they asked him if he did not want a pencil and paper to make some sketches.

Smilingly he said, "No thanks, you know I cannot draw from nature." A few days later the lithograph appeared with the ducks drawn to the life. What he meant when he modestly said that he could not draw from nature, was that he did not have to.

One does not know what turn the career of young Daumier might have taken if the times had not been crying out for an outstanding political caricaturist. France was getting heartily sick of the stupid and reactionary King Charles X. Political pamphleteering and caricature were in a ferment. In 1831 Daumier met Charles Philipon, founder and editor of *La Caricature* and *Le Charivari*, militant fighter for liberal democracy, ardent republican (which in 1835 excited the same opprobrium that the epithet communist does today); and so began the collaboration of these two kindred spirits which lasted a lifetime. Daumier found his metier. He was perhaps the greatest political caricaturist the world has ever seen; he had the faculty of dramatizing an abstract or political idea and clothing it in such convincing and universal terms that it still has meaning for us. Has there ever been a more vivid and complete embodiment of a prostitute press than in the picture of *Mlle Constitutionnel*, the "official" newspaper (illustration 385)? Look at those two great masterpieces, *Le Ventre Législatif* (illustration 386) and *Rue Transnonain* (illustration 387). They were separate prints issued by *La Caricature* at one franc apiece in order to defray the expense of fines that had been imposed upon the periodical. The *Ventre Législatif* —as superb in design as a grand fresco—was the caricatured portrait of a corrupt Chamber of Deputies. Daumier had made many careful studies of the members by visiting the Chamber day by day and returning to his studio to model busts of nearly everyone in clay (these busts exist today), and finally he composed the lithograph from these modeled sketches. It was by this means perhaps that he attained that plastic feeling, that tactile sense which is so marked a characteristic of his work. *Rue Transnonain* represented an incident of police brutality in which a whole family, man, woman, and child, were murdered by the civic guard. Burning with indignation Daumier drew the scene, so charged with emotion yet so grandly simple and monumental in feeling that it is one of the most moving pictures of all time. It is said that people lined up daily in long queues to see the picture when it was exhibited in Aubert's window in the Galerie Vero-Dodat. From this time on, Daumier's fame was secure. He had already served a six months' term in the prison of Ste. Pélagie in 1832 for a caricature against Louis-Philippe. This king with liberal pretenses had been swept into power by popular discontent in 1830, but he soon proved to be as reactionary as Charles X, and in 1835 he clamped down a censorship of the press so severe

that any political caricature was quite out of the question. Daumier therefore turned to social caricature and began the huge opus of over three thousand lithographs that appeared in *Charivari* from 1833, off and on, to 1872. He received at first forty and later fifty francs per stone, and his work for *Charivari* constituted his chief source of income during his life. He often brought out series of from ten to fifty lithographs on the same subject, as for example *Bluestockings, Les Artistes, Le Bon Bourgeois, Les Beaux Jours de la Vie, Histoire Ancienne, Croquis Parisiens, Landlords and Tenants, Hunting, Country Life, Railroads* (just being built), *Les Papas, Théâtre, Mœurs Conjugales, Bathers* (copied by Delacroix as studies of the nude), *Professeurs et Moutards, Croquis Musicaux*, and many others. There was one class which he was merciless in satirizing, *Les Gens de Justice* (illustration 384). Another famous series was that of Robert Macaire, a type whose adventures gave a complete picture of the rascality of the time. He also designed a large number of woodcut illustrations for books, notably the *Némésis Médicale, Les Français Peints par Eux-mêmes, La Grande Ville*, and the various *Physiologies*, and for magazines such as *Le Monde Illustré* in the years 1862–68 (illustration 389). But in spite of his manifest achievements Daumier never felt quite at home in this medium. He told Théodore de Banville that "he was sick and tired of designs on wood and did not wish to do any more; the lithographic crayon alone followed his thought, whereas the lead pencil was refractory and would not obey him; in short he had a violent dislike of this kind of design where nine times out of ten one is betrayed and dishonored by the engraver."

Daumier lived quietly and modestly on the Ile St. Louis. He liked to go to the theatre and to chat with a few intimate friends far into the night; or on a Sunday excursion, he would be with such confreres as Delacroix, Corot, Millet, Rousseau, Dupré, Daubigny, and Geoffroy-Dechaume. He painted also in his leisure moments and in those years (1860–63) when there was no demand for his caricatures. In his painting and drawing, *Don Quixote, Les Blanchisseuses, Christ Presented to the People*, he voiced those deep and moving intuitions which somehow never found expression in his lithographs. In his later years the style of his lithographs changed. Color, rich blacks, and minuteness of form no longer were important; the figures became bathed in atmosphere and light; only the barest essentials were given. His line became fluid, form-enclosing, and supremely vital. He always had the gift of creating types. His distortions, his deviations from the norm, always were convincing: every figure he ever drew had in it the breath of life. But now his expression became truly monumental. Take for example the *European Equilibrium* (illustration 390) or *The Witnesses* (illustration 391), an unpublished lithograph said to be the last one he

made: grandeur of conception and inspired breadth of execution lift them out of the limbo of ephemeral caricatures into the small class of the elect of all time. *The Witnesses* with its group of skeletons of men, women, and children picketing, as it were, the Council of War, is one of the grandest war pictures ever made. Great and satisfying as were these paintings and lithographs of Daumier, they brought him little material recompense. Old and blind, he eked out a modest existence with a tiny pension from the government in a cottage at Valmondois generously given to him by his old friend Corot. He died in 1879. Van Gogh in a letter has perhaps summed him up as well as anyone:

But I remembered being so very much impressed at the time by something so strong and manly in Daumier's conception that I thought: it must be a good thing to think and feel in that way, and to overlook or to pass by many things, in order to concentrate oneself on things that furnish food for thought, and that touch us as human beings much more than meadows or clouds.

A number of the great painters of the time also tried their hand at printmaking. Ingres made a notable portrait etching of Pressigny (illustration 392) and several lithographs including an *Odalisque* (illustration 400) similar to one of his paintings. It is a miracle of tight drawing and carefully built up effects. Ingres, the brilliant pupil of David, broke from the classical tradition of his master, and was considered a "Gothic" by him and others. However, as the Romantic School gained in favor and influence, Ingres became the chief bulwark of classicism against the Romantic vagary. His work was based on line and drawing highly finished, and, within its narrow limits, attained a rare perfection, but in Delacroix's words, it was "the complete expression of an incomplete intelligence." His great rival was Delacroix, the champion of the Romantic School. Eugène Delacroix was born in 1798, the natural son—according to one story—of Talleyrand. Delacroix was one of the most richly endowed personalities in the history of art. He was passionately devoted to music; he had a gift for writing, published many articles, and from his twenty-fourth year kept a diary which is a most revealing document on the temperament and character of an artist. "He was a man of general education," wrote Baudelaire in a sensitive appreciation of his genius, "unlike the other modern painters who are for the most part either illustrious or obscure daubers, sad specialists old or young, or pure artisans, some making academic figures, others fruits, and still others animals. Delacroix loved everything, and surrendered his mind to every kind of impression." His writings on art praising order, reason, and clarity, Baudelaire continues, reveal

that duality in most great artists, "which compels them, as critics, to praise and analyze with all voluptuousness the qualities of which as creators they are most in need, and which are the antithesis of what they possess in abundance."

If Delacroix had praised and extolled what we specially admire in him, the violence, the precipitateness of his gestures, the turbulence of his composition, the magic of his color, we would indeed be astonished. Why search for something one already has abundantly? . . . In the last years of his life all that might be called pleasure had disappeared from his life, a single, avid, exacting, terrible passion having taken its place—work— which was no longer merely a passion, but would have been better described as a fury.

In his one hundred and twenty-six etchings and lithographs Delacroix spoke the language of the Romantic artist. The Romantic School of artists, in reaction against the growing crystalization of bourgeois culture, sought either to combat it or shock it (as did Berlioz or Victor Hugo) or to run away from it to exotic lands or to a Gothic Middle Ages of their own imagination. Delacroix, although not indulging in the excesses and exaggerations of some of the Romantic fraternity, nevertheless was one of their acknowledged leaders. We find therefore in his work many of the leit-motifs of Romanticism, the portrayal of the elemental qualities of wild animals, the exotic note of African sketches (illustration 393) and illustrations for *Les Chroniques de France*, for *Hamlet*, and for *Faust*. The lithograph, *La Sœur de Dugesclin* (illustration 394), from *Les Chroniques de France* is a most inspired reconstruction of medieval romance. It has color, movement, drama, it is beautifully drawn; in a word a *chef d'œuvre*. Eckermann in his *Conversations with Goethe* in 1826 records the poet's reactions when the first proofs of the *Faust* lithographs (illustration 395) were sent to him from Paris:

The longer this excellent design was looked at, the greater seemed the intelligence of the artist; who made no figure like another, but in each expressed some different part of the action. "M. Delacroix," said Goethe, "is a man of great talent who has found in Faust his proper nourishment. The French censure his wildness, but it suits him well here. He will, I hope, go through all Faust, and I anticipate a special pleasure from the witches' kitchen and the scenes on the Brocken. We can see that he has a good knowledge of life, for which a city like Paris has given him the best opportunity." I observed that these designs greatly conduce to the comprehension of the poem. "Undoubtedly," said Goethe, "for the more perfect imagination of such an artist constrains us to think the situations as beautiful as he has conceived them himself. And if I must confess that M. Delacroix has in some scenes surpassed my own notions, how much more will the reader find all in full life and surpassing

his imagination."

In the career of that short-lived genius Théodore Chassériau (1819–56) the conflicting principles of Ingres and Delacroix were resolved and blended. He combined the purity of Ingres with the richness of Delacroix. His print *œuvre* consists of a series of etchings for *Othello* and a few other etchings and lithographs, of which the *Venus Anadyomène* is an outstanding example (illustration 396). It is interesting to discover that in the nineteenth century artists made more and more use of the nude as a compositional element. They might call their compositions by some fancy name such as *Odalisque, Olympia, Venus, Bather, The Horoscope*, but the chief interest after all was in the nude human figure. A group of prints (illustrations 396–403) give an idea of the great variety of approach to a single theme. The point of view expressed by these artists begins to approximate the concept of art for art's sake: subject matter is less important than the personality of the artist and a new and original manner of expressing it. Whistler was to establish the doctrine of art for art's sake in its most complete form. The theory works successfully in those cases where the artist's personality is richly endowed, where the artist's mentality and feelings become the lens which concentrates some leading idea of humanity or nature as a whole, a definite *Weltanschauung*. In the hands of a petty or incomplete personality, the result becomes banality.

The great painter Gustave Courbet (1819–77) made only one lithograph, *The Apostle Jean Journet Setting out for the Conquest of Universal Harmony* (illustration 404). Courbet, an expansive, robust, somewhat demagogic personality, championed the doctrine of realism (which viewed in the perspective of time turns out to be far from photographic realism). Not abstract or ideal or exotic subjects, he maintained, but real life, was important. However, when he thought that he was copying nature, he really was being only an honest, vigorous, and skillful painter. He was filled with the radical and humanitarian notions current in his time, was persecuted for his active participation in the short-lived Paris Commune of 1871, and died in exile in Switzerland.

One offshoot of the realistic movement was the program of the Return to Nature which animated a group of artists who went to live around the Forest of Fontainebleau. The leading members of this School of Barbizon, as they were sometimes called, were Jacque, Millet, Daubigny, Théodore Rousseau, and Dupré. The names of Corot, Diaz, Barye, and Daumier are often associated with them. They produced landscapes and rustic scenes in much the same spirit as the Dutch landscape etchers and painters of the seventeenth century. Charles Jacque, an industrious landscape and genre painter, made almost

a thousand etchings which, though not deep or profound, nevertheless exhibit a great variety of technical approaches in etching, drypoint, and roulette work. Jean François Millet (1814–75) in his dozen important etchings shows a greater depth and nobility of feeling. Norman, peasant-born, Millet, after years of struggle in Paris, returned to the country to consecrate himself to the epic of the soil.

Peasant subjects [he wrote] suit my nature best, for I must confess, at the risk of your taking me for a socialist, that the human side is what touches me most in art, and that could I only do what I liked, or at least attempt to do it, I would paint nothing that was not the result of an impression directly received from Nature, whether in landscape or in figures. . . . I have been reproached for not observing detail; I see it, but I prefer to construct the *synthesis* which as an artistic effort is higher and more robust. You reproach me with insensibility to charm; why, I open your eyes to that which you do not perceive, but which is none the less real: the dramatic.

Many of his famous prints were variations of subjects used in his paintings: the etchings of *The Gleaners, The Diggers, The Churner, The Man with the Wheelbarrow, The Shepherdess Knitting* (illustration 405), *Woman Feeding a Child, The Woolcarder,* and the lithograph of *The Sower.* Millet's work in a sense was a reflection of certain social theories of the time, as promulgated for example by P. J. Prud'hon:

To paint men in the sincerity of their nature and their habits, at their work, accomplishing their civic and domestic duties, with their actual countenances, above all without posturing; to surprise them in undress of their consciousness, as an aim of general education: such seems to me to be the real starting point of modern art.

The purely landscape aspect of the Barbizon School was expressed in the few etchings of Rousseau and the thirty-four etchings and lithographs of Jean Baptiste Camille Corot (1796–1875). Once during a discussion of Delacroix, Corot said, "He is an eagle and I am only a skylark." In a sense this gives the keynote of his character and achievement, at least as far as his prints were concerned. In his prints he was never the great figure painter, but rather the lyric poet celebrating the delicate and subtle moods of nature. In his etchings and in his *clichés verres* (illustration 406) he built up his effects with a free, almost careless interweaving of lines which suggested rather than defined the forms. He always painted from imagination rather than *en plein air.* When Corot was asked by a colleague for the secret of his painting he replied, "All you have to do is to look at the large masses with half-closed eyes." Yes, and when you want to see the

details? "Then I close my eyes completely." Similar in spirit to the Barbizon landscapes, though not by an artist associated with them, are the thirty-odd etchings of the Dutchman Johann Barthold Jongkind (1819–91). Like Corot's, his effects were built up by wild and wayward lines, though with greater economy than Corot and with a more vital and nervous stroke. The *Porte d'Honfleur* (illustration 407) is a marvel of direct and forceful approach to a landscape scene.

The discussion of landscape painting and etching inevitably leads us to England, for English poets and artists, especially in the last two hundred years, have shown a notable and sensitive appreciation of landscape. At the beginning of the century the activity in oil and watercolor painting was paralleled by the production of many prints, etchings by Crome (illustration 411), Daniell, and Read, soft ground etchings by Cottman, Girtin, and J. R. Cozens, aquatints by Alexander Cozens, Prout, and David Cox (the *Treatise on Landscape Painting* of 1814). But the two most important artists in landscape were Turner and Constable. Turner's *Liber Studiorum* was projected in direct emulation of Claude's sketches in his *Liber Veritatis* which had been translated into etching and mezzotint by Earlom in 1777. The set was planned to consist of one hundred combined etchings and mezzotints, but the project was abandoned by Turner owing to lack of popular support after seventy-one had been formally published between the years 1807 to 1819. In most cases the preliminary etched outline was made by Turner himself and proofs exist of the plates in this state. In ten subjects Turner himself then added the tone and washes by means of mezzotint. For the balance of the plates he employed such mezzotinters as Charles Turner, no relation (illustration 410), Say, Dunkarton, Clint, Lupton, and others. The *Liber Studiorum* expressed not Turner the great colorist and pathfinder admired by the modern artists of today, but Turner the traditionalist who summed up the landscape schools of the past (especially of Claude) and, in his delineations of wild scenery, the Romantic School current in his day. In his "Prospectus" to the series in 1807, he announced that he "intended in this publication to attempt a classification of the various styles of landscape, viz. the historic, mountainous, pastoral, marine, and architectural." It is as examples of composed or heroic landscapes rather than for their direct observation of nature that Turner's plates are valued today. For direct transcripts from nature, for the moving and subtle delineation of atmospheric effects, for wind and clouds and rain, for sunset and dawn, for the freshness of dew and the brightness of sun, we turn to the collaboration of the painter John Constable and the mezzotinter David Lucas. The first set, *Various Subjects of Landscape,* from which *Summer Evening* is taken (illustra-

tion 409), was published in its completed form in 1833. In a tribute to Lucas, Constable wrote, "His great urbanity and integrity are equaled only by his skill as an engraver; and the scenes transmitted by his hand are such as I have ever preferred. For the most part, they are those with which I have the strongest associations—those of my earliest years, when in the cheerful morn of life, I looked to nature with unceasing joy." Constable as a painter was to have considerable influence on Delacroix and others of the French School, for the freshness of his color and the fidelity of his observation of nature. It is to be regretted that Constable did not make more than two or three original etchings, for his *Milford Bridge near Salisbury* (illustration 408) is a vigorous work filled with atmosphere and light.

The revival of interest in the woodcut began in France and England in the 1830s. The way had been prepared by Thomas Bewick of Newcastle (1753–1828). This provincial engraver began in the tradition of the crude and popular woodcut, but in the course of his long life perfected a new style of xylography, the white line engraving. He was not the first to have made such engravings but he was the first to have worked up the technique into a practical method. By working on end grain wood with engraving tools instead of a knife, he was able to build up compositions in which white lines of hitherto unachieved fineness became the dominant motif. This procedure was more in the true spirit of the medium since it is easier to work from black to white on wood and engrave highlights and break up black masses with fine white lines than it is to scoop out wood on both sides of a black line. His two most famous works were the *History of British Birds*, 1797–1804, and the *History of British Quadrupeds*, 1790, written and illustrated by himself. His plates of natural history are interesting for their able rendering of textures, plumage, and the like. But we turn especially to the tailpieces and vignettes which he inserted at various places in his books. They are filled with charming, racy, and humorous observation of English country life (illustrations 413 and 414). It is England seen by a man of the people, which Bewick always was. In the hands of his followers in England and France white line wood engraving became an efficient reproductive medium especially in connection with book illustration. Xylography had always had this great advantage over lithography and the intaglio process—the cuts could be printed simultaneously with the letterpress. The regular woodcut, however, had the disadvantage of being crude and lacking in subtlety. With the new method this disability was obviated, since wood engraving could reproduce tonal effects with great flexibility. The impulse of a new technique combined with both the demand of the rising middle-class culture for cheap illustrated books and the

existence of a flourishing school of artists produced the so-called renaissance of French book illustration. In 1835 appeared *Gil Blas* with Gigoux's romantic illustrations; in 1838 Curmer's edition of *Paul and Virginia*; in 1842 Grandville's sprightly *Les Scènes Privées des Animaux*. There is not space enough to consider all the charming and interesting works that came out in the first half of the century with illustrations by Vernet, Raffet, Meissonier, Grandville, Daumier, Gavarni, the Johannots, and others. The name of Doré is associated with imposing illustrations of the Bible, Dante, Coleridge, Rabelais, and Balzac's *Contes Drolatiques*. Doré (1833–83) was an exuberant, fantastic, and at times melodramatic and superficial illustrator. His fertility of invention was remarkable. Less known are his extraordinary illustrations to Blanchard Jerrold's *London* (illustration 412), a spirited, comprehensive, and somewhat lurid commentary on the heights and depths of a great city. One of the most striking of his designs in the series, the *Prisoners Taking Their Exercise in a Courtyard*, was the inspiration for one of Van Gogh's famous paintings.

In Germany woodcut illustration also was popular. Inspired by Vernet's *Napoleon*, Kugler and Menzel brought out in 1840 their monumental *History of Frederick the Great*. Adolph Menzel (1815–1905) was in many ways an amazing artist, amazing in his mastery of minute and factual detail, which he marshaled, by patient research, into some of the most extraordinary historical reconstructions the world has ever seen. He had what might be called a factual imagination: facts inspired him to his highest flights. His reconstruction of the life and times of Frederick the Great in the aforementioned history as well as in the illustrations to Frederick the Great's literary works, and the costumes of his army, was truly unique. Other outstanding works out of an unusually productive *œuvre* are his illustrations to Kleist's *Der Zerbrochene Krug* and the series of lithographs entitled *Versuche auf Stein mit Pinsel und Schabeisen* (illustration 417). Mention should be made of the few woodcuts designed in a very personal style by the painter Casper David Friedrich (illustration 418). Ludwig Richter (illustration 420) stands revealed in his work as a charming, benevolent, and sentimental personality, a child who never grew up. It is interesting to note that in his drawings there are no grown-ups: his men and women are never of adult stature, they are merely bigger children. He is at his best when illustrating folk song or fairy tale. A sweet and sentimental charm shines through all his work, a nostalgia for the good old times when life was *gemütlich* and pleasures simple. The complement to Richter's pious and sentimental picture of German life is provided by the woodcuts and text of Wilhelm Busch (1832–1908). Here we find gentle satire and good-humored

insight into the foibles of Herr Biedermeyer and his family (illustration 416). The pictorial adventures of his characters, Max and Moritz, were prototypes of our comic strips.

Although the new technique of wood engraving was perfected in England, it did not at first stimulate the artists in the production of illustrated books; it was used rather in the interests of factual journalism such as the *Illustrated London News*. In the sixties, however, many designs were made on wood by Rossetti, Sandys, Whistler, Keene, and other *Punch* artists. Later William Morris, Walter Crane, Shannon, and Ricketts revived the use of the woodcut for book illustration. *When Adam Delved,* designed by Burne-Jones, with the decorative border by William Morris, was the frontispiece to the Kelmscott edition of Morris's stirring socialist romance, *A Dream of John Ball* (illustration 415).

The name of William Blake carries with it the magic of an ineffable secret: he was a man apart, a mystic whose values were created not of this world but of an inner and transcendent light. He would have been the same had he been born at any time and place. It was one of the ironic touches of history that he was born in 1757 and lived for seventy years in the city where Reynolds and Stothard were great and popular. He was an engraver by profession and spent a large part of his life doing hackwork for publishers to earn his daily bread. At the age of fourteen he was apprenticed to a second-rate engraver named Basire, whose rather mechanical system of engraving he absorbed. It is unfortunate that he had no better model, for it was not until the end of his life that he was able to shake off some of these mechanical mannerisms and evolve a more beautiful and flexible medium for the expression of his ideas. After his apprenticeship he studied for a time at the Royal Academy School. He already had very definite ideas about art and recounts an anecdote about Moser the academician (of whom we have already heard in connection with Rowlandson):

I was once looking over the prints from Rafael and Michel Angelo in the library of the Royal Academy; Moser came to me and said, "You should not study these old, hard, stiff and dry unfinished works of art. Stay a little and I will show you what you should study." He then went and took me down Le Brun's and Rubens' galleries. How did I secretly rage. I also spoke my mind. . . . I said to Moser, "These things that you call finished are not even begun. How can they then be finished? The man who does not know the beginning never can know the end of art. . . . I am happy to say that Rafael never was from my earliest childhood hidden from me. I saw, and I knew immediately the difference between Rafael and Rubens."

These two artists symbolized for Blake the difference

between good and bad art. Drawing, the firm and precise outline, was to him more important than color, tone, and chiaroscuro; in this he was truly Gothic. Art was never the imitation of natural objects, always the expression of an abstract idea. For this reason the sensuousness of Rubens repelled him.

Blake had two great vehicles of expression, poetry and art, and they went hand in hand. He had a momentary flash of acclaim with his *Poetical Sketches* in a circle of fashionable ladies and bluestockings. But the productions of his genius were not understood and he was driven to find a cheap way of setting down in permanent form the thoughts and images that teemed in his consciousness. To this end he perfected the method of "relief etching." John Thomas Smith describes it as Blake told it to him:

Blake, after deeply perplexing himself as to the mode of accomplishing the publication of his illustrated songs, without their being subject to the expense of letter-press, his brother Robert stood before him in one of his visionary imaginations, and so decidedly directed him in the way in which he ought to proceed that he immediately followed his advice, by writing his poetry, and drawing his marginal subjects of embellishments in outline upon the copper plate with an impervious liquid, and then eating the plain parts or lights away with aqua-fortis considerably below them, so that the outlines were left as a stereotype. The plates in this state were then printed in any tint that he wished, to enable him or Mrs. Blake to color the marginal figures in imitation of drawings.

In this manner he produced whole books with text, illustrations, and marginal decorations. The first work to be published was the *Songs of Innocence* in 1789. In 1794 he finished the complement to this, the *Songs of Experience*, in which appears that superb poem on the nature of evil, "Tiger! Tiger!" (illustration 421). He made numerous other books, *The Book of Thel*, 1789, *The Marriage of Heaven and Hell*, 1793, and the various *Prophetic Books* ending up with the *Milton* of 1808 and the *Jerusalem*, finished in 1821 (illustration 422). As illustrated books they are perfection, for the artist-author has completely realized his intention. If much of his writing and visual symbols are seemingly obscure, it is because we have not taken the trouble to learn his language or are not sensitive to mystical experience. Blake had a definite world-conception that was as complete as any single man has ever worked out. It was, however, so far beyond the ken of his contemporaries that he was for the most part misunderstood and neglected. Even when Blake exhibited and later engraved his large picture of the *Canterbury Pilgrims* (1810) —surely understandable enough in its delineation of types—he met with failure. He was given a commission

to illustrate the first Eclogue of Virgil for an edition of translations published by Dr. Thornton in 1821. He made seventeen small wood engravings which narrowly escaped recutting since they were not in the style of the mechanical wood engravings of the time. Underneath the first cut the following apology was printed:

The Illustrations of this English Pastoral are by the famous Blake, the illustrator of Young's Night Thoughts and Blair's Grave; who designed and engraved them himself. This is mentioned, as they display less of art than genius, and are much admired by some eminent painters.

Today the book is remembered only because of these wood engravings, for they are among the most lovely designs ever made (illustrations 425 and 426).

Blake's last years would have been passed in abject poverty, had it not been for the friendship and generous aid of John Linnell. It was he who commissioned Blake to engrave the *Illustrations of the Book of Job*, published in twenty-one plates in 1826. This is unquestionably Blake's masterpiece and one of the choicest treasures in the world of art. It is an epic of the imagination, outstanding in pictorial design and felicity of execution, and endowed with a profundity of hidden meaning that only years of study will reveal. Blake has made the problem of Good and Evil the central theme of his drama, for such it may properly be called; and he has resolved this everlasting problem by departing somewhat from the original Bible story and conceiving the conflict in terms of man himself, by making it, in the words of Joseph Wicksteed, "a primarily subjective experience; the account of a man's inward struggle and triumph; the conflict between his indwelling Good and Evil powers." It is Blake's great achievement, alas not recognized during his lifetime, that he not only conceived this stupendous cosmic drama of the human soul, but he also carried it out in a moving and beautiful and precise formulation. One of the loveliest engravings of the series is number fourteen, *When the Morning Stars Sang Together*, and it is reproduced herewith (illustration 423). Two years later Blake died while he was working on a series of engravings for Dante's *Inferno* (illustration 424). Samuel Palmer thus gives his recollection of the man:

He was energy itself, and shed around him a kindling influence, an atmosphere of life, full of the ideal. . . . He was a man without a mask, his aim single, his path straightforward, his wants few, so he was free, noble, and happy. His voice and manner were quiet, yet all awake with intellect. Above the tricks of littleness or the least taint of affectation, with a natural dignity which few would have dared to affront, he was gentle and affectionate, loving to be with little children and to talk about them. . . . Those may laugh at this who did not know such

a one as Blake, but of him it is the simple truth.

A small band of young artists gathered with John Linnell in admiration of the venerable Blake. Chief among them were Edward Calvert, George Richmond, and Samuel Palmer. Blake the mystic they did not understand, but they loved and revered the pastoral Blake of the *Songs of Innocence* and Virgil's *Eclogue*. Under the direct inspiration of Blake (for he never made a print after 1830) Calvert made a dozen engravings on copper and wood and two lithographs. *The Bride*, *The Cyder Feast*, *The Brook*, and *The Return Home* are filled with sweet arcadian charm. *The Chamber Idyll* (illustration 427) in particular for its delicacy and ecstatic mood and masterly execution is one of the most perfect little prints ever made. Calvert lived until 1883, very much introverted, destroying almost more than he produced. Samuel Palmer (1805–81) continued the pastoral tradition in his elaborate, minutely worked out etchings (illustration 428). "Those who have seen him," wrote his son, "sitting, sable in hand, hour after hour behind tissue paper, pencilling, in varnish, silver cloudets round a moon; or have seen him revelling in the ferocity of seething mordant with which he sometimes loved to excavate an emphatic passage, will not wonder that he achieved only thirteen etchings." He was a typical Victorian artist; and the *Memoir of Palmer* written by his son gave Victorians an insight into what they thought was artistic temperament.

In every century, as we have seen, there were one or two artists who stand apart from the main current of their time by the intensity of their inner life or their difficulties in adjusting themselves to their surroundings. In the sixteenth century there were Duvet and Baldung Grien; in the seventeenth century, Elsheimer, Seghers, and Rembrandt; in the eighteenth century, Gabriel de St. Aubin and possibly Goya; in the nineteenth century Blake. To this company of what might be called the Brotherhood of the Inner Life four more names must be added: Meryon, Bresdin, Redon, and Ensor. Charles Meryon (1821–68) had a tragic life: there was in him a strain of morbid melancholia, he suffered poverty, and he died insane. But no one has ever drawn a portrait of a city with such vivid intensity, or endowed every brick and stone with such personality. And this in spite of the fact that he had no great technical facility in etching. Such etchings as the *Petit Pont*, the *Galerie de Notre Dame*, the *Rue des Mauvais Garçons*, the *St. Etienne du Mont*, the *Abside de Notre Dame* (illustration 430), all etched in the years 1850 to 1854, are immortal. Especially moving is the *Morgue* of 1854, as successful in its evocation of a mood as it is in its superb rendering of buildings. Jules Andrieu reports Meryon's comment on his etching, *Le Stryge* (illustration 429), which gives a clue as to why his prints

have such a moving effect: it is because he was a visionary who lived not in the present but in the past or in a world of his own. Picking up an impression of *Le Stryge*, Meryon said:

You can't tell why my comrades, who know their work better than I do, fail with the Tower of St. Jacques. It is because the modern square is the principal thing for them, and the Middle Age tower an accident. Even if they saw, as I see, an enemy behind each battlement and arms through each loophole; if they expected, as I do, to have the boiling oil and the molten lead poured down on them, they would do far finer things than I can do. For often I have to patch my plate so much that I ought indeed to be a tinker. My comrades are sensible fellows. They are never haunted by this fellow [Le Stryge]. The monster is mine, and that of the men who built this tower of St. Jacques. He means stupidity, cruelty, lust, hypocrisy; they have all met in that beast.

A legend has been built up by certain critics around the name of Rodolphe Bresdin (1825–85). They nicknamed him Chien-Caillou and endowed him with an ultrabohemian character and a garret to live in after the manner of Murger. Redon, whose teacher he was, gives a more sensitive and reasonable estimate of his character. Like Redon himself, he was a gentle visionary, and Redon recounts how "his words directed the painter's eye toward the two worlds of life, toward two realities which it was impossible to separate without a diminution of our art." *The Good Samaritan* (illustration 431) is a masterpiece of miniaturelike workmanship and fantasy. Redon's own expression is more austere and noble. He sought to give form—always in plastic terms—to the contents of dream and to flights of imagination, inspired by Poe, Goya, the Bible, and Flaubert's *Temptation of St. Anthony*. Among his hundred lithographs are many of startling originality, notably the *Pégase Captif* (illustration 433), *Yeux Clos*, *L'Aile*, *Buddha*, *L'Arbre*, *Le Jour*, and *La Mort*. Technically they exhibit a range from delicate grays to rich vibrant blacks. Walter Pach has pointed out the extent to which Redon was a precursor of certain modern movements. Blake, of course, had said many of the same things as Redon, but Blake was not known in France. James Ensor was the last of the great visionaries. His highly personal and somewhat macabre art is represented in a characteristic etching, *Death Pursuing the Human Horde* (illustration 432).

In 1862 Baudelaire wrote an article with the title "L'Eau-forte est à la Mode"—Etching Is in Fashion—in which he speaks of the work of Meryon, Legros, Manet, Ribot, Whistler, and Jongkind and of the activities of the print-publisher Cadart. Quite a number of professional etchers were attracting notice: the amiable and accomplished Bracquemond (1833–1914), who etched some interesting birds and two striking portraits of Edmond de Goncourt and Meryon, and who gave technical instruction to Corot, Millet, Rousseau, Manet, and Degas. There was Lalanne, who produced a new textbook on etching and many uninspired plates, and Felix Buhot (1847–98), who etched a number of picturesque and whimsical scenes in Paris and London in the seventies and eighties (illustration 435). Alphonse Legros (1837–99) started by making crude but powerfully felt etchings of monastic life; later he went to England and turned out soft, innocuous landscapes. The leading British etcher of the time was an amateur, the well-known surgeon Sir Francis Seymour Haden (1818–1910). He was an able and somewhat dictatorial Victorian gentleman who had very definite ideas and knew how to express them, both with his pen and his etching needle. He liked etchings and collected them. He did not like engravings and reproductive work in general, and he wrote against them, exalting etching at their expense, and making a fetish of spontaneous originality. Perhaps a reaction against mediocre reproductive engraving was needed, but he went too far and condemned it all from Marcantonio to Moreau le Jeune. He himself also etched and used to carry around with him in his carriage a copper plate, ready to draw upon. He made over two hundred etchings and there was nothing amateurish about them except that they were done in his leisure time. Like many English country gentlemen he had a real feeling for landscape, and since he was never at a loss to express his feelings positively, the best of his etchings are vigorous and even tender transcripts from nature. Rembrandt was his master, and he made good use of his instruction. Such plates as *Egham, Water Meadow, Egham Lock* (illustration 434), *Sunset in Ireland, Kensington Gardens, Windmill Hill No. 1, Nine Barrow Down, Challow Farm*, and the five Welsh plates, are a contribution to landscape etching.

Haden's brother-in-law was the American James A. McNeill Whistler, and as they both had rather peppery personalities, they did not get along very well together. Whistler was born at Lowell, Massachusetts, in 1834. He attended West Point for a while, but not finding military discipline to his liking, went to Paris to study art. He made friends with Legros, Bracquemond, Degas, and Fantin-Latour. In 1858 he published a set of etchings, *The French Set*, containing such notable plates as *The Kitchen, La Vielle aux Loques, The Mustard Woman*, and *Street in Saverne*. In some of them the influence of Jacque's and Meryon's etchings is visible. In the same year he went to London which became more or less his headquarters until his death in 1903. He was as able with his tongue and pen as he was with his brush and etching needle, and remained a thorn in the flesh of British philistinism all his life. In his famous lawsuit with Ruskin, resulting in

an award of one farthing damages, he scored a moral triumph over the very British dictator of prevailing taste. Shortly after his arrival in London he made a series of sixteen carefully worked out etchings known as the *Thames Set* (published in 1871), of which the outstanding examples are the *Black Lion Wharf, Rotherhithe*, the *Lime-burner* (illustration 437), the *Hungerford Bridge* (illustration 436), the *Thames Police*, and *Limehouse*. In these early etchings, inspired by the bustle of London's shipping and industry, he made a complete statement of what he saw. In his painting he was influenced to a certain extent by Velazquez and Rossetti, by the Impressionists, and by Japanese prints. He painted a number of well-known portraits, including those of Carlyle, his Mother, Duret, and the Leylands. A reflection of this phase of his activity is seen in the drypoint of his niece Annie Haden (illustration 438). He was very fond of this plate, and wrote on the proof in the Avery collection, "One of my very best." Mansfield quotes him as saying that if he were required to rest his reputation on any one print, as a matter of technical achievement, he would be willing to rest it on that. Other notable portrait prints are *Bibi Lalouette, Becquet, Riault the Engraver, Drouet*, and *Fanny Leyland*. In the course of the years his artistic expression changed. His signature developed from the name Whistler into a stylized butterfly. He became interested not in protraying a scene in its detailed form but in suggesting a mood, in rendering and setting down a definite "impression" from which all but the contributing details were tastefully excluded. In this he was allied to the French Impressionists, but where their leading motive was a greater sense of reality or scientific management of light, his keynote was largely decorative, a poetic impression of exquisiteness and irresponsible beauty. He truly became the butterfly that composed lyrics in a lighter vein. His etchings have all the spontaneous charm of an improvisation, but many of his lesser plates suffer from this very quality, for the sketch can easily become trivial. "Taste," wrote Arthur Symons, "in Whistler was carried to the point of genius and became creative." The full expression of this attitude appeared in the twelve etchings known as the *First Venice Set* published in 1880, and which contained the *Palaces*, the *Nocturne*, the *Traghetto*, the *Doorway*, and the *Riva* (illustration 439). He repeated this success with another *Venice Set*, the *Twenty-six Etchings of 1886*. In these etchings the effect is greatly enhanced by Whistler's masterly printing. Indeed so dependent was he on printing that an etching like *Nocturne* is practically a monotype. In addition to his four hundred and sixty etchings he made about one hundred and sixty lithographs which have much the same qualities, fugitive visions, delicate and poetic effects of atmosphere, such as the *Thames, St. Giles in the Fields, Little Evelyn, The Horoscope*, and *Old*

Battersea Bridge. The effect produced by a lithotint such as *Nocturne: The Thames at Battersea* (illustration 440), he has also produced in words:

And when the evening mist clothes the riverside with poetry, as with a veil, and the poor buildings lose themselves in the dim sky, and the tall chimneys become campanili, and the warehouses are palaces in the night, and the whole city hangs in the heavens, and fairy land is before us—then the wayfarer hastens home; the working man and the cultured one, the wise man and the one of pleasure, cease to understand, as they have ceased to see, and Nature, who, for once, has sung in tune, sings her exquisite song to the artist alone.

Whistler, in his writing and in his work, carried to its extreme the doctrine of art for art's sake, where the artist's personality and taste become the sole source of value. In his reaction against the stodginess of the Victorian storytelling picture he went to another extreme. In spite of his ruthless wit and striving for effect, he had his integrity as an artist, and he was a patient and tireless and fastidious craftsman.

A picture is finished [said he] when all trace of the means used to bring about the end has disappeared. To say of a picture, as is often said in its praise, that it shows great and earnest labor, is to say that it is incomplete and unfit for view. Industry in Art is a necessity—not a virtue—and any evidence of the same, in the production, is a blemish, not a quality; a proof, not of achievement, but of absolutely insufficient work, for work alone will efface the footsteps of work. The work of a master reeks not of the sweat of the brow—suggests no effort—and is finished from the beginning.

Whistler has his place in history as an aristocratic and exquisite poet, a high priest of Personal Art, that "goddess of dainty thought—reticent of habit, abjuring all obtrusiveness, purposing in no way to better others—seeking and finding the beautiful in all conditions and in all times."

In France a group of Whistler's contemporaries were making art history. They were all great painters, and because they were distinguished artists their prints have an importance and significance greater than that of the often larger production of the professional printmakers. First there was Manet (1832–83). In his famous *Manifesto to the Public* in 1867 he wrote: "M. Manet has always recognized genius wherever he found it and he has never aimed to overthrow an ancient tradition of art or to establish a new one. He has merely sought to be himself and no other." This sums up his achievement in a few words. In neither his life nor his works was Manet deliberately subversive of tradition; viewed in the perspective of time, much of his art, that was so excoriated by con-

temporary criticism, is seen to be merely a purification of the academic tendencies of his day. The one thing he insisted on was that art be true to life and to the personality of the creator, and he sought for a technique that would most adequately give expression to this for himself. Manet had independent means and was essentially a gentleman of the world. He went to his studio and painted pictures, "as regularly," said Zola, "as other people go their offices and countinghouses." He made seventy-five etchings and twenty-one lithographs. His etchings are typically painter's etchings: he was more interested in color and tactile values than in line-work as an end in itself. He had what Baudelaire called "*un gout decidé pour la realité.*" With Manet this enhanced vision of form was instinctive and immediate: he did not have to perform a laborious synthesis in order to give it expression, and it is this that gives his prints their vigor, spontaneity, and verve (illustration 442). His etching, *Olympia* (illustration 402), a free translation of his famous painting, was etched as a frontispiece to a pamphlet that Zola wrote in defense of Manet's art.

Degas, like Manet, had independent means, but he was more aloof and sardonic in temperament. He had an absorbing passion to draw and paint, a passion to capture the elusive, to set down for all time the fleeting moment, to immortalize the significant gesture of movement. "You know how I hate to sell my work," he grumbled. "I always hope eventually to do better." Degas had a trenchant wit and many stories are told about him. Vollard relates:

Suddenly we heard someone call "Monsieur Degas!" It was Vibert, the well-known painter of the Cardinals. "You must come to see our exhibition of watercolors," he said. Then he gave a sidelong glance at the old mackintosh Degas was wearing, and added: "You may find our frames and rugs a little too fancy for you, but art is always a luxury, isn't it?" "Yours, perhaps," retorted Degas, "but mine is an absolute necessity."

He painted and made pastels; he modeled in wax; he made drawings, countless studies which he hoarded in his studio; he experimented with etching and aquatint and lithograph. He made about sixty prints altogether, some of them frankly experimental but others among the most perfect and completely realized prints ever made. Take, for example, the lithograph, *Mlle Bécat aux Ambassadeurs* (illustration 443). How complete and moving is the evocation of the scene in the *café chantant*, the sight, the smell, the sound of it; or the *Sortie de Bain* (illustration 398), what a wealth of meaning there is in that intimate picture of a fat woman. The etching and aquatint, *Au Louvre* (illustration 444), contains a portrait of his friend

and fellow-artist Mary Cassatt. "Cassatt has infinite talent," Degas remarked musingly. "I remember the time we started a little magazine called *Le Jour et La Nuit* together. I was very much interested in print processes then, and had made countless experiments. . . . You can get extraordinary results with copper." Mary Cassatt, though American born, lived most of her life in France and painted chiefly mothers and children. She made a number of charming etchings and drypoints and some aquatints in color inspired by Japanese prints (illustration 445).

Pissarro had the largest print *œuvre* of any of the Impressionists, having made 127 etchings and 67 lithographs (illustration 446). Renoir, the healthiest and most sensuous and natural of the group, put the stamp of his expansive personality upon everything he touched, be it oil painting, pastel, sculpture, or his few etchings and lithographs (illustration 397). He created instinctively and elementally. He loved color and sunlight and children and motherhood and the ruddy skin and rounded forms of buxom women; and this love of his radiated from his every work. No greater contrast can be imagined than between Renoir and van Gogh, both sun-worshipers. But where Renoir just basked in the sun, van Gogh reached for it passionately to illumine the dark night of his soul. Van Gogh made only one etching, the striking portrait of Dr. Gachet (illustration 449). Van Gogh wrote to his brother:

I have seen Dr. Gachet, who gives me the impression of being rather eccentric, but his experience as a doctor must keep him balanced enough to combat the nervous trouble from which he certainly seems to me to suffer at least as seriously as I do. . . . When he spoke of Belgium and the days of the old painters, his grief-hardened face grew smiling again, and I really think that I shall keep on being friends with him and that I shall do his portrait.

Dr. Gachet was the same doctor who knew Meryon at the asylum of Charenton.

The name of Gauguin has been surrounded with a halo of romantic legend. His life, to be sure, was picturesque enough, wild adventures between Europe and South America, a successful business career, the renunciation of business and family for the pursuit of art, and finally the renunciation of a whole civilization in favor of a savage Eden which Strindberg dramatically rejected: "You have created a new heaven and a new earth, but I do not enjoy myself in the midst of your creation. It is too sun-drenched for me, who enjoy the play of light and shade." In Gauguin's life there was much travail of flesh and spirit.

I have known [he wrote] extreme misery, that is to say I have been hungry and I have been cold and all that follows therefrom. That is nothing or almost nothing; one gets used to it. But what is terrible in one's misery is the frustration of one's work, and of the development of one's intellectual faculties. It is true that suffering sharpens the faculties. But it must not be too much, otherwise it kills you.

There is no trace of poverty, suffering, and sickness in his works from the South Seas: the forms are big and serene, the mood exalted. Out of odd flat bits of wood he made wood engravings such as never had been made before, blocks that were cut and scratched and sandpapered in unconventional ways, forms that were distorted in the interest of design or emotive effect, subjects that were taken from Tahitian life and legend.

It is because these prints go back to the most primitive time of engraving [he wrote to de Monfried] that they are interesting. Wood engraving for illustration has become like photogravure, detestable. A drawing by Degas beside a copy of the drawing done by hatchers! I am sure that in time my wood engravings being done now will have a certain value.

(At the time there were no buyers at eight francs apiece.) The best of these, such as *Noa Noa, Nave Nave Fenva* (illustration 450), *Maruru, Te Faruru,* and *Te Atua,* have a strange and moving beauty. Stripped of legend and fable the story of Gauguin is simply the story of a man with a terrific urge to create, the triumph of a demonic will.

Spend yourself, spend yourself again! . . . I believe that life has no meaning unless one lives it with a will, at least to the limit of one's will. Virtue, good, evil are nothing but words, unless one takes them apart in order to build up something with them; they do not win their true meaning until one knows how to apply them.

Cézanne was the painter's painter, that is to say his great contribution was technical and only indirectly in terms of the human spirit. He was absorbed during his whole life in what Read calls "the knitting together of form and color into a coordinated harmony," or as Cézanne himself put it, "to make a Poussin out of nature," to combine the architectonic concept of the classical painters with the color perception of the Impressionists.

Everything we see [said Cézanne] is dispersed and disappears. Nature is always the same, but nothing remains of it, nothing of what we see. Our art should give to nature the thrill of continuance with the appearance of all its changes. It should enable us to feel nature as eternal.

All this is related to the problem of Cézanne as a painter, but it is also reflected in his prints—he made but six—

such as the color lithograph, *The Bathers* (illustration 403). Here the artist has created a microcosm, as Wilenski calls it, of planes and forms and color in which each part is pleasurably and vitally connected with every other part. To do this successfully, to make the parts all fit together harmoniously, a certain amount of distortion is necessary. The distortion which most people notice is the deviation from their preconceived notion of the appearance of the human figure, although there are equally wide deviations from the appearance of other natural objects. If these people would stop fixing their eyes on the figures in their effort to correct the supposed defects of anatomy, and, instead, look directly into the picture beyond the figures and enjoy the pleasurable perspective of space, then the figures would take their proper place and seem strangely solid and real. This is the beginning of an adventure in perception and appreciation which will bring great delight and continued satisfaction to the seeing eyes. The people who are bothered by distortion are like the people who refuse to enjoy Chaucer because the words are so queer.

And now we come to the Gay Nineties. There were the posters, a new and fascinating art by Lautrec, Steinlen (illustration 456), Cheret (illustration 455), Willette, and Léandre. There were the woodcuts and wood engravings which the etcher and engraver Auguste Lepère and his associates were trying to revive as a popular art in the publication *L'Image.* Bonnard and Vuillard set down their breezy impressions of Paris in color lithographs (illustrations 447 and 448) so different from the precise statements of Boys or Girtin. Auguste Rodin, in the course of a busy sculptor's life, executed a few spirited drypoints (illustration 457). Forain was drawing and etching and Vallotton cutting woodcuts in *art nouveau* style (illustration 458). Across the channel Beardsley and Max Beerbohm were making drawings, and Conder and Rothenstein and Shannon making lithographs. But the artist who perhaps best summed up the period, its odd mixture of glamour and tinsel, its decadence and *fin de siècle* pose, was Henri de Toulouse-Lautrec. He was born in 1864, a descendant of the famous Counts of Toulouse. He died of drink and dissipation at the age of thirty-seven. He was crippled and conspicuously ugly: fate cast him for the role of observer. He watched life, but was never of it, the sporting life at the racecourse (illustration 454), the gay life of the theatre, music hall, and cabaret (illustrations 452 and 453). He lived for a while in a *maison close* and became the friend and confidant of the inmates. It was out of this intimate knowledge that he drew the set of ten lithographs, *Elles,* and the vividly realized *Etude de Femme* (illustration 399). He started making lithographs in 1892 and in the next nine years drew more than three hundred and fifty. He had a trenchant and vital line

and a sardonic sense of character. *"Vraiment, vous êtes le génie de la déformation,"* exclaimed Yvette Guilbert when she saw one of his caricatures of her, but she grew to like it just the same. Yvette Guilbert, the greatest of music hall singers, summed up the period, too, in her way. "Yvette begins to sing," wrote Arthur Symons, "and immediately the gay world that you see across the smoke of your cigarette, seems to unmask itself, becomes too suddenly serious, tragic, a piece of real existence."

So we come to the end of the nineteenth century, extraordinary in its variety and complexity, and brimming over with startling contrasts. No century has had richer material. There was a great impetus to printmaking not only through the enlargement of the buying public but also through the invention of new techniques, lithography and aquatint and the new wood engraving. But the technique which was to have the widest influence on the nineteenth-century art was photography. Through the development of photoengraving, the linecut and the halftone, it stripped regular printmaking completely of its reproductive function. It could make a facsimile of an artist's drawing more quickly and more cheaply than the other processes, and it had the further advantage that it could be printed simultaneously with letterpress. It was the Gillotype, or early version of the linecut, that supplanted lithography as the medium for political caricature in the fifties. Photography, as an art for itself, has passed through stages of experimentation, of commercialization, and of creative mastery.

No attempt has been made to trace the enormous development of the art and technique of photography during the nineteenth and twentieth centuries. That would require a separate book. Out of the wealth of material available, a few examples have been illustrated, both to signalize some of the pioneers of the process and also to typify the achievement of photography in such classes as the portrait and the documentary. Louis Jacques Mandé Daguerre, although he played a large role in the technical development of photography, does not fit into this book because *daguerreotypes* are unique positives and thus do not belong in the category of prints or multiple originals. "The first photographs made by a camera," writes Beaumont Newhall, "must be credited to Joseph Nicéphore Niepce. Although not a single example of these photographs remains today, his letters and eyewitness accounts leave no doubt that between 1816 and 1829 he succeeded many times in fixing the camera's image with comparative permanency." What he actually did was to fix, with bitumen, a negative image on a metal plate which could then be engraved and printed as one would a regular print. Several of these plates have survived, and a print from one of them is shown in illustration 459. It is a reproduction of a seventeenth-century engraved portrait of Cardinal d'Amboise. Therefore Niepce really was the progenitor of modern photoengraving, a reproductive process. Nonetheless he also is supposed to have made photographs (he called them heliographs) from nature, but they have not survived. They were of course negative images (the dark values were light and the light values dark).

The true photograph, that is to say, one made with a negative from which any number of positives could be printed, was first made and perfected by an Englishman, William Henry Fox Talbot, around 1840. He used paper as the base for his negative and light-sensitive silver chloride as the image-making agent, and then fixed the image by washing out all the silver salts unaffected by light, by means of sodium hyposulfite (hypo). He called the prints thus obtained calotypes. A calotype by Talbot is reproduced as illustration 460. Further advances, such as the collodion or wet-plate process, the dry-plate process, gelatine film, fast lenses, and the like, have brought the technique of photography to its present state of perfection.

As an outstanding example of portraiture one might cite the calotype photographs of David Octavius Hill (1802–70). Typical is the portrait of Mrs. Anna Jameson (illustration 461). Hill was a Scotish painter who turned to photography, in collaboration with the chemist Adamson, to help him in his painting. Now he is remembered for his photographs and not for his paintings. Eugène Atget (1856–1927) devoted most of his life to making a straightforward portrait of every aspect of Paris life with a stand camera and dry plates. In his photograph of a shopwindow on the Avenue des Gobelins (illustration 462), the skillful use of the accidentals of window reflections contributes greatly to the vividness of the scene.

Photography functions at its best as a more or less faithful transcript of external reality. Only in the hands of a few masters have its limitations been transcended. Photography is of the moment, a snapshot, an instantaneous cross section of the outward aspect of things. It records behavior, not motives. By its objective documentation it has driven the artist to find an outlet on a subjective plane, as it were, to analyze and synthesize his own feelings, to explore the resources of symbolic expression and psychological nuance—the very things that the camera cannot do. The effect of photography on printmaking has been tangible and definite. Photoengraving has made printmaking less of a business and more of an art. The artist who now makes prints, as we shall see in the next chapter, speaks not as a copyist but as a creative artist working directly in a graphic medium. This has necessitated a new orientation, a new justification for prints. They must stand or fall as an independent art. Photography has had still another effect on art and

culture. Photomechanical processes have made the arts of all the world, even the most obscure and exotic, and also of the totality of the past, readily accessible through reproduction. This has been a boon to scholars, but for the creative artist it has brought about a facile eclecticism and a melange of many styles.

7. The Twentieth Century in Europe

If the keynote of the nineteenth century was personality, the keynote of the twentieth century is flux. The tempo of civilization has been steadily accelerating: lightning changes, violence, tumultuous upheavals, epoch-making discoveries are the order of the day. An old order is crumbling. The individual is being submerged in the coalescing of vast collective forces. Two of the greatest and most devastating wars the world has ever known were fought in this century; perhaps they are but successive chapters of a world catastrophe, the climax of which is yet to come. Countries, nations, and peoples are shuffled about on the world map as never before. Treaties are made to be broken, wars are waged without being declared. Human beings are exterminated on a scale that staggers the imagination. International morality is declared bankrupt; diplomacy becomes a sordid and shoddy piece of chicanery. Individual heroism, self-sacrifice, and idealism flourish side by side with cruelty, profiteering, and exploitation. Speed and more speed, power and more power! Man talks to man in the antipodes. We travel across a continent in a few hours, and around the world in a few days. Supersonic speed and transcendent power have been gained under the stimulus of war, that is to say, of mass murder. The fission of the atom has become a reality. Man travels from planet to planet. The Frankensteins of destruction are creeping up on mankind, while it plays with power politics. Man has become master of stupendous forces which he knows not how to use. Nature is in harness for nationality and monopoly, and not for humanity at large. Overpopulation is despoiling nature at an alarming rate.

Values are shifting from day to day: concepts of morality, of courts and justice, of property rights and human rights, movements of labor, of the individual and totalitarianism—nothing is stable or secure. Everybody is bewildered—or indifferent—the leaders as well as the led. Orozco made a powerful lithograph, *Leaders*—a restless sea of sombreros above which, through the exigencies of time and chance, there have been tossed up two or three other sombreros, no bigger or better than the rest: these are the leaders. Values are changing in literature, music, and art. The artists are searching, perhaps in vain, for a unifying or stable principle. Styles are born and flourish in bewildering succession. In addition to the older styles still current, there have appeared in the course of the century such movements as Pointillism, Fauvism, Cubism, Expressionism, Futurism, Orphism, Suprematism, Constructivism, Dadaism, Surrealism, Purism, Neoclassicism, Neoromanticism, Neoplasticism, *Die Neue Sachlichkeit*, Social Consciousness, Nonobjective Abstraction, Abstract Expressionism, Pop Art, Minimalism. Once, as we have seen, an epoch or a century dominated the artist's expression; later he molded his own manner of speech. Now the artist—Picasso for example—runs through a half dozen styles during his lifetime. Not only in their work but also in their lives are the artists drawn into participation. They are forced to reckon with a community relatively unresponsive to their real contribution; to reinterpret the old patterns of collector, patron, and dealer; and come to terms with society economically as well as esthetically. Gone are both the *bottega* and the ivory tower of yesterday. Art has become a business.

It was during the twentieth century that the strange manifestation known as modern art burst upon the world. For those who have traced the mutations of style, century by century, the development of this so-called new phenomenon at the end of the nineteenth century and the beginning of the twentieth century can come as no great surprise. Its history can be interpreted in terms of action and reaction, and the impact of certain discoveries upon the creative youth of the time. There was, for example, a revolt by the Impressionists against the official Salon tradition. When the Impressionists became successful and were imitated by a host of lesser fry, a younger generation reacted against the preoccupation with surface and light in favor of a more profound study of form and design. They turned for inspiration to a more plastic and possibly more universal art tradition than the bankruptcies of the Salon or the color researches of the Impressionists. Thus arose Postimpressionism, which includes much of modern art. They harked back to primitive woodcuts, to folk art in general, to the hitherto neglected sculpture and applied arts of Africa,

Persia, Mexico, or the South Pacific. Thus, modern art is not really a bolt out of the blue, but a logical development in keeping with the trend of the times. It is no mere coincidence that the decades before and after 1900 witnessed an unparalleled outburst of creative energy in the arts. It set a trend that is decisive even today. It established once and for all that the artist did not imitate nature but created something on his own. His aim was not the representation of nature but its transformation: nature or life seen through temperament. The artist insisted that a work of art was an entity separate from nature, an entity that had a life and function of its own, and obeyed its own laws and conventions. As Whistler aptly said: "Nature contains the elements, in color and form, of all pictures, as the keyboard contains the notes of all music. But the artist is born to pick and choose, and group with science, these elements, that the result may be beautiful. . . . To say to the painter that Nature is to be taken as she is, is to say to the player, that he may sit on the piano." And likewise a story is told of Matisse's reply to a question by an irate amateur at an exhibition. "Monsieur Matisse," said he, pointing to one of the artist's more daring distortions of the human figure, "did you ever see a woman like that in real life?" "No," replied Matisse, "I never did. But this is not real life: this is a picture."

Distortion was one of the stumbling blocks in the early acceptance of modern art. The average layman could not understand why the artist should want to deviate from the norm which the laymen had formed from looking at Salon or calendar art. To take liberties with the human figure was unpardonable. He might accept distortion when he saw it in Wilhelm Busch's *The Virtuoso* (illustration 416) because he knew it was intended to be funny. But to distort in a picture supposed to be high art was an insult to the human race. At the beginning of the century, the appreciation of art by the general public was limited to Salon and academic art. Three generations later, the average man can accept the distortions of modern art as a matter of course, even though he does not know why. In the course of years, modern art has become extremely well publicized. Today the public will accept anything that is called art.

As an introduction to the problem of modern art, let us consider for a moment the state of Great Britain around the beginning of the century. The world was on the whole a comfortable place to live in. The idea of unlimited progress developed by the Victorian Age was still dominant: no one anticipated the debacle of the second decade. Etchings were in vogue: architectural etchings of landscape or picturesque types. These prints of architecture were addressed to a lay public more or less as souvenirs of old-world monuments and places once visited and enjoyed. The pattern of subject matter was set by the "picturesque scene" first delineated by Isabey, Bonington, and the travel books of the Romantic period (illustration 377). The technique and treatment were derived from two nineteenth-century etchers: Meryon by his meticulous use of detail and masterly evocation of architectural mood, and Whistler by the charm of his etched line, tasteful selection of detail, and the compositional device of the vignette. A vast amount of this kind of etching was produced. Some of it, in the hands of such artists as Bone and Brockhurst (illustrations 463 and 464) is technically acceptable, but much of it is mediocre and commercial. It is always the second- and third-rate imitators who dilute the achievements of the masters and bring discredit on the school. They have nothing new to say and have not even discovered a new way of saying it. When an artist works in a pattern or formula that is well established, he must speak with unusual creative intensity in order to overcome in the beholder the indifference of familiarity. As with architectural prints, so with landscapes, which tended to become innocuous and repetitive, or with figure etching which degenerated into sweetness and sentimentality. Yet, if one had grown up with such prints, and had come to find pleasure, solace, and even escape in them, it would seem quite natural to be shocked on seeing examples of modern art, and to feel that the whole edifice of familiar beauty and art was crumbling. Possibly it was, but so were many other values. The world was not standing still.

The moderns, then, have tried to interpret this new world in the idiom and tempo of today: to interpret, rather than portray, although portrayal or reporting also has its place. The camera has to a large extent taken over the reporting function, and left the artist free to explore new fields and to record experiences, moods, feelings impossible to express by means of purely realistic art. The artist's task is to dramatize his esthetic thoughts and feelings, whether it be for stylistic self-expression or for purposes of documentation. As John Marin once wrote: "If these buildings move me . . . it is this moving of me which I try to express, so that I may recall the spell I have been under, and behold the expression of the different emotions that have been called into being." For example, in Feininger's *Village Church* (illustration 501) the interest is not in the church or the emotions associated with old architecture but in the abstract pattern, the dynamic balance of light and dark, the equilibrium of thrusting lines and shapes. The artist has used a building with a tower as a springboard to create a fascinating and exciting design.

In order to help him in this dramatization and in the reinforcement of his message, the artist makes use of certain qualities inherent in the conventions of art. It is

known that a picture, by its design or arrangement of lines and forms, can, within certain limits, suggest distress, restlessness, serenity, ecstasy, melody, and the like, quite apart from the meaning. The medium, the form, has an evocative power of its own. A simple example is Hokusai's *Wave* (illustration 730) where a variety of curves are used with telling effect. The chief tools employed by the artist, however, are abstraction, distortion, and rhythm. To abstract means to draw out, to concentrate on essentials, to eliminate everything which does not contribute to the desired effect. There are various degrees of abstraction. In the most advanced state, a natural form is transformed into pure geometric ornament: a mountain becomes a triangle. To distort means to deviate from an accepted norm either to emphasize the meaning or to reinforce compositional lines. The function of abstraction and distortion is not new, though it may seem so to those who are familiar with only one kind of art— the art they grew up with. There is distortion in an Ingres lithograph (illustration 400) as well as in a Gothic woodcut (illustration 23), and, one might add, in a Salon painting based upon photography. The modern artist thus has many more powerful tools at his disposal than the appeal of association which a mirrorlike copy might possess. He can and does reinforce his message through form and stylization. After this rather elementary introduction to the modern point of view let us find out what happened in the world of twentieth-century prints.

During the early part of the century Paris was the center of the art and print world. The outstanding characteristic of French graphic art, as well as of French painting, during those years has been untrammeled research into new modes of expression. Most of the new movements were originated by artists living in Paris: *Ecole de Paris* is a term much in use. Being all-around artists with a definite feeling for style, they had a different attitude than the professional printmaker. They did not produce prints with a specific market in mind; they made them as they painted in oil, executed sculpture or drawings, or designed for the ballet: in order that they might try out all media and put the impress of their style on them all. Courageous and farsighted dealers also played a positive role in French graphic art. Edmund Sagot and his successor Maurice Le Garrec, Henry Kahnweiler, Ambroise Vollard, and Galerie Maeght deserve special praise for their part in commissioning and publishing prints, singly, in sets, and in books. Many painters might not have made any prints but for their intervention.

Postimpressionist ferment continued into the twentieth century. Groups and schools were constantly forming and re-forming. Among the group of *Fauves* (so named at the *Salon d'Automne* of 1905) were Henri Ma-

tisse, André Derain, Maurice Vlaminck, Raoul Dufy, Georges Rouault, Albert Marquet, Kees van Dongen, and Othon Friesz. Their association, though it lasted only about three years, was influential. Matisse was by far the most important, and achieved early notoriety by his strongly distorted paintings and sculpture. His distortions, however, were motivated by design and not by incompetence for he was an academically trained artist and a marvelous draughtsman. His printmaking career began with distorted linoleum cuts and trenchant outline etchings of heads and figures, and continued with lithographs of odalisques and interiors beautifully organized and vividly suggesting color. He made well over three hundred prints displaying the female figure in every conceivable pose, and executed in various ways and mediums from the incisive sketch to the fully realized composition—a magnificent set of variations on a single theme (illustrations 465, 467–470). In his old age he worked with collages of colored paper, some of which were reproduced by stencil in *Jazz* 1947 (illustration 471); they display an exquisite sense of color. He illustrated numerous books with original prints. All in all, Matisse was a dedicated printmaker and one of the greatest masters in twentieth-century graphic art. Derain somehow lost his early *fauviste* verve (illustration 486) and lapsed into conventional eclecticism. The same thing is true of Vlaminck, who ended up painting repetitive landscapes. Raoul Dufy also changed his style but with less diminution of quality. His stylized woodcut illustrations to Apollinaire's *Bestiary* (1911) are of high quality, and his later lithographs executed in free calligraphic line are equally attractive (illustrations 466, 481).

Around 1910 the emergence of the cubist style was reflected in prints. Cubism, as is well known, was developed simultaneously by Braque and Picasso (illustrations 472, 473) and further developed by Léger (illustration 475), Jacques Villon (illustration 485), Gris, Gleizes, Marcousis, and the painters Duchamp, Picabia, and Metzinger. Cubism was an attempt to break up a figure or form into a series of component facets in order to represent various viewpoints. Taking a cue from certain paintings of Cézanne and from Negro sculpture, the painters began a drastic simplification of natural forms into vague cubes and cylinders which they organized into an esthetically satisfying whole. There were two aspects in prints of what might be called the early phase of cubism. The first in the suggestion of three-dimensional design, a play of planes and their intersections in prints by Braque (illustration 473), Picasso (illustration 472), Villon (illustration 485), Gris, and Marcoussis. The other in flat color patterns exemplified by the pochoirs of Picasso (illustration 474), Gleizes (illustration 476), and Braque.

Concurrently, Paul Signac and Henri Edmond Cros

were translating the *pointilliste* style into color lithography (illustration 478). Bonnard (illustration 448) and Vuillard (illustration 447) were continuing to make impressionist lithographs in color. Many famous painters and sculptors tried their hand at making prints in their characteristic styles. Some, like Douanier Rousseau, Robert Delaunay, Henri Laurens (illustration 482), Charles Despiau or Maurice Utrillo made only a few, others became dedicated printmakers. Jacques Villon became one of the most distinguished burinists and virtuosos of intaglio technique (illustrations 484, 485). Sculptor Aristide Maillol made monumental nudes in lithograph (illustration 487) and many woodcuts for books. His lifework was one great affirmation of fecund Earth, of sun-drenched land and the fruits thereof. Jules Pascin (illustration 483), a facile and witty draughtsman, etched scenes from city life and drew sensuous nudes in a highly personal vein. No matter how carelessly he drew, his lines came to life. André Dunoyer de Segonzac also had a personal style, based upon elegance and lucidity, in his etchings of landscape and figures (illustration 480). Fernand Léger (illustration 475) found inspiration in mechanical forms. As he said: "I invent images of machines as others with their imagination have invented landscapes. The mechanical element in my work is not a prejudice or an attitude, but a means of giving the sensations of force and power." Georges Rouault, after his early involvement with the *Fauve* group, stood apart from most of the modern experimentors in that he seemed to live in a medieval world of his own. Yet in his lithographs and intaglio prints of circus and religious themes he showed himself to be one of the greatest graphic artists of our time. His prints were intensely felt and executed by methods all his own. They combined a tragic sense of life with a feeling of monumental grandeur. Perhaps his greatest work was the set of *Miserere*, fifty-eight large copper plates from which our illustrations are taken (illustrations 488, 489). The creative ferment of the early part of the century simmered down after the World War. The great figures have become old masters, as it were, and few of a younger generation have achieved international reknown. Jean Dubuffet, however, has become a master in his own right. The following printmakers also are worthy of mention: Henri-Georges Adam, Mario Avati, Pierre Courtin, Jean Fautrier, Johnny Friedaender, Germaine Richier, Pierre Soulages, and Roger Vieillard.

Surrealism, created by writers and painters, was reflected in the prints of Joan Miró, André Masson (illustration 494), Yves Tanguy, Jean Arp (illustration 492), Max Ernst, and Salvador Dali (illustration 493). Of course there exist surrealist phases in the *œuvre* of numerous other masters such as Picasso, Chagall, and Klee, but among the avowed surrealists Miró's work is most important in quality and quantity. He is an artist of unusual inventiveness and sensibility. His whimsical color lithograph, for example, *Personnage aux oiseaux* (illustration 490) is presented in the guise of a child's drawing. It is far from being so simple: it is sophisticated in feeling, deliberate in method, and subtle in its coloring. Much of the artist's imagery is saturated with sex symbolism, but the leading metaphor of this print seems more fanciful than sexual.

Surrealism is difficult to define. It makes use of the unconscious as a creative impulse. It is doubtful whether Surrealism would ever have been possible if it had not been for the discoveries of Freud and the psychoanalysts. The disclosure of man's subconscious, of his powerful irrational impulses, of the devious motivation of sex instincts, of antisocial tendencies that flare up sometimes in spite of all social conditioning, has had a marked effect upon the culture of our time. It is on some such basis, combined with the ironic irrationalism of Dada, born of disillusion after the First World War, that the surrealists built their program. They stress the pathological and insane, psychic automatism, emotional shock for the sake of shock, the grotesque outpourings of unfettered imagination, and the attack on reason in general. Man, as we know, is an irrational as well as rational being. He spends about one-third of his life in the state of sleep and dream where much of the surrealist point of view is approximated. There are certain intuitions about life that can be expressed in no other manner but the surrealist. There are elements, drawn from the unconscious, or expressed more or less in surrealist terms, in the works of Shakespeare, Swift, Coleridge, Blake, and Lewis Carroll, just as there are in the pictures of Dürer, Bosch, Bruegel, Callot, Goya, Grandville, Bresdin, and Redon.

André Breton has stated the fundamental aim of the movement as "the future transmutation of those seemingly contradictory states, dream and reality, into a sort of absolute reality, of Surreality, so to speak." The difficulty is to give free voice to the subconscious, to find some way to get past the censor, which is conscious reason. Various methods are employed to accomplish this purpose. One is through psychic automatism, as for example the "doodles" on a telephone pad, the theory being that such forms are a true index to psychic states. Related to this is the elaboration of the eidetic or persistent image. The surrealists claim to distinguish between valid and invalid images by their persistence and compulsive momentum. The valid images, they say, are part of a collective human subconscious, and should therefore strike a responsive note in every beholder. It is an interesting theory if one grants the premise that there is a collective subconscious; not all authorities are in agree-

ment over this point. It was more or less on this question, however, that the main body of surrealists rejected Dali around 1936 for his exploitation of purely personal neuroses, or what he called "paranoiac-critical activity."

A compositional device sometimes used by the surrealists is the juxtaposition of objects seemingly unrelated but really conjoined by unconscious motivation. An interesting anticipation of this principle—the unity of inner meaning—is to be found in a stone rubbing of the Han Dynasty, *Five Omens of the Frog Pool* (illustration 677). Images of double meaning are often used to evade the censor; such ambiguous forms are really metaphors based on visual association, just as puns in the Freudian sense are valid through sound. Finally there are the use of the hypnagogic image or remembrance of dream upon waking and the development in general of material located near the threshold of consciousness.

Of the two main methods for producing surrealist pictures, Breton, the orthodox theorist of the movement, maintains that psychic automatism is the surer; the other, namely the use of dream material, is more liable to error and corruption in its transmutation. There has been considerable bickering among the surrealists—which seems natural considering the material with which they deal. One of the great schisms occurred in 1931 when Louis Arragon and his followers broke away to espouse communist theories. It was perhaps inevitable that such an antagonism should develop, for Freudianism represents one of the few serious ideological challenges that communism has received. If the psychoanalysts' contention regarding the irrational factor in man's essential makeup is accepted, then the communists' extrovert faith in the complete social and economic conditioning of man is untenable. The surrealists are pioneers in the discovery of a new mode of expression. Some of them are pathological and extreme—exhibitionists literally and figuratively; nonetheless they are laying the groundwork of a new symbolic language useful to the world at large.

Earlier I touched upon the subjective approach of the modern artist, how he focuses attention on his own reaction rather than on the external object. This assertion of individuality is at the opposite pole from the medieval artist's complete effacement. Yet curiously enough, the concept of art's function is similar in both eras: the expression of an idea rather than the imitation of nature. St. Thomas Aquinas's dictum, "Art imitates nature [not in its form but] in its processes" is matched by Stuart Davis's "Our pictures will be expressions which are parallel to nature, and parallel lines never meet." A subjectively creative attitude is effective in the evocation of the intangibles of thought and feeling for their own sake. In Franz Marc's *Annunciation* (illustration 502) the emphasis

is directed upon the inner feelings of Mary, feelings so exalted that for the moment they have become cosmic and are shared by all creation. Everything in the picture —the design, the darting rays, the staccato accents—contribute to the feeling of tingling rapture. The artist has dramatized ecstasy. In another vein Edvard Munch in *The Cry* (illustration 550) dramatizes a feeling of dread and anxiety. The analysis of emotions was carried to extreme lengths in Germany, where the movement was called Expressionism.

In Germany, too, there was creative ferment around the turn of the century. Impressionism had been welcomed there chiefly through the championship of Max Liebermann; and there likewise had been a reaction to the surface aspects of Impressionism similar to Postimpressionism in France. It took a different turn in Germany. The French had emphasized chiefly the formal architectonic elements, adopting what might be called the classical attitude, whereas the Germans emphasized the psychological approach, an almost Gothic preoccupation with inner meaning. Out of such distortion and abstraction—for emotive effect rather than for sheer joy of organizing formal elements—grew what is loosely called the Expressionist School. It happened in several stages. Around 1905 the group known as *Die Brücke* (the Bridge), Kirchner, Schmidt-Rottluff, Heckel (later Nolde [illustration 498], Pechstein, and Otto Müller) first reacted against the Impressionist group or *Secession* (Liebermann, Corinth, Slevogt, and Meid). The rebels found inspiration among other things in Munch's strongly emotionalized paintings and prints. Kirchner was the most original and dynamic of the group, also the most prolific with an *œuvre* of about twenty-four hundred prints in all mediums, most of which he printed himself (illustrations 495–497). Heckel (illustration 499) showed more sensibility than monumentality with an *œuvre* of about six hundred. Schmidt-Rottluff's temperament was sturdy and imperturbable but with a capacity for exalted vision. His compositions have a dynamic balance of black and white. The formal abstract elements are strong, but are kept from lapsing into a formula by the artist's deep feeling and striving for monumental figural form (illustration 500).

Around 1911, Kandinsky, Kubin, Klee, Marc, Macke, Campendonk, and Jawlensky coalesced into the *Blaue Reiter* group, mingling mysticism with inspiration drawn from primitive art and cubism. In the following year they organized a big exhibition in Munich to which the *Brücke* group were invited and a yearbook, *Der Blaue Reiter*, was published. Whatever plans they had for a grand synthesis of all the arts, new and revolutionary, including music (Schoenberg), were blasted by the war. The Russians, Kandinsky and Jawlensky, had to leave

the country, and Marc and Macke fell at the front. In Vienna, Oskar Kokoschka evolved from the decorative stylizations of the *Wiener Werkstatte* to such highly charged subjective expression as the lithographs to the *Bach Cantata* (illustration 519).

All these movements reached their fullest development during the febrile postwar years. There was terrific emotional tension all over Germany, which found one outlet in feverish activity by artists, good and bad. Inflation and the consequent urge to convert money into tangible objects caused a great demand for works of art. Such dealers as Paul Cassirer, Hans Goltz, J. B. Neumann, and Alfred Flechtheim, also helped to encourage modern printmakers by exhibitions and the publication of prints. The older artists who had survived the war continued to produce prolifically. The war, in a sense, made Expressionism international. Some of the artists of the *Bauhaus* group, first at Weimar and later at Dessau, Kandinsky, Klee, Feininger, Albers, and Marcks, were artists of prime stature. Kandinsky had only an indirect relation with Expressionism in its strictest sense. During the *Blaue Reiter* period (illustration 522) he was already developing his concept of abstract, or absolute painting, as he called it, in which all representation of natural objects was eliminated, and in which color, line, and plane in themselves produce emotional response. His work revolutionized the whole of modern art (illustrations 523, 524). Paul Klee was one of the most original and important artists of the expressionist generation, or indeed of twentieth-century art in general. His expression was intensely and uniquely personal, a perfect blending of form and content. He was endlessly inventive. Seemingly naive and childlike, his work displayed the ultimate sophistication. He aimed to incarnate the intangibles of fantasy, dream, and memory. "Art," he once said, "plays an unwitting game with ultimate things, but reaches them nevertheless" (illustrations 505, 506). The woodcuts of Gerhard Marcks (illustration 503) are cast in linear terms, neither boringly old nor blatantly new. They display wit and humor and a quiet detached wisdom that stands apart from the hectic tempo of the time. Feininger was American and later returned to his native country. Albers and Gropius also went to the United States.

Kaethe Kollwitz, apart from all movements, made her compassionate and deeply felt prints of sorrowing humanity (illustrations 509–513). The new objectivists saw life in a more bitter mood: George Grosz in his satiric lithographs executed with a deceptively childlike schematic line (illustrations 514, 515), Otto Dix in his gruesome set of war etchings (illustration 517), Max Beckmann in his harshly ironic etchings and lithographs (illustrations 507, 508). In Germany as in France there were relatively few professional printmakers (as for instance

Hermann Struck, Emil Orlik, or Max Slevogt). It was as painters that they made their prints. The sculptors—and there was a strong school of sculpture there—Lehmbruck and Barlach notably, and also Kolbe, Mataré, Marcks, and Sintenis, have made a distinct contribution to graphic art (illustrations 504, 516). The German dadaist, Kurt Schwitters, also had relations with the *De Stijl* group in Holland, and made some geometrically abstract lithographs (illustration 521). All this creative activity came to an end with the advent of the Nazi regime. The artists were silenced, exiled, or died. During the Nazi regime, the young artists were isolated from all outside influences, and consequently were retarded in their artistic development. Many did not achieve their personal style until after the period covered in this book. Mention should be made, however, of the realistic serigraphs of Gerd Winner, the macabre lithographs of Paul Wunderlich, and the abstract color lithographs of Ernst Wilhelm Nay. The painter, Julius Bissier (1893–1965), who carried on the tradition of Paul Klee with sensitive color and calligraphic elements, also made a few woodcuts.

In Austria during the first half of the twentieth century, the expressionist Oskar Kokoschka and the surrealist Alfred Kubin continued their activities. The painter Egon Schiele (illustration 520) before his untimely death in 1918 made about a dozen powerfully drawn prints of figural subjects. The sculptor Fritz Wotruba has made a few lithographs. Emil Fuchs and Anton Lehmden executed etchings under the banner of "fantastic realism." Noteworthy is Lehmden's *Roman Cycle*, a series of etchings, fascinating for their evocation of Roman ruins.

In Russia at the beginning of the century there was little professional print activity. Several artists connected with the Russian Ballet in Paris, Natalia Gontcharova and Michail Larionov made a few prints. Marc Chagall first came to Paris about 1910 and has been there off and on ever since. His series *Mein Leben* was published by Cassirer in Germany. The more than three hundred etchings commissioned by Vollard as illustrations to Gogol, La Fontaine, and the Bible (illustration 526) were not published during Vollard's lifetime. After their later publication by Teriade, 1948–56, Chagall has issued numerous other prints (illustration 527). Chagall's work has a unique, almost magical quality, a seemingly naive yet esthetically sophisticated charm, based on folk art, a fantastic dreamlike humor, and a wealth of imagery drawn from Jewish life and mysticism. His series on the Old Testament are perhaps the most truly Hebraic interpretations of the Bible ever made.

After the Revolution, there was for a while a bewildering succession of experimental schools, such as Suprematism and Constructivism, which found little expression in prints. El Lissitsky and Alexander Archipenko made

some abstract color lithographs in Germany (illustration 525). Later, a more realistic art, which could be understood by the people, was encouraged. The great demand for illustrated books stimulated graphic production, first along the lines of folk art in lithography with Vladimir Lebedev and E. I. Charushin but chiefly in wood engraving which fitted easily with type. Foreign as well as Russian classics, often in cheap but excellent editions, were published: Shakespeare, Homer, Chaucer, Fielding, Dickens, Heine, Zweig, de Maupassant, Mark Twain, as well as Gogol, Pushkin, Gorky, Tolstoy, and Chekov. In the hands of such artists as Vladimir Favorsky, Alexei Kravchenko (illustration 529), Pyotr Staronossov, David Sterenberg, Fedor Konstantinov (illustration 528), and many others, Soviet wood engraving has become a strong movement, combining vigor, taste, and technical skill. During the German invasion of the Soviet Union, book and print production was necessarily suspended. Since then socialist realism has been the only style officially encouraged, although in recent years some sporadic attempts have been made by artists to experiment in more modern or unorthodox modes. Leningrad has been more flexible than Moscow in this respect. It was in Leningrad, for instance, that Anatol Kaplan was able to produce his lithographs to Sholom Aleichem's stories and other scenes from Jewish life.

After the First World War and the reconstitution of the Polish nation, a flourishing school of wood engraving was launched by W. Skoczylas, S. Mrózewski, S. Ostoja-Chrostowski, T. Ciéslewski, T. Kusiliewicz, W. Podoski, Domjan, and others. The prints were sometimes decoratively heraldic, sometimes in the style of religious images, and sometimes executed with all the resources of modern technique. This promising movement was nipped in the bud by the Germans. Mention should be made of the Polish artist, Joseph Hecht, resident in Paris, one of the leaders in the revival of burin engraving (illustration 479) and of Jacques Lipchitz and Jankel Adler who have made prints.

Nearly all the great Spanish artists have lived in Paris. Witness Juan Gris with lithographs, Joan Miró with etchings, woodcuts, and lithographs, and Salvador Dali with etchings. Indeed, the etcher Quintanilla is about the only one who showed no trace of the School of Paris. Picasso, however, was the most famous artist of Spanish birth. He was a born printmaker: his work totaled almost two thousand prints. What is most striking was his universality in theme and execution. He had qualities of genius in the field of visual art such as Mozart, for example, displayed in the field of music—a rare combination of seemingly effortless technical mastery and inexhaustible invention. He has spanned all the changes in the problem of representation from realism to every kind of abstraction—a relentless drive to fathom every metamorphosis of visual representation: outer form, inner form, abstract form, broken-up form, movement, simultaneity. No matter how many liberties he took in his distortions, he endowed all his lines and forms with compelling life. It was characteristic of his exuberant imagination that it often took the form of variations on a theme—again the analogy with music. He played with a theme, stressing sometimes one, sometimes another element. No artist has more fully realized the potentialities of such graphic mediums as etching, engraving, aquatint, and lithography. But he was not an artist whose sole motivation was esthetic: he had human feelings and they found expression in his art. His sympathy for the underdog, his reaction to the cruelty and destruction of war, his tribute to the beauty of woman, to the joy of life, to Pan and the elemental forces of Nature, his probing into the dark chthonian forces of the subconscious, into the enigma of man and woman and their relationship, into the bare essence of mankind from childhood to old age— all these and more give depth and dignity to his art. It is not strange, therefore, that Picasso, with his protean esthetic mastery and humane impulses, has loomed as a major influence upon the younger generation and upon modern art in general. Picasso is supposed to have said: "*la jeunesse, c'est moi*" (illustrations 530–538).

In Italy around 1910 a group of artists, Giacomo Balla, Umberto Boccione, Gino Severini, and Carlo Carra under the leadership of a poet, Filippo Marinetti, banded together to form the Futurist School. Their aim, among other things, was to suggest motion and simultaneity. Little if any of this was reflected in prints, although Boccione had made a number of prefuturist etchings. Around the same time Giorgio de Chirico developed the "metaphysical" style of painting, emphasizing loneliness and mystery in terms of Renaissance realism and perspective. This again found little counterpart in prints. In Giorgio Morandi, however, we find a dedicated printmaker. He started as a painter vaguely metaphysical, but made his mark by his small and highly plastic etchings, still lifes of old bottles and other junkshop materials, all drawn with precision and inevitability of placement (illustration 540). The sculptor Marino Marini (illustration 539) has made a number of lithographs of a man on horseback which have grown more and more abstract as time goes on. The sculptor Giacomo Manzu likewise has made etchings of figural interest. Renzo Vespignani has executed some interesting etchings, modern in feeling. Massimo Campigli has executed color lithographs in a distinctive style inspired by old Egyptian art. Two Italian artists of today have achieved some measure of international renown, Giuseppe Capogrossi with abstract lithographs, and Renato Guttuso with prints and radical

political activity.

In Switzerland the painter Hodler made a few lithographs with his usual emphasis on repetitive rhythm. Steinlen and Vallotton drifted to Paris and Klee to Germany. More recently Alberto Giacometti (illustration 543) has become renowned as a sculptor but he has also executed a large *œuvre* of etchings and lithographs. Similarly Le Corbusier took up printmaking late in life. On the contemporary scene and with more specific graphic interest may be mentioned Hans Fischer, Max Hunziger, Hans Erni, and Leo Maillet. In Switzerland there is considerable interest in collecting prints and rare illustrated books.

Dutch printmakers range from Joseph Israels, Jan Toorop, and Marius Bauer of an older generation to Karel Appel, Cornelis Corneille, and George Constant, all members of the Cobra group of violent Expressionism. The activities of the *De Stijl* group were not reflected in prints. M. C. Escher, an independent artist of strong individuality, has made a number of woodcuts and lithographs probing aspects of illusion and reality, visual ambiguities, and metamorphoses of forms. His studies of scenes using false perspective are rendered with such convincing illusion that one must look sharply to discover the flaw. He is also concerned with contrasts as in *Order and Chaos* (illustration 542). Anton Heyboer has made etchings in a very personal style by including lettering in his compositions (illustration 541). Belgium has strong ties with Paris, and little of international significance has been produced that has not been already mentioned. Frans Masereel, however, developed a new kind of illustrated novel without words in woodcut sequence. In Sweden Anders Zorn carried on from the end of the nineteenth century. His brilliant but superficial technique, adapted from the Impressionists, made him internationally known. The Norwegian Edvard Munch, also a holdover from the nineteenth century, was undoubtedly a more creative artist, and his influence on other artists has been more widespread. His lithographs, etchings, and especially his woodcuts executed in bold and seemingly crude flat patterns—always directed toward the expression of inner psychological reactions—were one of the foundations of the Expressionist school (illustrations 546–550). His work was original and of Strindbergian intensity. Rolf Nesch is a Norwegian artist of international renown. He left his native Germany when Hitler came into power and has lived in Norway ever since. He started out as an Expressionist and admired Kirchner so much that he made a pilgrimage to Davos to see him. He is a dedicated printmaker, and has made well over five hundred prints. He found his personal style in what he called "metal prints"—indeed he was a pioneer in the technique—a collage of found objects and various materials attached to a metal plate for the purpose of making prints. His first metal prints (with collages of wire) were the set of twenty *Hamburg Bridges* of 1932. Since then his metal prints have grown steadily in complexity and range, as may be seen in the difference between *Skaugum* (from the "Snow" series) 1923 and *Dark Lady* 1953 (illustrations 544, 545). The technique of collage produces an embossed effect on the printed paper and extends the range of effects possible in printmaking. He was the first to make deliberate use of holes in a metal plate (printing white) in 1926. In spite of his concern with and mastery of technique, he considers it merely a means to an end. He is an intuitive creator of great inventiveness and sensibility. His color sense is exquisite. His subject matter —he often works in series—ranges from affectionate delineations of nature, the pastoral life, and the fisherman's occupation to the theatre and the fantasy of grotesque masks, trolls, and other creatures of Norse folklore.

The British etchers of collector's prints never regained their status or prices after the Great Depression of 1929. Several able painters, however, who also made a few etchings, such as Augustus John, Walter Sickert (illustration 551), and C. R. W. Nevinson (illustration 552), stood apart from the downward trend, the first with figure etchings in the spirit of Rembrandt, the second with vibrant genre and city scenes in the spirit of Degas and the Impressionists, and Nevinson with strongly designed prints and occasional ventures into cubist Vorticism. The English have always favored wood engraving, both as single prints and in connection with book illustration. Earlier representatives were C. Lovat-Fraser, William Nicholson, with his flat-patterned portraits of celebrities, and Gordon Craig, with his engravings for "The Mask" and woodcuts displaying contours softened with sandpaper. A fuller development came with a younger generation nourished on the more dynamic design of the moderns. Among these may be mentioned Eric Gill (illustration 554), renowned for lettering as well as for engraving and sculpture, Robert Gibbings of the Golden Cockerel Press, Leon Underwood, Blair Hughes-Stanton, Gertrude Hermes (illustration 553), Paul and John Nash, both distinguished painters. Around midcentury some powerful lithographs in color were made by Graham Sutherland, Henry Moore (illustration 555), and others. For many years Anthony Gross has been making etchings in a very individual style.

One of the most influential of British printmakers is Stanley William Hayter. Equally at home in London, Paris, and New York, he had a studio in Paris from 1917 to 1940, to which many artists, including Picasso, Miró, Kandinsky, Masson, Ernst, and Tanguy came to get technical advice and to work on plates. Through his infec-

tious enthusiasm and instructive zeal, Studio 17 took on the aspect of a collective movement, which continued when he came to America in 1940 and initiated many Americans into the craft. Hayter has undertaken to revive and explore a creative approach to the handling of the burin. He maintains that after the great achievements of Mantegna and Pollaiuolo, the direction of line engraving was diverted by Dürer and Raimondi toward purely reproductive values, thereby ignoring the plastic and spatial resources of the medium. His comments on the engraving of the past and present are penetrating and challenging. His manipulation of the graver displays unusual variation of linear expression and bravura of curve. He and his associates have also made researches in the textures produced on copperplate by burnishing and graining with carborundums, and especially by the impress on soft grounds of many materials including textile weaves, wood grains, and other natural forms, pieces of string, crumpled paper, and the like (see the impress of textile and leaf in Masson's etching, illustration 494). The artist has an all-absorbing interest in questions of technique, though he admits that technique alone will not produce a work of art. His own work is abstract with surrealist overtones. He usually starts by making a random doodle on the plate and then develops the composition as he proceeds. He has enumerated the operations performed in making *Pavane* (illustration 556) as follows: "Started with a line engraving on a copperplate, whole plate then coated with soft ground and a wood grain pressed into it, certain parts stopped out, rest bitten in Smillie's bath until almost black, work continued in line engraving, background worked back with burnisher, stone, and charcoal, certain parts darkened by planing with coarse carborundum stone (prints like drypoint), and the whites finally hollowed out of plate." *Pavane* was selected for reproduction rather than larger works, as *Combat, Tarantelle,* or *Laocoön* because it would suffer less by reproduction.

During the Mexican Revolution there was a resurgence of creative activity that brought about the Mexican school of painting. It was primarily a social art in which the human figure—humanity—has been the keynote. Landscape, still life, and all the technical virtuosities of the School of Paris, found comparatively little favor. The latent pictorial genius of the Mexicans flared up during the storm and stress of the revolution, and was fortunately encouraged by mural commissions and by other indirect means. Its influence in the United States was considerable, and the States in turn did much to keep the movement alive by the purchase of pictures. The existence of a graphic tradition is demonstrated by the wood and metal cuts of the folk artist, José Guadalupe Posada, from 1887 to 1913 (illustration 560). Rivera and Orozco

have testified to the influence which Posada had upon the direction of their own art. Nearly all the great painters of the Mexican Renaissance have made prints as well: José Clemente Orozco with his intensely felt, powerfully stylized, and often satirical lithographs (illustration 559); Diego Rivera with his skillfully organized scenes of Mexican life and history, some based on themes from his murals (illustration 557); David Alfaro Siqueiros with his colossal heads and compositions (illustration 558). French-born Jean Charlot, now living in Hawaii, is the most prolific printmaker of the original group, working in wood but chiefly in lithograph, including color prints made by lithographic offset (illustration 562). Among the painters who have made a few prints may be mentioned Carlos Merida, Julio Castellanos, and Miguel Covarrubias. Emilio Amero now in the U.S.A. has made color lithographs, and instructed many others in the technique of lithography. Francisco Diaz de León, as director of the *Escuela de las Artes del Libro*, has initiated many into the graphic arts. During the late 1930s the *Taller de Gráfica Popular* (Workshop of Popular Graphic Art) was flourishing. Among its members may be cited Leopoldo Mendes (illustration 561), Francisco Dosamantes, Gonzalo de la Paz Perez, and the American-born Pablo O'Higgins. They were radically inclined and made posters, broadsheets, and prints, chiefly lithographs, in great number. Mention should be made of Rufino Tamayo (illustration 563), a distinguished painter who early made woodcuts in the Mexican style and who later developed ties with Paris and made abstract color lithographs. The young Mexican artists of today work in the International Style and have lost all Mexican flavor.

One salient phase of twentieth-century art, as well as of literature, has been the growth of social consciousness. To be sure, the expression of social ideals had been anticipated in the work of such nineteenth-century artists as Millet, Daumier, Goya, Courbet, Pissarro, Steinlen, and William Morris; but it received a powerful impetus through devastating world wars, the economic depression of the 1930s, and the success of the Mexican and Russian revolutions. In its broadest aspect it envisages the essential solidarity of all human beings, a conviction that the world might be made a better place to live in by the abolition of injustice and discrimination and exploitation. As an ultimate goal, their quest for an Earthly Paradise would no doubt be endorsed by all men of good will. The disagreement is in the means: whether it be Marxian socialism, revolutionary communism, Maoist revolution, anarchism, social credit, economic democracy, or the primitive communism of early Christianity. The idea thus seems to be a seminal one, a possible source of inspiration to the artist. And there is no reason why the Brotherhood of Man could not become as powerful

and sustaining an emotional drive as Nirvana or the Redemption. There are various levels of absorption in the theme. With most artists, as with most people, the impulse goes no further than a generalized sympathy for the downtrodden and oppressed and a painful realization of the horrors of war. With a limited few the attitude stems from a more specific conviction as to the cause of injustice and the method of its eradication. The theme at this level—insofar as it is expressed in terms of art and not mere propaganda (which is the result of convictions either ill-digested or imposed from without)—has a dual aspect. The first is critical and satirical, a denunciation of the flaws in the present social order. The second is in a more positive vein, a glorification of the heroes of the class struggle, and a faint adumbration of a better world to come. This last must necessarily be expressed in general terms since, with so complicated a structure as modern society, the artists, no more than the political economists themselves, have no clear idea of the working out of any new order. Along these lines, then, a new mythology is being built up around the left movement, with heroes and martyrs and villains, and various inspiring and edifying parables.

In completing the roundup of twentieth-century prints, a word should be said about graphic art and books. As in the past, numerous books containing etchings, woodcuts, and lithographs have been issued during the century. The enterprise of publishers has always been an incentive in the production of prints. The subject is capable of extended study, but can be treated only briefly here. Of our illustrations, the following prints appeared in book form: Léger's for Malraux's *Lunes de Papier* (illustration 475) published by Kahnweiler, Paris; Dufy's for Apollinaire's *The Hare* from *Le Bestiaire* (illustration 466) published by Deplanch, Paris; Derain's for Apollinaire's *Enchanteur pourrissant* (illustration 486) published by Kahnweiler, Paris; Pascin's for *Cendrillon* (illustration 483) published by Tremois, Paris; Dali's for *Les Chants de Maldoror* (illustration 493) published by Skira, Paris; Chagall's for *The Old Testament* (illustration 526) unpublished at Vollard's death but published by Tériade, Paris, in 1956. Most civilized countries have produced enormous quantities of books, whether in popular or limited editions, containing process illustrations or original prints. One would wish that they were fewer and better. How can one define the perfect illustration? First of all it should be an integral part of the book; it should fit harmoniously on the printed page in scale and color and weight. If the text is subordinate to the illustration, as might happen with a distinguished original print, then the typography should be built around the picture. But beyond all technical or typographical considerations, there is required a certain quality of pertinent inevitability: not just *an* illustration but *the* illustration, the perfect interpretation of the spirit and content of the author. As a norm for the ideal illustrated book of the twentieth century, one might suggest the following works as interpreted in original prints by great artists: Bonnard for Verlaine's *Parallèlement*, Derain for Apollinaire's *Enchanteur Pourrissant*, Dufy for Apollinaire's *Bestiare*, Matisse for Mallarmé's *Poésies*, Rouault for Suares's *Passion*, Picasso for Ovid's *Métamorphoses*, Maillol for Virgil's *Eclogues*, André Girard for *Héraclite d'Ephèse*, Chagall for *The Old Testament*, Eric Gill for *The Four Gospels*, John Sloan for Maugham's *Of Human Bondage*, June Wayne for *Songs and Sonnets of Donne*.

In the view of Soviet critic A. Solodovnikov, there is "a clash of two general trends in art. One of these trends is founded on the principle that the chief purpose of art is to carry man away from reality, to provide amusement and relaxation; the other claims that art is called upon to educate society." In my opinion both alternatives are but partial statements. Art ministers to the whole man, to the play instinct as much as to the serious business of life. Propaganda (or education) has its time and place, but it is not the whole story of art. Pure escapism, likewise, is infantile and unworthy of any mature conception of art. The artist, less bound by the interests and prejudices of a class, and infinitely curious about all phenomena, contrives to render a fairly impartial cross section of life as a whole. In one respect only may the artist be called partisan: in the assertion of his individuality and freedom, in his faith in the integrity of his expression. The world is witnessing an unparalleled aggrandizement of the forces of regimentation and collectivization. This anti-individualistic tendency may eventually be revealed as the major trend of the century, overshadowing the conflicts of rival nations or economic theories, because it is universal and functions as much under capitalism as under communism. The individual is being submerged in the mass, his life regimented, his outlook and tastes standardized, as much through the by-products of capitalist democracy—radio, cinema, newspaper syndicates, mass production and assembly lines, book clubs and digests, national advertising, and packaged products—as through the plan and program of a totalitarian state. The artist by instinct and training stands apart from this collective drift. He believes in freedom—which does not necessarily mean laissez-faire. Individuality, that is to say, a personal viewpoint is his greatest asset. The artist's is one of the few voices that can speak for freedom and the individual.

In concluding this survey of twentieth-century art, let me add a personal note. I have more or less arbitrarily terminated it around the half-century mark, approximately 1950. I have several reasons for doing this. First of

all, the succeeding material is so vast and complex that it would require another big book to cover it adequately. Also I believe that it would take a perspective of much more than twenty years to evaluate judiciously. Furthermore, in my opinion, a revolutionary break in the very concept of art has occurred. For untold centuries the basic assumption of painting has been the projection of three-dimensional forms upon a flat surface by various devices, such as perspective and modeling; its pleasurable effects have been enhanced by means of composition, or the organization of color, rhythm, accent, balance of light and dark values, and the like. Subject matter provided some measure of conventional reality. From time to time some of these devices may have been deliberately disregarded, but the basic assumptions still remained. After the mid-century, however, many movements (heralded by Kandinsky)—such as Action Painting, Abstract Expressionism, Neoplasticism, Concrete Art, L'Art Brut, Assemblage and Junk sculpture, Primary Structures, Color-Field Painting, Minimalism, Optical Art, and Systemic Painting—just cannot be judged by traditional criteria. The new movements have rejected tradition and must be approached from a new point of view. There is a clear analogy with modern music. Dodecaphony (Twelve-Note Technique), Serialism, Musique Concrète and Aleatory music (introducing elements of chance) are not only irritating but also unintelligible to one who has been brought up on tonality, thematic structure, and traditional harmony. I am not introducing moral judgments and saying that the old is good and the modern is bad. I merely assert that they are totally opposed concepts. Neither can be enjoyed or understood except in its own frame of reference.

8. American Prints

I. FROM THE BEGINNING THROUGH THE NINETEENTH CENTURY

American printmaking during colonial times and during most of the nineteenth century was an art for the common people. In early times there were no public collections or art museums. Almost the only pictures that people saw were engravings, and they were few in number. The cultural climate of the colonies, based as it was upon that of the mother country, was not slanted to any great degree toward a pictorial or graphic tradition. Architecture and the decorative arts, the production of furniture and fine silver flourished in the colonies as it did in England. But even in England, printmaking as a distinctively native art was limited during the eighteenth century largely to mezzotint, which indeed was often called "engraving in the English manner" on the Continent. Mezzotint was almost entirely an art of portraiture, reproductions of paintings. Thus it happened that the earliest prints made in this country were portraits. The first known print was a woodcut, crude but powerful, the *Rev. Richard Mather*, made probably by the printer John Foster about 1670 (illustration 564). There must have been a demand for likenesses of influential divines in New England, as the mezzotints by Peter Pelham, William Jennys, and John Singleton Copley testify. These particular prints (executed by the artist after his own design, for, contrary to the usual practice, he was here both painter and mezzotinter) were surprisingly well done, displaying a strong sense of character, albeit sober and austere (illustrations 565 and 567). Pelham's portrait of the Rev. Cotton Mather is generally considered the first mezzotint and framing print made in America; and indeed it could hold its own in any collection of mezzotint portraits. Somewhat more lusty and satiric in spirit is John Greenwood's original print of *Jersey Nanny* (illustration 566). There was apt to be more demand by greater numbers of people—and therefore more incentive for printmaking—in the urban and middle-class area of New England than in the agricultural regions of Virginia and the South. The aristocratic owners of the plantations were more likely to satisfy their need for culture through oil paintings and direct importation from England.

Besides portraits the colonists were interested in maps and views, battles and notable events, and, as they became increasingly conscious of separation from the mother country, the memorable events of the American Revolution. When one compares the graphic documentation of the American Revolution with that of the French Revolution occurring but a few years later, one realizes how inadequate was the technical tradition which the American craftsmen took over from England. Amos Doolittle's engravings (based on drawings by Ralph Earl) of the battles of *Lexington* and *Concord* are absurdly crude, but they are nonetheless part of our historic heritage. The same holds true of the earlier Johnston-Blodgett engraving, the *Battle of Lake George* (illustration 570), and the amusing Dawkins portrayal, the *Paxton Expedition*. Perhaps the most famous of all Revolutionary prints is Paul Revere's *Boston Massacre* (illustration 571). Revere was a silversmith and patriot, renowned in history and legend, but he was an indifferent engraver. It turns out that Revere copied his picture from a larger and better engraving by Henry Pelham. Doolittle's engraving (after a drawing by Peter Lacour) of *Federal Hall and the Inauguration of Washington as President* (illustration 572) does have considerable charm and the vividness of a contemporary rendering. With the documentation in portraiture of some of the key figures of the Revolution, such as Franklin, Washington, and Jefferson, we are on sounder esthetic ground, for Charles Willson Peale (illustration 568) and Edward Savage were accomplished painters as well as competent printmakers.

Topography, or the production of views, was an important and favored category of graphic art. The citizens of the young nation began to take pride in their country, and demanded delineations of its picturesque scenery and flourishing cities. Perhaps the most impressive early enterprise of this type was the set of twenty-eight engraved views of Philadelphia issued by William and Thomas Birch in 1800 (illustration 573). J. L. Bouquet de Woiseri followed with an aquatint, the *First Cities of the United States*, in 1810. In the prospectus to *Picturesque Views of American Scenery* (aquatints by Hill after Shaw, 1819) the publisher wrote:

Our country abounds with Scenery, comprehending all the varieties of the sublime, the beautiful, and the picturesque in nature, worthy to engage the skill of an Artist in their delineation; and as no well-executed work of this description has ever been produced, it is confidently hoped that the present will meet with due encouragement.

The *View near Fishkill* (illustration 574) is taken from another even more famous series, the *Hudson River Portfolio*, 1825, with aquatints by Hill after Wall. Still another work containing aquatints by the accomplished engraver John Hill is the *Progressive Drawing Book* by Fielding Lucas, Baltimore, 1827. Such instructive books, of which a number were issued at this time, did much to set a standard pattern for landscape composition, since they were used not only by art students for professional training but also by amateur painters for copying.

Meanwhile, during the 1830s and 1840s, there was considerable production of excellent aquatint views of cities. Conspicuous in this field was W. J. Bennett, whose accurate and esthetically satisfying views of New York, Boston, West Point, Baltimore, Washington, and New Orleans are justly famous (illustration 575). Mention should be made of Yeager's aquatint after Krimmel, of an even earlier date, 1821, *Procession of Victuallers of Philadelphia* (illustration 576). Notable, too, are the Hornor view *Broadway*, 1836, J. Rubens Smith's *Franklin House, Philadelphia*, 1842, and several by Robert Havell, who, having finished his monumental folios of Audubon's *Birds*, settled in this country and executed charming views of Boston, West Point, and Niagara Falls. Toward the end of this period, lithography began to supplant aquatint because it was cheaper and yielded more impressions. Many fine views appeared in this medium, especially the early (1829) and impressive *Battery and New York Harbor* by Thomas Thompson, the highly finished Köllner series *American Cities*, Henry Walton's singular views of upstate New York (*Ithaca*, for example), and New England ports by such painters as Fitz Hugh Lane and J. Foxcroft Cole. Production of good views continued into the 1860s.

One cannot ignore Audubon's monumental incursion into natural history, the four elephantine folios of *American Birds*, 1827–38, created through the ideal collaboration of the engraver, Robert Havell, with the artist naturalist, J. J. Audubon (illustrations 579, 580). It was a unique and stupendous undertaking. In this task of depicting, in natural size and in their proper setting, all the birds of America, Audubon achieved a perfect fusion of esthetic sensibility and scientific recording. One may measure the full extent of his accomplishment and the breathtaking originality of his conception by comparing a plate of Audubon's *Birds* with similar subjects by M. E. D.

Brown and by Audubon's rival, Alexander Wilson, as engraved by Lawson. It was the activity of Wilson's partisans in Philadelphia which forced Audubon to have his work engraved in England.

Mention was made of the development of lithography in the second quarter of the nineteenth century. The first lithograph made in America, *The Mill*, was by Bass Otis and appeared in the *Analectic Magazine* in 1819. Benjamin West had already made a lithograph in England in 1801 (illustration 585). Rembrandt Peale was the first artist of established reputation to take up the medium in America. His portrait, *Washington, Pater Patriae*, of 1827 is an accomplished piece of work (illustration 586). One may cite for their early proficiency on stone such painters as Inman, Doughty, and Thompson, and such professional lithographers as Newsam, Lehman, Swett, and Bufford. Several unusual lithographs appeared in the 1830s. William Mason's *Horizontorium*, lithographed by J. J. Barker, 1832 (illustration 581), is a perspective illusion: viewed from a certain angle close to the horizontal, the building appears more or less in its natural form. Edward Clay's *The Times* is a satiric cartoon on the Panic of 1837 (illustration 582). Two portrait collections of the 1840s are noteworthy for their originality and competent projection of character: the lithographed silhouettes with appropriate backgrounds by W. H. Brown, as for instance *John Randolph* 1844 (illustration 587), and the *Portrait Gallery*, lithographed in Washington by Charles Fenderich.

Engraving on metal and wood continued to be used for all manner of applied art, posters, fashion plates *(Godey's Lady's Book)*, and illustrations in books and periodicals. This last field is so vast and complicated that treatment must necessarily be summary. Typical examples are Asher B. Durand's engraving after S. F. B. Morse's *The Wife* and Alexander Anderson's wood engraving, *Uncle Tom's Cabin*. J. G. Chapman dominated the field of illustration in the 1840s, as F. O. C. Darley did in the 1850s and 1860s. But the Harper Bible of 1846, celebrated as it was for its 1400 wood engravings after Chapman, somehow has little to say to us today. Darley, on the other hand, was a talented draughtsman, the best of whose work still has an appeal in our time. Special mention should be made of John La Farge's imaginative and felicitious illustration of *The Fisherman and the Genie*. Toward the end of the century, the perfection of photomechanical methods of reproduction supplanted old-fashioned engraving for illustration. The achievement of the school of illustrators then dominant—which was considerable and worthy of note—may best be studied in their original drawings (Abbey, Blum, Frost, Pennell, Pyle, Remington, and Vedder) rather than in their process reproductions. Two of the white line wood engravers, Henry Wolf and Timothy Cole (illustration 601), held out by sheer force of

personality, and were collected as late as the first decade of the twentieth century.

The ferment and expansion of the 1830s and 1840s were reflected in prints in various ways. The young nation took pride in the martial and naval achievements of its immediate past. It was the period when generals became presidents, "Old Hickory" Jackson, "Tippecanoe" Harrison, and "Old Rough and Ready" Taylor. The War of 1812 was a glorious memory. Those events which could be glamorized, chiefly naval victories, were painted by Thomas Birch and Reinagle, and popularized in engravings by Lawson, Tanner, and Thiebout. *The United States Military Magazine and Record of all the Volunteers,* 1839–41, serves to recall the popularity of the volunteer companies who drilled in gorgeous uniforms and had fun in summer encampments.

Along with their pride in martial achievement and in their cities and scenery, the Americans gloried in their American way of life. The genre picture became popular. Since the nation was still predominantly rural in culture, and since the country was still close to the city, much of the genre was rural in feeling. The paintings of Mount or Edmonds as engraved by Jones or Burt (illustration 583), of Bingham as engraved by Sartain or Doney (illustration 584), the lithographs of Lillie Martin Spencer, and later of Eastman Johnson, Durrie, Fanny Palmer, Tait, and Maurer are typical of this class. These, together with large patriotic prints such as Durand's engraving of Trumbull's *Declaration of Independence* (illustration 578) and with sporting prints and "westerns," give a cross section of the framing prints favored by the people.

Prints were indeed popular during this period. Among the various factors which brought about this active interest in prints and art in general, not the least was the activity of the American Art Union from about 1844 to 1852. This organization, under the distinguished direction of William Cullen Bryant and others, bought hundreds of paintings and sculpture by American artists and distributed them to its members by lot. For an annual fee of five dollars, a member received an impressive engraving of some famous painting as a premium and also a chance to acquire an original painting (witness Matteson's lithograph *The Distribution of American Art Union Prizes at the Broadway Tabernacle* December 24, 1847). At one time its membership counted 16,000, when Thomas Cole's series *The Voyage of Life* was announced for distribution. Among the premium prints issued by the society may be cited Woodville's *Mexican News* engraved by Alfred Jones, Bingham's *Jolly Flatboatmen,* engraved by Doney (9666 impressions), and Darley's lithograph in illustration of the *Legend of Sleepy Hollow.* These prints often entered homes where there had not been any art

before. The example of the New York society was followed by similar organizations in Philadelphia, Boston, and Cincinnati. There is no telling to what extent the movement might have expanded, if it had not come in conflict with antilottery laws. The Union was dissolved by court order in 1852.

Where the Art Union left off, private enterprise took over the task of purveying prints to the American people, with perhaps a little more emphasis on the common touch. Nathaniel Currier, his successor, Currier and Ives, Sarony and Major, Endicott and Co., the Kelloggs of Connecticut, Wagner and McGuigan, Prang and Co., Kurz and Allison, and a host of ephemeral firms issued thousands of prints and prospered. Of these, Currier and Ives were the most famous and enduring, in both quality and quantity of their output, so much so that the name has become a synonym for a certain class of print. The range of their subject matter is extensive and furnishes an illuminating index of the taste of the average American: historical events and portraits, landscapes and city views, sporting subjects, clipper ships, Western and Indian scenes, railroads, sentimental or fancy subjects, and comics. The heyday of their production was in the 1850s and 1860s; later their prints became mediocre. The approach of their leading artists was essentially romantic; they were really purveyors of the American Dream. With the celebrated rural subjects of Durrie and Fanny Palmer, for example, it would seem as if they were imbued with nostalgic perspective at the very time they were made, a feeling of the good old days down at the farm. At their best the sentiment was genuine and not at all sentimental, as it was in most of the run-of-the-mill productions. But one need only compare them with Winslow Homer's wood engravings, similar in subject and equally factual in rendering, to sense the difference between healthy realism and romantic glamour. One wonders who bought the Currier prints when they were issued; could they have been the people who were born on a farm and left it to go to the city? The sporting artists, Tait, Palmer, and Maurer were themselves keen and active sportsmen, and their pictures, filled with satisfying detail, always depict the returning hunters or fishermen laden down with the trophies of the chase for fireside sportsmen to dream about. Most of the Currier Western and Indian subjects were studio products, for, as far as is known, none of the artists, Tait, Maurer, or Cameron, were ever actually in the West. They projected in graphic form the American's idea of the West as the region of adventure and romance; in a sense perhaps, they even molded the idea. For an on-the-spot recording, one turns to the Indian sketches of Bodmer and Catlin (illustration 588) whose work is known to have been used by the Currier designers as source material.

The tremendous interest of the American people in the expansion of their country—the Prairies and the Far West, the excitement of the Gold Rush in 1849, the development of modes of transportation, the clipper ships, the transcontinental railroads, Mississippi River boats and the canals—has been delightfully and dramatically documented by Currier and Ives and other publishers. It should be emphasized that for every creditable print issued, there may have been a hundred others which had little or no merit as a work of art. Lithography was a business as well as an art. Louis Maurer has revealed that, even with the best of firms, the work was often the product of many hands, one specialist doing backgrounds, another doing figure work, and so on. Publishers often copied other prints in whole or in part, and were not always scrupulous about giving credit for their borrowings. The best of the Currier and Ives, however, will always have a place in any survey of American printmaking, not only for their graphic quality and historical importance but also for their romantic appeal. The charm these works exert upon the collector of today is largely sentimental and romantic: a glimpse of an ideal world now gone forever, which indeed may never have existed, but which is now definitely part of our legendary heritage.

The Civil War was well recorded in photography by William Brady and his assistants, Alexander Gardner and T. H. O'Sullivan, in the cumbersome collodion or wet-plate process. It was also recorded by a new type of artist war correspondent—Winslow Homer, Edwin Forbes, Alfred and William Waud—sent to the front by the illustrated weeklies. The conflict between the North and South also evoked some bitter caricature by Thomas Nast and Adalbert Volck and that curious half-fantastic, half-satiric lithograph by Blythe, *Abraham Lincoln Writing the Emancipation Proclamation.* The effect of the war on printmaking and art in general was harmful and, in its aftermath, disastrous. The gilded age was at hand, and a great social change was taking place. We were entering what Oliver Larkin called a "chromo civilization." It was an age of gaudy ostentation and vulgar taste; moneymaking was the ruling passion. In such an atmosphere, the artists, and particularly the printmakers, were thrown back on themselves. They lost touch with their public. The lithographic firms had turned completely commercial, and were developing a particularly insensitive form of color printing which became known as the chromo. Engraving was relegated to mechanical bank note engraving. Etching was moribund in spite of the French dealer Cadart's efforts to stimulate the interest of American artists during a visit in 1866. Wood engraving had turned into a routine reproductive craft in the service of the illustrated weeklies where factual rendering and speed were essential. Winslow Homer, after designing a notable and quite delightful group of wood engravings (some of them poorly engraved) for *Harper's Weekly* and other periodicals in the late 1860s and early 1870s, gave up graphic art to devote himself entirely to painting.

Henceforth the impulse to create prints had to come more or less from the artist himself. In making a so-called painter-etching, the artist had no specific market in mind; he was merely doing something to satisfy his own esthetic impulses. To be sure, there had been some previous examples of such work. John G. Chapman, after a highly successful career as a painter and illustrator, had retired to Italy and etched some intimate scenes in the Roman Campagna (*Ostia*, 1885). William Morris Hunt, back from France and his friendship with Millet, made several lithographs in the mid-1850s, *Flower Seller*, *Woman at Well* (illustration 597). J. Foxcroft Cole in 1870 made a series of pastorals in lithography, inspired possibly by the example of Charles Jacque. Dr. William Rimmer surely must have made his curious lithograph *Female Figure on a Couch*, 1859, to please himself.

Around the beginning of the 1880s, there occurred the so-called revival of etching. In 1877 the New York Etching Club was formed under the leadership of James D. Smillie. Similar organizations were formed in other cities. The whole movement was given active encouragement by S. R. Koehler, curator of prints at the Museum of Fine Arts in Boston, and editor of the short-lived but influential *American Art Revue*, 1880–82. The organizations died out in a few years chiefly because most of the members were second-rate artists, but the idea of original etching was in the air, and more and better artists began experimenting with the medium. George Innes made his first and only etching in 1879. Stephen Parrish, the father of Maxfield Parrish, initiated Charles Platt into the craft. The latter made a number of charming if somewhat dated etchings, and might have become one of our leading etchers if he had not given up printmaking to become a distinguished architect. Meanwhile, abroad, Otto Bacher and Frank Duveneck met Whistler, while they were etching in Venice. Of the two, Duveneck was an artist of greater stature and less influenced by Whistler's technique and personality. Duveneck's thirty-odd etchings place him in the front rank of nineteenth-century etchers (illustration 598). Some of his prints on exhibition in London were mistaken by Seymour Haden for Whistler's—it is difficult now to see just why, except for a similarity of Venetian subject matter—and became the occasion of one of Whistler's celebrated quarrels. Joseph Pennell already had quite a group of etchings to his credit when he fell under the spell of Whistler and became his acknowledged disciple.

In the 1890s, a number of well-known painters tried

their hand at printmaking. John Singer Sargent made a few lithographs including the characteristic *Study of a Seated Man* (illustration 600). Henry W. Ranger executed two atmospheric lithotints of the Seine in Paris. Arthur B. Davies, a young romantic, made a group of tenderly poetic lithographs in 1895. John Sloan began making etchings before the turn of the century, but did not attain his personal style until about 1905. Incidentally, Robert Blum, back in 1885, made an etching, *Scene at a Fair*, which seems an anticipation of the later subject matter of Sloan and Glackens. J. H. Twachtman, presumably under the prompting of his friend Weir, made a number of etchings in a delicate and sketchily calligraphic hand. J. Alden Weir, himself, had the instincts of a true graphic artist (illustration 599). There is a high seriousness to his finished work and an elegance, a sensitive feeling for the potentialities of the various mediums—etching, drypoint, and lithograph—and above all a projection of a living personality. He might have become a major graphic artist if his eyesight had not prevented his continuing with a medium to which he had become genuinely devoted. Mary Cassatt was one of the major graphic artists of the late nineteenth century (illustration 445). She devoted much of her art to a sympathetic delineation of women and children without lapsing into sentimentality. Her sound draftsmanship, her instinctive sense of style, and her technical mastery of such mediums as drypoint, soft-ground etching, aquatint, and color printing earned the respect of Degas and the approbation of critics and collectors.

Of all the printmakers of the second half of the nineteenth century, Whistler is perhaps the best known, both here and abroad, the most influential, the most prolific in quantity of prints. He has been the object of extravagant adulation and equally uncritical denigration. Some seventy years after his death, we may now strike some reasonable balance in between. For such an evaluation there are, on the credit side, his pioneering discovery of the Thames and its industrial structures (illustrations 436, 437) as esthetic material; the distinguished and vigorous portraits of the 1860s, *Riault* and *Annie Hayden* (illustration 438); the mood and atmosphere of the Venice scenes (illustration 439); the delicacy and sensibility of the lithographs (illustration 440); the resolute fight against the anecdotal in art and for an Impressionism, not of scientific color but of exquisite taste and decorative charm. On the debit side: the sketchiness and triviality of many of his subjects, especially during the late years; the essential rootlessness of his art, for, as the expatriate par excellence, he had roots neither in his native America nor in Paris and London where he lived; and his fundamental weakness as a creator, for his power came more from taste and connoisseurship than from creative imagination.

The art of the Pennsylvania Germans (illustration 577) has not been mentioned. The people who made the woodcuts and *fraktur* drawings certainly were American, even though their art was strongly influenced by German peasant tradition. Their baptismal certificates and religious mottoes have the intensity of feeling, the directness of expression with limited technique, the essential poetry which mark the best of true folk art.

In the final analysis, American printmaking in the nineteenth century was in the main practical and purposive. The printmaker was useful in the community as the middleman or mediator between the painter in his studio and that vast body of unknown potential called the public. When graphic art was in a flourishing state, as it was in the second quarter of the century, the painter sometimes even painted a picture specifically for reproduction. It also happened at various times that the painter-designer and the printmaker were one and the same. Today with our high regard for originality, we set great store by such "original" graphic works, but in their day they had no such special virtue. Thus, up to the time of Whistler and his militant advocacy of art for art's sake, printmaking in America had a definite purpose and a specific use. Competent rendering of subject matter was paramount, not pure creation, and achievement should be judged on that basis. As far as technique was concerned, the Americans were proficient and resourceful; they did their job well and were in no sense inferior to their contemporaries in England, Germany, and elsewhere. In other words American graphic art during the nineteenth century could hold its own in comparison with most other national schools. French printmaking alone seems to have transcended national boundaries, largely because France possessed many artists of major stature at all times during the century.

Of the original etchers of the late nineteenth century, Cassatt, Duveneck, and Weir do seem to stand above the rank and file. But towering above the rest in the importance of their achievement are three figures: Audubon, who combined art and science to produce one of the world's greatest works of ornithology; Whistler, who made a lasting contribution to etching and lithography; and Winslow Homer, whose graphic records of American life have come to possess universal appeal. In many ways Homer was the exact foil to Whistler: numerous parallel contrasts between the two could be traced, if space were available. With his independence of mind and eye, Homer was one of the most original figures in American art. It is unfortunate that more was not demanded of him as a printmaker, for he had the instinct and technical equipment of a great graphic artist. Homer was a popular artist, and his public unfortunately made no great demands on his technique. He began as an apprentice in Bufford's lithographic shop and did some

commercial work. The only lithographs which he made later were the six *Campaign Sketches* of 1862 (illustration 593). It is regrettable that he did not continue with the medium, for his wood engravings lack the textural quality and autographic drawing of the lithographs. He also made six large etchings in the 1880s after his own paintings, but did not feel at ease with the medium or the reproductive technique required. His greatest contribution to graphic art—in addition to his drawings early and late—were the two-hundred-odd wood engravings which he designed (but did not cut) for various periodicals: *Harper's Weekly, Ballou's Pictorial, Appleton's Journal, Every Saturday,* and others from 1860 to 1875. The best of these are among the most charming genre pieces ever printed in America. They show the American way of life in its best light, a veritable American idyll: glimpses of the farmer at work, the sociabilities of country life, skating in Central Park, camping experiences, the Saratoga races, and the watering places—all delineated with freshness and honesty of vision, with masterly draftsmanship and compositional skill. There were memories of childhood, too, in these engravings, of simple rustic and seaside pleasures, berry picking, clambakes and the like. In Lloyd Goodrich's words: "He expressed the grave, matter-of-fact poetry of childhood with a simplicity that is captivating and a tenderness that is all the more poignant for being entirely unconscious." After 1875, Homer devoted himself largely to a delineation of the sea in drawings, water colors, and oil paintings.

II. THE TWENTIETH CENTURY

The progression of printmaking does not always fit into neat categories of centuries. Thus the decisive date ushering in twentieth-century art was not 1900 but 1913 on the occasion of the Armory Show in New York. The state of American graphic art in the late 1890s and early 1900s was at a low ebb. At the bottom level were innocuous landscapes and banal storytelling pictures by etchers no longer heard of. Foreign influences gradually became dominant. The prints of Meryon, Haden, Cameron, Dendy Sadler, Haig, Zorn, and the American expatriates, Whistler and Pennell, were being collected. Reproductive prints were still popular, particularly wood engravings. In the Pan-American Exposition at Buffalo in 1901, half the awards went to wood engravers, Timothy Cole (illustration 601) getting the gold medal; in the Louisiana Purchase Exposition in St. Louis in 1904, four awards were given to wood engravers compared with seven to etchers (none to lithographers), Cole again receiving a special grand prize. But by 1915 etching was definitely in the ascendent as shown by the awards at the Panama-Pacific Exposition at San Francisco, where the prizes to etchers outnumbered those to reproductive wood engravers thirty-five to four.

Etching thus became a favored medium. Not only foreign etchings but also those of native architectural etchers, Herman Webster, D. S. MacLaughlin, Ernest Roth, Louis Rosenberg, Samuel Chamberlain, and John Taylor Arms (illustration 603), were collected. Though the subject matter of the latter group was largely European, they were not much collected in Europe because American art had not yet attained an international market. Other American etchers of traditional tastes also achieved fame and success with non-European subjects: Frank Benson (illustration 605) and Richard Bishop with sporting scenes, duck shooting, and the like; George E. Burr, B. J. Nordfeldt, and Mahonri Young (illustration 643) with prints of the Arizona desert and American Indian life; Ernest Haskell with etchings of California and Maine; or Kerr Eby with New England landscapes.

The First World War helped jolt the country out of its provincialism, or rather out of its complacent acceptance of a genteel art tradition. In a sense, the war took the glamour out of Europe; it no longer was something remote and awe-inspiring where the beauty of centuries dwelt. The United States suffered less than the other nations engaged in the war, and emerged with pride in its own achievements. A dynamic idea spread, namely that printmakers could find their subjects close at hand, that their own way of life and background could furnish exciting esthetic material. It was the rediscovery of a continent, the unfolding of a great pageant: landscape, people, city and country life, industry, transportation, social forces—portrayed in many different ways, factually, heroically, sketchily, lovingly, humorously, and

satirically. Here were graphic illustrations of the Face of America so eloquently described by Walt Whitman.

Around 1910, a movement in reaction against academicism was started by the New York realist painters who found their material in the homely, sometimes sordid, but always vital realities of city life. Several of them also made prints: John Sloan (illustrations 607, 608), Edward Hopper (illustrations 609, 610), and Jerome Myers made etchings, George Bellows (illustration 611) and, later, Glenn Coleman made lithographs. The almost 300 prints, which John Sloan made, mark him as one of the major printmakers of America, not only because of their content (transcripts of life vividly drawn) but also by reason of the formal relations exhibited in the later works (the sense of color and plastic solidity). The etchings of Edward Hopper likewise have commanded the respect of both modern and conservative critics because of his feeling for light and for the flawless pattern of his design. The tradition of genre and urban life was carried on in various media with compassion, with humor, with monumentality, or with rowdy gusto by other printmakers: Raphael Soyer (illustration 629), Mabel Dwight, Isabel Bishop, Paul Cadmus, Earl Horter, Reginald Marsh (illustration 627), Peggy Bacon, Harry Wickey, Martin Lewis, and others. The American Impressionist painter Childe Hassam also translated his particular idiom to the copperplate (illustration 606).

The prestige of etching, however, was challenged by the rising star of lithography. George Bellows, along with Joseph Pennell and Albert Sterner, were pioneers in the revival of lithography in America after its lapse into commercialism and disfavor. Bellows was not our greatest artist, but he was in many ways characteristic of the emergence of an American art. His boyish enthusiasm, his discovery of new subject matter, and the vigor of his execution drew the attention of artists and the public to the possibilities of lithography (illustration 611) Almost all of the younger generation of artists took to the medium with enthusiasm, approaching it not as craftsmen but as artists with a sense of creative adventure. Another factor that contributed was the existence of able lithographic printers such as George Miller and Bolton Brown (both of whom printed for Bellows), Theodore Cuno (who printed for Pennell) in Philadelphia, Linton Kistler in California, and Lawrence Barrett in Colorado. The artist-lithographers Francis Chapin, Max Kahn, Russell Limbach, Emil Ganso, Albert Carman, and Will Barnet also helped by their own work and by their teaching. As a result there emerged a group of varied aim, such as Adolf Dehn (illustration 636), Wanda Gág (illustration 619), George Biddle, William Gropper (illustration 635), Rockwell Kent (illustration 612), Yasuo Kuniyoshi (illustration 630), Max Kahn (illustration 631), Benton Spru-

ance (illustration 646), Robert Riggs, Albert Barker, and Stow Wengenroth, all of whom have done special things with the lithograph stone.

Rudolph Ruzicka, also a distinguished typographer and type designer (illustration 602), Allen Lewis, J. J. A. Murphy (illustration 622), J. J. Lankes, Rockwell Kent (illustration 621), and later Howard Cook, Thomas W. Nason, Paul Landacre (illustration 623), Fritz Eichenberg, and Lynd Ward, freed wood engraving from its servitude as a reproductive medium and raised it to the dignity of a creative vehicle. Linoleum blocks in color were used by Alfred Frueh to produce some trenchant portraits of theatre folk.

As early as 1910 reports began to drift in from Paris about new and strange ways of painting and drawing. Exhibiting centers of experimental work came into being, such as Stieglitz's "291" Gallery, where Marin's modern etchings were shown, and likewise drawings by Max Weber (illustration 614) and Abraham Walkowitz. The big Armory Show of 1913, organized by Arthur B. Davies (illustration 615), Walter Pach, and Walt Kuhn, put modern art dramatically on the map. The innovations of the Postimpressionists shocked and bewildered an unprepared public. But, equally important, the same exhibition introduced to a wider audience the work of the American realists and independents, outside the pale of the National Academy and the conservative etching societies. The Armory showing inspired and encouraged the younger artists but did not at once win over popular taste. The liberating influence of Fauvism and Cubism made its way slowly against violent and scurrilous opposition. But these were not the only factors that helped to modify the taste of the time. The Jazz Age was in many ways a period of revolutionary ferment and foreign innovation. If Cézanne, Matisse, and Duchamp were avant-garde, so were Russian ballet and its decor, so were peasant art and folk art and primitive sculpture in general, so was picturesque adventure in foreign lands (Rockwell Kent, George Biddle, Pop Hart, Boardman Robinson). All these influences played a part in breaking down the restrictions of the academicians. By the end of the 1920s the battle for the freedom of art expression had been won.

Meanwhile the younger generation was absorbing the principles of the Postimpressionists: dynamic design, accentuated three-dimensional feeling, distortion and stylization for formal or emotive effects. The works of Charles Sheeler (illustration 617), Niles Spencer (illustration 620), Yasuo Kuniyoshi (illustration 630), Wanda Gág (illustration 619), Howard Cook (illustration 626), and Stuart Davis (illustration 616) are noteworthy in this respect, and of course many of the printmakers already mentioned continued to produce. The period was by way

of becoming a golden age of printmaking. Money was plentiful and prints by both conservative and advanced artists were actively collected. This expansion was arrested catastrophically by the financial crash of 1929 and the resultant depression. It wiped out the old-fashioned collector. Since the financial worth of his collection, often inflated beyond true value, was dissipated, he suffered monetary loss as well as great disillusion. The professional printmakers, who were dependent on the patronage of the collector, likewise suffered a setback from which they never fully recovered. The young collectors, who grew up after the depression and had the means to buy art, usually acquired only sufficient pictures to cover the walls. The serious collector who aimed at a full coverage of a printmaker's work was no more.

Two trends were evident in the 1930s. One of these was the revolt against the dominance of the big cities, New York and Chicago, and the emergence of regional schools. Perhaps the most publicized of such schools was the midwestern trio, Benton (illustration 642), Curry, and Wood, but numerous other artists, as for instance Harry Wickey, Henry G. Keller, Howard Cook, Adolf Dehn, Caroline Durieux, Peter Hurd, Everett Spruce, and Carol Cloar also depicted the "American scene" without quite so much fanfare. The list could be extended indefinitely. Insofar as regionalism represented the establishment of local centers of printmaking all over the country, it was a gain to American graphic art, for it increased exposure to art and encouraged artists to make use of neglected pictorial material close at home. The other trend was the appearance of socially conscious art in urban areas where the incidence of economic depression was greatest. A few of the artists even joined the Communist party. But social protest did not prove to be a lasting influence for it dwindled when conditions improved. The Federal Art Projects, established in the second half of the 1930s as relief measures during the depression, did, however, contribute certain tangible benefits to printmaking in America, chiefly by aiding many young artists at a critical period in their careers. The list of important printmakers who received their start on the art projects is impressive: to name but a few, Max Kahn, Misch Kohn, George Constant, Louis Schanker, Lawrence Kupferman, Mitchell Siporin, Fred Becker, Russell Limbach. Another contribution was the development of new graphic techniques, such as the carbograph (in Philadelphia) and the serigraph or silk-screen stencil print. The latter medium, an extension of an old stencil method used commercially, was adapted for artists' use chiefly by Anthony Velonis (illustration 637) on the New York Art Project around 1938. Velonis is an engaging personality, a tireless experimenter for whom the search is the prime incentive. Like S. F. B. Morse, he has gifts

both as an artist and as an inventor. There can be little doubt as to his practical ability to organize and adapt means to an end. The name serigraph (silk-drawing) by analogy with lithograph (stone-drawing) was invented to avoid the awkward term silk-screen-stencil-print and to distinguish between commercial productions and original prints made by artists. Among the early pioneers of serigraphy were Guy Maccoy, Elizabeth Olds, Ruth Chaney, Hyman Warsager, Harry Sternberg, Ruth Gikow, Leonard Pytlak, Doris Meltzer, Bernard Steffen, and Robert Gwathmey (illustration 638). The Silk Screen Group was founded in 1940, changed into the National Serigraph Society in 1944, and flourished for about ten years. The wide range and diverse styles of the first decade of serigraphy can be typified by two examples: the abstract solidity of Eugene Morley's *Execution* (illustration 640) and the random freedom and delicacy of Sylvia Wald's *Tundra* (illustration 639). Later another group was organized in California, The Western Serigraph Society (Dorothy Bowman and Howard Bradford), and flourished for a few years. After a period of quiescence, the medium has come to life again through its use by the artists of the 1960s.

The decade of the 1940s witnessed the phenomenal rise in popularity of the School of Paris among collectors, a fact that has had considerable influence on American art as well. The German Expressionists, whose work began to be seen more frequently in this country, also gained in influence. And it was in 1940 that the Englishman S. W. Hayter arrived in this country to preach his gospel of creative engraving and mixed techniques. He soon had an eager following among printmakers. He organized the group, "Atelier 17," which carried on research in soft-ground textures, relief etching, and other technical innovations. Among the contemporary printmakers who at one time or another were connected with Atelier 17 may be mentioned: Mauricio Lasansky, Gabor Peterdi (already in Paris), Fred Becker, André Racz, Sue Fuller, Reginald Marsh, Karl Schrag, Ezio Martinelli, Abraham Rattner, Seong Moy, and Norma Morgan. Through his stimulus and that of his erstwhile pupil Lasansky of Iowa State University (who in turn has taught such pupils as Glen Alps, Lee Chesney, John Paul Jones, and Malcolm Myers) a new kind of print, sometimes abstract, sometimes expressionist, but always based on complex intaglio techniques, has spread like wildfire. Lasansky (illustration 650) is a highly gifted and emotionally intense artist whose creative output has been curtailed by his dedicated teaching. Gabor Peterdi (illustration 649) teaches at Yale and has also written an excellent book on technique. Both Lasansky and Peterdi have been important influences in American printmaking.

During the 1940s and 1950s print production had

reached almost astronomical proportions, and it is difficult to survey adequately contemporary printmaking. There is multiplicity of technique as well as of idiom. In addition to complex elaboration of the intaglio processes, combinations of intaglio and relief printing, and improvements in serigraph manipulation, new materials, plastics, have been used, cellocut by Boris Margo, and Lucite engraving by Harold Paris (illustration 655), or new pigments have been applied, such as the encaustic colors of Milton Goldstein.

A complete revolution in taste has taken place since the beginning of the century. This can be strikingly demonstrated by the following tabulation. In 1914 a yearbook by Forbes Watson came out, reproducing groups of prints by each of the following artists: Aid, Burr, Chandler, Cotton, Gleeson, Goetsch, Goldthwaite, Haskell, Higgins, Hornby, Horter, Hunt, Hurley, Levy, Lewis, MacLaughlin, Manley, Marin, Merrill, Nordfeldt, Pearson, Plowman, Reed, Stevens, Trowbridge, White, Winslow, and Mahonri Young. Most of these are virtually unknown today, and all of them, including the early Marin etchings, were in the traditional manner. In 1936, the magazine *Prints* conducted an elaborate survey of the state of printmaking. In this survey ten artists were rated as having the widest national acclaim in the following order: Rockwell Kent, John Taylor Arms, Kerr Eby, Frank Benson, Peggy Bacon, Arthur Heintzelman, Adolf Dehn, Thomas Nason, Wanda Gág, and John Sloan. Supplementary to this were listings in six regional groups, in which the following stood first in each: Howard Cook, Thomas Handforth, Alfred Hutty, Levon West, Emil Ganso, and Martin Lewis. Not many even of these would be known at present! No such survey exists for today. Besides, it would be outside the scope of this book, which ends approximately at mid-century for reasons which I have explained elsewhere. In a sense it is a pity that the survey ends arbitrarily at mid-century, for the 1950s and 1960s witnessed a variety of movements and an upsurge of experimentation and possibly a touch of commercial speculation and exploitation. It was during that period that Abstract Expressionism and Pop Art flourished and achieved international renown and influence—America's contribution to world art. But the issues are so complex and wide ranging and the critical standards so revolutionary that a separate book would be required to treat the subject adequately.

For another print medium, photography, a separate book would also be required in order to record all the variations of American documentary and scientific photography, such as press photography, photomicrography, stroboscopic photography, and the like; or even a comprehensive survey of American photographs as creative art. Even the six photographers whose work is illustrated deserve more than six illustrations to suggest the range and quality of their work. Alfred Stieglitz was a genius of photography in technical skill, psychological insight, and creative vision. His control of every detail of selection, angle of view, exposure, and printing builds up definite esthetic and psychological values that haunt the imagination in *The Steerage* (illustration 662). A born experimenter and keenly alive to the significant currents of his time, he was among the first to photograph night and rainy scenes, airplanes, and skyscrapers. His portraits and those interpretations of nature's moods called *Equivalents* are among the great achievements of the camera. Edward Steichen started out as a painter, later turned to photography, and was associated with Stieglitz at "291." He, too, was famous for his portraits. Later, he became chief photographer of Conde Nast Publications, and then director of the department of photography at the Museum of Modern Art, where he arranged the famous exhibition *Family of Man* in 1955. His photograph of Alphonse Mucha was made in 1902 (illustration 665). Stieglitz gave Paul Strand his first exhibition at his "291" gallery and devoted a whole number of *Camera Work* to his work. Strand's photographs were stark and direct, and were projected with the utmost clarity. They shocked the Photo-Secession photographers who were used to soft-focus effects and esthetic manipulations. His *Wire Wheel*, 1918 (illustration 663), is striking in its organization of modern industrial forms in an abstract pattern. During his long life he has continued to record the world around him with fidelity, clarity, and understanding. In recent years he has been in the habit of making sequences of photographs, depicting life in various parts of the world (Mexico, France, Italy, the Hebrides, and Egypt), which were then reproduced in book form. Ansel Adams was a musician before he became a professional photographer. His name is associated with the Yosemite Valley in California, and indeed his *Branches in Snow* is taken from one of his Yosemite Portfolios (illustration 664). He loves nature and is an ardent conservationist. He is a great technician in pure photography and has had considerable influence through his teaching and the manuals he has written. Edward Weston was also an advocate of pure photography, that is to say, making prints without enlarging or cropping for composition. The final result is as the photographer sees it from the beginning. Weston's photographs, rock forms, nudes, vegetables creating abstract patterns, are notable for their inventiveness of design and precision of detail (illustration 666). Barbara Morgan is a painter, printmaker, and photographer with a joyously sensuous appreciation of life. Famous for her photographs of Martha Graham in her dances, she has also published *Summer's Children*, a photographic cycle of life in summer camp. In a more abstract and experi-

mental vein, her photograph *Samadhi* is actually a drawing with light (illustration 659). It is to be regretted that lack of space precludes a consideration of numerous other important photographers such as Brett Weston, Charles Sheeler, Walker Evans, Dorothea Lange, Bernice Abbott, Minor White, and Robert Frank. Man Ray, an American living in Paris, made some abstract photographs without a camera by laying miscellaneous objects upon sensitized film and exposing to strong light. Lazló Moholy-Nagy also made similar experiments independently at the Bauhaus in Germany.

It might be expedient, after having surveyed the broad aspects of twentieth-century American printmaking up to mid-century, to focus a little more closely upon the important artists and their work. I have already mentioned Sloan, Hopper, and Bellows, who were little affected by the innovations of the Armory Show. To this group should be added Rockwell Kent, a kind of universal personage for whom painting and printmaking were but two activities among many others, such as writing, adventure in faraway places, and social protest. A romantic realist, he followed another, possibly more Nordic, tradition than that of the School of Paris (illustrations 612, 621). Similarly Mahonri Young, a grandson of Brigham Young, showed no influence of modernist theories (illustration 643).

For another group, all established artists and trained in traditional schools, the principles of modern art were a great revelation. Arthur B. Davies (illustration 615), one of the sponsors of the Armory Show, was a successful romantic painter and assiduous printmaker (his earliest prints date from about 1895). He was a tireless experimenter both in technique and in style. His work has an almost feminine sensibility and poetic charm. The influence of the Armory Show, however, upon his prints was only superficial. Walt Kuhn was also a sponsor of the Armory Show but its influence was confined largely to his few prints, for his paintings were in general vigorous and realistic, with subjects drawn largely from the circus and performer's world. The painter Charles Sheeler, famous for his precise rendering of industrial structures, made a few lithographs of abstract patterns, such as *Yachts*, 1924 (illustration 617). He took a characteristic of sailboats, their billowing sails, and made from them a pattern of graceful curves. Similarly *White Factory* by Niles Spencer (illustration 620) is an abstract arrangement of planes and textures with strong three-dimensional implications. Stuart Davis, as a young Independent artist, made drawings for the *Masses Magazine* and exhibited in the Armory Show. He eventually developed a personal style of abstraction, and made what he called "compositions celebrating the resolution in art-stresses set up by some aspects of the American scene" (illustra-

tion 616).

John Marin began as a conventional etcher of European urban scenes but soon began to evolve a more inventive and personal style. He started to make watercolors and eventually became one of the leading watercolorists of America. After his return to the United States in 1911, his graphic production became less in number compared with his watercolors and later oils, but it had great significance. His later prints are rare but important. His etching *Woolworth Building: the Dance* of 1913 (illustration 625) is Expressionist in feeling, whereas in the *Sailboat* of 1932 (illustration 618) the keynote is abstraction and synthesis for essentials. Marin's development came from within himself and was not prompted by outside influences. He therefore did not learn any lessons from the Armory Show: he knew them already. Max Weber also did not need the Armory Show for inspiration. From 1905 to 1909 he was in Paris where he studied with Matisse. He was especially influenced by Cézanne and primitive African sculpture (illustration 614). Arnold Ronnebeck came to this country as a full-fledged modern sculptor in the early 1920s. He made stylized lithographs of New York. Eventually he moved to Colorado, close to the Indian country where he made a number of lithographs. *Chicken Pull* (illustration 641) is a game played by the Taos Indians, in which they, riding on horseback, try to snatch a chicken from each other. It is interesting to compare this lithograph with Benton's *Going West* (illustration 642). Both Ronnebeck and Benton have made use of certain modern devices to suggest speed.

One of the great benefits of the Armory Show and its aftermath was that it encouraged individuality in painters, sculptors, and printmakers. They discovered that it was possible for them to do their own thing in spite of the academicians. The work of Wanda Gág, for example, has exuberance and vitality. Her design is never static. Her delight in repetitive rhythms is readily apparent (illustration 619). Two themes ran through Adolf Dehn's work: landscape and caricature, nature and human nature (illustration 636). He was a powerful satirist and he could render, with all the resources of the lithographic stone (often by unorthodox means), the subtler moods of nature—dawn, mist, dusk, night with half-lights and shadows, the changing accents of the seasons. William Gropper has been called the American Daumier. Gropper is in no sense an imitator of Daumier, but there are numerous analogies between the two artists. Both gained their chief living as cartoonists, and both espoused causes unpopular in their day. In *For the Record* (illustration 635), one of a series called *The Senate*, the orator is making remarks which will be immortalized in the *Congressional Record*. Note how the emotional tension is heightened and the humor intensified by the contrast between the

vehemence of the speaker and the indifference of his colleagues. Louis Lozowick in his lithograph *Tanks* (illustration 633) has rendered, with precision and formal interest, modern industrial structures. Note the symbolism of the presence of the horse and airplane, the contrast between natural and mechanical power. Harry Sternberg, a painter and all-around printmaker, also had an interest in industry, especially in its human side (illustration 634); in his maturity he has reflected on the grandeur of mountains and on larger social issues, including satire on the littleness of man. Hyman Warsager, in addition to his pioneering serigraphs, has made some expressionist aquatints in color (illustration 628). He seeks to convey the impressions of the stifling summer atmosphere of a city night. Every detail contributes to this effect, the hot glare amid the murky darkness, the oppressive downward thrust of all the shapes, weighing down the figures on the fire escape. Reginald Marsh was a sort of reporter extraordinary. He marshaled facts without taking sides. He depicted a raucous Bowery scene, *Tattoo, Shave and Haircut* (illustration 627), with the same detachment with which he drew a locomotive or the audience of a burlesque show. Prentiss Taylor's work is characterized by sensibility and taste, a style blended of baroque and romantic elements, with whimsical details and witty juxtaposition of details (illustration 648). Benton Spruance's whole life was dedicated to lithography, not only through his *oeuvre* but also through his teaching. He did not have an instinctive sense of style and had to find his personal idiom by long and persistent effort. He achieved it in his later color prints. He was intelligent and keenly aware of the issues of today. He often interpreted ancient legends in contemporary terms (illustration 646). Federico Castellón, precociously gifted, started out with symbolic and surrealist prints and drawings; later he turned to expressionist modes, all with a distinctive style. *Rendezvous in a Landscape* (illustration 645) is an early work with dreamlike overtones of a surrealist approach. It seems to evoke that moment of wonder when Adam first met Eve. The lithographs of Raphael Soyer have the same qualities that mark his paintings. There is the same touching feeling of sympathy and humanity, the same vibrant suggestion of atmosphere, the same evocation of types from the Bowery bum to the young woman of today (illustration 629). John J. A. Murphy combined the use of religious and modern subject matter with significant research in technique and optics, in the breaking up of forms for emotive effect, and in the application of optical focus for the rendering of planes in recession (illustration 622). The wood engraving *Counterpoint* (illustration 623), with its suggestion of pivotal movement, is by Paul Landacre of California. His prints are characterized by their originality, intriguing design, and faultless

execution. Howard Cook, a notable mural painter and proficient printmaker, was born in New England and now lives in the Southwest. He has a genuine feeling for the essential characteristics of a place, from *New England Church*, a wood engraving, to *Mexican Interior*, an etching. It is interesting to compare the plastic solidity of his lithograph *Lower Manhattan* (illustration 626) with Marin's more fanciful interpretation (illustration 625). Max Kahn, sculptor and printmaker, has lived and taught in Chicago. His color lithographs have an expressionist slant, such as *Judith on the Way to the Tent of Holofernes* or the amusing *Cat Walk* (illustration 631). Will Barnet is a gifted artist who has passed through several stylistic phases: one of deliberate simplification or primitivism, one of elaborate abstraction, and one of stylized realism (illustration 632). He has taught printmaking at the Art Students League and elsewhere. Yasuo Kuniyoshi has a personal vision which may be due in part to his Oriental heritage. There are in his prints a sure realization of form, sensitiveness to tone and color, and racy idiomatic draftsmanship (illustration 630). There is also a slightly strange accent in the work of Twohy (Two-vy-nah-auche, "Land Elk" of the Ute Indian tribe), for in his lithograph *Indian Village* (illustration 644) he makes use of certain pictorial conventions employed by the old Indian tribes in their paintings on buffalo hides, such as the so-called "winter counts."

There are about a half dozen artists who are outstanding for the quality and quantity of their contribution and for their teaching and influence on the printmakers of the 1940s and 1950s. I have already spoken of Lasansky in Iowa and Peterdi of Yale. There is also Misch Kohn of Chicago. He has an incredible virtuosity of technique that reinforces the originality of his invention. He has made, for instance, some very large wood engravings (illustration 652), which become more difficult to print as they increase in size. He solved the problem by printing the wood blocks in a lithographic press. Later he worked in aquatint by the lift-ground process, producing animal and figural compositions with calligraphic curls and swirls dripped directly onto the metal. Antonio Frasconi, South American born but living in the United States, expresses his *joie de vivre* in whatever he does, be it in woodcuts of the wine country of California, the fish markets of New York, or *Some Well-known Fables* (illustration 651). He has taught in New York. Caroline Durieux has a delightful sense of the absurd. She is a born satirist, although she claims that she is not a satirist but a realist. She is also notable for her technical innovations. She has perfected a new medium of printmaking, the electron print (illustration 657), by using radioactive isotopes as the duplicating principle. She has also done research on a new method of color printing. It employs the principle

of the *cliché verre* (used by Corot and Millet) applied to exposed Matrix film. The coating is loosened but not separated from its transparent base, and then manipulated by hand into various shaped areas and wrinkles to make an abstract composition. For color she uses an extension of the dye-transfer process. She is professor emeritus at Louisiana State University. June Wayne has ideas and the technique and esthetic feeling to project them as works of art. She has done research in optics and crystalline modules, and often works in series of paintings or prints (illustration 658). Her creative work has to a certain extent been curtailed by her abilities in other fields than art, for instance her executive ability in founding the Tamarind Lithographic Workshop in Los Angeles. This institution has had great influence on American printmaking not only by printing lithographs for artists and establishing fellowships, but also by training lithographic printers, who in turn have established workshops all over the country.

There are several artists not previously mentioned who have made their name as painters or sculptors and who also have a considered body of prints to their credit. Ben Shahn and Jack Levine both can be called humanists because of their antipathy to geometric abstraction and their interest in social questions. Shahn works in silk screen (illustration 653) and Levine in etching (illustration 647). Shahn has translated his particular style into prints, posters, and book illustrations. Leonard Baskin could also be called a humanist for his preoccupation with the human figure—often greatly distorted—in his sculpture and prints (illustration 654). Many of them convey the feeling of agony. He began as a wood engraver and then also worked in etching in a continuing series of portraits of artists whom he admires. He loves books and has established a press of his own, the "Gehenna Press," where he designs and issues books in limited editions, sometimes illustrated with his own wood-blocks. Josef Albers of Bauhaus fame has made geometric abstractions in woodcut, lithograph, and silk screen, sometimes with a slight pedagogical overtone. His early woodcut *Aquarium*, 1934 (illustration 660), was no doubt inspired by the elegant curves made by darting fish. Adja Yunkers, Latvian-born painter and printmaker, is an artist of great sensibility, subtle color sense, and incredible technique. His earliest prints were woodcuts, including the *Rio Grande Portfolio*, when he first came to the United States. In 1960 he made a set of lithographs of *The Skies of Venice* on a Tamarind Lithographic Workshop Fellowship. His *magnum opus* in printmaking is his *Credo* of 1953, a huge pentaptych, of which *Magnificat* is the center panel (illustration 661). This work, executed with nine blocks and fifty-six colors (achieved by skillful overprinting) loses greatly by reproduction in black and white. In recent years he has taken to painting exclusively, and America has lost one of its great printmakers.

There are a number of painters and sculptors whose involvement with printmaking has not been so great, but who nonetheless have made noteworthy prints. Examples of three such artists have been reproduced. Ivan Albright has carried over the minute and sometimes macabre realism of his painting into his lithograph *Heavy the Oar to Him Who Is Tired* (illustration 613). Likewise Rico Lebrun reflects his intense and agonized style in his lithograph *Beggars Turned into Dogs* (illustration 656). Franklin Watkins's expressionist woodcut *Softly-Softly* (illustration 624) was based on a mural cycle, *Death and Resurrection*. It is regrettable that lack of space precluded showing examples of Milton Avery, Gifford Beal, Eugene Berman, Alexander Brook, Louis Bunce, Charles Burchfield, Sandy Calder, Ralston Crawford, Wharton Esherick, Philip Evergood, Ernest Fiene, Dorothea Greenbaum, Pop Hart, Marsden Hartley, Eugene Higgins, Joseph Hirsch, Leon Karp, Karl Knaths, Jacques Lipchitz, Peter Lipman-Wolf, Fletcher Martin, Ezio Martinelli, Kenneth Hays Miller, Louise Nevelson, Abraham Rattner, Bernard Reder, Andrée Ruellan, Louis Schanker, Kurt Seligman, Mitchel Siporin, David Smith, Maurice Sterne, John Storrs, Mark Tobey, A. Walkowitz, Karl Zerbe, and William Zorach. All have translated their characteristic style into prints.

Among the printmakers of the 1940s not previously mentioned may be cited Alfred Bendiner, Jolan Bettelheim, Morris Blackburn, Fiske Boyd, Hubert Davis, William Givler, Thomas Handforth, Clement Haupers, A. W. Heintzelman, Victoria Huntley, Mervin Jules, Gene Kloss, Armin Landeck, Barbara Latham, Clare Leighton, Charles Locke, Merrit Mauzey, Willard Nash, Ralph Pearson, Carl Pickhardt, Moishe Smith, Moses Soyer, Maybelle Stamper, and John Winkler.

Of the younger generation the list is endless. Many are on the borderline where their work extends far into the 1950s and 1960s. The following are but a few: Garo Antreasian, Edmond Casarella, Bernard Childs, Albert Christ-Janer, Warrington Colescott, Edward Colker, Mary Corita, Worden Day, Arthur Deshaies, Leonard Edmondson, Eugene Feldman, Terry Haas, Jules Heller, Ynez Johnston, Jerry Kaplan, Jacob Landau, Gerson Leiber, James McGarrell, Sam Maitin, Michael Mazur, Dean Meeker, Peter Milton, Seong Moy, Barbara Neustadt, Nathan Oliveira, Peter Paone, Michael Ponce de Leon, Rudy Pozzatti, Clare Romano, John Ross, Anne Ryan, Angelo Savelli, Karl Schrag, Aubrey Schwartz, Doris Seidler, J. L. Steg, Carol Summers, Ansei Uchima, Claire Van Vliet, Romas Viesulas, J. Von Wicht. They represent a fraction of the future in American printmaking.

9. The Orient

I. CHINA

The Orient is a far distant region whose philosophy and thought-forms, whose total outlook on life differ widely from our own Occidental culture. It possesses many secrets not easily revealed—that East where all things have been done, all emotions felt, all thoughts expressed from time immemorial. The East of asceticism and sensuality, of mysticism and rationalist ethics, of fecund life and the equally overwhelming sense of the futility of life, of experiments and theories of government from absolute monarchy through theocracy, aristocracy, militarism, and socialism to anarchy. The East of the great inventions, gunpowder, the compass, printing, and paper money. "To look for the first time at the art of Asia," said Coomaraswamy, "is to stand at the threshold of a new world. To make ourselves at home here requires sensibility, intelligence, and patience." The East that expresses itself in prints is China and Japan; the graphic arts for one or another reason did not flourish in India, Persia, and the Mohammedan countries. Here we are face to face with one more esthetic that definitely subordinates realistic representation to contemplative insight, metaphysical vitality, a quest for essentials or the innate spirit of things. There is an analogy, as Coomaraswamy has pointed out, between Oriental art and Gothic or Scholastic art: they both contain linear, calligraphic, and symbolic elements, and are expressive of inner truth rather than external reality. And, as we have seen, modern twentieth-century art in certain of its aspects seems to have approached the Oriental conception. The emphasis on the creative rather than the imitative can be illustrated by a dialogue from *Essay on Landscape Painting* by the Sung painter Ching Hao, translated by Siren.

When an old sage meets in the forest the young painter who tells the story, he asks: "Do you know the method of painting?" To which I answered: "You seem to be an old uncouth rustic; how could you know anything about brushwork?" But the old man said: "How can you know what I carry in my bosom?" Then I listened and felt ashamed and astonished; he spoke to me as follows: "Young people like to study in order to accomplish something; they should know that there are six essentials in painting. The first is called Ch'i (spirit or vitality), the second is called Yün (resonance or harmony), the third is called Ssu (thought or plan), the fourth is called Ching (effect of scenery or motif), the fifth is called Pi (brush), and the sixth is called Mo (ink)." I remarked: "Painting is to make beautiful things, and the important point is to obtain their true likeness, is it not?" He answered: "It is not. Painting is to paint: to estimate the shapes of things, to really obtain them; to estimate the beauty of things, to reach it; to estimate the reality (significance) of things and to grasp it. One should not take outward beauty for reality. He who does not understand this mystery will not obtain truth, even though his pictures may contain likeness." I asked: "What is likeness and what is truth?" The old man said: "Likeness can be obtained by shapes without spirit, but when truth is reached, both spirit and substance are fully expressed. He who tries to express spirit through ornamental beauty will make dead things." I thanked him and said: "From this I realize that the study of calligraphy and painting is an occupation for virtuous men."

The Chinese invented paper and printing and the technique of making woodcuts. The earliest dated woodcut extant appeared in the Diamond Sutra, a Buddhist scripture with the date 868 (illustration 669), discovered by Sir Aurel Stein in the Cave of Ten Thousand Buddhas at Tun Huang in Chinese Turkestan, and now in the British Museum. But there must have been other and cruder woodcuts before that time printed by stamping. We can therefore safely say that the Chinese have been making woodcuts for well over a thousand years. Printmaking in China was largely interpretive or didactic, and not an instrument for original creative work. Paintings and drawings were reproduced in woodcut by specialized craftsmen (illustration 671). Since so few of the early paintings have survived, the print often remains the only record of an artist's pictures or style still existing. The technical competence of these woodcut craftsmen varied greatly. Many of the blocks were very crudely cut and none too faithful in their interpretation of the original. Nor can productions be dated on the basis of cruder or more primitive style. Exquisitely cut blocks are to be found in early times as well as crude work in later eras. It depended upon the skill of the individual craftsman.

The vast majority of Chinese woodcuts were made for books. The earliest printing of books occurred in the eighth century, when the idea of taking impressions on paper from wooden blocks seems to have arisen, chiefly in connection with Buddhist tracts and images. A large number of these early books were destroyed in 845 during the reign of the Taoist T'ang Emperor Huei Ch'ang, who ordered the destruction of over 4500 Buddhist temples. Production of printed books, however, did not become general until 932 when the Confucian Canon, and 972 when the Buddhist Canon or *Tripitaka*, was printed for the first time. In these early days a page of text was cut on a single block; these books were what we call block-books. Movable type of baked clay was invented about 1043, and some centuries later was made of wood or metal; but its use was never so general as the block-book method. T'ang, Sung, and Yüan illustrated books are now very rare. During Sung times it became customary to fold over the sheets and tie together the loose ends to make pages—a style of binding that has continued in use ever since. Previously books were in the form of rolled hand scrolls or were folded in bundles accordion-fashion.

A fragment of a *Tripitaka*, in hand-scroll form at the Fogg Art Museum, contains four large woodcuts which (according to Prof. Max Loehr, who has written a book about them) may be among the earliest landscape woodcuts known. The text is part of a commentary written by the Sung Emperor T'ai-tsung, or Chao Huang (976–997), on the *Tripitaka* published during his reign. This fragment, however, must belong to a later reprint from the original wood blocks, since it is dated 1108 in the cartouche at the end of the chapter. The original wood blocks of the text and pictures must have been cut between the years 984 and 991, but not one of the earlier printings has survived. The four pictures are well designed and expertly cut, and are specially noteworthy in that, although they accompany Buddhist scripture, the religious imagery is subordinate to the landscape. In the example shown (illustration 668), note the relative unimportance of the only bit of religious imagery, the hermit's hut, in the upper left corner, and the proficient rendering of trees and rocks and stylized cloud forms.

There was a great expansion of illustrated book production during the Ming dynasty, particularly during the reigns of Hung Wu (1368–99) and Wan Li (1572–1622). The earliest illustrated books were almost all religious in character. In the Ming and succeeding dynasties, the field was enlarged to include history, poetry, encyclopedias, drawing manuals, and other books on the arts and sciences.

There was another print medium used in China long before the invention of the woodcut—the stone rubbing, T'a. About the year 175 the six Confucian classics were engraved on stone by imperial authority, and the slabs were set up at the entrance of the academy in order that scholars might have the benefit of an accurate and enduring text. Copies were struck off for the use of scholars when lampblack ink was perfected during the fourth and fifth centuries, and it was discovered that impressions of inscriptions and designs incised in flat slabs or rock could be obtained. A dampened sheet of thin but tough paper was laid on the stone and forced into all the incisions, whereupon black ink (occasionally red or green or blue) was applied with a flat pad to the surface of the paper (that side of the paper which we would call the back). Because the ink could not reach into the incisions, the design appeared in white against a background of black. In this way was avoided that reversal of image which always takes place when ink is applied *between* the block and the paper. Although there are references to stone rubbings in early Chinese literature, the earliest actual stone rubbing now in existence, discovered by Pelliot at Tun-Huang, dates from the reign of the T'ang emperor, T'ai Tsung (Li Shih-min) (627–49). In 992 there is a record of the publication of books of stone rubbings after calligraphy of the Tsin and Wei dynasties.

It is not known when stone engraving was first used for the reproduction of designs by well-known artists; possibly it was as early as T'ang. Tablets exist dating from Sung times with engravings supposedly after originals, now lost, by Wu Tao Tzu and other artists. From the Ming dynasty onwards stone engravings were made to perpetuate famous paintings in increasing numbers. In certain places, such as The Grove of Stone Tablets (Pei Lin) at Sian-fu or the Confucian Temple at Ch'ü-fu, whole collections or museums of incised tablets exist, from which stone rubbings are still taken. Rubbings were made not only from stones prepared for this purpose but also from famous sculptured monuments, wherever flat incised or low-relief stones existed. For instance, as early as 1064 the Sung scholar Ou-yang Hsiu referred to stone rubbings in his possession from the funerary chamber of the Wu family (illustration 678). Similarly, rubbings have been made of sculpture in the caves of Yün Kang in Shansi (illustration 679) or of Lung Mên near Lo-yang in Honan (illustration 680). Rubbings are still being made today. Similarly, stone rubbings are also being made in countries south of China such as Cambodia and Thailand.

One of the most famous and seemingly authentic designs ascribed to Wu Tao Tzu is the *Tortoise and Serpent*, symbol of the North (illustration 681), taken from a stone in the Municipal Office at Ch'êng-tu, capital of Szechwan. Another work, a Kuan-yin, exists in several stone versions. Wu Tao Tzu is perhaps the most renowned of

all Chinese painters, and many fantastic legends are told of him, though no authentic work of his (much of it having been in fresco) exists today except for such translations as the stone rubbings. As early as 1085 the Chinese painter and critic Su Tung P'o could write that he knew of only one or two genuine pictures by Wu Tao Tzu. In a reconstruction from various sources Waley describes his style as realistic, strongly sculpturesque and three-dimensional, imaginatively original, and facile in technique; he quotes Su Tung P'o's estimate: "Wu Tao Tzu's figures might have been drawn from lantern shadows on the wall. They seem to walk out of the picture and back into it; they project, can be seen from each side. The flat planes and tilted angles fit into one another as though by a natural geometric law." The T'ang dynasty during which he worked was one of the most creative in Chinese history. Among his famous contemporaries were the landscape painter Wang Wei, the poets Li Po and Tu Fu, and the Emperor Ming Huan, poet and musician, whose mad infatuation for the concubine Yang Kueifei, "the most beautiful woman in the world," led to his downfall.

Of Wu's contemporary, Wang Wei, equally known as a poet and a painter, likewise, no authentic original has survived, and we can estimate his greatness only by his reputation and influence, which has been enormous. He has been called the father of the Southern Sung Landscape School and of poetic landscape in general. His mature paintings, chiefly in monochrome (p'o-mo or broken ink style), were of a subtlety and delicacy which made translation into another medium well-nigh impossible. The Wang Ch'uan hand scroll, an early work in miniature style, portraying his villa and gardens, from a Ming stone rubbing (dated 1617), is based probably on a Sung copy of the original. As Tung Ch'i Ch'ang, the Ming critic said, the beloved contour lines were there but the execution was so poor that the engraving could not be made the standard for Wang's style.

The woodcut based on a stone rubbing, the *God of Fortune* (illustration 684), is attributed to Su Tung-P'o (1036–1101), a universal genius of the Sung dynasty, a poet, essayist, art critic, calligrapher, and painter. The print, distinguished for its exquisite placement of seals, design, and script, illustrates the close relation between calligraphy and drawing in Chinese art. In his practice with written character, every Chinese scholar acquires a sensitive appreciation of the formal and artistic aspects of writing, of individuality of brush stroke, rhythm, symmetry, asymmetry, balance, and vitality of line. Where every written character is in itself a work of art, calligraphy ranks as a fine art. In China there are people who collect examples of writing as we collect works of art. In this picture the artist first drew an ideograph or written character, and then upon that drew a head, thus

creating the character of the God of Fortune, both as symbol and as representation. Another example of this kind of artistic punning is a stone rubbing dated 1864 of *Chung K'uei* (illustration 687) after a painting by K'uei Hsing. The portrait is a fanciful adaptation of the ideograph for Chung K'uei, the Demon Queller, whose effigy is often hung at the portals of houses to ward off evil spirits.

Three cultural traditions run through Chinese art and history, and are, in a sense, recapitulated in the personal attitudes of cultivated Chinese: Confucianism, Taoism, and Buddhism. The modern scholar T. C. Lin's dictum: "We are socially Confucian and individually Taoist," is matched by the T'ang poet Po Chü Yi, who wrote in his epitaph that he used Confucianism to order his conduct, used Buddhism to cleanse his mind, and then utilized history, paintings, mountains, rivers, wine, music and song to soothe his spirit.

Confucianism has been a force in China for about twenty-five hundred years—the Doctrine of the Golden Mean (the Mean-in-Action or morality), a system of rational ethics, a reliance on good breeding, art, and ritual for the cementing of human relations. When asked if there was not one word which could be the keynote to conduct, the Master said: "Is not reciprocity such a word? What you do not wish done to yourself, do not do to others." Pragmatic in his attitude, Confucius was quoted by his grandson Tsesze as saying: "I know now why the moral life is not practised. The wise mistake moral law for something higher than what it really is; and the foolish do not know enough what moral law really is. I know now why the moral law is not understood. Noble natures want to live too high, high above their moral ordinary self; and ignoble natures do not live high enough. There is no one who does not eat and drink. But few there are who really know flavor." Such in brief was the teaching of Confucius, projecting the ideal of a cultivated man true to his own nature, aiming neither too high nor too low, and enjoying the pleasant life of a scholar and a gentleman. As early as Han times, the great historian Szuma Ch'ien could say: "All people in China, who discuss the six arts, from the Emperor down, regard the Master as the final authority." Significant, too, is the examination system for public office, instituted in the T'ang Dynasty and in use ever since, whereby candidates for public service are selected on the basis of their knowledge of the Confucian classics. Everything relating to the life and works of Confucius has been the subject of diligent compilation by Chinese scholars. It is natural, therefore, that many books exist portraying his life in word and image. The portrait of Confucius (illustration 683) is a characteristic example of the use of a flowing linear rhythm and the emphasis on an inner likeness. The Chi-

nese ideal of portraiture is expressed by a writer of the twelfth century, Hu Ch'üan. How different it is from Albrecht Dürer's dictum engraved on his portrait of Philip Melanchthon: "The trained hand of Dürer can depict the features of the living Philip but not his mind."

There is no branch of painting so difficult as portrait painting. It is not that the reproduction of the features is difficult; the difficulty lies in painting the springs of action hidden in the heart. The face of a great man may resemble that of a mean man, but their hearts will not be alike. Therefore, to paint a likeness which does not exhibit these heart-impulses, leaving it an open question whether the sitter is a great man or a mean man, is to be unskilled in the art of portraiture.

The portrait of Confucius also has a technical interest: it is small enough to have been issued in book or album form. Rubbings were not always made from large stone slabs. Apparently books were printed either from wood or stone. Among the finds of Sir Aurel Stein in the Tun Huang caves was an edition of the text of the Diamond Sutra made up of stone rubbings.

Taoism, in contrast to the urbane worldliness of Confucianism, represented a mystical strain in the direction of simplicity and passivity in harmony with a universal principle, Nature. Convinced of the relativity of all attributes, the pure Taoist turned away from the rational and intellectual: he desired to *be* rather than to know or to do. In the *Tao Tê Ching*, attributed to that mythical personality, Lao Tzu, and in the delightfully written and profound parables and reflections of the Chuang Tzu (ca. 300 B.C.), this contemplative and unworldly ideal is expounded in such maxims as "Those who know do not speak; those who speak do not know," or "The sage does nothing but achieves everything," or the following, in Hughes's translation:

> To know men is to be wise,
> To know one's self is to be illumined.
> To conquer men is to have strength,
> To conquer one's self is to be stronger still,
> And to know when you have had enough is to be rich.

There were, however, other aspects to Taoism besides a mystical philosophy. Taoism as mythology and a special technique of soothsaying dated back to before Han times. This established religion degenerated—as did Buddhism, each borrowing from the other—into the practice of meaningless ritual, magic incantations, and a superstitious belief in demons and sorcery. Taoism in this debased form bore no relation to lofty concepts of Lao Tzu and Chuang Tzu; the purer strain of their teaching was carried on in the appreciation of nature and the cult of mystical simplicity of many poets and artists, and in

particular was to have considerable influence on Sung landscape painting. Among our illustrations are several that exhibit Taoist influence. One is a rubbing from the relief sculptures in the funerary chamber of the Wu family at Chia Hsiang in Shantung, dated A.D. 147, depicting in a courtyard the Ho Huan Tree (illustration 678) with forked trunk and interlacing branches, the sacred cosmic tree of Taoist lore. Another rubbing, likewise displaying the vigor of Han dynasty art, is the so-called Li Hsi Stone at Ch'ên-hsien in Kan-su, which has been dated A.D. 171. *Five Omens of the Frog Pool* (illustration 677) is one of the earliest representations of landscape and of the dragon, chiefly a Taoist symbol, here representing beneficent rain. Among the other omens may be recognized a deer, bespeaking length of days, two trees growing together, a stalk laden with ears, and a man making a votive gesture. A world of magic and myth, of animals and demons is revealed in a woodcut illustration. Readers of Wu Ch'êng-ên's folk novel *Hsi Yu Chi*, Record of a Journey to the West, translated by Arthur Waley under the title of *Monkey*, will remember it as a fantastic mingling of Taoist and Buddhist lore. The framework of the novel is based on a historical fact, the pilgrimage of Hsüan Tsang to India in the seventh century in order to gather Buddhist scriptures (*Tripitaka*). By the tenth century, as Waley points out, Hsüan's pilgrimage had become the subject of a whole cycle of legends. The woodcut *Scene in a Spiral* (illustration 672), from *Shu I Chi* or Record of Marvels, has been identified by Dr. Fêng Yulan as being related to the corpus of legend associated with the monkey hero. It is not an illustration to Wu Ch'êng-ên's novel, since the author lived in the sixteenth century, and this woodcut dates from early Ming times (reign of Hung Wu, 1368–99). It is interesting technically, too, in that the red and yellow coloring seems to have been applied through stencils.

Buddhism was officially introduced into China during the reign of Ming Ti, who in A.D. 61–67 had sent a mission into India to discover, as the legend runs, the god whose golden image had been revealed to him in a dream. Buddhism, first regarded as an alien religion, gradually grew in power and influence. The form of Buddhism current in China was the Mahayana, or Great Vehicle, with a wider scope and larger pantheon of divinities than the austere intellectual doctrine of Nibbana taught by Gautama himself, and thus more sympathetic to plastic expression in the arts. Most Chinese sculpture reveals Buddhist elements. The stone rubbing *Buddha* (illustration 679) from the caves at Yün Kang shows a strong Indian influence. This carving is in higher relief than most others from which rubbings have been taken, which accounts for the almost completely white background. It was under the Bo or Bodhi tree, the Tree of

Wisdom at Bodh Gaya, that Shakyamuni after a colossal mental struggle attained Buddhahood. From another cave, Lung Mên, comes a stone rubbing, *Maitreya*, dated A.D. 542 (illustration 680). It is indeed a most moving dramatization of a hermit's rapt contemplation. Completing a trio of pictures of the Buddhist inner life is *Lohan* (illustration 686) after the Buddhist priest, poet, and painter Kuan Hsiu (832–912), from a sixteen-sided stele in Hang-chou engraved by order of Ch'ien Lung and dated 1764. In Buddhist mythology, the Lohan or Arhats were the sixteen disciples commanded by the Buddha to remain in the world without entering Nirvana until the coming of the future Buddha Maitreya, to protect his Law. One is impressed by the powerful characterization of these grotesque ascetic types, who are supposed to have appeared to the artist in a vision.

The woodcut *Kuan-yin* (illustration 670), from the set *P'u-sa Hsiang-tu* (Images of Bodhisattvas), dates apparently from early Ming times (there is an attribution to the reign of Hung Wu, 1368–99), and thus is an earlier version of a similar set entitled *Tsu Yung Wu-shih-san Hsien* (Fifty-three Manifestations of Kuan-yin), dating from the second half of the seventeenth century. It is sensitively cut by an expert craftsman and, like the rest of the set, the result of special care in production, since each bears the inscription "Joyfully dedicated by the Marquis Huai Hsi, of Sei Yang, a disciple of Buddha." It likewise differs from the later set in that each Bodhisattva (including others beside Kuan-yin) is attended by a Lokapala or Guardian of the Four Corners of the World. Buddhism was a great stimulus to the graphic arts. From the earliest known woodcut onwards countless prints have been produced to illustrate the Sutras, to recount the life of Buddha, and to portray the hierarchy of Buddhist divinities. Images of Buddha were also used as charms (illustration 667). The single image produced by hand stamping with a seal and the carving of multiple images on a single block may have been preliminary steps in the development of the pictorial woodcut.

Bodhidharma, the great apostle of Dhyana Buddhism, came to China from India in A.D. 520. A fanciful representation of him crossing the Yangtse River on a reed is given in a T'ang stone rubbing (illustration 682). A native strain of this same school of Contemplative Buddhism developed in China under the name of Ch'an (and Zen in Japan). It taught that monastic rules and ascetic practices belonged to the World of Being; salvation was only through mystic contemplation: Buddha was pure thought, Buddha was the Way. Ch'an Buddhism, mingled as it was with the individualistic and mystic elements of pure Taoism, had a great influence on Sung landscape painting and indeed on all subsequent landscape painting. It gave the artist that spiritual background and emotional *timbre* essential for *feeling-into* a landscape, and for the imaginative and sympathetic comprehension of the forces of nature—the grandeur of mountains, the softness of mist, the silence of snow, the music of a waterfall, the innate character of pine or plum or bamboo.

There are certain conventions used by Chinese landscape painters that often prove a stumbling block for Western appreciation. One of these is what is assumed to be absence of or ignorance of perspective, but which in reality is the use of a system of perspective different from the Western geometric convention. In Chinese pictures distant objects do not recede along converging parallel lines, but are merely placed a little higher up in the picture. The convention of superposed registers, as Vernon Blake points out, dates back to Egyptian and Assyrian times, and is, in the hands of its practitioners, quite as flexible and expressive an instrument as the equally artificial geometric convention which we have come to regard as infallible. To a certain extent the customary shapes of Chinese pictures were a determining factor, either very tall and narrow or the very wide and not so tall, in neither of which would Western perspective have been very effective. An approximate way of explaining Chinese perspective is to assume that one is on a vantage point and looking down at the picture, in other words that the horizon line is high. Sometimes when the distortions inherent in the system might become unpleasant, the artists will resort to the device of breaking up the whole composition by means of cloud bands and sheets of water into several smaller units, each with its own perspective system. This is one of the reasons for the frequent use of bands of cloud and mist; and they, together with the perspective which, for example, makes mountains even more awe-inspiring than they are, add greatly to the mystery and dreamy unreality of Chinese landscape art.

The Chinese also made color woodcuts. Already in Ming times books were printed in black and red, the red being used for notes and comments. Toward the end of the Ming dynasty experiments in color printing with wood blocks to reproduce designs and paintings were being made, culminating in the publication in 1633 of a landmark, the *Shih Chu Chai Hua P'u* or Collection of Prints from the Ten Bamboo Studio. It was a collection in sixteen volumes of designs by Hu Yeh Tsung, Kao Yu, and others of birds, flowers, rocks, bamboo, prunus, orchids, and fruit (illustration 673), with an accompanying text of notes and advice to artists. Some time later, from 1679 to 1701, the first three volumes of the *Chieh-tzu-yuan Hua-chuan*, or Painting Manual of the Mustard-Seed Garden, were issued. This was specifically an encyclopedia on painting for artists, with many woodcuts in color and

monochrome in the style of various painters, and with instructions on how to paint bamboo, pine, landscape, and the like. The color woodcut *Squirrel Shrew and Grapes* (illustration 674) is based on a composition by the Sung artist Chao Ch'ang. Both works, and others like them, were popular and exist in numerous editions. The color work and technique, particularly in the early editions, were of a high order. The colors were delicate and subtle. Many of the pictures were executed in the "boneless style," that is to say without the use of a black key block. Some very interesting textures were achieved perhaps by wiping the blocks in a special way or by cloth impresses before printing.

Single prints in color were also produced during the late seventeenth century, possibly to be used as wall decorations. There are a number in the British Museum which were purchased by the traveler Kaempfer in Japan before 1693—still lifes of vases and baskets of flowers with other accessories, elaborately printed in color, including *gaufrage*. It is strange that so few have survived. A woodcut dating from the eighteenth century is reproduced as illustration 676. Nanking and Soochow were the great centers of printing, and no doubt many prints of theatrical subjects or popular superstition were produced for general consumption during the eighteenth and early nineteenth centuries. In fact, there is a type of woodcut known as the Soochow Print. One great factor which contributed to the deterioration of the art was the Tai Ping Rebellion (1851–64) which completely devastated Nanking, Soochow, and Hangchow. Most of the craftsmen were killed and the traditions of the technique interrupted and in many cases lost. The popular prints of today are undistinguished in design and garish in color.

Chinese prints, with a few notable exceptions such as those of the Ten Bamboo Studio, seem to lack print quality, that personal touch which works out a conception purely in terms of the medium. They were a means to an end, never an end in themselves. Great artists never worked directly on or for wood. Printmaking in China was a minor art, reproductive, a surrogate for something greater than itself. Nor was it ever popular art in the sense that it was cherished by the people: it was a scholars' art, remote from everyday life and closely bound up with books. In the 1920s a Chinese artist, Teng K'uei, has used a Western medium, the lithograph and lithotint, to make a series of original and technically accomplished prints (illustration 675). Conceived in the great tradition of Chinese painting, they have, nevertheless, the vitality and freshness of a personal approach. Likewise, during the Japanese invasion, numerous wood blocks were cut by Chinese artists, chiefly in the Western manner, for documentation and propaganda. It is possible that out of the flux of China a new and more widely popular print form may emerge. Several artists of Chinese birth, such as Zao Wou Ki, Walasse Ting, or Seong Moy work entirely in modern Western style.

II. JAPAN

Much of Japanese art and culture was derived indirectly from Chinese sources. As far as the graphic arts are concerned, the basis of woodcut technique and probably of color printing (there was a reprint of the Mustard-Seed Garden in Japan in 1748, and Chinese editions must have penetrated even earlier) came from the Chinese. The art took a different turn in Japan, however, and was animated by a different purpose. Japanese prints of the *Ukiyo-e* School, which is the glory of Japanese graphic art, were specifically designed to be cut on wood and were definitely produced for a popular audience. Simultaneously with *Ukiyo-e*, some prints and albums were published, which reproduce drawings and designs by famous Japanese artists who were primarily painters and not print designers, such as Korin or Kano Tanyu. Yet if Japanese graphic art were to be judged solely by these reproductive examples, it would rate a position not much more important than that of a minor adjunct to the Chinese School.

The best Japanese printmakers, then, followed a graphic rather than a reproductive tradition, and made full use of the esthetic conventions inherent in the woodcut medium. Japanese prints were the result of the skilled cooperation of three people, a designer, a woodcutter, and a printer. In the Orient there was always a division of labor: the designer never cut his own wood blocks, nor did he ever attend to the printing. In general only the name of the designer has been recorded. Around the beginnings of the full polychrome woodcut with Harunobu, the name of the cutter or printer was sometimes given, probably because the importance of their share in the perfection of the technique was recognized. Later, however, the practice was seldom observed, and the cutter and printer remained anonymous though technically accomplished craftsmen.

A word about the names of Japanese artists. In Japan, as in China, the patronymic or family name comes first and the given name comes second. According to Western nomenclature Torii Kiyonobu should read Kiyonobu Torii. Through a misunderstanding of Japanese terminology, we in the West have fallen into the habit of calling all Japanese artists by their first or given names,

as we might say Raphael (Santi) or Rembrandt (van Rijn). Also one might add, the Japanese (and the Chinese) adopt and discard names in ways that are somewhat incomprehensible to the Occidental mind.

The Japanese have definite names for the various sizes of prints. Since these are often referred to in the literature, it might be well to give the names and approximate dimensions of the commonest shapes: *hoso-e*, 12 × 6 inches, much used, for instance, by the Primitives or Shunshō; *chūban*, about 11 × 8 inches, as used by Harunobu and many others; *oban*, about 15 × 10 inches, used on larger Kiyonagas, for example. Frank modern reproductions and deceptive forgeries, as well as late reprints of many important prints, exist, and the collector must be on guard against them. The real collector of Japanese prints is very much concerned about standards of print quality. Louis V. Ledoux has summarized the matter as follows: "In selecting prints, distinction of subject, excellence of impression, excellence of condition, loveliness of color, all have been considered." In addition to the defects to be avoided, common to all prints, such as holes, mended spots, rubbed areas, trimmed margins, impressions from blocks in which lines are worn or broken, there are several considerations that refer particularly to Japanese color prints. The chief of these are accuracy of register in the successive color blocks, and condition of the coloring. Some of the pigments, particularly the violet, were fugitive, and seldom are found in their original hue. A harmony of colors, as opposed to crude or harsh contrasts, is considered eminently desirable, and appears only in the best of prints. Pristine condition—cleanness of paper and freshness of coloring—is highly prized, perhaps because it is so rarely to be found after the vicissitudes of a century or two.

The prints of the *Ukiyo-e* School, or Pictures of Transient (or Floating) World of Everyday Life, are among the most beautiful and original manifestations of popular art in the history of prints. It was an impulse toward vitality in the midst of decadence, toward realism as against idealism, but a realism of subject, never of treatment, which remained symbolic and suggestive as in all Oriental art. Arthur Davidson Ficke has aptly described the imaginative appeal inherent in the Japanese print:

This almost symbolic quality is the chief element of the pleasure to be derived from Japanese art. Japanese designs are metaphors; they depict not any object, but remote and greater powers to which the object is related. Often the artist produces his effect by the exaggeration of certain aspects, or by expressing particular qualities in the terms of some kindred thing. If his subject happens to be an actor in some great and tragic role, he will not hesitate to prolong the lines of the drapery unconscionably, to give the effect of solemn dignity, slow movement, and

monumental isolation. Westerners may smile at the distortion of such a figure; but they must acknowledge that an atmosphere of lofty and special destiny surrounds the form, precisely because the artist has dared to use these devices. The Japanese artist will draw a woman as if she were a lily, a man as if he were a tempest, a tree as if it were a writhing snake, a mountain as if it were a towering giant. This is the very essence of poetical imagination; and the result of it is to endow a picture with obscure suggestions and overtones of infinite power. Symbols of existence beyond themselves, these designs are charged with an almost mystical command upon the emotions of the spectator. Western art has employed such a method comparatively little in painting. In poetry it appears frequently. The poet, when he wishes to convey the impression of a beautiful woman, does not set out her features and her stature and all the details of her aspect. He tries to awaken some realization of her by a bold and fantastic leap of the imagination straight to the heart of the matter—he makes her a perfume, a light, a music, a memory of goddesses. The prosaic mind will never greatly care for work produced in accordance with this principle; the conventions will seem distortions, the imaginative generalizations will seem inaccuracies, and the transcending of reality to shape a more universal and significant statement will appear nothing more than ineptitude in grappling with fact. But to the poetical mind, all these things will come with a unique and irresistible fascination.

Ukiyo-e prints were a popular and ephemeral art similar to the theatrical posters and "funnies" of today. They were sold for a few *sen*, and little value was attached to them; they were pasted on wooden pillars and on the screens that protected the kitchen fire; they were bought, as are picture postcards today, by visitors as souvenirs to take back to the provinces; they were used as costume plates or as advertisements for houses in the Yoshiwara or other licensed quarters. It is extraordinary that a popular art should exhibit such refinement and subtlety of treatment. The rise and development of the *Ukiyo-e* School occurred entirely within the period of the Tokugawa Shoguns (1603–1867), when the urban or middle class was growing in wealth and power. Trade and manufacture flourished during the long peace which followed the devastating civil wars that were ended by the accession of Tokugawa Iyeyasu. The prosperous city dwellers of Edo, Kyoto, or Osaka, shut off by a rigid code from aristocratic pleasures, began to devise for themselves their own pastimes and amusements. The rise of the popular theatre (*Kabuki*), as opposed to the *No* drama of the aristocracy, coincided with the development of the Japanese print. Well-known historical legends, such as the *Chushingura* (Forty-Seven Ronin), the vendetta of the *Soga Brothers*, or the vicissitudes of *Sugawara Michizane*, as well as other even more lurid and melodramatic themes were dramatized. The acting likewise was melodramatic

and colorful, with much recourse to *aragoto* (rough business), sound and fury and vehement gestures, or to *nuregoto* (moist business). Actors, in spite of being at the bottom of the social scale, were immensely popular; and pictures of them in characteristic roles were eagerly sought for. The other popular class of subject matter was the *Bijin-e* or Pretty Girl Picture, either as models of dress and fashion or·as frank advertisements for houses of assignation. The inhabitants of the Yoshiwara and other licensed quarters were in no sense considered merely as prostitutes; they were more like the *hetairae* of the Greeks, professional entertainers, boon companions, women of wit and culture, accomplished poets and musicians. The teahouses, too, were centers of elegance and gaiety and cultured amusement. An eighteenth-century Japanese writer thus describes the quarters of the Yoshiwara: "their splendor was by day like Paradise and by night like the Palace of the Dragon King." The most famous of the courtesans—they were called *Oiran*—lived in indescribable luxury. They set the fashion in costume and elegant manners for the demi-monde; their appearances on the streets were triumphal processions. The situation was not without its sordid aspects, but the whole was invested with a glamour and elegance that has never been surpassed in its particular sphere.

Thus the theme of *Ukiyo-e* was the ephemeral world of actors and the theatre, of courtesans and the glamour of the Yoshiwara, of changing fashions in dress and hair-do, occasionally of sweet and lovely genre scenes, glimpses of domestic life, and later of familiar landscapes, the landmarks of Japan. This "transient world" was portrayed with power and grace and poetic charm by the artists of the *Ukiyo-e* School. The "eternal world," the pure contemplation of nature, the invocation of religious emotion, and all the themes regarded as lofty and idealistic by Chinese precedent, was still the prerogative of the classical or aristocratic schools of painting. During the seventeenth century, various painters began to react against the growing decadence and stereotyped themes of the Kano and Tosa painting schools in favor of more vital and realistic subject matter. The germ of *Ukiyo-e* was in the air. The real founder of the School was Hishikawa Moronobu (1625–94). It was he who around 1660 first had the idea of using the woodcut medium for making Floating-World pictures and thus channeling *Ukiyo-e* into a popular art. Most of his work as a print designer appeared in books (illustration 722) or in albums, such as *Shunga* (illustration 689). He may thus be accounted the father of Japanese book illustration, since the art before his time was crude and lacking in character and variety. The difference in woodcut technique between his early and late work points up the advance made by the artisans of knife and chisel during the same period. The earliest

works are clumsily engraved. In the later works, one feels, the brushstroke in all its idiosyncracies has been translated to the wood. Henceforth the self-effacing skill of the woodcutter interposed no barrier to the perfect rendering of an artist's style.

The existence of a rival of Moronobu, Sugimura Jihei (illustration 690), has been discovered by the scholar and collector, Kiyoshi Shibui. It is strange that so popular an artist in his day should have been so completely forgotten. One reason for his obscurity may have been that he often signed his name in subtle ways by weaving it in the design of sashes and kimonos. He was somewhat influenced by Moronobu's style, and his rare prints have sometimes been attributed to the other master.

Moronobu's prints have a heavy-handed vigor and boldness of characterization in contrast to the almost feminine sensibility and grace apparent in the designs of his younger contemporary Nishikawa Sukenobu, who also worked almost exclusively for books (illustration 723). Both were trained as painters in the classical schools, and both exerted considerable influence on succeeding artists in spite of the fact that they designed relatively few single prints. Indeed, book illustration was as much a medium for *Ukiyo-e* as was the separate woodcut; and many great artists, such as Shunshō, Kiyonaga, Shigemasa, Utamaro, and Hokusai (illustration 724) were also prolific and distinguished illustrators.

The first artist, perhaps, to design single prints (*ichimai-e*) in great numbers was Kiyonobu I (1664–1729). Most of his work was connected with the theatre: he painted signboards for theatres and designed programs. After some experience as a book illustrator, he started, around 1695, to design single prints of actors, which were hawked about on the streets. Their immediate success started the fashion for theatrical subjects (illustration 691). His draftsmanship—as was consistent with his poster training—was bold and vigorous, emphasizing large masses by exuberant lines. Kiyonobu was the founder of the Torii School which was active for six generations in carrying on a tradition more or less connected with the theatre. The second head of the Torii clan was his son, or possibly son-in-law, Kiyomasu (illustrations 692, 693). A detailed study of the work of Kiyonobu and Kiyomasu and of the meagre family records and other extant sources reveal problems which have agitated scholars for many years. It has been discovered, for instance, that there are variations of style and treatment and also chronological discrepancies in different phases of their work. The existence of prints signed Kiyonobu after his death in 1729 postulates the activity of a second Kiyonobu. The similarity between certain prints of Kiyomasu and Kiyonobu II suggests that they were designed by one person. There also exist certain

differences between the early, middle, and late periods of Kiyomasu's *oeuvre* which imply the existence of possibly three artists of the name. Several theories have been offered to solve the problem. Some scholars maintain that there were only two artists involved: Kiyonobu-Kiyomasu I and Kiyonobu-Kiyomasu II who used the two names interchangeably. Another school asserts that such simultaneous use of two names is contrary to all Japanese custom, and has advanced an ingenious theory reconstructing Kiyomasu I, II, III, and Kiyonobu I and II (the latter having first been Kiyomasu II but after his father's retirement or death having adopted his name). The latter hypothesis has much to recommend it, though neither theory completely reconciles all the known facts. The whole question is brought up as an example of the problems encountered in tracing the history of a folk art such as Japanese prints.

Around the beginning of the Hōyei period, or 1704, two other important artists, Kaigetsudō and Masanobu, began to issue prints. Relatively little is known about Kaigetsudō; the name probably represents not a single person but rather a workshop or clan. Their production was meagre and their works are very rare. All of the twenty-three subjects which have come down to us are *bijin-e* or pictures of courtesans. They are among the greatest of Japanese prints for sheer vitality of brushstroke, power of curving line, and monumental three-dimensional design. A large *sumi-e* of a stately Oiran, superbly designed with swirling drapery, and signed Kaigetsudō Doshin, is reproduced as illustration 695.

The third great figure of the early period was Okumura Masanobu. As an artist he probably was self-taught; he undoubtedly studied the works of his elder contemporaries, Moronobu, Sukenobu, and Kaigetsudō. He was a bookseller and print publisher as well as an artist. As a consequence, no doubt, of his interest as a publisher, in questions related to wood cutting and printing, his name has been associated with a number of important technical innovations. But beyond all technical considerations, he was a designer of great distinction. His figures convey the impression of elegance and reserve strength (illustration 697). He further extended the range of *Ukiyo-e* subject matter to include, besides actors and women, portraits and outdoor scenes suggesting landscape. In keeping with his self-taught background and open-minded response to different forms of art, he must have had some familiarity with Chinese art. He must also have seen some European pictures and have studied the conventions of European perspective. He was the first to make *uki-e*, or perspective prints, in which these conventions were employed (illustration 721). This tradition, though not common, did run through all periods of Japanese printmaking. Other well-known artists who made *uki-e* were Shiba Kokan, Shunshō, Toyoharu (illustration 720), and Hokusai. Masanobu is credited with having invented a special form, or rather shape, of Japanese woodcut, *hashira-e* or pillar print. The shape is very tall and narrow; and such prints were made to be hung on columns in Japanese houses. An unusually large *naga-e* (tall picture) by Masanobu, though not the exact proportions of a *hashira-e*, is reproduced as illustration 694. This woodcut was undoubtedly used as a pillar print, for it portrays *Shōki*, the equivalent of the Chinese *Chung K'uei*, the Demon Queller, whose effigy was placed by the door to ward off evil spirits. Many later artists, including Kiyomitsu, Toyonobu, Harunobu, Koryūsai, Kiyonaga, Shunshō (illustration 704), Chōki, and others, designed pillar prints to supply popular demand, fascinated no doubt also by the challenge of the unusual proportions to their powers of invention and composition. Of similar shape is a so-called stone-print in color by Koryūsai (illustration 703). Stone-prints were made in imitation of Chinese stone rubbings in color, but in Japan were probably cut in wood. Prints not in *hashira* shape, but executed in *ishi-zuri* technique (where the design is engraved, showing white against a flat background of black) were made earlier by Masanobu, Shigenaga, and others.

The earliest Japanese prints were in black and white only *(sumi-e)*. Kiyonobu is supposed to have been the first to add color by hand. Among the colors used in early times were a red or orange pigment called by the Japanese *tan*, sometimes a yellow pigment was used with *tan*, sometimes a rose-red called *beni* in combination with a greenish yellow or with low-toned blues and purples. Masanobu first had the idea of mixing a little lacquer, *urushi*, with some of the pigments to give them brilliance and also dusting bronze powder on them, thus creating another classification of hand-colored prints, the *urushi-e*. Shigenaga also made some (illustration 698).

At the beginning of Kanpō (1741), true color prints, in which the colors are printed from separate color blocks and not added by hand, made their appearance. It is not known with certainty who was responsible for this important innovation. Masanobu, if not the actual inventor, was one of the first to sense its possibilities. Though a veteran of the primitive black and white era, he was flexible and inventive enough to master the conventions of a two-color compositional scheme, and design some of the most charming *benizuri-e* ever made (illustration 696). At first the *beni* color scheme, rose and green, with a black key block, was used. Later other color combinations and even three color blocks with black were employed, thus leading up to the inception of the full polychrome print in the Meia era. In addition to Masanobu and Shigenaga a group of very able younger artists—

Toyonobu, Kiyohiro, and Kiyomitsu (illustration 699)—fully exploited the possibilities of the two- and three-color-block woodcut.

The artists whom we have hitherto been considering are generally classified as the Primitives. They are primitives with reference to technique and not to treatment, since Japanese prints were from the beginning highly sophisticated. The black and white prints and those colored by hand may be considered the first phase in the development of the Japanese print; to the second or transition stage belong the two- and three-color prints—thus covering the periods in history from Genroku through Horeki (1688–1763). The earlier prints, monumental or heraldic in character, display a boldness of execution and a dynamic interplay of linear rhythms. The designs were mostly of single figures; and little attempt was made at pictorial composition except in book illustrations or in *shunga* or erotic albums and other series. At the beginning of the Meia period, or about 1765, a further improvement in the printing process was made, which rendered possible polychrome effects with as many as eight to eleven blocks (later many more blocks were used), thus inaugurating the era of the "Brocade Picture" *(nishiki-e)* or full color print, which was to hold sway ever after. Harunobu was the first of the great designers to take advantage of this improvement, and it gave scope to his exquisite and lovely sense of color, in some of the most beautiful prints ever made (illustrations 700–702). (Illustration 702 is a *mitate:* see later under Utamaro and illustration 717 for explanation, and see illustration 682 for a Chinese prototype.) Harunobu first used color-printed backgrounds, and was also the first to make effective use of *gaufrage*, blind stamping, the impress of a woodblock without ink to make embossed patterns on the paper, thus giving textural variety. This device was used by many succeeding artists, notably Utamaro, and particularly on the kind of print known as *surimono*. The use of mica colors has been ascribed with no great certainty to Harunobu and even Masanobu. The fullest exploitation of mica pigments, particularly as backgrounds in a range of yellow, pink, or silver gray, came later with Utamaro and Sharaku. Their use was forbidden after 1794. With the mention of "gradation printing," first used by Sekiyen in his book *Sekiyen Gafu*, 1773, and later most effectively employed by Hokusai and Hiroshige, the account of the technical innovations in Japanese prints is fairly complete. But beyond and overshadowing questions of technique is the chronicle of the various artists' approaches to the perennial problem of self-expression.

Suzuki Harunobu (1725–70) was the dominant figure of the Meia period (1764–72). He broke away from the Torii tradition of actor prints, and, following the lead of Sukenobu, devoted himself to genre scenes of idyllic charm. There is magic in his girlish figures, exquisite in their sensitive gestures. It is astonishing how much feeling and sensibility can be expressed by the pose, the posture, the outline of the figure, for in these woodcuts, as in all Japanese prints, the faces are like masks, expressionless according to Western ideas. Louis V. Ledoux has beautifully summed up Harunobu's salient quality:

He is the artist of young girlhood, the poet of youth. His figures, untouched by sorrow, move through an earthly paradise, a fairyland of loveliness, the world that might be rather than the world that is. He has caught and rendered for us the evanescent charm of youth; he has sought to preserve, with the freshness of the morning on it, that fleeting moment between the opening of the bud and the fall of the first petal, in which alone beauty is perfect, unalloyed.

After the death of Harunobu and during the Anyei period (1772–81), though there was no all-pervading personality such as his, there was nevertheless no dearth of distinguished designers. Isoda Koryūsai, the Samurai pupil and friend of Harunobu, carried on his tradition (illustration 707), yet with an individual touch in his coloring and later in his style. Kitao Shigemasa (1739–1820), equally renowned as a calligrapher, draughtsman, and illustrator, unfortunately designed relatively few single prints. He collaborated with Shunshō in the illustrations to *Seiro Bijin Awase Sugata Kagami*, Mirror Reflecting the Forms of Fair Women of the Green Houses, 1776, one of the most beautiful of Japanese color print books. Another famous illustrated book is the *Yehon Butai Ogi*, Picture Book of Stage Fans of 1770, in which Bunchō and Shunshō collaborated. Samurai-born Ippitsusai Bunchō, whose life exhibited elements of a strange psychological conflict, combined, one might say, the exquisite sensibility (particularly as regards color) of Harunobu with the form and subject-matter of Shunshō (illustration 706). The most important artist, perhaps, who came to full maturity during the Anyei period, was Katsukawa Shunshō. He was a prolific designer for books, *shunga* albums, and theatrical prints, chiefly in *hoso-e* shape (illustrations 704, 705). His actor portraits display an intensity unknown to the Torii masters, an emotional *timbre* conveyed by superb draftsmanship, placement, and conscious use of color. In Ficke's words: "all his figures are dynamic—the storehouses of volcanic forces whose existence he suggests by restless line-conflicts. . . . In repose they are like statues; in action they have the vigor of those natural forces—waves, river currents, storms of thunder—which so often form their backgrounds." Shunshō has an austere and possibly limited appeal, for he concentrated not on beauty but on dramatic effect. At his best he is unsurpassed.

The Temmei period (1781–89) was dominated by Torii Kiyonaga (illustrations 708–710). He was a pupil of, though little influenced by, Torii Kiyomitsu. At his death, Kiyonaga became head of the clan as Torii IV, and did much to restore its waning prestige. Of the younger generation, Shunchō, Chōki, Shunman, Eishi, and Toyokuni, all fell under the spell of his style. Before Kiyonaga retired around 1790, he had designed, besides numerous book illustrations, a total of approximately eight hundred prints—figure and genre pieces from daily life, courtesans, as well as theatre subjects, *joruri* plays, actors in character, and actors in private life. He represented the full flowering of the *Ukiyo-e* School—the stage at which Phidias, for example, summed up Greek sculpture—by a perfect fusion of strength and refinement. His is an art of balance, of idealized grandeur, not the tumultuous grandeur of the Primitives, but a calm and poised serenity, static withal, in its conscious symmetry. "Kiyonaga," in Binyon's words, "rarely invents motives beyond the simplest to relate his figures to one another; and his most characteristic women are proudly impassive. He is content with the solid pose of his majestic forms, as if to bend or sway them toward or away from each other would mar their dignity. But out of these so simple harmonies what a magnificent whole he creates, consummate in its equilibrium and authority!" Kiyonaga was one of the first to explore the possibilities of the diptych, triptych, and pentaptych forms of composition on separate blocks, each unit functioning as a separate composition yet so tied together in design as to form part of an overall picture. The diptychs of the *Minami Juniko* series are justly famous (illustration 710), and so are such triptychs as *Boating Party on the Sumida, Visitors to Emoshima, Party Viewing Moon across the Sumida River.*

Utamaro and the meteoric Sharaku were the leading artists of Kansei (1789–1801), but again they were not alone in the field. Katsukawa Shun'ei carried on the tradition of his teacher Shunshō. Hosoda Eishi, Samurai-born, and trained in the classical Kano school, carried over a certain nobility of treatment into his popular productions, particularly when under the sway of Kiyonaga's style (illustration 718). Like him he was an accomplished designer of triptychs and of such delightful pentaptychs as *Yoshitsune Playing Before Joruri-hime.* When, however, Eishi lapsed into the taste of the day in order to vie with Utamaro, he was apt to become mannered and overly sweet. Kubo Shunman, as described by Fenollosa, "is, like Shigenaga and Bunchō, one of those strange personalities who infuse their art with a nameless individual charm. Everything he does has a strange touch. The Kiyonaga face becomes distorted with a sort of divine frenzy; trees grope about with their branch tips like sentient beings; flowers seem to exhale unknown perfumes."

A poet as well as an artist, he designed relatively few prints, but of rare distinction, restrained in color and with an intriguing complexity of rhythm, as in the six-sheet *Tamagawa* or the triptych *Cup Floating Game.* The eclectic, Eishosai Chōki, in a style compounded of Kiyonaga, Eishi, Sharaku, and Utamaro, designed some prints with a haunting beauty of coloring, *New Year's Sunrise* and *Fireflies* (illustration 719).

In Toshusai Sharaku we meet one of the most extraordinary figures in Japanese art. We know little about him other than that he was a *No* dancer in the service of the Daimyo of Awa. In the last ten months of the year 1794 he designed about 136 prints of actors, including 23 bust portraits with mica backgrounds (illustrations 711, 712). We do not know how or why he suddenly burst in, full fledged as it were, upon the print world with his terrific characterizations, nor why he ceased in so short a time, to be heard of no more. His prints evidently were not popular, yet he must have had some measure of contemporary appreciation, since his work, issued by one of the most discriminating publishers of the time, Tsutaya, influenced Chōki and was imitated by Toyokuni and Kunimasa. It was not that the form of his work was new and strange, for much of it was in conventional *hoso-e* shape, and his use of the bust portrait had been anticipated by Shun'ei. It is possible that the public and the actors vaguely sensed in his pictures something that cut deeper than the mere re-creation of a dramatic role, and penetrated behind the actor's mask to lash at the being underneath. Brutally realistic satire is rare in Japanese art. Sharaku's mood may have been something different and more akin to that of Goya or Grosz, a savage irony directed against a whole class, or even the human race. His work disturbed or repelled. A critic wrote of Sharaku but a few years after his brief appearance: "He drew portraits of actors, but exaggerated the truth, and his pictures lacked form. Therefore he was not well received, and after a year or so he ceased to work." On the other hand another critic, not later than 1802, wrote: "The power of his brush strokes and of his taste is praiseworthy." It is likely that his work, though not popular, was appreciated by the discriminating few. And it may well be, as Ledoux has pointed out, that the cessation of Sharaku's activity as a print designer was caused not by his unpopularity but by the ban of his feudal lord, as an occupation unworthy of his rank as a *No* dancer. These biographical speculations may add a dash of mystery to the Sharaku legend, but are in the last analysis subordinate to the timeless appeal of his great artistic creations. His delineations of actors in their roles transcend the confines of the *Kabuki* stage and become awe-inspiring personifications of demonic forces, of baleful passions and odious instincts—brutality, duplicity, vainglory,

bestiality, lust, and revenge. His designs, for all their disturbing effect, have a haunting impressiveness, a kind of fearsome beauty. The lines are restrained but powerfully intense, and display an inspired grasp of the essentials of physiognomy and character. Seldom have the depths of human emotions been revealed with such objective yet expressive power.

Kitagawa Utamaro was discovered by the West in the 1880s and 1890s, and was endowed with *fin de siècle* decadent tendencies by some of the critics. Utamaro was not, in my opinion, a decadent at all, but an artist of great sensibility and sensitivity to the currents of his time, a restless and daring experimenter in the same sense that Picasso was. In a print *œuvre* totaling about a thousand pieces he showed himself a designer of unusual inventiveness and a master of complex rhythm. Only one year younger than Kiyonaga, Utamaro did not reach the maturity of his style until about 1790 when the Torii artist retired. For a decade he reigned supreme. His work was immensely popular. On several of his prints he indulged in boastful and disparaging remarks about his rival contemporaries. He had many imitators, even forgers, during his lifetime. He gave to the perennial theme of woman a new significance and form. "It is this seizure," as Binyon has said, "of the aboriginal, the essential, the instinctive, in feminine humanity that distinguishes Utamaro among all the artists of the world." The types he designed were varied: the *petite* grace of *Okita the Tea-House Waitress*, the stateliness of *The Hour of the Snake* (illustration 713), the willowy languor of the *Woman Seated on a Veranda*. In some, the characteristics were exaggerated almost to the breaking point; but the series of half-length figures and large heads with silver or yellow or pink mica backgrounds (illustration 716) display to the full his rare power of draftsmanship and subtle coloring. But there was more to Utamaro than his projections of feminine beauty: there were the snow and moonlit landscapes, the fusion of scientific precision and esthetic style in the illustrations to the *Insect Book* and *Gifts of the Ebb Tide* (shells and rocks), the great set in twelve sheets of *Silk Culture*, the consummately designed triptychs, *Awabi Fishers* (illustration 715), *The Printmakers, The Dressmakers, The Summer Storm, The Women on the Bridge, The Fishing Party on the Sumida*, and finally the tender domestic scenes, mothers and children, including the powerful *Yamauba and Kintoki* series (illustration 714) inspired by the legend of the boy giant of the mountains.

The rare large woodcut *Famous Beauties Enacting the Oxcart Scene* (illustration 717) is an example of a kind of subject fairly common in *Ukiyo-e*. It is called *mitate* or "Brother Picture," that is to say a scene from a play or well-known legend (in this case Scene 6 of the *Sugawara* tragedy) brought up to date or reenacted by courtesans

or sometimes by children. It is no doubt a form of parody, not so much of manner as of content; and it gives a fair indication of the cultural level of the audience for whom Japanese prints were made. The treatment is in terms of everyday life, brought down to earth as it were, and sometimes with a touch of irreverence or "spoofing." But the implication is plain that the artists, the courtesans, and public were familiar with the allusions contained in these and many other prints referring to themes and parables in Chinese and Japanese philosophy and poetry. It is as if a movie magazine of today were to publish regularly impersonations of episodes from Shakespeare, Milton, or Homer. A further measure of popular culture is given by the many illustrated anthologies of poetry that were published from Moronobu onwards, and by the frequency with which poems of incomparable beauty appeared on prints.

Utamaro was a many-sided artist, constantly trying out new effects, uneven in production. His best work, which is rare, ranks among the masterpieces of *Ukiyo-e*. His mediocre productions, combined with those of his imitators, have given a distorted picture of his genius. His total work must be judged in relation to the taste of his age, which he both reflected and, to a certain extent, dominated. The times had indeed changed since the austere grandeur of the Primitives was popular; now the populace, somewhat blasé and already accustomed to complicated colorings from twenty to thirty blocks, demanded novelty in any form. Unrest and revolutionary ferment, too, were stirring, agitation against the continued usurpation of power by the Shoguns, which was suppressed but eventually culminated in their overthrow in 1867. In 1804 Utamaro published, in spite of the censorship, several satiric prints which gave offense to the Shogun. He suffered imprisonment, and died in broken health in 1806. After his death there was a marked decline in the quality of figure design. The leading artist, Toyokuni I, who had made some notable prints in rivalry with—and imitation of—Utamaro, succumbed to the general deterioration of taste, reflected also in banal textile patterns and overladen coiffures. The later Toyokuni, his pupils and namesakes (there were four who bore his name) lost their mastery in exaggerated and meaningless gestures, in elaboration of unessential detail, in uninspired realism, and in inferior coloring. It is most unfortunate that these are the prints most commonly known in the West, for they give a false idea of the true worth of *Ukiyo-e*. Even their subject matter became stereotyped and trivial: these artists were most successful when they did not aim too high, but contented themselves with still life arrangements on *surimono* or such fanciful semihumorous compositions as Utagawa Kuniyoshi's *Goldfish Story* (illustration 725) and other fish

or bird-and-flower designs (illustration 734).

Mention should be made of Osaka prints. Not all *Ukiyo-e* were made in Edo. There were other groups in Osaka and Nagasaki, but they have been generally ignored. Recently, Roger Keyes has revived interest in Osaka prints by a book on the subject. Osaka had been a book publishing center in the eighteenth century, witness Sukenobu's books. According to Keyes, the first single sheets were published by Chōbei after designs by Ryūkōsai and his pupil Shōkōsai beginning in 1793. The leading designer of the period, however, was Shunkō, who, after meeting Hokusai in 1817, called himself Hukushu (illustration 727). Other designers of the first half of the century were Shigeharu, Kunihiro, Hoku-ei, Hirosada (in the late 1840s) and, after mid-century, Yoshitaki. Most of them were influenced by the prevailing taste of the day, Toyokuni and Kunisada. What characterizes the Osaka style and its artists are the literalness of their portraiture and the marvelous cutting and printing of their designs. Part of this may be due to the presence of an extraordinary engraver, Kasuke, who combined the exquisiteness of the *surimono* technique with the melodrama of the theatre prints. *Surimono* are a special kind of print—in vogue from the time of Moronobu onwards—commissioned by a private person as greeting cards for the New Year or other special occasions. They generally were smaller than the average print, and no expense was spared in the number of blocks or colors and in the use of embossing or metallic effects to make them as sumptuous and beautiful as possible. Kasuke started as a pupil of Hukushu, and himself designed *surimono*. He engraved one hundred and fifty blocks between 1820 and 1834, and toward the end of his career signed himself Blockmaster Kasuke. He would cut off his name from the block if it showed any signs of wear. Perhaps another reason for the printing excellence of Osaka prints was the great interest taken in them by the public. The *Kabuki* theatre played a great role in the popular cultural life of Osaka in the early nineteenth century. Actors were also poets and playwrights; poets also designed actor prints. Even before Kasuke, individuals or groups of admirers commissioned Ashikuni to design *surimono* of actors for them. The production of Osaka prints, devoted exclusively to the theatre, began about 1790 and lasted till the end of the nineteenth century. At their best they were remarkable for the beauty of their color printing. In the second half of the century they shared in the general decline of Japanese prints. Around 1864 aniline dyes were introduced; by the late 1870s and 1880s the dyes could be produced cheaply, and further cheapened the prints.

To return to Edo, in one branch of printmaking only was there any sign of freshness and vitality—landscape.

After 1800 a shift of interest away from the figure is noticeable. A landscape school arose, which portrayed the land—as others had portrayed the people—the city and the country, its streets and highways, its harbors and landmarks, the ever-changing aspects of the great mountain, Fuji. The landscapists gained favor with the populace. A landscape tradition of long standing had been laid down by the classical Kano and Tosa schools; and to a certain degree it influenced the new movement. But the new *Ukiyo-e* artists gave it a character of their own: not the mood of lofty communion with nature, but an intimate, localized, and human touch; not the mountain as a symbol of sublimity, but the mountain seen from a spot famous for its view. And thus arose the many series of *Edo Views*: or the scenes along the highways between Edo and Kyōto (*The Fifty-three Stations of the Tokaido or Eastern Highway, The Sixty-nine Stations of the Kisokaido via Kiso Gorge);* or *The Thirty-six Famous Views of Fuji.* Several figure designers of the Utagawa School, Kunisada I and Kuniyoshi, also made a few notable landscapes, but the two greatest designers were Hokusai and Hiroshige. Each had pupils and followers who carried on but never equaled their performances.

Katsushika Hokusai, "the Man Mad about Painting," as he sometimes signed himself, was born in 1760. He was a pupil of Shunshō, but in his final development was largely self-taught, drawing upon many sources including European and Chinese. He was always poor, always changing his name and his lodging, and he was always drawing. No artist has ever shown a more unflagging and a more undiscriminating delight in the delineation of humanity and all natural objects. The thirteen volumes of his sketchbooks, *Manga* (illustration 724), were a veritable encyclopedia of graphic representations of birds, insects, animals, fish, flowers, trees, rocks, mountains, architecture, ghosts, and every possible trade and craft and expression and gesture of man. In his celebrated epilogue to the first volume of the *Hundred Views of Fuji*, 1834, he spoke of his own artistic development, saying that as early as his sixth year he felt the impulse to draw the form of things; when he was fifty he had already published innumerable sketches. At seventy-three he began to comprehend approximately the true form and nature of birds, fish, and plants; consequently he hoped to make great progress after the age of eighty, and when he should have reached the age of one hundred and ten, every dot and every line would be alive. Hokusai was a fecund, tirelessly inventive artist who had to digest the entire visible world before he could arrange it in the hierarchy of its importance. His work is a triumph of extrovert externalization. In his later phase he somewhat overcame his unselective lack of taste to produce magnificent designs in landscape. Justly renowned are his

Thirty-six Views of Fuji (illustrations 729, 730) portraying the majestic mountain in various aspects, often in contrast with the puny occupations of man. This set and the ten supplementary plates are remarkable for their originality of composition and the sprightly counterpoint of their linear rhythms. Other famous series are the *Waterfalls* (illustration 731), the *Bridges*, the *LuChu Islands*, and the *Flowers*. Early and late he designed *surimono*, a class of print in which his pupils, Hokkei (illustration 728), Gakutei, and Shinsai, also excelled. His other great masterpiece, one in which he for once undertook, successfully, a lofty theme, is the rare set of ten *Images from the Poets of China and Japan.*

Where Hokusai, one might say, approached landscape as a draughtsman in stressing linear structure with a limited palette of color blocks, Hiroshige looked at the problem more with the eye of a painter in playing off color against color. Few artists have ever portrayed such a range of atmospheric effects, day and night, wind and sun, snow and rain; or controlled such delicate manipulations of aerial perspective with so limited a means as the flat color block. Hiroshige accomplished this by stylization and suggestion, by the unerring selection of essential details and by the subtle juxtaposition or blending of colors. The most successful realization of the artist's intention is to be seen only in the rare early impressions. Among his most famous series were *Eight Views of Lake Biwa*, several *Tokaido* sets including the great *Tokaido* of 1834 (illustrations 732, 733), the *Thirty-six Views of Fuji*, and many sets of *Edo Views* (illustration 735). He was a prolific designer, and made, besides countless landscapes, a *Chūshingura* set, numerous bird and flower prints (*kacho*) in narrow upright *tanzaku* form, which may have some relation to the paintings of the Shijo School (illustration 734), some charming fan-shaped compositions or *uchiwa-e*, and several notable triptychs, including *Kiso Gorge in Snow* and *Banks of the Sumida in Winter.* After Hiroshige's death in 1858 even the landscape school suffered a decline, and Japanese prints in general ceased to have esthetic significance. To be sure, one sometimes encounters a later print of lovely quality, a *Crow* by Kyosai, *White Mice* by Zeshin, or in modern times a *Nude* by Goyo, but they are definitely exceptions. The opening of Japan to the world in 1854 unloosed a torrent of Western influences which eventually overwhelmed what was left of a stylistic tradition. The so-called Yokohama prints graphically recorded the reaction of the Japanese, after their long isolation, to the foreigners (American, English, Dutch, French, and Russian) and their strange habits and costumes. Among the artists who portrayed these exotic scenes for popular consumption were Hiroshige II, Sadahide, and Yoshikazu (illustration 726).

Hokusai and Hiroshige were the two artists whom the Occidental world found easiest to understand and appreciate. Recognition of Utamaro, Harunobu, and Kiyonaga came later, and of the Primitives and Sharaku last of all. Hokusai's prints were among the first to reach Europe. The story is told that Bracquemond in 1856 had acquired from the printer Delâtre a little volume of Hokusai's *Manga* which had been used for packing china, and which he was wont to show with great enthusiasm to Whistler, Degas, and all his artist friends in Paris. The artists, particularly the Impressionists, were early and eager collectors of Japanese prints, both landscapes and figure pieces, fascinated by their often daringly asymmetrical compositional schemes and their frank reliance on stylization and design to carry the burden of their message. Some even found inspiration for their own work in them. The influence on Whistler can be traced in much of his work, but is most obvious in his etchings and lithographs of the Putney and Battersea bridges. Degas had a collection of Japanese prints, including the rare *Nude Bathers* of Kiyonaga. Gauguin owned Hokusais and Utamaros, and was influenced by their flat color patterns, and so was Van Gogh, who painted a portrait of Père Tanguy, dealer in artists' colors and Japanese prints, against a background of Japanese pictures. Mary Cassatt, who had in her possession some choice Utamaros, made color prints directly inspired by Japanese woodcuts. Toulouse-Lautrec was perhaps most akin to *Ukiyo-e* in choice of subject and sense of style; the *japonisme* that pervaded his work was perhaps most evident in such lithographs as the cover to *Estampe Originale*, the posters, and the set of *Elles.* Thus the esthetic qualities of Japanese prints were discovered by the artists and critics of Paris (and to a lesser degree those of London) beginning about the middle of the nineteenth century. From there, recognition spread through Europe and America and eventually back to Japan, where *Ukiyo-e* had originally been held in little esteem by collectors. These prints of popular and ephemeral appeal have at last been found to have enduring value. The painter Camille Pissarro, writing of an exhibition of Japanese prints in 1883, has summed up their quality: "I find in the art of this astonishing people a repose, a calm, a grandeur, an extraordinary unity, a rather subdued radiance which is nevertheless brilliant. What astounding balance, and what taste!"

In the twentieth century, printmaking in Japan has revived again, but not in *Ukiyo-e* style. The keynote is set by the title of the new movement, *Sōsaku Hanga*, Creative Prints. Self-expression is the motive. Its subject matter is not limited, as were the Floating World Pictures, and its technique and style have been influenced by modern European art. Ignoring the old Japanese tradition of a division of labor in print production, the modern print-

makers make a point of executing and printing their designs themselves. They work chiefly on wood, although stone and metal are sometimes used. James Michener and Oliver Statler have introduced the movement to the Western world in their books. The first artist to make a *sōsaku hanga* was Yamamoto Kanae in 1904. He was the founder, along with Minami, Kunzo, and others, of the *Sōsaku Hanga* Association, which held its first exhibition in 1919. They were the pioneers who had to overcome the prejudice of critics and collectors against the woodcut medium as trivial and vulgar on account of its association with debased *Ukiyo-e*. A slightly younger generation of able artists, such as Hiratsuka, Unichi; Maekawa, Sempan; and Onchi, Koshiro (illustration 736) gave the movement more substance and prestige. The generation born in the 1900's, such as Azechi, Umetaro; Yamaguchi, Gen; and Saito, Kiyoshi (illustration 737) were much more free to follow their own bent, and even became known outside of Japan. Of this group, Munakata, Shiko is outstanding, and has really achieved international renown. He is a very original artist, a Zen adept with a passionate sensibility that ranges from sensuous nudes to impressive renderings of the ten disciples of Buddha. Another masterpiece is his huge woodcut *Flower Hunting Mural* (illustration 738). During the 1940s and 1950s the movement has proliferated into the hundreds—one can mention but a few names: Uchima, Ansei; Hagewaru, Hideo; Kawano, Kaoru; Maki, Haku; Sekino, Junichiro; Yoshida, Chisuko; and Yoshida, Hodaka. Their approach and style are as varied as those of their Western colleagues. One senses in much of their work during this period—even in work of an abstract quality—a subtle Japanese overtone which is lacking in the abstract and impersonal productions of the 1960s.

CHINESE DYNASTIES

Han	206 BC–220 AD
Six Dynasties	220 AD–618
(including Wei 386–534)	
T'ang	618 –906
Five Dynasties	907 –960
Sung	960 –1279
Ming	1368 –1644
Yüan	1280 –1368
Ch'ing	1644 –1911
Republic	1912

JAPANESE CHRONOLOGY

Tenna	1681–1683	Temmei	1781–1788
Jōkyō	1684–1687	Kansei	1789–1800
Genroku	1688–1703	Kyōwa	1801–1803
Hōei	1704–1710	Bunka	1804–1817
Shōtoku	1711–1715	Bunsei	1818–1829
Kyōhō	1716–1735	Tempō	1830–1843
Gembun	1736–1740	Kōka	1844–1847
Kampō	1741–1743	Kaei	1848–1853
Enkyō	1744–1747	Ansei	1854–1859
Kan-en	1748–1750	Man-en	1860
Hōreki	1751–1763	Bunkyū	1861–1863
Meia	1764–1771	Genji	1864
An-ei	1772–1780	Keiō	1865–1867

Bibliography

This bibliography is chiefly for the beginner or intelligent layman who wishes to learn more about prints, and not for the specialist who would require a whole library of reference works. Therefore monographs on single artists are not included.

INTRODUCTION TO THE STUDY OF PRINTS

Getlein, Frank and Dorothy. *The Bite of the Print*, 1964. *Introduction to prints by way of their social meaning.*

Hind, A. M. *Guide to Processes and Schools of Engraving*, British Museum, 1952. *A well-ordered syllabus of 52 pages.*

Ivins, William M., Jr. *Prints and Books*. Informal Papers, 1926. *Stimulating essays by a great authority.*

————.*How Prints Look, Magnified photographs of details of prints with commentary on techniques*, paperback, 1962.

Mayor, A. Hyatt. *Prints and People*, 1971. *Fresh commentary by a life-long student of prints.*

Sachs, Paul J. *Modern Prints and Drawings*, 1954. *Delightful introduction to nineteenth- and twentieth-century graphic art.*

Shikes, Ralph. *The Indignant Eye*, 1969. *The artist as social critic from the fifteenth century to Picasso.*

Weitenkampf, Frank. *How to Appreciate Prints*, 1942. *Old-fashioned but still useful introduction arranged by techniques.*

Zigrosser, Carl. *The Appeal of Prints*, 1970. *The appreciation of prints, with comparisons between old and modern styles.*

————, and Gaehde. *Guide to the Collecting and Care of Original Prints*, 1965.

GENERAL HISTORIES

Bock, Elfried. *Geschichte der Graphischen Kunst*, 1930. *Best anthology of European prints from beginnings to 1930.*

Glaser, Curt. *Die Graphik der Neuzeit*, 1923. *Well-illustrated survey of nineteenth- and twentieth-century European prints. Scholarly but not pedantic.*

Kristeller, Paul. *Kupferstich und Holzschnitt*, 1921. *The standard book in German, and indispensable to the serious student of prints up to 1800.*

Laran, J. *L'Estampe*, 1959. *Standard work in French.*

Lugt, Frits. *Les Marques de Collections*, 1921. *The great book on collectors' marks with many sidelights on the history of collecting and the mutations of taste.*

Roger-Marx, Claude. *Graphic Art of the Twentieth Century*, 1962.

Zigrosser, Carl, editor, *Prints: Thirteen Essays*, 1962. *Sponsored by the Print Council of America.*

STUDIES OF SINGLE MEDIUMS

Bliss, Douglas Percy. *History of Wood Engraving*, 1928. *Charmingly written, touching on unusual subjects, such as* Livres d'Heures, *Chapbooks,* Imagerie, Herbals, *etc.*

Halm, Peter. *Bild vom Stein*, 1961. *Short survey including twentieth century.*

Hind, A. M. *History of Engraving and Etching*, 1963, paperback. *Standard work in English; bibliographies, etc.; good up to 1900.*

————. *Introduction to a History of Woodcut*, 1963, two volumes, paperback. *Detailed survey of fifteenth-century work with many illustrations and bibliographies.*

Lumsden, Ernest. *The Art of Etching*, 1962, paperback. *The conventional technique, and informative historical survey.*

Man, Felix. *150 Years of Lithography*, 1952. *Extensive bibliography and many illustrations.*

Pennell, Joseph. *Lithography and Lithographers*, 1915. *A breezy and unorthodox history with many illustrations.*

MONOGRAPHS ON SEPARATE COUNTRIES

Bock, Elfried. *Deutsche Graphik*, 1922. *Illustrated survey of printmaking in all periods.*

Courboin, F. *La Gravure en France*, 1923. *Short history of French printmaking up to 1900.*

Gray, Basil. *The English Print. Best short study of subject. Few but excellent illustrations.*

PERIODICALS

Print Collector's Quarterly, 1911–1942. *Contains a wealth of information on all periods and an invaluable corpus of handy illustrations.*

The Print Collector's Newsletter, 1970—. *Six numbers per annual volume. News of prints and publications, with selected auction prices.*

TWENTIETH-CENTURY PRINTS

Buchheim, L. G. *The Graphic Art of German Expressionism*, 1960.

Koepplin, Dieter. *Kubismus: Zeichnungen und Druckgraphik*, 1969. *Exhibition catalogue at Kunstmuseum, Basel.*

Stubbe, Wolf. *Graphic Arts in the Twentieth Century. Sumptuous review of modern prints, chiefly European.*

Zigrosser, Carl. *The Expressionists*, 1957. *Their graphic art.*

See also the recent technical handbooks for examples of modern prints.

ILLUSTRATED BOOKS

Hardie, Martin. *English Colored Books. A delightful work incorporating much research.*

Hofer, Philip. *The Artist and the Book: 1860–1960*, Boston, 1961. *Comprehensive survey.*

Rümann, Arthur. *Das Illustrierte Buch des Neunzehnte Jahrhunderts*, 1930. *Well-illustrated and documented work on nineteenth-century books.*

Skira, Albert. *Anthologie du Livre Illustré par les Peintres et Sculpteurs de l'Ecole de Paris*, 1946.

Worringer, W. *Die Altdeutsche Buchillustration*, 1919. *Illustrated survey of German woodcuts in books up to the middle of the sixteenth century.*

ORNAMENT PRINTS

Berlin Museum. *Katalog der Ornamentstichsammlung*, 2 vols., 1936. *An indispensable work for the study of ornament.*

Guilmard, D. *Les Maîtres Ornemanistes*, 1880. *A pioneer work on ornament but still useful. Illustrated.*

Jessen, Peter. *Der Ornamentstich*, 1920. *Concise and systematic account of ornament and architectural prints.*

THREE LANDMARKS OF TECHNIQUE

Bosse, A. *Traicté des Manières de Graver en taille-douce*, Paris, 1645. And later editions, revised by Cochin, Paris, 1745 and 1758. *A famous technician codifies for the first time the technical basis of etching and engraving.*

Papillon, J. M. *Traité Historique et Pratique de la Gravure en Bois*, 3 vols., Paris, 1766. *The great eighteenth-century woodcutter sums up the theory and practice of his art.*

Senefelder, Aloys. *Lehrbuch der Steindruckerey*, Munich, 1818. *Technical exposition of lithography with autobiographical notes and examples printed from stone.*

RECENT TECHNICAL HANDBOOKS

Antreasian and Adams. *The Tamarind Book of Lithography: Art and Techniques. The last word on lithographic printing.*

Auvil, Kenneth. *Serigraphy: Silk Screen Techniques for the Artist*, 1965, paperback.

Brunner, Felix. *Handbook of Graphic Reproduction Processes*, 1962. *Extensive survey of techniques and their identification.*

Buckland-Wright, John. *Etching and Engraving*, 1953. *Technique and the modern trend.*

Curwen, Harold. *Process of Graphic Reproduction in Printing*, 1958. *Both fine arts and process techniques.*

Daniels, Harvey. *Printmaking*, 1971. *Sumptuously illustrated treatise by an English printmaker.*

Hayter, S. W. *New Ways of Gravure*, 1949. *Modern methods of engraving with highly personal comments by a famous practitioner.*

Heller, Jules. *Printmaking Today*, 1966. *All-around handbook.*

Peterdi, Gabor. *Printmaking*, 1959. *One of the earliest and best handbooks on all modern techniques.*

AMERICAN PRINTS

Beal, Karen F. *American Prints in the Library of Congress*, 1970. *Catalogue of the collection, illustrated.*

Dreppard, C. W. *Early American Prints*, 1930. *A chatty informal introduction to the subject but containing, nonetheless, much pertinent information.*

Johnson, Una. *Ten Years of American Prints: 1947–1956.* Brooklyn Museum, 1956. *Illustrated exhibition catalogue with notes on unusual techniques.*

Peters, Harry T. *America on Stone, The Other Printmakers to the American People*, 1931.

————. *Currier and Ives, Printmakers to the American People*, 1929.

Pierson and Davidson. *Arts of the United States, A Pictorial Survey*, 1960. *Covering 17 categories of American art, including photographs and prints, old and modern.*

Shadwell, Wendy. *American Printmaking: The First 150 Years*, 1969. *Many illustrations from the Middendorf Collection.*

Stokes and Haskell. *American Historical Prints*, 1932. *Record of a great public collection.*

Weitenkampf, Frank. *American Graphic Art. Useful reference work with information collected over a lifetime.*

Zigrosser, Carl. *The Artist in America*, 1942. *Twenty-four profiles of contemporary American printmakers.*

PHOTOGRAPHY

Newhall, Beaumont. *Photography 1839–1937*, New York, 1937. *A survey by a great authority.*

Consult also the publications of the Steichen Center at the Museum of Modern Art, and the Stieglitz Center at the Philadelphia Museum of Art, as well as periodical literature such as the quarterly publication, *Aperture*, edited by Minor White, and the fifty volumes of *Camera Work*, edited by Alfred Stieglitz.

CHINESE PRINTS

Binyon, L. *Catalogue of Japanese and Chinese Colour Prints in the British Museum*, 1916. *Brief list of Chinese prints, including the Tun Huang finds and the Kaempfer purchase.*

Carter, Thomas F. *The Invention of Printing in China*, 1931. *An admirable piece of research. Unfortunately the author touches only indirectly upon woodcut and illustration.*

Fischer, Otto. *Ausstellung Chinescher Steinabklatsche*, Zurich, 1944. *Short historical survey of stone rubbings written with understanding.*

Loehr, Max. *Chinese Landscape Woodcuts*, 1968. *Enlightened commentary on some Sung woodcuts.*

Rijksmuseum voor Volkenkunde, Leiden. *Chinese Houtsneden*, 1956. *Old and new. Illustrated.*

Siren, Oswald. *The Chinese on the Art of Painting*, paperback, 1963. *Chinese writings on art from the Han through the Ch'ing dynasties.*

Tschichold, Jan. *Die Bildersammlung der Zehnbambushalle*, 1970. *The last word by a great authority. Marvelous color facsimilies in a beautiful book.*

Waley, Arthur. *Introduction to the Study of Chinese Painting*, 1958. *Chinese painting with philosophical background based on Chinese sources.*

Wang, Chi-chen. *The Technique of Chinese Rubbings and Its Application*, 1938. *Short exposition with some excellent large reproductions of rubbings.*

Wu, K. T. *Colour Printing in the Ming Dynasty*, in *T'ien Hsia Monthly*, August, 1940. *Important study by a Chinese scholar.*

JAPANESE PRINTS

Binyon and Sexton. *Japanese Colour Prints*, 1923, reprinted 1960. *Handy all-around work, slightly outdated; excellent table of signatures, chronology, actors' crests, and publishers' seals.*

Brown, Louise Norton. *Block Printing and Book Illustration in Japan*, 1924. *A pioneer work, not always accurate, illustrated.*

Ficke, Arthur Davison. *Chats on Japanese Prints*, 1915, reprinted 1958. *Charmingly written introduction to the subject by a poet and lifelong student of Japanese prints.*

Hillier, Jack. *The Japanese Print, a New Approach*, 1960. *Readable introduction to the subject.*

Keyes and Mizushima. *The Theatrical World of Osaka Prints*, 1973. *A marvel of scholarly research, bringing to life a neglected class of Japanese prints.*

Lane, Richard. *Masters of the Japanese Print*, 1962.

McNulty, Kneeland. *Foreigners in Japan*, 1972. *Philadelphia Museum Exhibition Catalogue displaying the native reaction in pictorial terms (Yokohama prints) of the opening of Japan to the Western world.*

Michener, James. *The Floating World*, 1954. *One of the pioneers in the new orientation toward Japanese prints.*

————. *Japanese Prints from Early Masters to the Moderns*, 1959. *Notes on prints by Richard Lane.*

Muneshige, Narazaki; English adaptation by C. H. Mitchell. *The Japanese Print: Its Evolution and Essence*, 1969. *The most comprehensive of recent works on the subject.*

Statler, Oliver. *Modern Japanese Prints*, 1956. *The sōsaku hanga movement.*

Toda, K. *Catalogue of Japanese and Chinese Illustrated Books in the Ryerson Library of the Chicago Art Institute*, 1931. *A scholarly work giving detailed information, illustrated.*

Volker, T. *Ukio-e Quartet*, 1949. *The roles of the publisher, designer, engraver, and printer.*

Index of Illustrations

Titles of books and of national schools are given in italics. Anonymous book illustrations are usually listed under author or title or printer, but occasionally under national school. Japanese artists (except those of the twentieth century) are known and listed under their given names, followed (without comma) by their family names.

All other artists (except Rembrandt, Raphael, and Titian) are listed under their family name followed by a comma and their given name.

Reproductive prints are generally listed under the name of the designer, although there are few exceptions where the engraver seemed more important than the designer. In many cases there are cross-references to the reproductive engraver.

In all cases the first word in the title under the picture locates the place in the index.

Index of Names

135

1. *Etruscan School.* Engraved Back of Bronze Mirror

2. *Romanesque School.* Nativity

3. *Coptic School.* Textile Design of Birds

4. *Austrian School*. Lectern Cloth with Marriage at Cana

5. *Austrian School.* Rest on the Flight into Egypt

6. *Bavarian School.* St. Dorothy

7. *German School.* St. Christopher

8. *French School.* Dispatch Box with Woodcut of Crucifixion

9. *German School.* Crucifixion

10. *German School.* Christ and the Woman of Samaria

11. *Fra Pelbartus.*
The Author Writing in a Garden

12. Graf. Standard Bearer of Bern

14. *Block Book*. Song of Songs

15. *Block Book*. St. John Sailing to Patmos

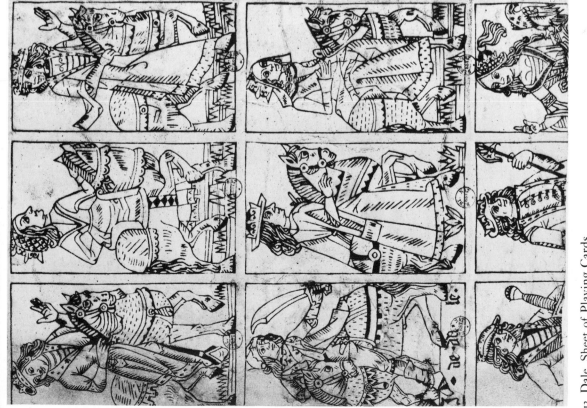

13. Dale. Sheet of Playing Cards

16. *Terence, Comoediae.* Phaedra and Pythias

17. *Directorium Statuum.* Students Carousing

18. *Buch der Weisheit (Bidpai).* Wood Gatherers

19. Wolgemut. Solomon Banqueting with His Wives

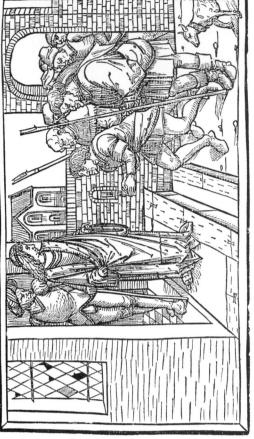

21. *Bible, Lübeck*. Joseph and His Brethren

23. *Zamorensis*. Tumblers

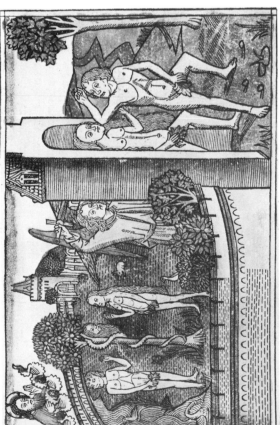

20. *Bible, Cologne*. Adam and Eve

22. *Ingulds Guldin Spiel*. A Party Playing Cards

24. *German School.* Bookplate of Brandenberg

25. Reuwich. The Holy Sepulchre

26. *Bartholomaeus Anglicus.* A Garden

27. *Regimen Sanitatis.* Patient Between Two
Physicians

28. Reuwich. Group of Thirteen Physicians

30. *Danse Macabre, La Grant.* Death and the Printers

32. *Historie van Troyen.* Si= Hercules Fighting Three Lions

29. *Danse Macabre des Hommes.* The Doctor and the Lover

31. *Les Loups Ravissans.* Death and the Soldier

33. *Terence, Comoediae.* The Theatre (Lyon)

34. *Bible en Françoys.* The Root of All Evil, Adam and Eve

35. *Terence, Comoediae.* The Theatre (Strassburg)

36. *Composte des Bergères.* The Month of August

37. *Horae B.V.M.* Dives and Lazarus

38. *Horae B.V.M.* Adoration of the Shepherds

39. *Horae B.V.M.* David and Bathsheba

40. *Horae B.V.M.* Adoration of the Magi

42. *Savonarola, Compendio di Revelazione.* Savonarola Preaching

41. *Contrasto di Carnevali e Quaresima.* Fishmonger's Shop

45. *Medici, La Nencia.* Man Offering a Flower to a Woman

46. *Savonarola, Sermone.* Agony in the Garden

47. *Chevalier Délibéré.* Author Dines with Hermit "Understanding"

48. *Dante.* Inferno, Canto II

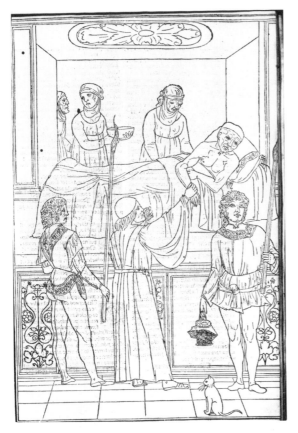

49. *Ketham, Fasciculus Medicinae.* Physician Visiting Plague Patient

50. *Petrarch, Trionfi.* Triumph of Death

51. *Hypnerotomachia.* By a Stream

52. *Bible, Malermi Version.* Illustration to Psalms

53. *Boccaccio, Decameron.* The Assembly

54. *Valturius, De Re Militari.* Warrior Before a Door

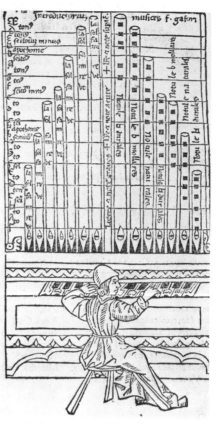

55. *Gafurius, De Re Musica.* The Organist

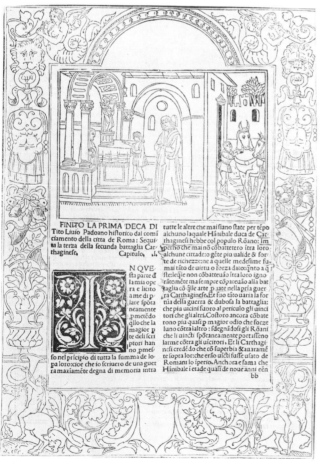

56. *Livio, Deche.* Beginning of Livy's Second *Decade*

57. *Forestis, De Claris Mulieribus.* Paula Gonzaga

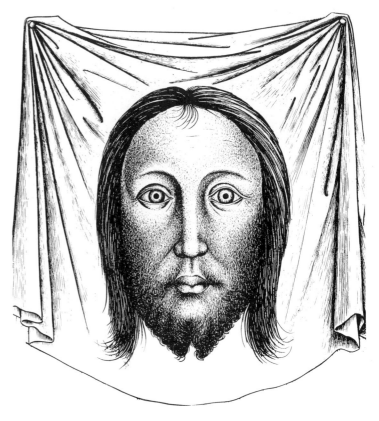

59. Master of the Playing Cards. The Sudarium

58. Master of the Playing Cards. Queen of Flowers

60. Master of the Balaam. St. Eligius

61. Master E.S. The Madonna of Einsiedeln

62. Master E.S. The Letter Q

63. Master of the Love Gardens. Garden of Love

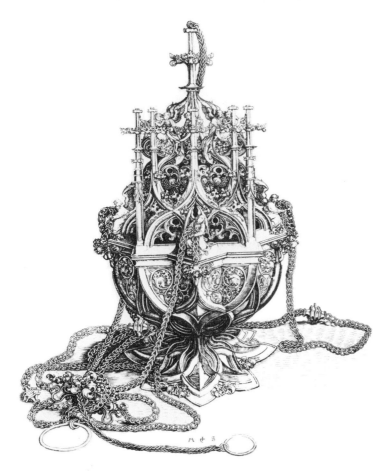

64. Schongauer. The Censer

66. Schongauer. The Nativity

65. Schongauer. Christ Appearing to the Magdalen

67. Meckenem. The Birth of the Virgin

68. Master of the Hausbuch. The Lovers

69. Master of the Hausbuch. Young Man Confronted by Death

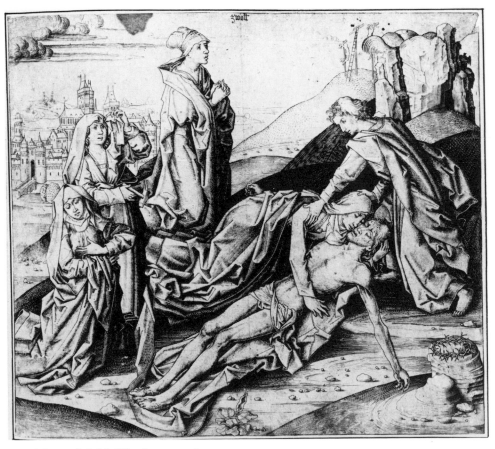

70. Master I.A.M. The Lamentation

71. Meckenem. The Enraged Wife

72. Meckenem. The Lute Player and the Harpist

73. Schongauer. Tribulation of St. Anthony

74. Master L.Cz. Temptation of Christ

75. Meckenem. Self-Portrait with Wife

76. Meckenem. Ornament with Morris Dancers

77. Meckenem. Dance at the Court of Herod

78. Dürer. The Second Knot

79. Dürer. A Fool Builds a House

80. Dürer. Birth of the Virgin

81. *Bible, Nuremberg.* Four Horsemen of the Apocalypse

82. Dürer. Four Horsemen of the Apocalypse

84. Dürer. The Nativity

83. Dürer. Virgin and Child with Monkey

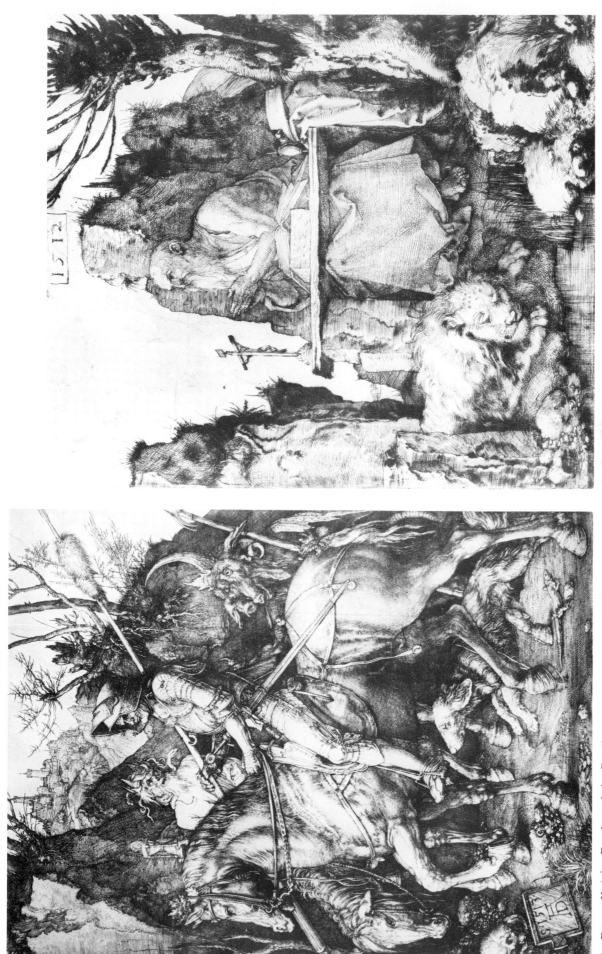

86. Dürer. St. Jerome

85. Dürer. Knight, Death, and the Devil

87. Dürer. Adam and Eve

88. Dürer. Melancholia

89. Dürer. Christ on the Mount of Olives

90. Dürer. The Great Cannon

91. Hopfer. Trophies

92. Altdorfer. Landscape

94. Van Leyden. Portrait of Emperor Maximilian

93. Dürer. Portrait of Pirkheimer

ALTERIVS NONSIT QVI SVVS ESSE POTEST

EFIGIES AVREOLI THEOPHRASTI AB HOHEN:
HEIM SVÆ ÆTATIS 47
OMNE DONVM PERFECTVM A DEO
INPERFECTVM A DIABOLO

1 SA 40

96. Hirschvogel. Portrait of Paracelsus

AETHERNA IPSE SVAE MENTIS SIMVLACHRA LVTHERVS
EXPRIMIT AT VVLTVS CERA LVCAE OCCIDVOS.

·M·D·X·X·

95. Cranach. Portrait of Martin Luther as a Monk

97. Hirschvogel. Landscape

98. Lautensack. Landscape with Vineyard

99. Bosch–van der Heyden. Shrove Tuesday

100. Van Leyden. Jezebel and Ahab

101. Van Leyden. The Milkmaid

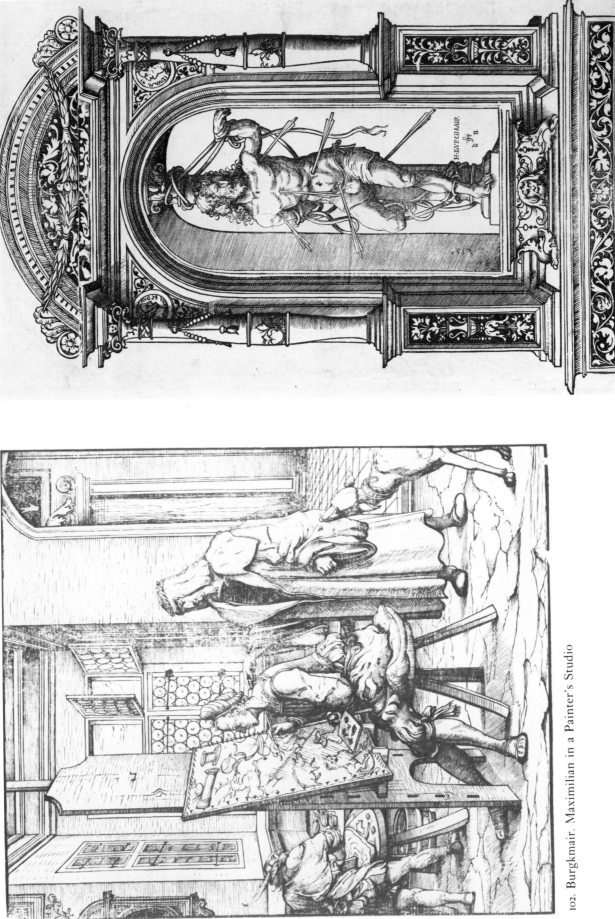

103. Burgkmair–de Negker. St. Sebastian

102. Burgkmair. Maximilian in a Painter's Studio

105. Cranach. Penance of St. John Chrysostom

104. Cranach. Venus and Amor

106. Holbein. Portrait of Erasmus

107. Holbein. Title Page Design of *Cebetis Tabulae*

109. Holbein–Lützelberger. Ruth and Boaz

108. Holbein–Lützelberger. Death
and the Plowman

110. Holbein–Lützelberger. Death and the King

111. Graf. Soldiers and Death

112. Baldung. The Fifth Commandment

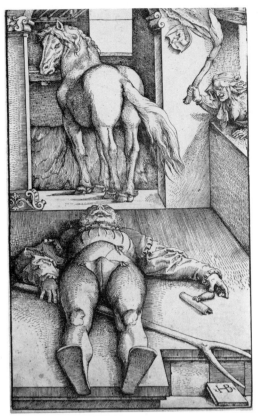

113. Baldung. The Bewitched Groom

115. Baldung. Conversion of St. Paul

114. Baldung. Wild Horses

118. Baldung. The Fall of Man

116. Baldung. St. Sebastian

117. Baldung. Portrait of Brunfels

119. Vellert. Faun on Wine Barrel

120. Delaune. La Musique

121. Pencz. Luna

122. B. Beham. Madonna by Window

123. H. S. Beham. Drummer and
Standard-Bearer

124. Weiditz. The Man with a Beautiful Wife

125. Weiditz. Painter's Studio

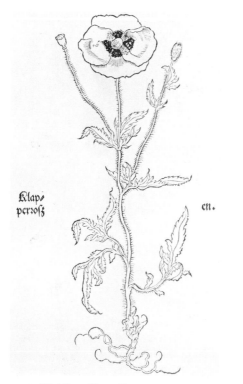

126. Weiditz. Corn Poppy

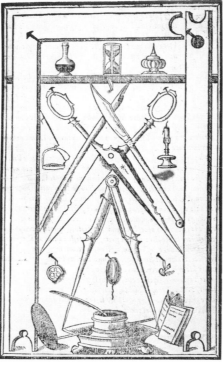

127. *Tagliente.* The Tools of the Scribe

129. *Tagliente.* Chancellery Hand

128. Aldegrever. Ornament with Lettering

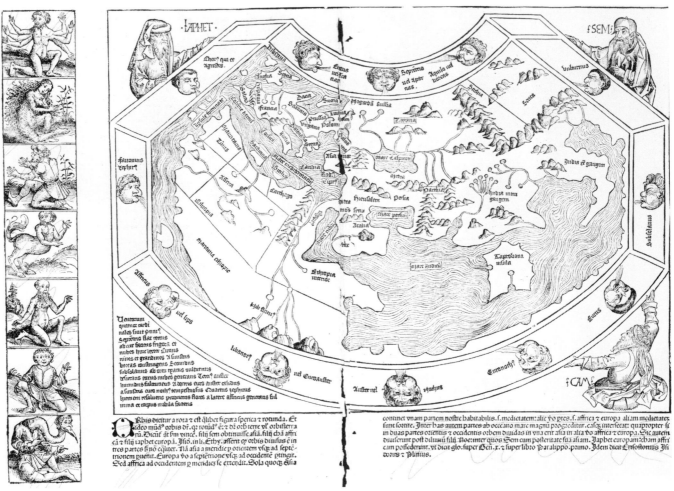

130. *Schedel, Nuremberg Chronicle.* Map of the World

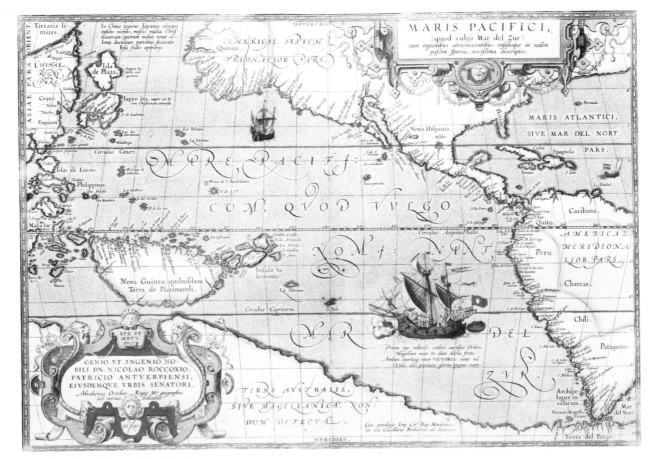

131. Ortelius. Map of Pacific Ocean

132. Flöttner. Design for a Bed

133. Vecellio. Lace Pattern

135. Altdorfer. Holy Family at the Fountain

134. Altdorfer. Virgin and Child in Landscape

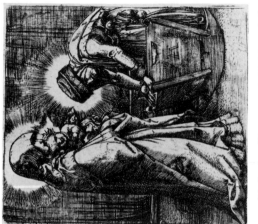

137. Altdorfer. Virgin and Child with St. Anne

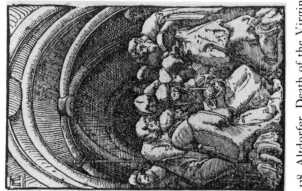

138. Altdorfer. Death of the Virgin

136. Altdorfer. The Beautiful Virgin of Regensburg

139. Primaticcio. Diana

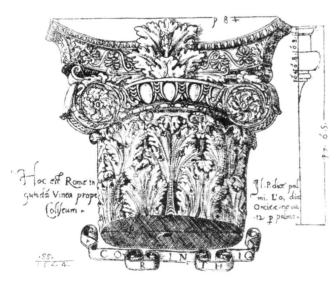

140. Serlio. Corinthian Capital

141. Cousin. The Lamentation

142. Viator. Perspective Interior

143. Duvet. Winepress of the Wrath of God

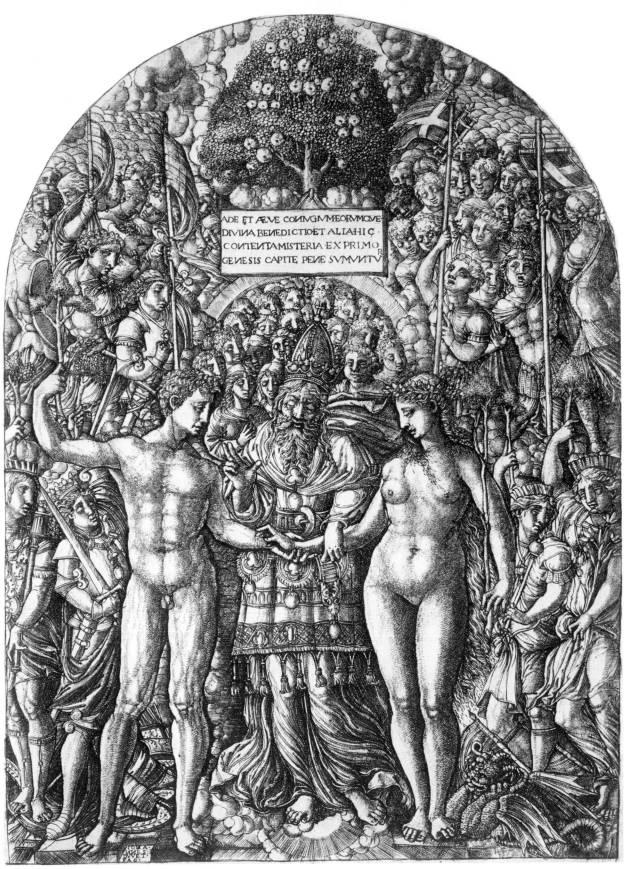

ADE ET ÆVE CONIVGVM MEORVMQVE
DIVINA BENEDICTIOET ALIAHIC
CONTENTAMISTERIA EX PRIMO
GENESIS CAPITE PENE SVMVNTV

144. Duvet. Marriage of Adam and Eve

Iulius, Augustus, nec non et Iunius Aestas · AESTAS Adolescentiæ imago · Frugiferas aruis fert Aestas torrida meßeis ·

145. Bruegel–van der Heyden. Summer

IVSTICIA

SCOPVS LEGIS EST, AVT VT EV̄ QVE PVNIT EMENDET, AVT POENA
EIVS CAETEROS MELIORES REDDET AVT SVBLATIS MALIS CAETERI SECVRIORES VIVAṬ.

146. Bruegel–Galle (?). Justice

Die dâr luy en lacker fyt bôr cryfman oft clercken Die tuijnen fijn worsten die huijfen met vlaijen
die gheraêkt daer en fmaeckt clâr van als fonder werken cappuijnen en kieckens t vliechter al ghebruijen

147. Bruegel–unknown engraver. Luilekkerland

148. Bruegel–unknown engraver. Kermesse of St. George

149. Bruegel. Rabbit Hunters.

150. Goltzius. Landscape with Shepherd

152. Goltzius. The Farnese Hercules

151. Goltzius. The Standard-Bearer

153. *Florentine School.* The Planet Mercury

154. Pollaiuolo. Battle of the Naked Men

155. Rosselli–Botticelli. Assumption of the Virgin

156. *Dante, Divina Commedia.* Canto II, Inferno

157. *Tarocchi Card.* Primo Mobile

158. Peregrino. Ornament

159. *Florentine School.* Garden of Love.

160. Peregrino. Orpheus

161. Mantegna. Virgin and Child

162. Mantegna. Risen Christ Between St. Andrew and St. Longinus

163. Mantegna. The Entombment

164. Mantegna. Bacchanal with Winepress

165. Campagnola. St. John the Baptist

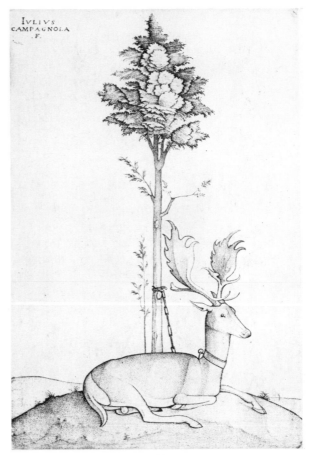

166. Campagnola. Stag at Rest

167. Campagnola. Christ and the Woman of Samaria

169. Robetta. Adoration of the Magi

168. Barbari. Apollo and Diana

171. Montagna. St. Benedict Expounding His Rule

170. Master of 1515. Fortuna

172. Raimondi. Giovanni Achillini

173. Raphael–Raimondi. Lucretia

174. Raphael–Raimondi. The Judgment of Paris

175. Raphael–Raimondi. St. Cecilia

176. Raimondi. Two Fauns

177. Raimondi. The Vintage

178. Raphael–Raimondi. Morbetto

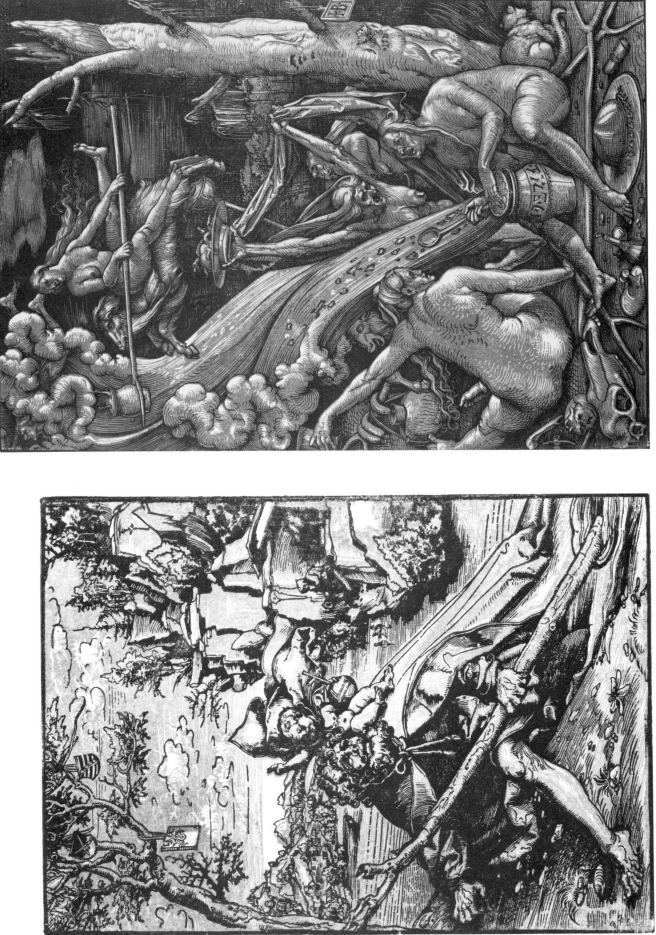

180. Baldung. The Witches

179. Cranach. St. Christopher

181. Raphael–da Carpi. Miracle of the Fishes

182. Pordenone–da Carpi. Saturn

183. Parmigianino–da Trento. Madonna and Child with St. John

184. Montagna. Pan and Apollo

185. Campagnola. The Astrologer

186. Ghisi. Melancholy of Michelangelo

187. Titian–Boldrini. Venus and Amor

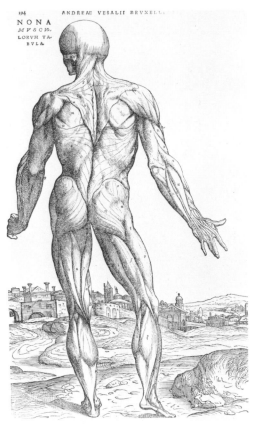

188. Titian Workshop. Ninth Plate of Muscles

189. Titian–Boldrini. Landscape with Milkmaid

TITIANI VECELLII PICTORIS CELEBERRIMI AC
FAMOSISSIMI VERA EFFIGIES.

ILL.ᵐᵉ ET R.ᵐᵒ D. Dⁿᵒ HENRICO CAETANO S.R.E. CARD. AMPL.ᵐᵒ BON.ᵉ LEGATO
EXIGVVM HOC MVNVS IMAGINIS TITIANI PICT. CVIVS NOMEN ORBIS CONTINERE NON VALET SVB MISSE DICAT SACRATQVE
HVMILL DEDIT. Q.SERVVS AVGVST. CARRATIVS.

191. Carracci. Portrait of Titian

190. Titian–de Nanto. Portrait of Ariosto

193. Cambiaso. The Conversion of St. Paul

192. Scolari. The Rape of Proserpina

194. Parmigianino. The Entombment

195. Baroccio. Christ Appearing to St. Francis

196. (de) Bry. Peter Calyce's Cruelty to the Indians

198. Kilian. Engraver's Studio

197. Vredeman de Vries. Printshop of Jerome Cock

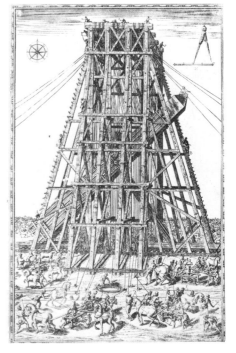

199. Fontana. The Raising of the Obelisk

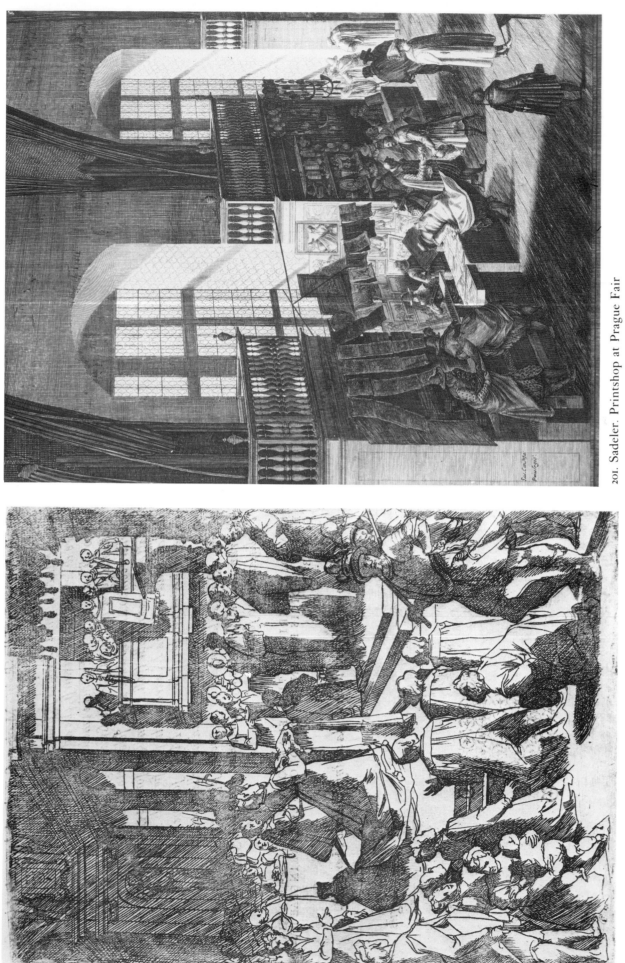

201. Sadeler. Printshop at Prague Fair

200. Balducci. Marriage of Grand Duke of Tuscany

202. Rubens–Jegher. Temptation of Christ

203. Rubens–Bolswert. Village Dance

P.Paul Rubens fecit.

204. Rubens. St. Catherine

Judocus de Momper Pictor.
montium Antuerpiæ.

Ant. van Dyck fecit aqua forti.

205. Van Dyck. Portrait of de Momper

207. Callot. La Bénédicité

206. Hollar. Winter

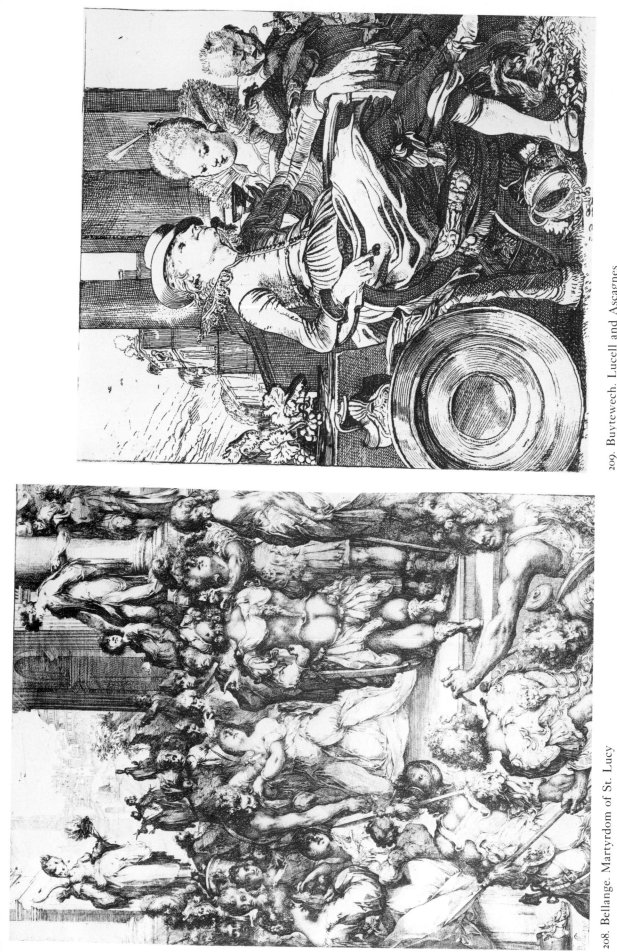

209. Buytewech. Lucell and Ascagnes

208. Bellange. Martyrdom of St. Lucy

Voyla les beaux exploits de ces cœurs inhumains L'vn pour auoir de l'or, inuente des supplices, Et tous d'vn mesme accord commettent mechamment
Ils rauagent par tout rien nechappe a leur mains L'autre à mil forfaicts anime ses complices; Levol, le rapt, le meurtre, et le violement. 5

Israel ex. Cum Priuil. Reg.

210. Callot. Pillage of a Farmhouse

Au bout du comte ils treuuent pour destin
Qu'ils sont uenus d'Aegipte a ce festin

Callot fe.

211. Callot. Gypsy Encampment

213. Callot. Riciulina and Metzetin

212. Callot. Beggar with Head and Feet Bare

214. Rembrandt. Beggar with Wooden Leg

Ce dessein façonné des honneurs des printemps,
Enioliué d'obiectz de diuers passetemps;

C'est uostre aage, Madame où les douceurs encloses
Nous sont autant de fleurs, ou Rosiers precieux

Qui pousseront sans fin des doux-flairantes roses
Dont l'odeur aggrera aux hommes et aux Cieux

215. Callot. Parterre, Nancy

216. Callot. Temptation of St. Anthony

217. Callot. The Fair at Impruneta

218. Bosse. Etching and Engraving Studio

219. Bosse. Hearing, from set of Five Senses

220. Bosse. Visite à l'accouchée

221. Seghers. Rocky River Landscape

222. Seghers. Three Books

224. Elsheimer. Nymph Dancing

225. Elsheimer–Goudt. Philemon et Baucis

223. Seghers. The Larch Tree

227. Rembrandt. Self-Portrait Leaning on a Stone Sill

226. Rembrandt. Portrait of His Mother

228. Rembrandt. Self-Portrait by a Window

229. Rembrandt. Dr. Faustus

230. Rembrandt. Christ Preaching

231. Rembrandt. Three Crosses

232. Rembrandt. Landscape with Farm Buildings and Tower

233. Rembrandt. The Gold Weigher's Field

235. Rembrandt. Woman with Arrow

234. Rembrandt. The Presentation in the Temple

236. Van Ostade. The Painter's Studio

237. Van Ostade. The Fisherman

238. Ruysdael. The Wheat Field

239. Roghman. Landscape with Column

240. Bega. Drinker

241. Blooteling. Smoker

242. Teniers. Kermesse

Een Vlotſchuÿt, Een Schietſchuÿt, 4

243. Zeeman. Vessels of Amsterdam

T. Bakhuizen fec: et exc: cum Privil: ord: Holland: et West-Frisiæ.

244. Backhuysen. Marine with Distant View of Amsterdam

245. van de Velde. June

246. Waterloo. The Linden Tree by an Inn

247. Everdingen. Water Mill

248. Potter. Frisian Horse

249. Gelée. Le Bouvier

250. Gelée. Campo Vaccino

252. Caravaggio. The Den al of Peter

253. Ribera. Drunken Silenus

251. Castiglione. Temporalis Aeternitatis

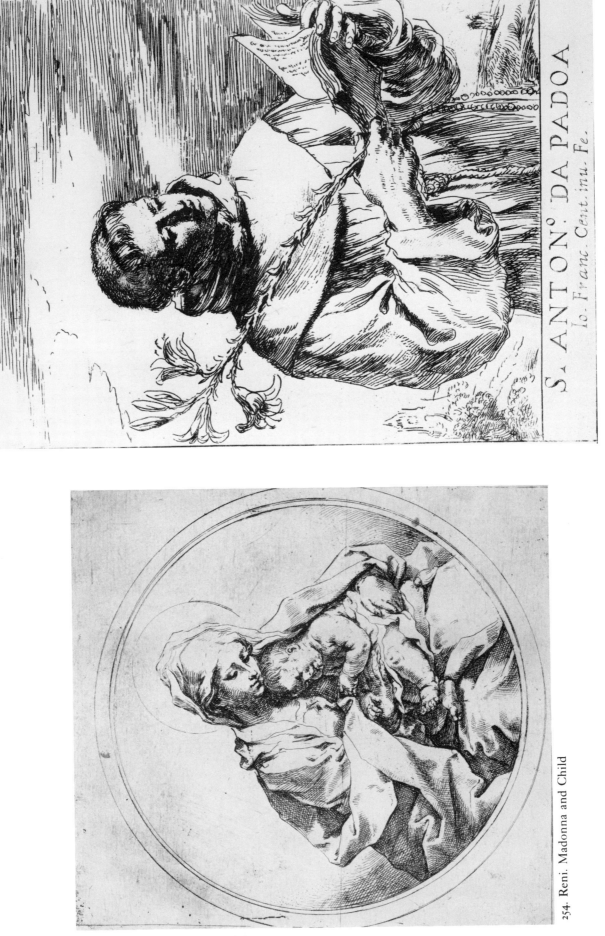

S. ANTON: DA PADOA
Io. Franc. Cent. inu. Fe.

255. Guercino. St. Anthony of Padua

254. Reni. Madonna and Child

257. van de Velde II. Portra t of Oliver Cromwell

256. Leoni. Portrait of Galileo

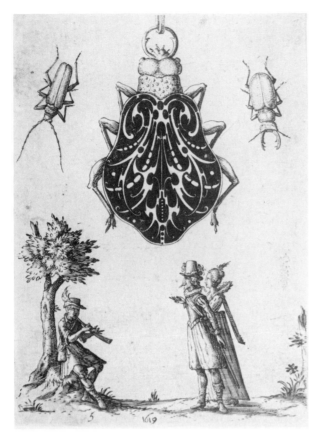

258. Tutin. Ornament

259. Bracelli. Bizarre Figures

260. Della Bella. Cartouche

261. Jacquinet. Gunsmith Shop

262. Chardin–Le Bas. *Etude du Dessin*

263. Le Pautre. Fountain

265. Mellan. La Sainte Face

AMELIA ELISABETHA, D.G. HASSIE LANDGRAVIA etc.
COMITISSA HANOVIÆ MVNTZENB:

264. Siegen. Landgravin von Hesse

MICHAEL DE MAROLLES
ABB. DE VILLELOIN An.Æ.4.8.
M. del et f. 1648

266. Mellan. Michael de Marolles

Antonius Vitré
Regis & Cleri Gallicani Typographus.

267. Morin. Antoine Vitré

268. Nanteuil. Thesis with Portrait of Louis XIV

269. Nanteuil. Portrait of Jean Loret

270. Drevet–Rigaud. Portrait of Robert de Cotte

271. Wille–Toqué. Marquis de Marigny

272. Watteau–Surugue. Italian Comedy

273. Watteau–Aveline. The Shop of Gersaint

FÊTES VENITIENNES

Gravées d'Apres le Tableau original peint par Watteau
haut de 1.pied 9.pouces sur 1.pied 5.pouces
de large.

FESTA VENETA

Sculpta juxtà Exemplar à Watteavo depictum cujus
altitudo 1.pedem cum 9.uncüs et latitudo 1.pedem
cum 5. continet.

A.Watteau pinxit.

Lau. Cars Sculp.

Du Cabinet de Mr de Jullienne
Avec Privilege du Roy

274. Watteau–Cars. Fêtes Venitiennes

275. Fragonard. Bacchanal

276. Boucher–Demarteau. Venus Desarmée par les Amours

278. Boucher. Le Petit Savoyard

277. Fragonard–Delaunay. Happy Accident of the Swing

279. Pillement–Allen. Chinoiserie Design

280. Pillement–Allen. Fleurs Idéales

281. Chippendale–Darby. Desk

282. Adam–Cunego. Chimneys in St. James's Palace

284. Prévost–Teillard. Vase of Flowers

283. Casteels–Fletcher. August Flowers

285. Eisen–de Longueil. La Courtisane Amoureuse

286. Gravelot–le Mire. La Galerie du Palais de Justice

287. Boucher–Cars. Le Malade Imaginaire

288. Gravelot–Duclos. Elle donne les Lois, aux Bergères aux R●

289. Eisen–Ponce. Headpiece to *Les Baisers*.

291. Prud'hon. Phrosine et Mélidor

290. Moreau le Jeune. Foire de Gonesse

292. Lavreince–Delaunay. Consolation de l'Absence

293. Baudouin–Delaunay. Le Carquois Epuisé

294. Augustin de St. Aubin–Duclos. Le Bal Paré

296. Baudouin–Simonet. –a Soirée des Tuileries

295. Lavreince–Delaunay. Le Billet Doux

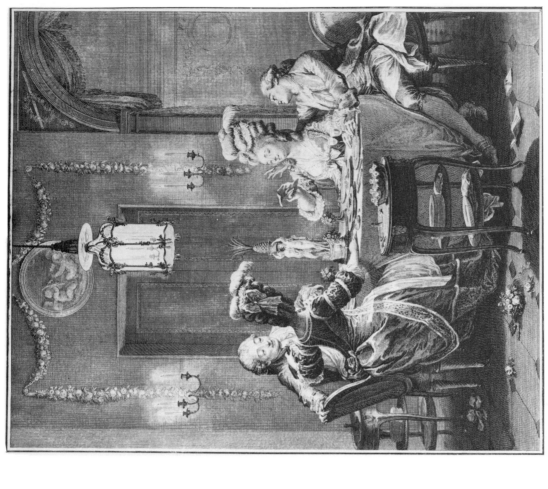

297. Moreau–Helman. Les Délices de la Maternité

298. Moreau–Helman. Le Souper Fin

300. Moreau–Delaunay. Les Adieux

299. Moreau–Malbeste. La Sortie de l'Opéra

301. Cochin. Ballet: The Princess of Navarre

303. Carmontelle–Delafosse. The Mozart Family

302. Cochin–St. Aubin. Portrait of Benjamin Franklin

304. Moreau–Gaucher. Crowning of the Bust of Voltaire

Peint par Chardin.

Gravé par Le Bas 1741

LE NEGLIGÉ

OU

TOILETTE DU MATIN

Avant que la Raison l'eclaire,
Elle prend du Miroir les avis Séduisans.

Tiré du Cabinet de Monseigneur le Comte
de Tessin

Dans le désir et l'Art de plaire,
Les Belles, je le vois, ne sont jamais Enfans.

305. Chardin–Le Bas. Le Negligé

306. Chardin–Lepicié. La Gouvernante

307. Gabriel de St. Aubin. Spectacle des Tuileries

308. Gabriel de St. Aubin. Le Salon du Louvre

311. Gabriel de St. Aubin. Théâtre Italien

309. Gabriel de St. Aubin. Académie Particulière

310. Gabriel de St. Aubin. Les Nouvellistes

312. Cochin–Augustin de St. Aubin. Portrait of Cochin

313. Cochin–Augustin de St. Aubin. Portrait of Beaumarchais

314. Cochin (supervised by). The Conquests of Ch'ien Lung

CONCOURS pour le PRIX de l'Etude des TÊTES et de l'EXPRESSION.

Fondé à l'Academie Royale de Peinture et Sculpture par Mr. le Comte de CAYLUS Honoraire Amateur en 1760.

315. Cochin–Flipart. Competition for Caylus Prize

316. Choffard. Printshop of Basan

317. Chodowiecki. Cabinet d'un Peintre

P.J. MARIETTE

Controlleur general de la grande Chancellerie,
Honoraire de l'Academie Royale de Peinture et Sculpture,
ne à Paris le 7.e Mai 1694.

318. Cochin–Augustin de St. Aubin. Portrait of Pierre Jean Mariette

319. Daullé–Pesne. Portrait of Jean Mariette

320. Bartsch. Self-Portrait

321. St. Memin. Portrait of Jefferson

322. Janinet–Hoin. Mme Dugazon in the Role of Nina

323. Bonnet–Drouais. Portrait of Mme du Barry

324. Debucourt. Promenade Publique

325. Sergent–Marceau. Les Peuples Parcourant les Rues

326. Fragonard, fils–Berthault. Revolutionary Committee under the Terror

327. Le Prince. La Vue

328. *Vue d'Optique.* Fontainebleau du coté du parterre

330. *Image Populaire.* O Crux Ave

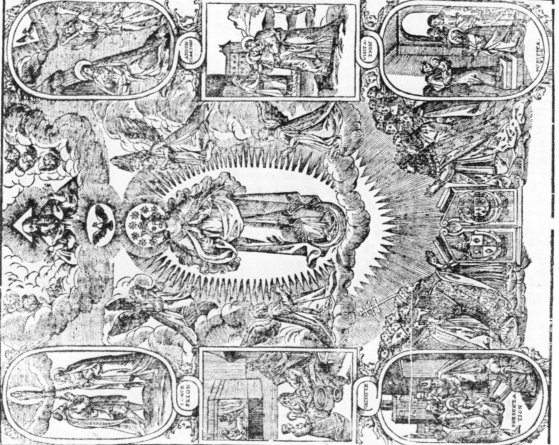

329. Papillon. Notre Dame de Bonne Délivrance

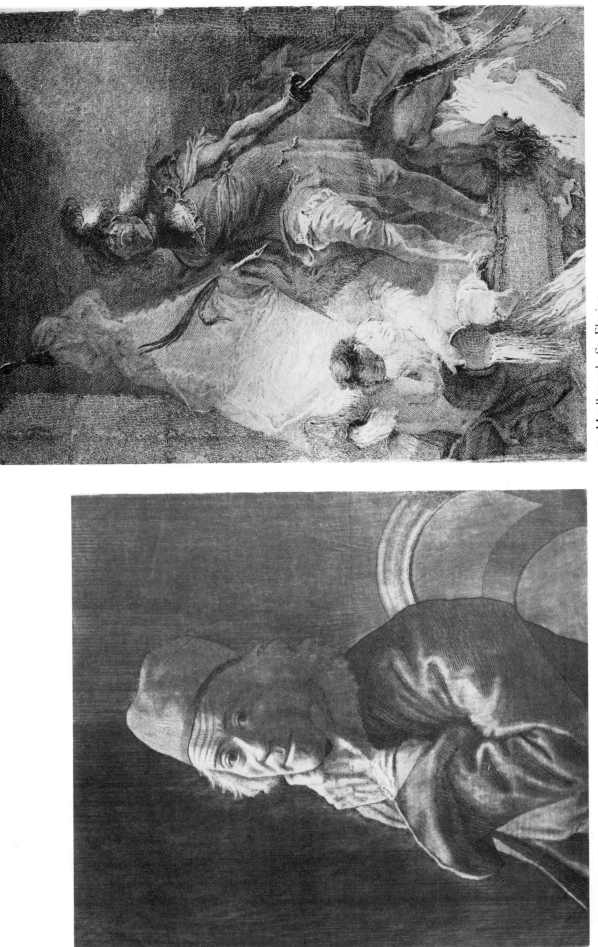

332. Maulbertsch. St. Florian

331. Liotard. Self-Portrait

333. Bibiena–Ospel. Royal Gallery, stage set

335. Romney–Meyer. Lady Hamilton as Nature

334. Reynolds–Watson. Lady Bamfylde

336. Reynolds–Doughty. Samuel Johnson

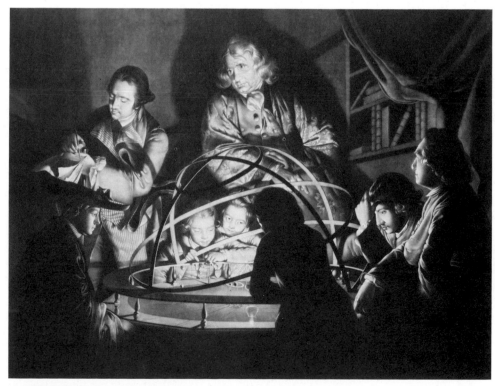

337. Wright–Pether. The Orrery

338. Hogarth–Baron. The Morning After

339. Hogarth. Strolling Actresses Dressing in a Barn

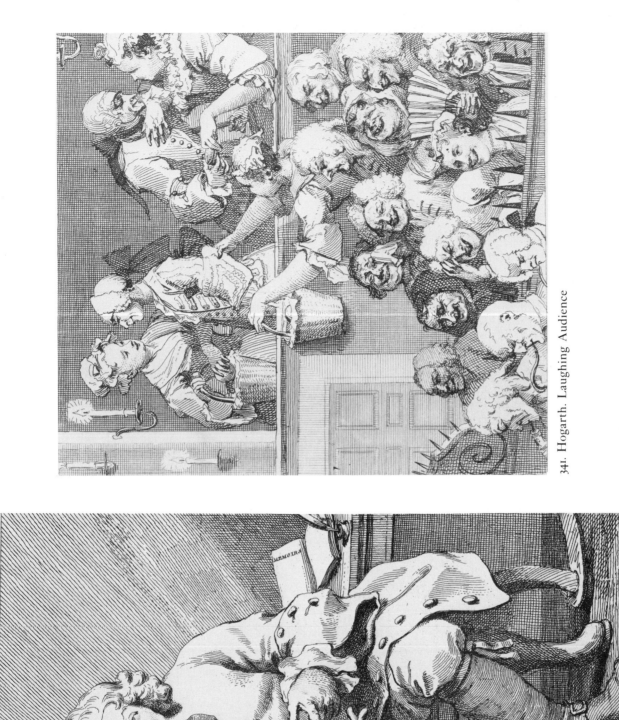

341. Hogarth. Laughing Audience

340. Hogarth. Portrait of Lord Lovat

342. Gainsborough. Cows in a Landscape

343. Hogarth–Bartolozzi. Shrimp Girl

344. Down-nman–Tomkins. Mrs. Siddons

345. G.B. Tiepolo. Death Gives Audience

346. G.D. Tiepolo. Flight into Egypt

347. Canaletto. Torre di Malghera

348. Canaletto. The Terrace

349. Piranesi. Carcere IX

350. Piranesi. Carcere XIV

351. Piranesi. The Colosseum

352. Piranesi. Piazza Navona

353. Goya. Coloso

Fran.co Goya y Lucientes,
Pintor.

354. Goya. Self-Portrait

355. Goya. Will No One Unbind Us?

356. Goya. As Far as His Grandfather

357. Goya. Bravo Toro

358. Goya. Modo de Volar

359. Goya. Disparate de Bestia

360. Goya. Thanks to Millet Seed

361. Goya. And There Is No Remedy

362. Raffet. Revue Nocturne

363. Goya. The Wreckage of War

364. Rowlandson–Jukes. Vauxhall

365. Rowlandson and Pugin. Christie's Auction Room

366. Rowlandson. Sign of the Four Alls

367. Rowlandson. A Seriocomic Scene in Norwich

368. Hodges–Reeve. Hare Hunting

369. Newhouse–Reeve. False Alarm on the Road to Gretna Green

371. Reinagle and Pether–Dunkarton. Night-Blooming Cereus

Rosier Centifolia Bipinnata *Rosier à feuilles de Céleri*

370. Redouté–Langlois. Rosa Centifolia

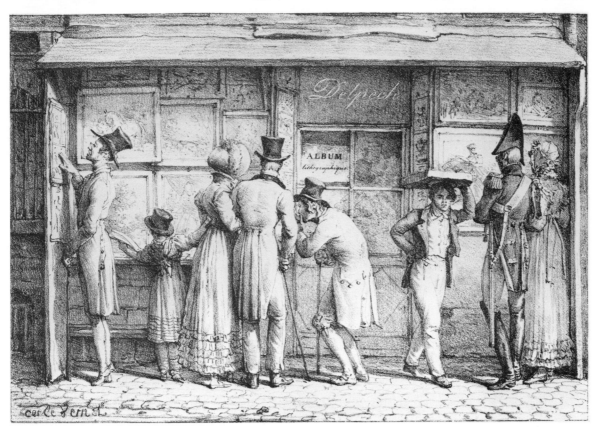

372. Vernet. The Printing Shop of Delpech

373. Quaglio. Portrait of Senefelder

374. Kriehuber. Matinée chez Liszt

375. Denon. Denon Drawing a Portrait

376. Géricault. Retour de Russie

377. Bonington. Tour de la Grosse Horloge

378. Isabey. Eglise de St.-Nectaire

379. Boys. Pavillon de Flore

381. Gavarni. A Montmartre

380. Gavarni. The de Goncourt Brothers

382. Gavarni. "This is how I will look on Sunday"

383. Gavarni. "I've cancanned until I have no more legs"

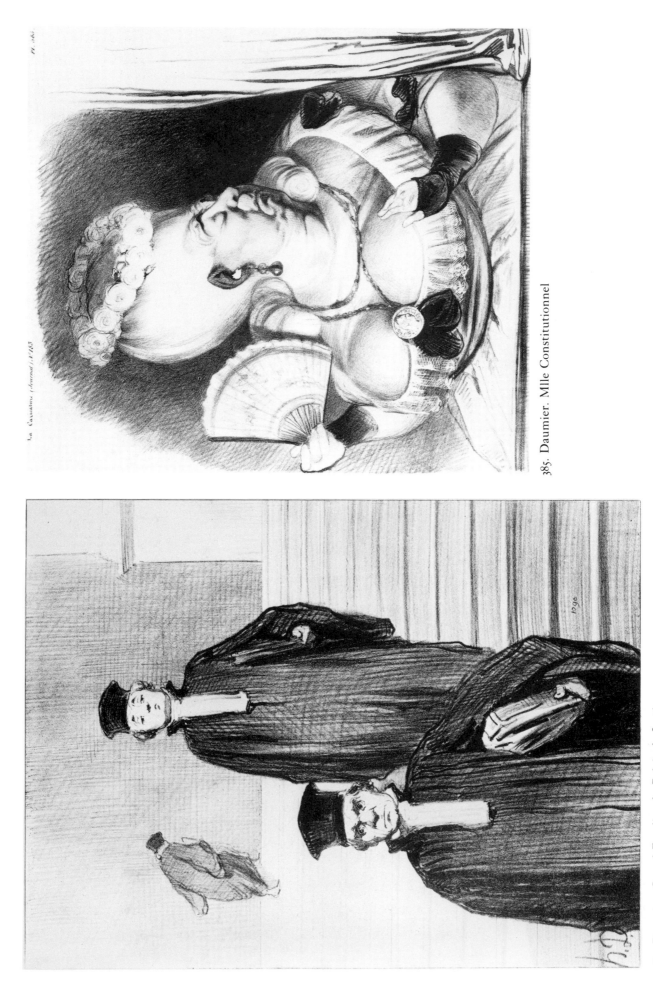

385. Daumier. Mlle Constitutionnel

384. Daumier. Grand Escalier du Palais de Justice

386. Daumier. Le Ventre Législatif

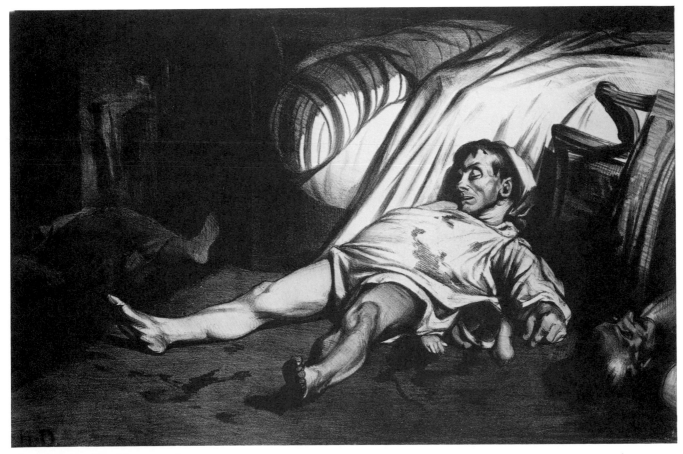

387. Daumier. Rue Transnonain

388. Daumier. Nadar Elevating Photography to the Height of Art

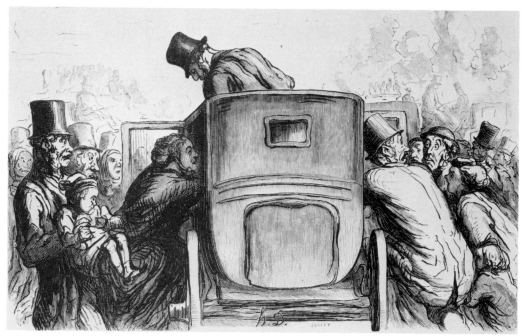

389. Daumier. Cab Shortage at the Exposition

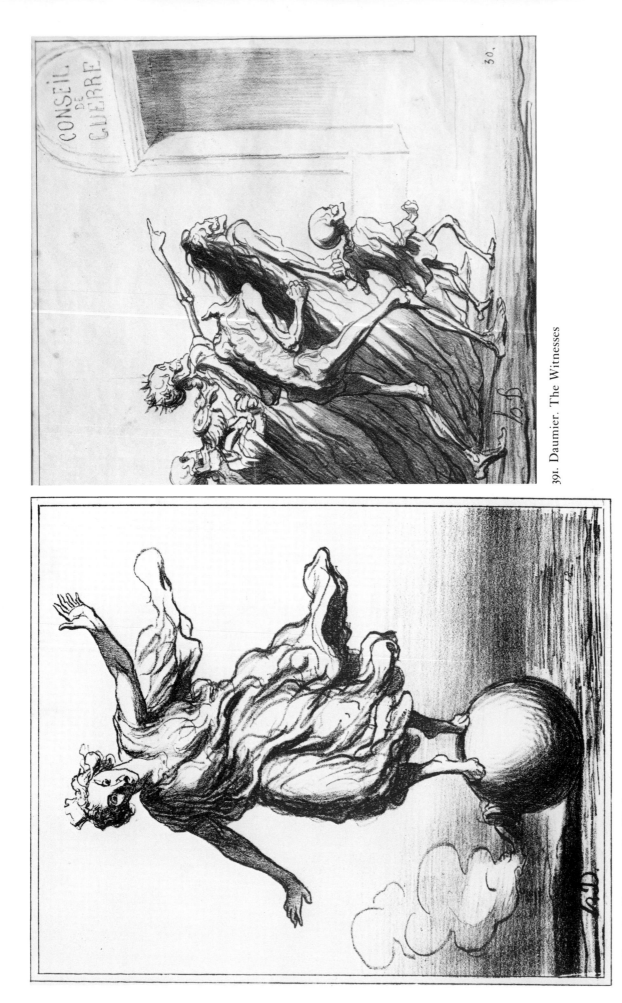

391. Daumier. The Witnesses

390. Daumier. European Equilibrium

392. Ingres. Portrait of Cortois de Pressigny

393. Delacroix. Lion d'Atlas

395. Delacroix. Faust in the Hartz Mountains

394. Delacroix. La Sœur de Dugesclin

397. Renoir. Baigneuse

396. Chassériau. Venus Anadyomène

399. Toulouse-Lautrec. Etude de Femme

398. Degas. Sortie de Bain

400. Ingres. Odalisque

401. Gauguin. Manao Tupapau

402. Manet. Olympia

403. Cézanne. Bathers

405. Millet. Shepherdess Knitting

404. Courbet. Jean Journet

406. Corot. Demeure du Poète

407. Jongkind. Porte d'Honfleur

408. Constable. Milford Bridge

409. Constable–Lucas. Summer Evening

410. Turner. Little Devil's Bridge near Altdorf

411. Crome. Mousehold Heath

412. Doré. London Slum

413. Bewick. Wayfarers

414. Bewick. Fisherman

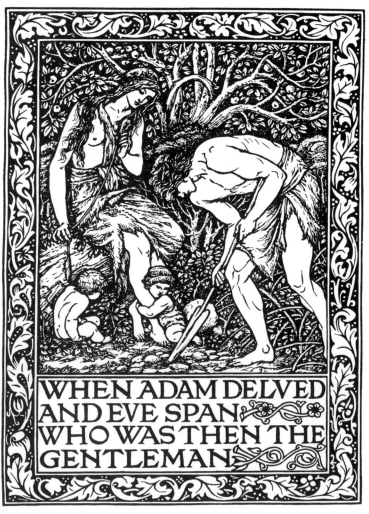

WHEN ADAM DELVED
AND EVE SPAN
WHO WAS THEN THE
GENTLEMAN

415. Burne-Jones. Adam and Eve

Silentium.

Introduzione.

Scherzo.

Adagio.

Adagio con sentimento.

Piano.

Smorzando.

Maëstoso.

Capriccioso.

Passagio chromatico.

Fuga del diavolo.

Forte vivace.

Fortissimo vivacissimo.

Finale furioso.

Bravo-bravissimo.

416. Busch. The Virtuoso

418. Friedrich. Melancolia

417. Menzel. Bear Pit

420. Richter. St. John's Festival

419. Schinkel. Liebliche Wehmut

422. Blake. The Union of the Soul with God

421. Blake. Tyger, Tyger

423. Blake. When the Morning Stars Sang Together

424. Blake. Paolo and Francesca

425. Blake. Storm-blasted Tree

426. Blake. Sabrina's Stream

427. Calvert. Chamber Idyll

428. Palmer, Samuel. Sleeping Shepherd

429. Meryon. Le Stryge

430. Meryon. Abside de Notre-Dame

432. Ensor. Death Pursuing the Human Horde

431. Bresdin. The Good Samaritan

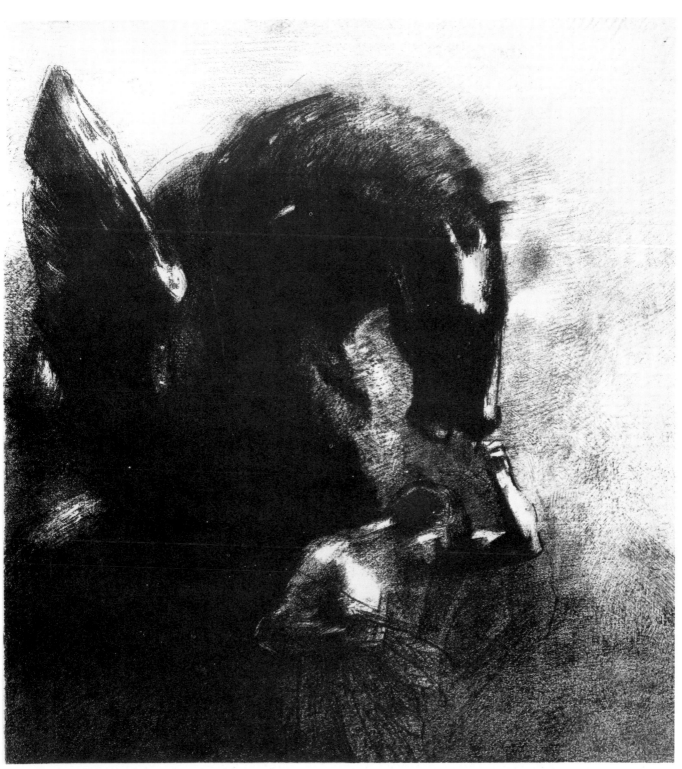

433. Redon. Pégase Captif

434. Haden. Egham Lock

435. Buhot. Winter in Paris

436. Whistler. Old Hungerford Bridge

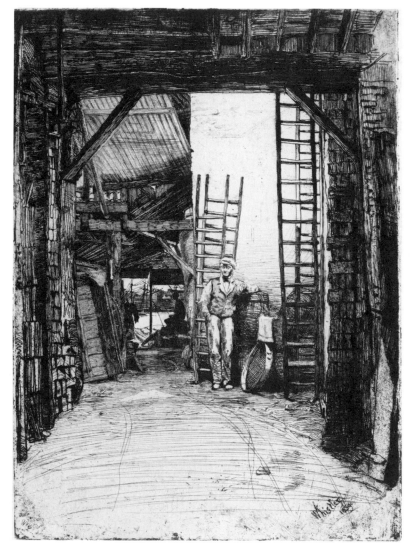

437. Whistler. The Lime-Burner

438. Whistler. Annie Hayden

439. Whistler. Riva No. 1

440. Whistler. Nocturne, The Thames at Battersea

441. Manet. Au Paradis

442. Manet. Portrait of Berthe Morisot

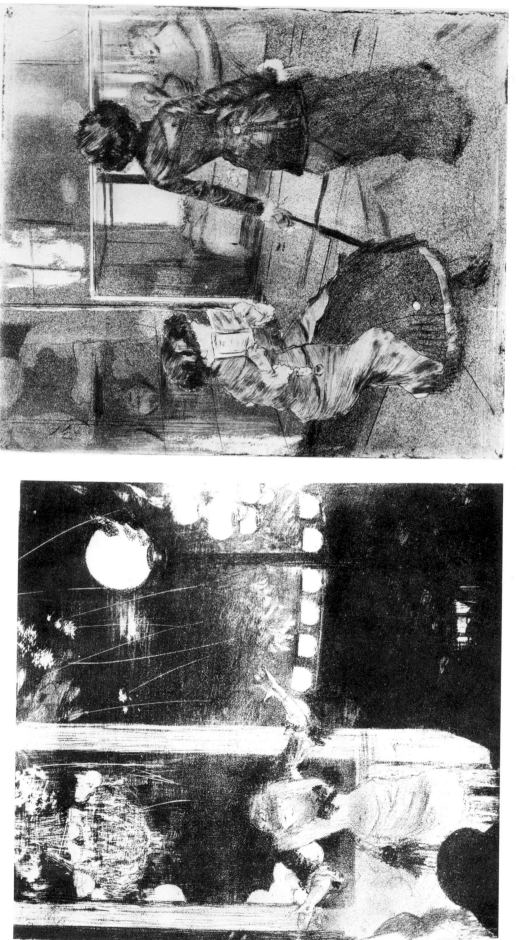

444. Degas. Au Louvre

443. Degas. Mlle Bécat

445. Cassatt. The Fitting

446. Pissarro. Place de la République, Rouen

447. Vuillard. The Cook

448. Bonnard. Street at Evening

449. Van Gogh. Portrait of Dr. Gachet

450. Gauguin. Nave Nave Fenua

451. Toulouse-Lautrec. May Milton, poster

452. Toulouse-Lautrec. Yvette Guilbert

453. Toulouse-Lautrec. Jane Avril

454. Toulouse-Lautrec. Jockey

456. Steinlen. Lait Sterilisé, poster

455. Cheret. Cleveland Cycles, poster

458. Vallotton. La Paresse

457. Rodin. Portrait of Victor Hugo

459. Niepce. Cardinal d'Amboise

460. Talbot. Chess Players

461. Hill. Mrs. Jameson

462. Atget. Avenue des Gobelins

463. Bone. Spanish Good Friday

464. Brockhurst. Adolescence

465. Matisse. Nu au fauteuil

466. Dufy. The Hare

467. Matisse. La Persanne

468. Matisse. Seated Nude, Back

469. Matisse. Nu Etendu

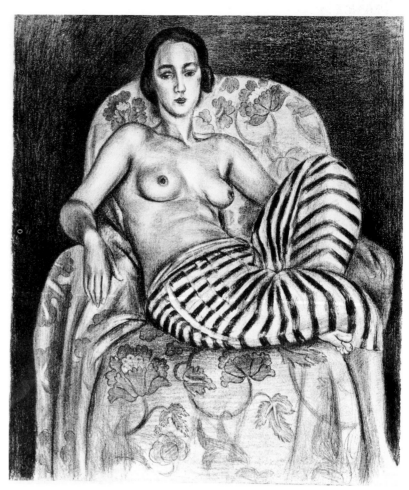

470. Matisse. Grande Odalisque au Fauteuil

471. Matisse. The Knife Thrower

472. Picasso. Tête d'Homme

473. Braque. Paris

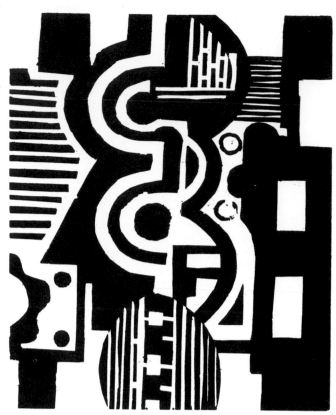

475. Léger. Lunes de Papier (Abstraction)

474. Picasso. Pierrot and Harlequin

476. Gleizes. Decoration for a Railroad Station

477. Braque. Athénée

479. Hecht. Mont-St.-Michel

481. Dufy. Golfe de Juan

478. Signac. Bords de la Seine

480. Dunoyer de Segonzac. Farm in the Afternoon

483. Pascin. Cinderella

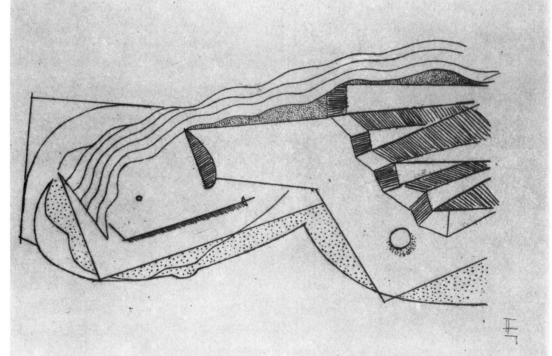

482. Laurens. Woman with a Fan

484. Villon. Baudelaire with Pedestal

485. Villon. Chessboard

486. Derain. Enchanteur pourrisant

487. Maillol. Juno

488. Rouault. Il arrive parfois

489. Rouault. De Profundis

490. Miró. Personnage aux Oiseaux

491. Miró. Book Decoration

492. Arp. Illustration to *Dreams and Projects*

493. Dali. Illustration to *Chants de Maldoror*

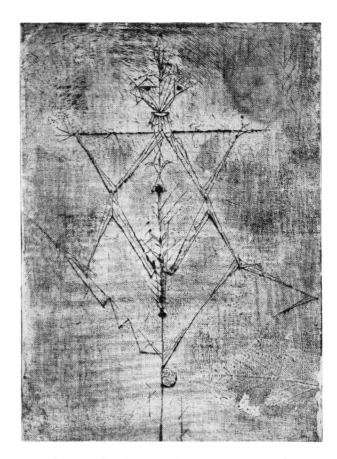

494. Masson. Le Génie de Blé

495. Kirchner. Portrait of Arp

496. Kirchner. Bathers by the Sea

497. Kirchner. Landscape near Glarus

498. Nolde. Jestri

499. Heckel. Girl by the Sea

500. Schmidt–Rottluff. The Way to Emmaus

501. Feininger. Village Church

502. Marc. The Annunciation

503. Marcks. Cats

504. Barlach. Christ on the Mount of Olives

505. Klee. Old Man Reckoning

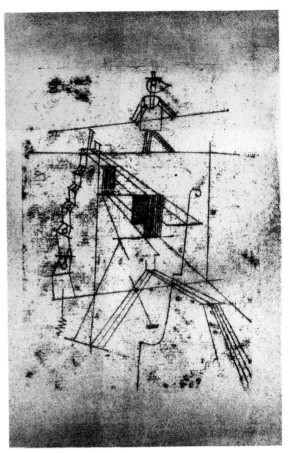

506. Klee. Seiltänzer

507. Beckmann. Dream

508. Beckmann. Königinen II

509. Kollwitz. The Volunteers

510. Kollwitz. Woman and Death

511. Kollwitz. The Call of Death

512. Kollwitz. Beggars

513. Kollwitz. The Mothers

514. Grosz. Self-Portrait for Charlie Chaplin

515. Grosz. Workers

517. Dix. Dance of Death, 1917

516. Lehmbruck. Four Women

518. Kokoschka. Resurrection

519. Kokoschka. Hope Leading the Weak One

520. Schiele. Reclining Nude

521. Schwitters. Abstraction

522. Kandinsky. Lyrical from book, *Klänge*

523. Kandinsky. Composition: Chessboard—Orange

524. Kandinsky. Violet

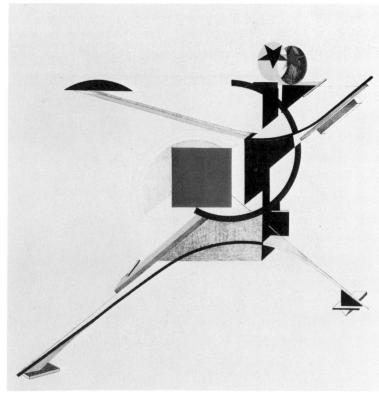

525. Lissitsky. Neuer

526. Chagall. Jacob's Dream

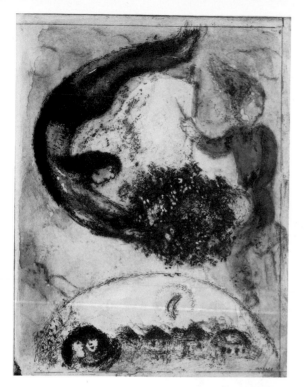

527. Chagall. The Offering

528. Konstantinov. Harvest, Collective Farm

529. Kravchenko. Dneprostroy
(Building the Dam)

530. Picasso. Repas Frugal

531. Picasso. Nude Woman Crowning Herself with Flowers

532. Picasso. Salomé

533. Picasso. Femme au Tambourin

534. Picasso. Dancing Centaur

535. Picasso. Minotauromachia

536. Picasso. Woman by Window

537. Picasso. Owl on Chair

538. Picasso. Little Head of Woman

539. Marini. Horse and Rider

540. Morandi. Still Life

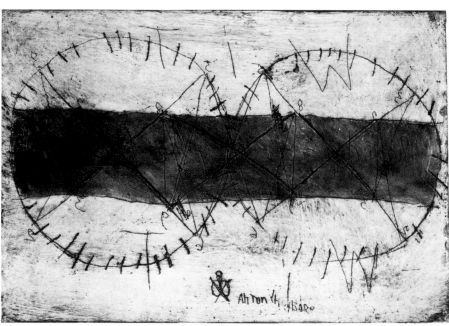

541. Heyboer. Composition of Circles

542. Escher. Order and Chaos

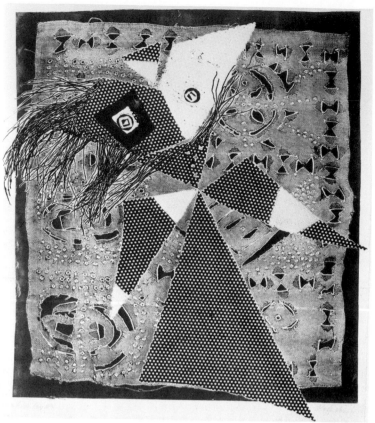

544. Nesch. Dark Lady

543. Giacometti. Femme Couchée

545. Nesch. Skaugum

546. Munch. Head of Girl, on the Beach

547. Munch. The Sick Child

548. Munch. Young Model (Study of Puberty)

549. Munch. The Kiss

550. Munch. The Cry

551. Sickert. "That Old-Fashioned Mother of Mine"

552. Nevinson. Swooping Down

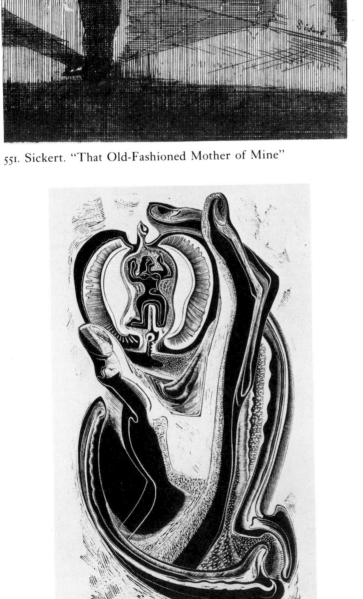

553. Hermes. Adam and Eve

554. Gill. Venus

556. Hayter. Pavane

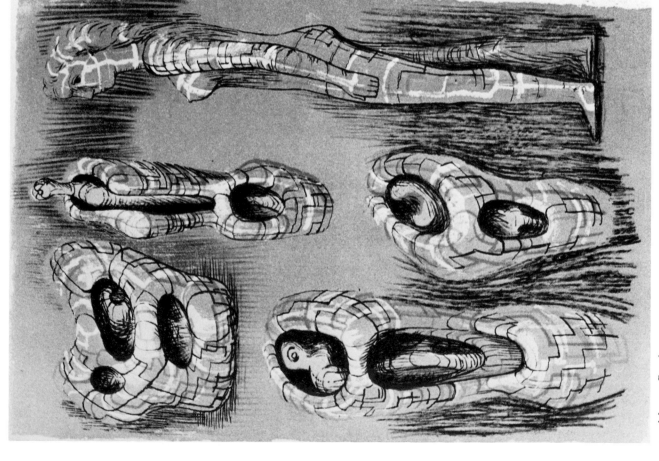

555. Moore. Pandora

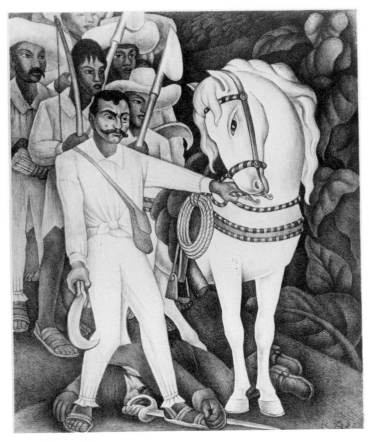

557. Rivera. Zapata

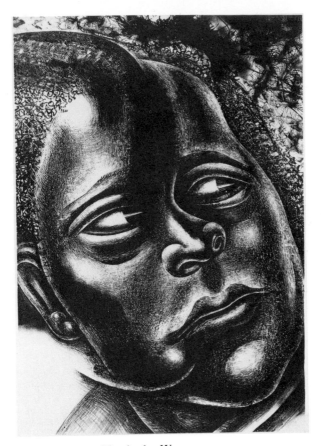

558. Siqueiros. Head of a Woman

559. Orozco. Requiem

560. Posada. Calavera Huertista

561. Mendez. Dream of the Poor

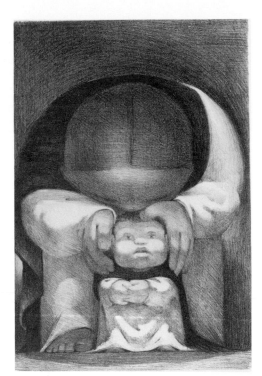

562. Charlot. First Steps

563. Tamayo. Bleu Paysage Aztèque

564. Foster. Richard Mather

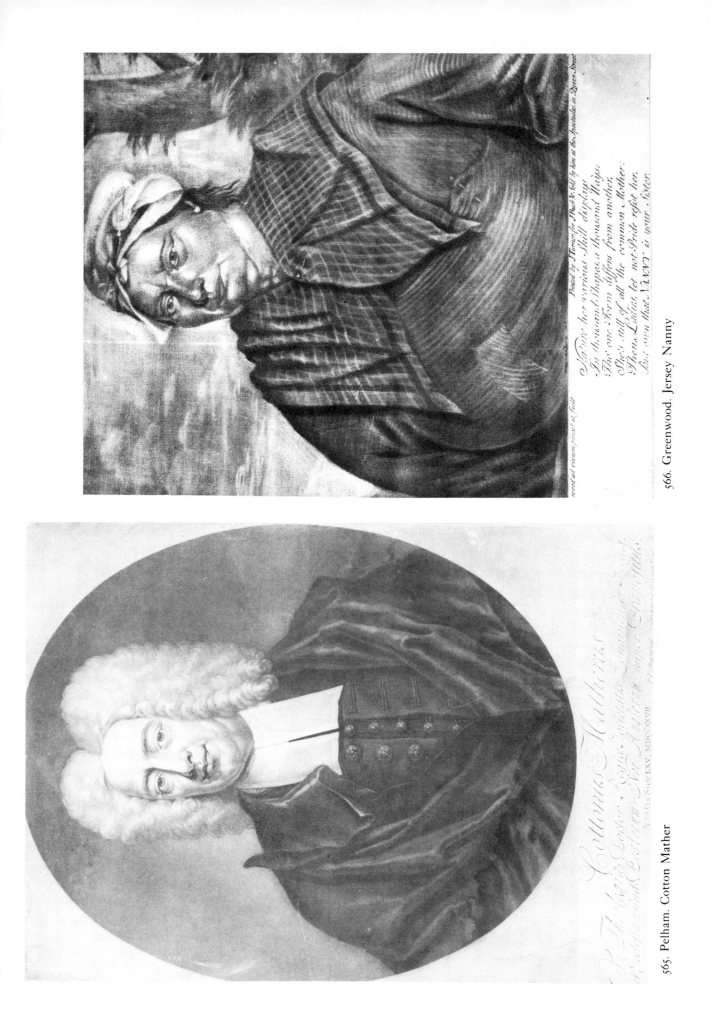

Nature her various Shapes displays
In thousand Shapes a thousand Ways:
Tho' one Form differs from another;
She's still of all the common Mother:
Then Ladies, let not Pride reject her,
But own that NANNY is your Sister.

Greenwood ad vivum pinxit et fecit

Printed by Harvey for J Buck to sold by him at the Spectacles in Queen Street

566. Greenwood. Jersey Nanny

Cottonus Matherus

565. Pelham. Cotton Mather

567. Copley. Rev. William Welsteed

568. C. W. Peale. Benjamin Franklin

569. Burgis. Boston Light House

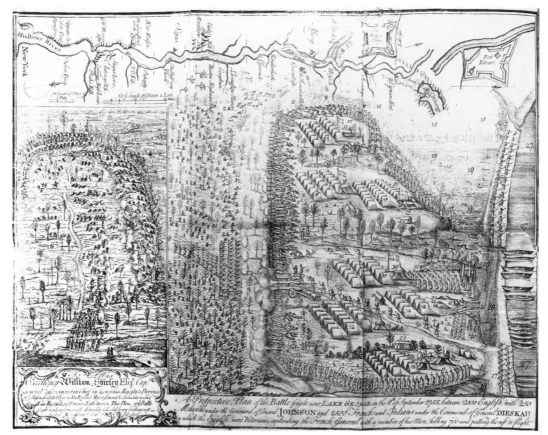

570. Johnston–Blodgett. Battle of Lake George

571. Revere. Boston Massacre

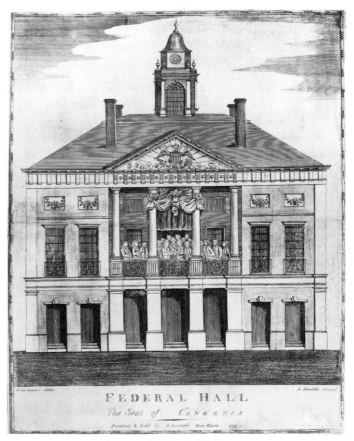

572. Doolittle–Lacour. Federal Hall

575. Bennett. South Street from Maiden Lane

576. Yeager–Krimmel. Procession of Victuallers, Philadelphia

577. *Pennsylvania-German School.* Adam and Eve

578. Trumbull–Durand. Declaration of Independence

579. Audubon–Havell. Loggerhead Shrike

580. Audubon–Havell. White-Headed Eagle

581. Mason–Barker. Horizontorium

582. Clay. The Times, 1837

583. Edmunds–Jones. "Sparking"

584. Bingham–Doney. The Jolly Flatboatmen

586. Rembrandt Peale. George Washington

585. West. Angel of the Resurrection

587. Brown. John Randolph

588. Catlin. Buffalo Hunt, Chasing Back

589. Parsons–Currier. Clipper Ship *Lightning*

590. Durrie–Currier and Ives. Home to Thanksgiving

591. Frances Palmer. Across the Continent

592. Maurer. Life in the Woods

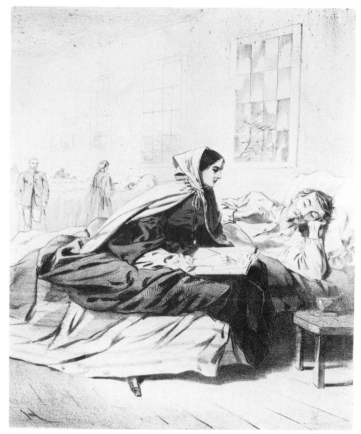

593. Homer. Letter for Home

594. Homer. The Life Line

595. Homer–Lagarde. Waiting for a Bite

596. Homer–unknown engraver. "Dad's Coming"

597. Hunt. Woman at Well

598. Duveneck. Laguna, Venice

599. Weir. Woman Sewing

600. Sargent. Study of a Seated Man

601. Cole–Gainsborough. Mrs. Siddons

602. Ruzicka. Louisburg Square, Boston

603. Arms. Colegiata, Toro

604. Pennell. Edgar Thomson Steelworks

605. Benson. Broadbills

606. Hassam. Easthampton

607. Sloan. Nude and Etching Press

608. Sloan. Night Windows

609. Hopper. Evening Wind

610. Hopper. Night Shadows

611. Bellows. Stag at Sharkey's

613. Albright. "Heavy the Oar to Him Who Is Tired"

612. Kent. Pinnacle

614. Weber. On the Shore

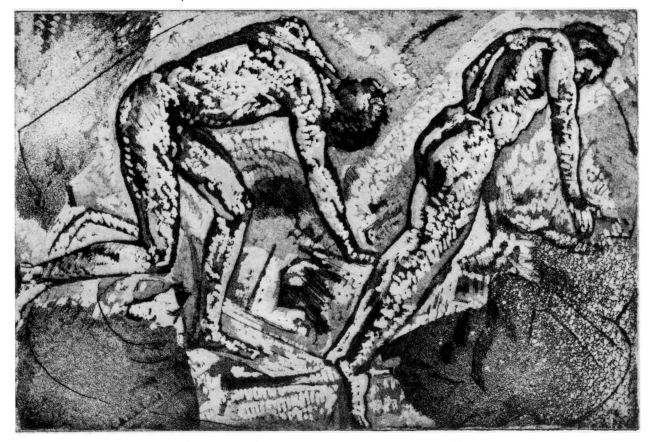

615. Davies. Up-Rising

616. Davis. Barbershop Chord

618. Marin. Sailboat

620. Spencer. White Factory

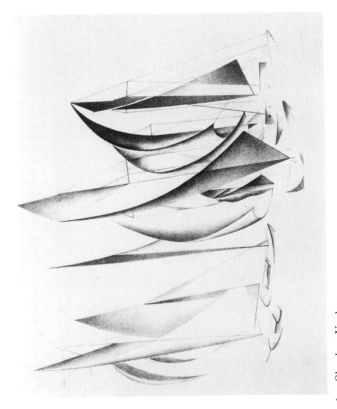

617. Sheeler. Yachts

619. Gág. Elevated Station

622. Murphy. Wild Horses

621. Kent. Over the Ultimate

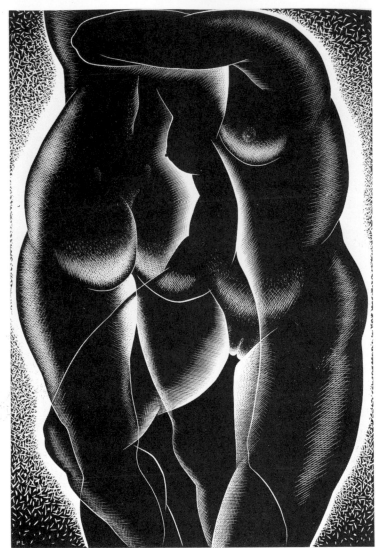

623. Landacre. Counterpoint

624. Watkins. Softly-Softly

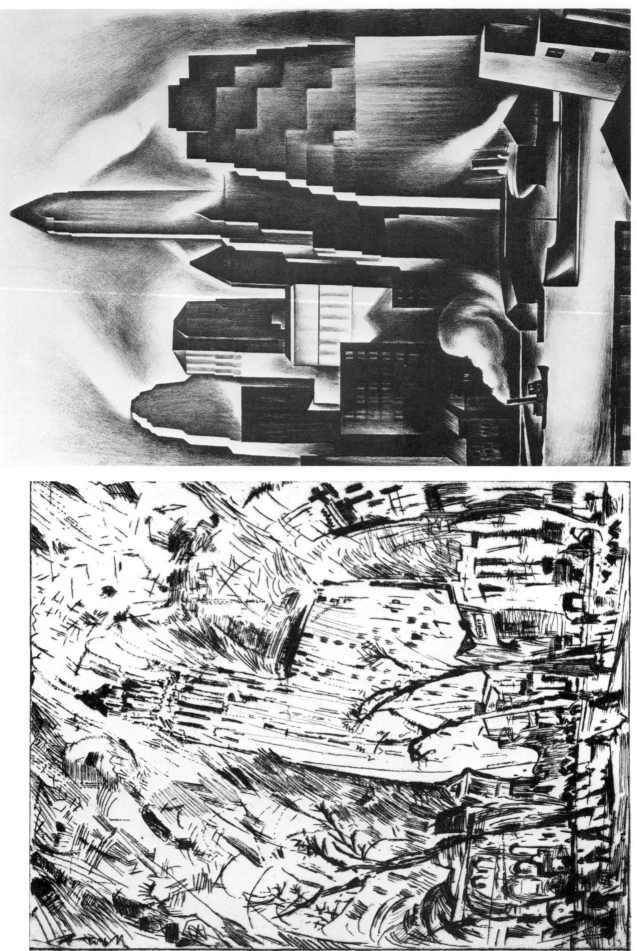

626. Cook. Lower Manhattan

625. Marin. Woolworth Building: the Dance

628. Warsager. Manhattan Night

627. Marsh. Tattoo, Shave and Haircut

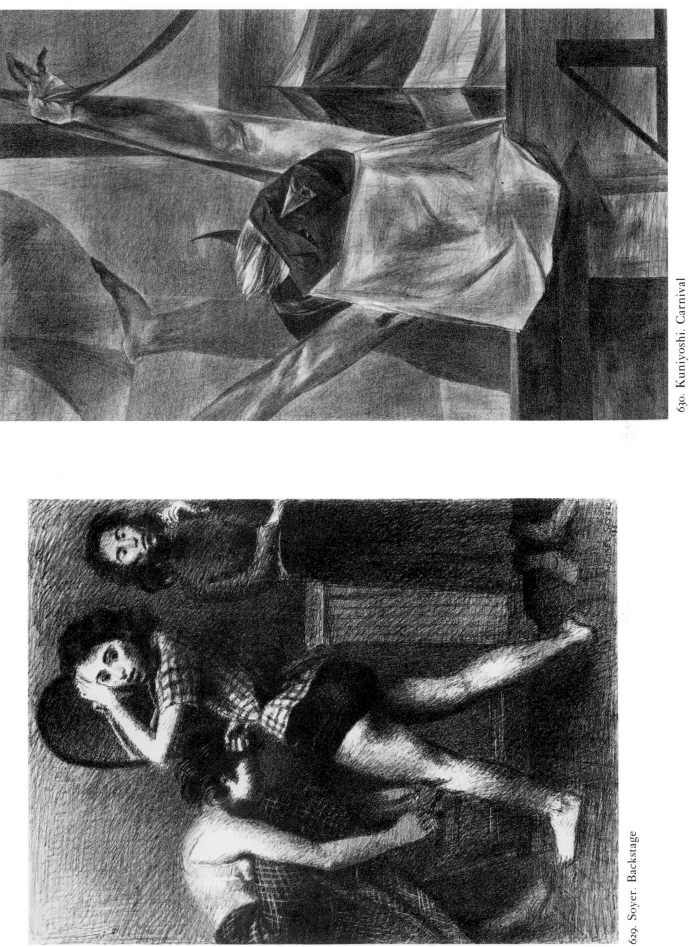

630. Kuniyoshi. Carnival

629. Soyer. Backstage

631. Kahn. Cat Walk

632. Barnet. Woman and Cats

633. Lozowick. Tanks

634. Sternberg. Steel

635. Gropper. For the Record

636. Dehn. All for a Piece of Meat

637. Velonis. Decoration: Empire

638. Gwathmey. End of the Day

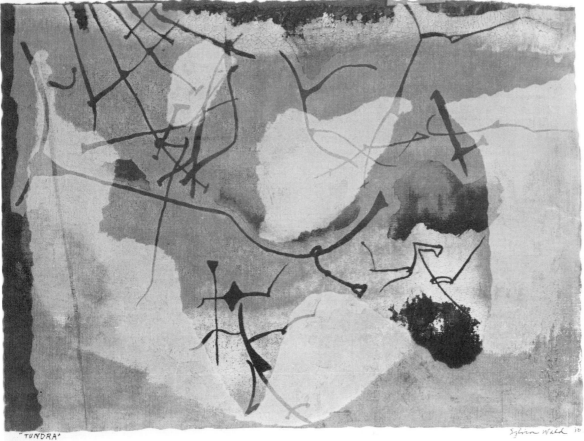

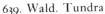

639. Wald. Tundra

640. Morley. Execution

641. Ronnebeck. Chicken Pull

642. Benton. Going West

643. Young. Navajo Watering Place

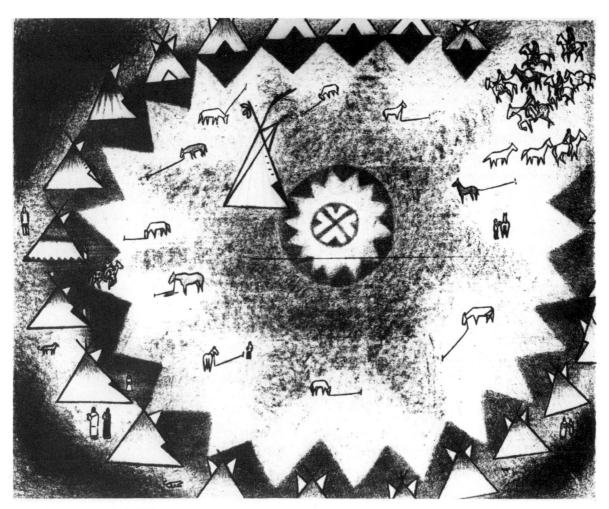

644. Twohy. Indian Village

645. Castellón. Rendezvous in a Landscape

646. Spruance. Penelope

647. Levine. The General

648. Taylor. Supper in Port

649. Peterdi. Vision of Fear

650. Lasansky. Bodas de Sangre

651. Frasconi. The Sun and the Wind

652. Kohn. Tiger

653. Shahn. Silent Music

654. Baskin. Poet Laureate

655. Paris. Lost

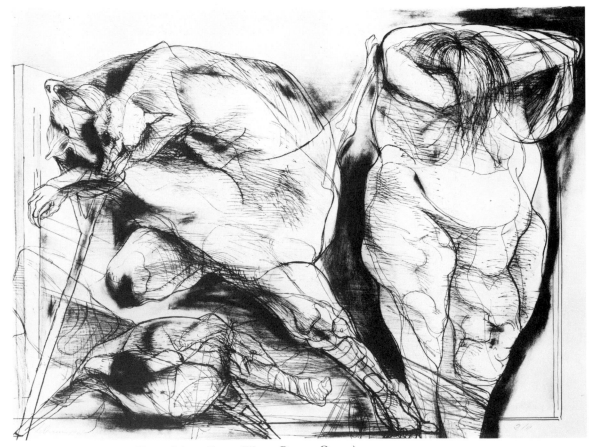

656. Lebrun. Beggars Turned into Dogs (Three-Penny Opera)

657. Durieux. Impasse

658. Wayne. Last Chance

659. Morgan. Samadhi

660. Albers. Aquarium

661. Yunkers. Magnificat

662. Stieglitz. Steerage

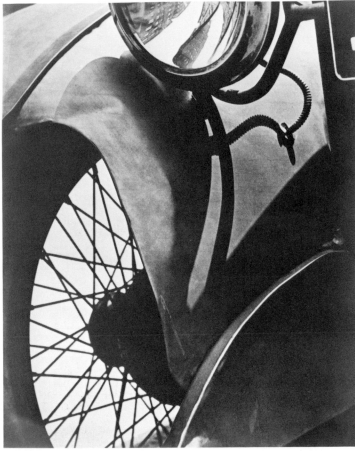

663. Strand. Wire Wheel

664. Adams. Pine Branches in Snow

665. Steichen. Portrait of Alphonse Mucha

666. Weston. Dinosaur (Eroded Rock)

667. *Japanese School.* Hundred Buddha Charms

668. *Chinese Woodcut.* Landscape with Hermit's Hut

669. *Chinese Woodcut.* Buddha Discoursing, from the *Diamond Sutra*

慈客六現

月裏姮娥不
盡眉只將雲
霧作羅
衣

不
知夢逐
青鸞去猶把
花枝笑拈歸
鼓山珪

670. *Chinese Woodcut.* Kuan Yin

671. Ch'ung Huan. Waterfall

672. *Chinese Woodcut.* Scene in a Spiral

673. *Ten Bamboo Studio.* Snake-Gourd Vine

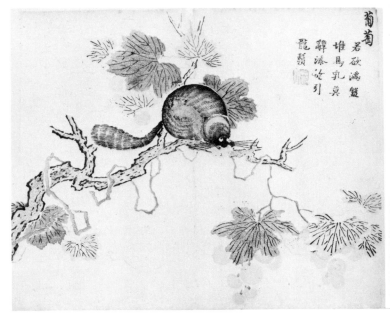

674. *Mustard Seed Garden Manual.* Squirrel Shrew and Grapes

675. Teng K'uei. Appurtenances of a Meal

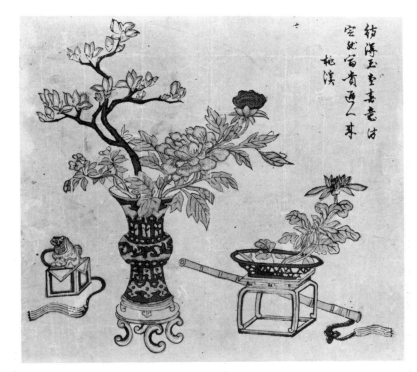

676. *Chinese Woodcut.* Spring Decorations

677. *Chinese Stone Rubbing.* Five Omens of the Frog Pool

679. *Chinese Stone Rubbing.* Buddha under the Bodhi Tree

678. *Chinese Stone Rubbing.* The Ho Huan Tree

681. Wu Tao Tzu. Tortoise and Serpent

680. *Chinese Stone Rubbing*. Maitreya

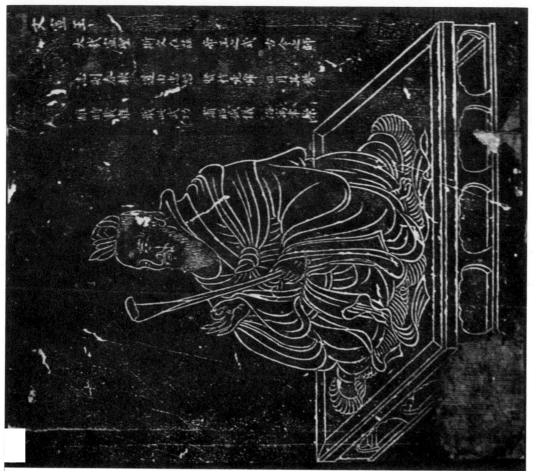

683. *Chinese Stone Rubbing.* Confucius

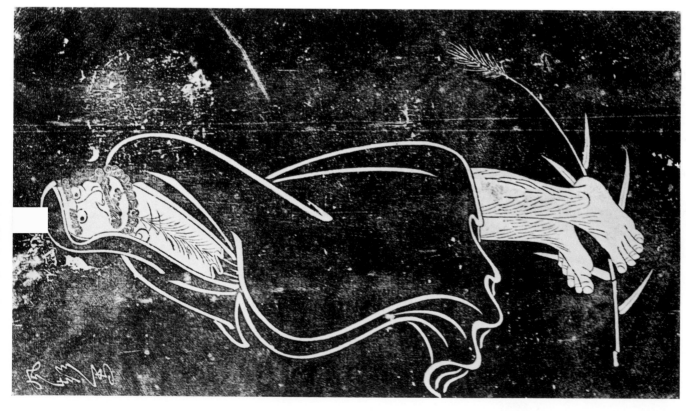

682. *Chinese Stone Rubbing.* Bodhidharma Crossing the Yangtse River on a Reed

684. Su Tung P'o (attributed). The God of Fortune

685. Chia Li. Bamboo

686. Kuan Hsiu. Lohan

687. K'uei Hsing. Chung K'uei

688. Moronobu (?). Warrior Subduing a Demon

689. Moronobu. The Lovers

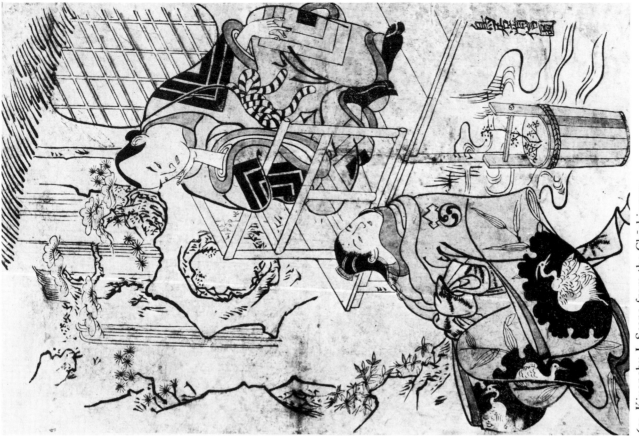

691. Kiyonobu I. Scene from the Chūshingura

690. Jihei Sugimura. Strolling Woman

692. Kiyomasu I. Handayū in a Female Role

693. Kiyomasu II. Golden Pheasant

694. Masanobu. Shōki, the Demon Queller

695. Kaigetsudō. Oiran Walking to the Left

696. Masanobu. Ono no Komachi

697. Masanobu. Kyōto, the Song

698. Shigenaga. Dog Bringing Love Letter

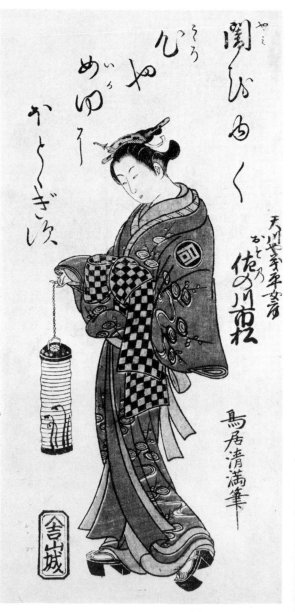

699. Kiyomitsu. Osono in the Chūshingura

701. Harunobu. Girl with Lantern

700. Harunobu. Lover Departing

702. Harunobu. Courtesan as Daruma Crossing the Sea

703. Koryūsai. Falcon

706. Bunchō. Fox Dance

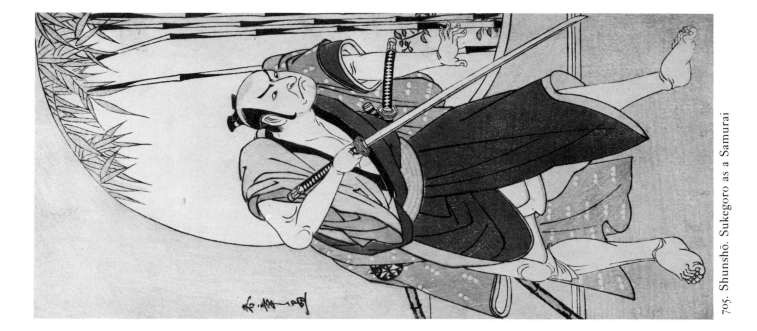

705. Shunshō. Sukegoro as a Samurai

704. Shunshō. Courtesan

708. Kiyonaga. Shigeyuki Practising Calligraphy

707. Koryūsai. "Telescope Not Used"

709. Kiyonaga. Public Bathhouse

710. Kiyonaga. Terrace by the Sea

712. Sharaku. Ichikawa Ebizō as Washizuki Kandayo

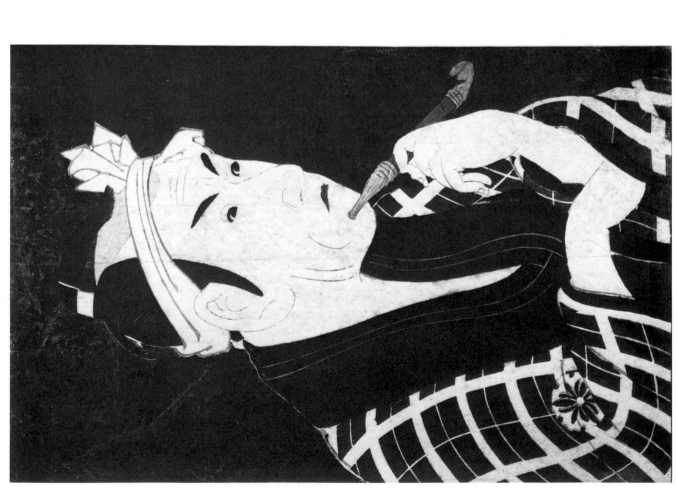

711. Sharaku. Kōshirō IV as the Fishmonger Gorobei

713. Utamaro. The Hour of the Snake

714. Utamaro. Kintoki and Yamaubi

715. Utamaro. Awabi Fishers

716. Utamaro. Osan no-sō

717. Utamaro. *Famous Beauties Enacting the Oxcart Scene*

719. Chōki. Fireflies

718. Eishi. Prince Yoshitsune Playing Music

720. Toyoharu. Prince Yoshitsune Serenading Joruri Hime

721. Masanobu. Perspective View of Kabuki Theatre

722. Moronobu. Illustration to a book on Landscape Gardening

723. Sukenobu. Illustration to a book, *Yehon Tokiwagusa*

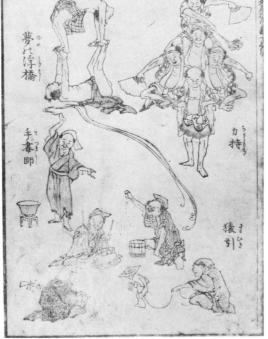

724. Hokusai. Acrobats, from *Manga*, Volume X

725. Kuniyoshi. Goldfish Story

726. Yoshikazu. Cooking in a Foreign Residence

727. Hokushu. A Scene from *Isse Ichidai*

728. Hokkei. Fan and Yeboshi Hat

729. Hokusai. Fuji above the Storm

730. Hokusai. The Wave

731. Hokusai. Amida Falls, Kiso

732. Hiroshige. Evening Snow at Kambara

733. Hiroshige. White Rain at Shono Pass

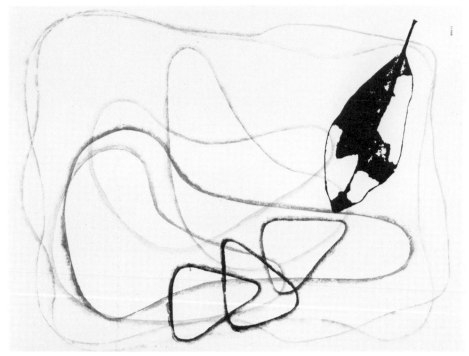

736. Onchi, Koshiro. Poem No. 22, Leaf and Clouds

735. Hiroshige. Shower at Ohashi Bridge

734. Hiroshige. Mandarin Ducks

737. Saito, Kiyoshi. Winter in Aizu

738. Munakata, Shiko. Flower Hunting Mural